ginal code for quick reference. Of particular value are direct quotations of every important point in each pamphlet. The author provides an illuminating introduction, a chronological list of Popiana, a compendious bibliography together with locations of the pamphlets, and an exhaustive index.

This comprehensive contribution to the literature will quickly establish itself as an authoritative and essential work of reference and an indispensable guide to Pope's works.

———

JOSEPH VINCENT GUERINOT is Associate Professor of English at the University of Wisconsin-Milwaukee. He received his Ph.D. at Yale University in 1962 and he has taught at several schools and universities in the United States and France.

Pamphlet Attacks on
ALEXANDER POPE
1711–1744

J. V. GUERINOT

Pamphlet Attacks on
ALEXANDER POPE
1711–1744

A DESCRIPTIVE BIBLIOGRAPHY

NEW YORK · NEW YORK UNIVERSITY PRESS
1969

First published 1969
© *1969 J. V. Guerinot*
Library of Congress Catalog Card Number 69–12700
Manufactured in Great Britain
and bound in The United States of America

SBN 416 42840 1

To Maynard Mack

CONTENTS

PREFACE

Certain methods followed here probably need a word of explanation. I have attempted a descriptive bibliography of the attacks published against Alexander Pope in pamphlet form during his lifetime.

I have also included attacks in book form, but excluded except for several rare and important items before 1728 all attacks published only in newspapers. My title, I must grant, is misleading, but I have found no solution. 'Attacks on Pope published between 1711 and 1744 mostly in pamphlet form but sometimes as broadsides, as books, or as parts of books, excluding all but several newspaper attacks' is accurate, but as a title impossible. In my attempt to provide a plain man's pathway through Popiana, I had to set aside the newspaper attacks, making an exception only to present fully the earliest attacks. And it seemed wrong to press too hard the definition of 'pamphlet'.

As my Introduction explains, the pamphlets exist in so few copies and are so widely scattered from Oxford to California and Texas that few students of Pope can have managed to see them all. Published information about their contents is very scanty. Yet the attacks on Pope play an important part in his poetical career, influenced Pope both as man and poet, and help to elucidate his major satires. It has seemed best, then, to include a summary of each attack, illustrated with generous quotations.

I have tried to include every point of importance that the pamphlet makes, and for ease of reference, have included before each summary a list of the works by Pope mentioned in the pamphlet, assigning to each a letter of the alphabet (omitting I and numbering H, J), and a list of the charges made, assigning to these arabic numerals. These letters and numerals subsequently appear in the left-hand margins to guide the reader quickly to the point that interests him. This method is sometimes graceless but seemed a necessary supplement to the index. Since I have located almost one hundred and sixty items, the bibliography,

even after every effort at condensation short of crabbedness, is of necessity rather long.

I have omitted discussion of only two Pope quarrels, the complicated controversy with Curll over the publication of Pope's letters, and the Crousaz attacks on the *Essay on Man*. The first, which plays a very small role in the pamphlet attacks, has been amply treated by C. W. Dilke in *Papers of a Critic* and by George Sherburn in his recent edition of *The Correspondence of Alexander Pope*. The second was hardly a personal attack and is of more interest to the historian of philosophy. Adequate information exists in the standard works on the *Essay on Man*.

My bibliographical descriptions make no claim to completeness. I have attempted only an elementary description which, I hope, is sufficient to allow the reader to identify the copy I have used. I have given for each item the full title-page, without, however, any attempt to indicate type faces or line divisions (except for verse) and with, in several cases, the omission of quotations in Greek.

Square brackets in my collations indicate that the gathering is unsigned, in pagination that the page is unnumbered. (Because of their many unnumbered pages, I have not given exact pagination for Welsted's *Epistles, Odes, &c.*, 1724; Cooke's *Tales, Epistles, Odes*, 1729; or *Mr. Cooke's Original Poems*, 1742.) I have silently reversed italics in quoting from prefaces, footnotes, and quotations within the pamphlets. Capitalizations I have attempted to preserve, but in titles and drop-titles I have capitalized only the first letter of words printed in small capitals. The publication dates of the pamphlets I have sometimes been obliged by the great difficulty in finding complete runs of newspapers to take from other writers on Popiana, giving my authority in each case; some I have been able to date only by the year. 'Rogers', without pagination, in my bibliography, refers to the dated list of 'Pamphlet Campaigns Concerning Pope, 1728–1744', in Robert W. Rogers, *The Major Satires of Alexander Pope* (Urbana, Illinois, 1955), pp. 134–54.

Unless otherwise indicated all quotations from a pamphlet are taken from the first edition. In the chronological list of pamphlets preceding the bibliography, intended only as a quick check-list

of first editions, I have given the location for the pamphlets not
to be found in the Yale University Library; locations of editions
other than the first, if not Yale, are given in the text. Pamphlets
in American libraries other than Yale I have read only in Xerox
or microfilm. Annotation of my excerpts from the pamphlets and
cross-referencing of the charges have necessarily been kept to a
minimum. I have throughout been forced to suppose that the
reader had available the standard editions of and works on Pope.

Professor Maynard Mack and Professor William Frost have
very kindly identified for me several quotations from Pope's *Iliad*
and *Odyssey*; since these poems are not included in the Pope con-
cordance I have been forced to leave unidentified a handful of
quotations from them.

The number of people who have helped me with this bibliography over the past several years is embarrassingly large. My
debt to my parents, *parentibus bene merentibus*, I cannot even begin
adequately to record here; the Father which seeth in secret will
reward openly. I must at least thank Mr and Mrs George Hersey,
Yale University, who encouraged and consoled during one
happy year in New Haven; Mr and Mrs Karl Patten, Bucknell
University, who read the introduction and helped me make it
sound a little less like something from the Left Book Club; Mr
Randolph Osman and Miss Patricia Crotty, student assistants
at Bucknell and Milwaukee respectively; Miss Jeanne K.
Welcher for invaluable advice, support, and help at many times
and in many places; the Benedictine community at Portsmouth
Priory, Rhode Island, especially Dom Alban Baer, for hospitality over many years and kindnesses too important and too frequent to record; Mr and Mrs Justin Replogle for the warm support of their friendship during the apparently interminable task
of making this ready for the press; Dom James Forbes, Master of
St Benet's Hall, Oxford, for Benedictine hospitality during happy
Oxford summers; Mr David Foxon who gave me the locations of
many of the pamphlets; Miss Marjorie Wynne and the wonder-
fully co-operative staff of the Beinecke Library; Professor Edward
Ruhe of the University of Kansas who helped with several Curll
problems; Professor Robert W. Rogers of the University of Illinois who identified for me the copies of the pamphlets he had

used; Dean Hartley Simpson for a timely grant-in-aid for the purchase of microfilm; the American Philosophical Society and the University of Wisconsin, Milwaukee, for summer grants; and, above all, Professor Maynard Mack, 'The *clearest Head*, and the *sincerest Heart*'. He proposed the subject of the dissertation on which this book is based and has directed my work over many years with unfailing kindness and enthusiasm.

ABBREVIATIONS

The following short titles have been everywhere used:

Ault	Ault, Norman. *New Light on Pope*. London, 1949.
Bond	Bond, R. P. *English Burlesque Poetry, 1700–1750*. Cambridge, Mass., 1932.
Case	Case, Arthur E. *A Bibliography of English Poetical Miscellanies, 1521–1750*. Oxford, 1935.
Corr.	*The Correspondence of Alexander Pope*, ed. George Sherburn. 5 vols. Oxford, 1956.
EC	*The Works of Alexander Pope* ..., ed. W. Elwin and W. J. Courthope. 10 vols. London, 1871–89.
Griffith	Griffith, R. H. *Alexander Pope: A Bibliography*. 2 vols. Austin, Texas, 1922–7.
Halsband	Halsband, Robert. *The Life of Lady Mary Wortley Montagu*. Oxford, 1957.
Hooker	*The Critical Works of John Dennis*, ed. E. N. Hooker. 2 vols. Baltimore, 1939–43.
Irving	Irving, William Henry. *John Gay, Favorite of the Wits*. Durham, N.C., 1940.
Jones	Jones, R. F. *Lewis Theobald, his Contribution to English Scholarship*. New York, 1919.
Letters of Thomas Burnet	*The Letters of Thomas Burnet to George Duckett, 1712–1722*, ed. David Nichol Smith. The Roxburghe Club, 1914.
Prose	*The Prose Works of Alexander Pope*, ed. Norman Ault. Vol. 1, The Earlier Works. Oxford, 1936.
Rogers	Rogers, Robert W. *The Major Satires of Alexander Pope*. Urbana, Ill., 1955.
Sherburn	Sherburn, George. *The Early Career of Alexander Pope*. Oxford, 1934.

xiii

Straus   Straus, Ralph. *The Unspeakable Curll*. London, 1927.

Teerink   Teerink, H. *A Bibliography of the Writings in Prose and Verse of Jonathan Swift*. The Hague, 1937.

Twick.   *The Twickenham Edition of the Poems of Alexander Pope*, General Editor, John Butt. 10 vols. London, 1939–67.

Wimsatt   Wimsatt, W. K. *The Portraits of Alexander Pope*. New Haven and London, 1965.

INTRODUCTION

I

Pope himself by writing the *Dunciad* calls our attention to the importance of the attacks published against him. He filled the apparatus of the *Dunciad Variorum* with references to them and included as Appendix II 'A List of Books, Papers, and Verses, in which our Author was abused, printed before the Publication of the *Dunciad*: With the true Names of the Authors', as well as a list of publications after the *Dunciad*. His later poems, especially the *Epistle to Arbuthnot*, also make necessary some acquaintance with Popiana, but little effort seems to have been made after his death by his editors and commentators to list or describe the attacks. Probably even then the pamphlets were getting hard to find. Pope's own list was not always accurate about dates and titles, and he included very little published after 1729.

In October 1836 the anonymous reviewer in the *Gentleman's Magazine* of Croly's *The Works of Alexander Pope* announced that he owned a moderate collection of Popiana pamphlets and suggested that 'an amusing and useful volume might be formed from them.'[1] He included in his review a list of thirteen Popiana pamphlets with extracts. In June 1855 B.H.C. writing in *Notes and Queries* asked, 'Has any collection of pieces written in praise or blame of Pope been published? Could not a supplemental volume of such writings be issued uniformly with his *Works*?'[2] In July 1879 P.A.H. in the same magazine recalled this 'capital suggestion', adding that it was unlikely from its very size ever to be carried out, and called for a bibliography of Pope's quarrels similar to the bibliography of the *Dunciad* that had been running in the magazine.[3]

His suggestion was taken up with enthusiasm and the 5th Series, Vol. XII, and the 6th Series, Vol. I, contained numerous contributions to a bibliography of Popiana. Then interest seems to have dropped off, and writing in 1934 George Sherburn could say, 'Fundamental study of Pope's quarrels must continue to start

[1] *Gentleman's Magazine*, VI (1836), 344.
[2] *Notes and Queries*, Ser. 1, XI, 485.   [3] *Ibid.* Ser. 5, XII, 6.

in the pages of *Notes and Queries*, at least until Professor Griffith publishes his promised bibliography in this field.'[1]

In 1922 in the introduction to his great bibliography of Pope R. H. Griffith had explained that he had originally intended to publish 'a list of the books, pamphlets, and articles involved in Pope's quarrels', but soon realized that a bibliography of Pope's own writings would have to be made first.[2] He promised a companion volume of Popiana which, most unfortunately, has never appeared. The result is that over a hundred years after the first expressed need for a guide to the literature of Pope's quarrels (and over two hundred and twenty years after his death), we are still without one. The present study attempts to fill the gap.

There have been a number of contributions to the subject without which my work would have been impossible. My indebtedness to *The Twickenham Edition of the Poems of Alexander Pope* will be apparent on every page, particularly to James Sutherland's edition of the *Dunciad*, where, however, by its very nature, complete annotation of Pope's Appendix II to this poem is not attempted and where the attacks are never brought together into a list. The British Museum Catalogue's entries under 'Pope' are indispensable, as is the catalogue of the Dyce Collection in the Victoria and Albert Museum. Besides catalogues of special collections such as the Lefferts Collection at Harvard, and those of T. J. Wise,[3] there is Professor Griffith's bibliography of Popiana in the *CBEL* and, more recently, R. W. Rogers has included as an appendix to his *Major Satires of Alexander Pope* a check-list of 'Pamphlet Campaigns Concerning Pope, 1728–1744'.[4]

I should explain immediately how the present work differs

---

[1] Sherburn, p. 20.   [2] Griffith, Vol. I, Pt I, vii.

[3] *Alexander Pope. Notes Towards a Bibliography of Early Editions of his Writings. A Catalogue of Marshall C. Leffert's Great Collection of First and Later Editions of the Works of Alexander Pope* (New York, n.d.); *A Pope Library. A Catalogue of Plays, Poems, and Prose Writings by Alexander Pope. Collected by Thomas James Wise* (London, 1931); *An Exhibition of the First Editions of The Works of Alexander Pope (1688–1744) Together with a Collection of the Engraved Portraits of the Poet and of his Friends. The Grolier Club. January 26 to March 4, 1911* (New York, 1911); *Pope Commemoration. 1888. Loan Museum. Catalogue of the Books, Autographs etc., Exhibited in the Town Hall, Twickenham, July 31st to August 4th, 1888* (London, 1888).

[4] Rogers, pp. 134–54.

from those above. The *CBEL* bibliography announces at the beginning that it is a selected list only, and the Rogers list, which does not extend back beyond 1728, includes 'only published pamphlets in which the principal business is to defend or to attack Pope'.[1] Besides their selectivity, there is another more important point of difference. Both lists include under 'Popiana' defences of as well as attacks on Pope, and give titles of pamphlets which are dedicated to Pope, imitations of his style, etc.

Such is, to be sure, the usual meaning of 'Popiana', but I have for convenience narrowed the definition and have here limited myself to pamphlets (and, for the sake of completeness, the few books) which attack Pope. A bibliography of tributes to Pope, imitations, defences, and purely association items would be a useful thing to have, but it should, for convenience, be kept separate from a list of the attacks. I have included in Appendix B a list of the most important pamphlets which turn up in Popiana lists but which are not attacks on Pope and, therefore, in my sense, not Popiana.

I have excluded entirely, except for a few rare and important items before 1728, attacks on Pope that appeared only in newspapers and, with one or two exceptions, newspapers reprinted in book form. A bibliography of all the newspaper attacks on Pope would have its uses, but the labour of compiling it would be out of all proportion to its value.

It would be comforting to feel that within these limits the present bibliography is complete, but I know that no such thing is true. It is more complete than any previous list, however, and will, I hope, help to turn up still unknown or unlocated pamphlets. I have been able to locate copies of several pamphlets not previously found.

Besides the stricter definition of Popiana and an attempt at completeness in my listing of pamphlets, the present bibliography attempts for the first time to describe and analyse at some length the contents of every attack. I have also included in each case an elementary bibliographical description. Almost all of the pamphlets studied are so rare as to be obtainable in only a very few libraries. Some exist in only one known copy. Very few have ever

[1] *Ibid.* p. 134.

been reprinted. The reader and teacher have thus been limited in their acquaintance with a part of Pope's life which everyone has agreed to think important to a few excerpts and general comments in the standard works on Pope. It is hoped that the present study will make generally available everything of real importance in these obscure and widely scattered books and pamphlets.

II

Perhaps the easiest way to begin a study of Popiana is to arrange the pamphlets chronologically and to set them against the work Pope was publishing at the same time. It becomes clear that, as one would expect, the pamphlet attacks correspond fairly closely in date and subject to Pope's own publications. It also becomes easy to group pamphlets together as directed against the same work and to see them as part of a larger attack, although the pamphlets do not always make clear the immediate motive for their composition and only rarely confine their criticism to a single poem.

Popiana begins in 1711 with John Dennis's first attack on Pope, the notorious *Reflections Critical and Satyrical, Upon A Late Rhapsody Call'd, An Essay Upon Criticism*. 'There is nothing more wrong, more low, or more incorrect than this Rhapsody upon Criticism,' Dennis declared (p. 2). 'As there is no Creature in Nature so venomous, there is nothing so stupid and so impotent as a hunchback'd Toad,' he continues (p. 26), and in his ruthless and mostly wrong-headed dissection of Pope's precocious poem he reverts frequently to the shape of his 'little Author'. Pope 'has reason to thank the good Gods that he was born a Modern. For had he been born of *Graecian* Parents, and his Father by consequence had by Law had the absolute Disposal of him, his Life had been no longer than that of one of his Poems, the Life of half a day' (p. 29). For over thirty years attacks on Pope would not differ greatly from this; there would be the same desire to humiliate and wound, the same eagerness to find errors in Pope's verse, however unfairly, the same scurrilous personal abuse.

Pope had given Dennis mild provocation, but, so far as is known, had in no wise offended Charles Gildon who in 1714 in his *A New Rehearsal* had Pope figure ludicrously as Sawny Dapper, an intolerably conceited young poetaster. Gildon is chiefly interested in *The Rape of the Lock*: '. . . you must make the Ladies speak Bawdy,' Dapper advises (p. 43). But there are rumours of the projected translation of Homer: '. . . if I did not understand

Greek, what of that; I hope a Man may Translate a *Greek* Author without understanding *Greek* . . .' (p. 41). Then in March 1715 *Aesop At The Bear Garden* appeared, a crude parody of *The Temple of Fame*. It must by now have seemed to Pope as though no major poem of his could escape attack, and this was, in fact, to be true.

By this time we have reached the first collective attempt to discredit Pope, the campaign against the Homer, begun, as everyone knows, well before Pope had even published his translation. Here we have for the first time a phenomenon of which Pope would recurrently be the victim, not an isolated attack – one pamphlet by one indignant author, as Dennis's pamphlet had been – but a whole series of attacks, stretching over several months or years, which in this case looked very much as if it had been planned, and indeed there is some evidence that it was.[1]

There were squibs in such papers as *The High-German Doctor* and *The Grumbler* and the epigram in Oldmixon's *Poems and Translations*:

First take the Gold – then charm the list'ning Ear.[2]

The same point was made by Burnet and Duckett in their heavily facetious *Homerides: Or, A Letter To Mr. Pope*, which Addison had seen: 'There are indeed but two Things to be considered in every Heroick Poem; first, how to *write* the Poem, secondly, how to make it *sell*.'[3]

Along with the attack on the Homer went a smaller warfare on Gay's *What D'Ye Call It*, in which Pope was popularly supposed to have had a hand. Apart from minor help from Pope and perhaps his encouragement of its publication, the play is Gay's, but Pope's collaboration remained a popular charge, to be confused later with his collaboration in *Three Hours after Marriage*.

The next major event in Popiana, although there appeared in 1716 the virulent *The Catholick Poet* and *A True Character Of Mr. Pope*, was caused by the performance and publication in January 1717 of the supposedly indecent *Three Hours*, in which Gay acknowledged the collaboration of Pope and Arbuthnot. In a little

[1] For the clearest summary of the available evidence, see Ault, pp. 101–19.

[2] John Oldmixon, *Poems And Translations. By Several Hands* (London, 1714), p. 245.

[3] Thomas Burnet and George Duckett, *Homerides: Or, A Letter To Mr. Pope* (London, 1715), p. 6.

over two months nine pamphlets appeared, devoted in whole or in part to that not very successful play.

> That Play, retorted Fopling, was so lewd,
> Ev'n Bullies blush'd, and Beaux astonish'd stood,

protested Leonard Welsted in his *Palaemon to Caelia* (p. 11). 'I pass over a whole *Dunghill* of this Ribaldry,' says the author of *A Letter To Mr. John Gay* (p. 24), weary of compiling his florilegium of what he chose to consider the play's blasphemies and obscenities. Pope, of course, receives most of the blame for the play, especially in Breval's *The Confederates*.

The next years, until 1728, are relatively quiet ones; Pope was busy with his translating and editing. Even in these years, however, there were at least one or two attacks annually, on the Homer, for example, in *Madame Dacier's Remarks Upon Mr. Pope's Account of Homer* (1724) and Bezaleel Morrice's *An Epistle To Mr. Welsted* (1721), or on his morals, in *The Life Of the late Celebrated Mrs. Elizabeth Wisebourn* (1721). One of the most striking features of Popiana is the sheer persistency of the attacks. It is much as though a quarterly magazine devoted entirely to attacks on one author should run for over thirty years. The objections to a poem or, even better, to Pope himself, once made, the same charges could be used over and over. What was said against the Homer and the *Rape of the Lock* in 1715 was still being said the year Pope died.

In 1726 Pope's editing of Shakespeare brought down on his head Lewis Theobald's *Shakespeare restored: Or, A Specimen Of The Many Errors, As Well Committed, as Unamended, by Mr. Pope In his Late Edition of this Poet*. Theobald never stoops to the purely personal, but the exposure was painful and bore important fruit.

The publication of the *Peri Bathous* and the 1728 *Dunciad* inaugurates the best-known phase of Popiana. Both books demanded replies in the spring and summer of 1728. The more damaging *Dunciad Variorum* in 1729 provoked still more pamphlets, and by the end of 1729 over thirty attacks had been published. Curll's chaste press had been busy turning out hasty *Popiads* and *Female Dunciads*, and authors like Smedley, Concanen, and Ned Ward made contributions to Popiana. The tone of the pamphlets becomes shriller, the attention more concentrated on Pope the

venomous satirist, and there are the unpleasant fantasies of Pope being flogged (*A Popp upon Pope*), committing suicide (*Sawney*), or, in the shape of a cur, being sadistically tormented by his victims (*The Metamorphosis*).

The warfare continued into 1730 and 1731. Then in 1732 Pope published another poem offering ideal material for pamphlets. The *Epistle to Burlington* contained what the dunces (and later generations) could assert was a vicious portrait of the Duke of Chandos. Everyone had always known Pope was ungrateful. His treatment of Wycherley and Addison had shown that, but who would have thought he would attack one of his patrons? Seven pamphlets in the next few months rejoiced in Pope's ingratitude.

> Ah! hapless they on whom unknown you smile,
> Whose yielding Hearts thy Flatteries beguile:
> Soon shall they see themselves with wild Surprise
> Adorn'd, as Victims, for the Sacrifice.[1]

Seventeen hundred and thirty-three, a year which produced more pamphlets for or against Pope than any other, saw the publication of the *First Satire of the Second Book* and the famous replies of Lady Mary and Lord Hervey, the *Verses Address'd to the Imitator Of . . . Horace*, and *An Epistle From A Nobleman To A Doctor of Divinity*. They were, of course, seconded by Grub Street in such things as *The Satirists* and *The Muse in Distress*. The *Imitations of Horace* with their rich personal and political allusions now provided constant ammunition until Pope's death. In 1735 Thomas Bentley in *A Letter To Mr. Pope* protested Pope's appropriation of his uncle's name in *Sober Advice From Horace*. 'An admirable Expedient, and worthy of your Sagacity, *to get upon the Back of Horace*, that you may abuse every body you don't like, with Impunity!' The poem is 'worse than any *Bacchanalian Song* made for a Bawdy-house' (p. 4). In the same year Curll published *The Poet finish'd in Prose*, the lengthiest of attacks on the *Epistle to Arbuthnot*, and commemorated the imbroglio over the publication of Pope's letters by beginning the tedious series of *Mr. Pope's Literary Correspondence*.

The *Essay on Man* next provided a fresh subject, as much for the not very theologically minded dunces because of its praise of

---

[1] *Of Good Nature* (London, 1732), p. 8.

Bolingbroke as because of its deism. In 1737 Crousaz published his first exposure of the poem's hidden heresy, and translations of his essays followed for several years, together with such ineptitudes as William Ayre's *Truth* (1739).

The later more explicitly political satires of 1738 provoked a fresh campaign. *A Supplement To One Thousand Seven Hundred Thirty-Eight* (1738), *A Dialogue On One Thousand Seven Hundred and Thirty-eight* (1738), *Characters* (1739), and, as late as 1742, *The Difference Between Verbal and Practical Virtue* all rush to the defence of the Walpole administration.

> Shall *Pope* and *Whitehead* with the rankest Hate,
> Disgorge a Stew of Satire on the State,
> As if a *Verres* or a *Nero* reign'd,
> Who all the Laws of God and Man profan'd ?[1]

The last phase of Popiana begins in July 1742 with the publication of Cibber's *A Letter From Mr. Cibber*, provoked by the *New Dunciad*. He charged, most spectacularly, that he had once rescued Pope, the eminent moralist, from a bawdy house, and protested his elevation to the throne of dullness in two succeeding letters. Over a half-dozen pamphlets attacking Pope greeted Cibber's defence and the publication of the *Dunciad in Four Books*. Cibber's third letter was published only four months before Pope's death.

The major quarrels of Pope, treated at length in the biographies, take up less space in Popiana than one would have imagined. Of Pope's major 'enemies' only Dennis, with five pamphlets, makes an important contribution to Popiana. Theobald never published a pamphlet against Pope. *Shakespeare restored* attacks him, of course, but like Theobald's letters in the newspapers, displays more reserve and good taste than is usual in Popiana.

Lady Mary Wortley Montagu and Lord Hervey, although their relations with Pope form one of the most interesting and mysterious parts of Pope's later biography, published very little against him. Lady Mary, as far as we know, was responsible only for the *Verses Address'd to the Imitator Of The First Satire Of The*

---

[1] *Characters: An Epistle To Alexander Pope Esq; And Mr. Whitehead* (London, 1739), p. 5.

Second Book of Horace, in which she probably had Hervey's collaboration. It is the only pamphlet attacking Pope that catches anything of Pope's own satiric brilliance. But however successful in their way the *Verses* were, we cannot assign to Lady Mary any other pamphlets here, though, on her own admission, she wrote several verses in *An Epistle to Alexander Pope* (1735).

Lord Hervey wrote the insipid *An Epistle From A Nobleman To A Doctor of Divinity* (1733), which occasioned several replies and imitations. He probably wrote as well *A Letter To Mr. Cibber*, and *The Difference Between Verbal and Practical Virtue*, both of these in 1742, in connection with Cibber's first letter; we may presume that he saw in the Cibber quarrel an opportunity to even scores with Pope.

The second hero of the *Dunciad*, Colley Cibber, also failed to publish much Popiana. There are the three letters published between 1742 and 1744, the second being only several pages long, the others of some eighty or ninety pages; *The Egotist* (1743) is also probably to be ascribed to him.

Aside from these attacks which the general reader is aware of, we are still left with over one hundred and thirty others. I do not wish to minimize the importance of the above pamphlets. Both because of authorship and of contents, they have great interest. It must also be emphasized that they elicited a great many other attacks and provided constant ammunition for the less original. Still, they must, in themselves, be seen as only a part of a much larger phenomenon. More important in a consideration of the attacks that Pope suffered are the frequently anonymous productions of Grub Street.

Before looking at the kinds of things the pamphlets said about Pope and his poetry and at the kinds of men who wrote them and their motives, it might be well to consider in passing the very idea of a pamphlet attack. The pamphlet, I take it, as it was known up through the nineteenth century, is dead. It once served a number of purposes, religious, political, literary. Almost always it was topical and controversial. It offered a cheap, quick, and effective way of reaching the public and in its more respectable forms has contributed enormously to our literature, as the pamphlets of Swift, to mention only one name, will demonstrate.

There can be no need to emphasize the immense importance of pamphlet literature to the historian. Today, however, we no longer tend to publish pamphlets on a lively political issue or a religious controversy; we write instead for newspapers and magazines.

The present work deals with another kind of pamphlet, the personal libel. And this seems, happily, dead entirely. It would be interesting to know the last major figure in English literature who was subject to libellous pamphlet attacks. The word 'libel' is perhaps too strong, and suggests an incidental problem too difficult to answer. Libel laws, although they existed in the eighteenth century, do not seem to have been invoked for personal abuse, except occasionally by the peerage. Even anti-governmental attacks were allowed considerable freedom. I do not know of any evidence that Pope seriously thought of recourse to law or that the people he himself satirized ever thought of it.

If 'libel' has too strong a legal connotation, it still helps to define our disreputable genre. The pamphlets we are considering make the most damaging statements about Pope's personal life. They attempt to destroy his public reputation and do it by resorting for the most part to lies. They therefore constitute to the moral theologian both detraction – an attempt to destroy the good fame of another – and calumny – the circulation of scandal which is untrue. Our pamphlets are not, then, properly literary criticism at all, and few of them pretended to be such.

We no longer treat our literary figures in this way. We have the occasionally vicious review and the attempt to dislodge an established reputation, but as a rule these move on an impersonal level and are meant to be serious treatments of the work, not of the man and his personal failings. In the eighteenth century, however, the libellous, almost purely personal, attack, usually in the form of a pamphlet, was a common thing. There is no study of the phenomenon, but it seems as though most famous Augustans were attacked in this way at some time or other. Gay was attacked occasionally, usually, it seems, in connection with Pope; Teerink's bibliography reveals a large number of attacks on Swift, but since he has included in his list serious criticism, imitations, parodies, etc., it is impossible to give a figure. Dryden is

probably the man who comes closest to Pope in the number and virulence of pamphlet attacks published during his lifetime.[1] But although such attacks constituted part of the Augustan literary scene, it is almost certain that no other literary figure was attacked with anything like the frequency that Pope was; it is, indeed, hard to think of any other figure in English literature who was so frequently attacked in his lifetime. His great and early fame and affluence, giving ground for envy and detraction, his own devious manœuvrings on occasion, and his vanity, his passionate concern with good writing which he persistently identified with moral and national health, all offer themselves as possible explanations. But first it will be necessary to consider the kinds of charges his attackers brought against him.

[1] Hugh Macdonald, *John Dryden, A Bibliography of Early Editions and of Drydeniana* (Oxford, 1939), lists about 140 items to Dryden's death, but includes praise of Dryden and allusions. See also his informative 'The Attacks on Dryden', *Essays and Studies by Members of the English Association*, xxi (1936), 41–74.

III

I

What did Pope's attackers say about him? A detailed treatment of each pamphlet is provided in my bibliography, but here we may consider some of the charges generally. Their comprehensiveness is striking. It must have seemed to Pope that there was almost nothing his enemies would not say. Or having once said, repeat forever. Nothing in his work, his personal life, or his character was spared. Even his life-long devotion to his mother was ridiculed in *Sawney and Colley*, two years before his death.

The portrait of Pope that emerges from Popiana is a familiar one, bearing striking resemblances to the version of Pope put forth in the nineteenth century and popular up until thirty years ago. 'How his editors and biographers have hated Pope!' exclaims Bateson.[1] I am not suggesting that Pope's critics used or very much read the pamphlet attacks, but they seem to have absorbed their point of view. Could one think of another figure in English literature the standard critical and biographical studies of whom would repeat, however unconsciously, the rumours and defamations of his avowed enemies? When Lytton Strachey draws for us his picture of Pope the monkey pouring down boiling oil on his victims,[2] how unedifying it is to hear Bloomsbury speak in the accents of Grub Street!

Postponing the literary and critical contents of the pamphlets, let us look at the most popular charges. We may take first the purely personal.

Pope's deformity probably deserves first place. It constitutes for the modern reader the most offensive single feature in Popiana. To hold up to ridicule and contempt a man's physical defects seems to us disgusting and inexcusable. I confess I do not understand the argument one sometimes reads that revulsion from the abuse of Pope as a cripple is sentimental because the

---

[1] *Twick.* III. ii. 171.

[2] Lytton Strachey, *Pope. The Leslie Stephen Lecture for 1925* (Cambridge, 1925), p. 2.

eighteenth century was more outspoken and robust than we. Of course it was, but making fun of cripples does not seem to have been otherwise a prominent literary feature of the Augustan Age.

> ... The Deformity of this Libeller, is Visible, Present, Lasting, Unalterable, and Peculiar to himself. 'Tis the mark of God and Nature upon him, to give us warning that we should hold no Society with him, as a Creature not of our Original, nor of our Species.[1]

Dennis not only seems incapable of writing about Pope without mentioning his deformity; he congratulates himself that he can do it with a clear conscience since Pope's shape is a mark of divine reprobation. Lady Mary expressed the same idea later:

> And with the Emblem of thy crooked Mind,
> Mark'd on thy Back, like *Cain*, by God's own Hand,
> Wander like him, accursed through the Land.[2]

Pope is a monkey and, by an obvious deformation of his name, an A P—E. He is not a man because he is not shaped like other men, and his name, the guarantee of his personal identity, must be twisted into the name of an animal. Hate, says Ortega y Gasset, seeks the annihilation of its object.[3] Pope must be reduced from the human to the animal.

His attackers would have been delighted to find that Pope had attacked others for their deformity, but all the evidence they could find was the innocuous reference to Roome, 'and Roome's funereal face' (*Dunciad* A, iii. 146).

Pope's religion constitutes the next – to us – most shocking object of attack. 'Most writers on the literature of this period have no idea, apparently, of the furious hatred of Catholics expressed in journals and pamphlets during the years here under consideration,' writes Professor Sherburn.[4] It was always useful to remind one's readers that Pope was a Roman Catholic. Here the attacks must be seen within their historical context. To say that someone was a Roman Catholic meant, if one wanted to be nasty, that he

---

[1] John Dennis, *A True Character Of Mr. Pope* (London, 1716), p. 10.

[2] Lady Mary Wortley Montagu, *Verses Address'd to the Imitator Of The First Satire Of The Second Book of Horace* (London, 1733), p. 8.

[3] Ortega y Gasset, *On Love, Aspects of a Single Theme* (New York, 1957), p. 19.

[4] George Sherburn, 'Notes on the Canon of Pope's Works, 1714–1720', *The Manly Anniversary Studies in Language and Literature* (Chicago, 1923), p. 170.

was a Jacobite. Pope's Tory friendships, especially his friendship with Bishop Atterbury, provided all the proof that was needed. Pope, like all his Catholic friends, must have been used to the gross and ignorant prejudice his religion excited, however deplorable such prejudice is; the political implications may well have been more disturbing. His name lent itself to an inevitable pun that never seemed to grow stale, a useful shorthand for reminding the reader that the monkey satirist was no true Englishman, no friend to the Glorious Revolution. The title of the pamphlet, *Pope Alexander's Supremacy and Infallibility examin'd* (1729), thus looks in two directions at once.

These charges aside, the charge that is omnipresent in the pamphlets, made overtly over and over, and implied even when not explicit, is that Pope had become a rich man. Of the importance of this to the writers themselves I shall speak later; here we may simply note that perhaps no charge is so common as that Pope had established his fortune with the Homer and continued to grow rich from his writing. A later variant of this charge has it that Pope deliberately printed successive versions of the same poem and multiplied editions of his works in order to make more money.

The other most common personal charge we may sum up by saying that Pope was a satirist. The more purely literary implications I will consider later; here we are interested in the personal abuse involved. Since he writes satire, he is a toad bursting with envy, a spiteful and malicious little monkey, the wasp of Twickenham. In 'Farmer Pope and his Son: Or, The Toad and the Ox, A Fable', for example, an ancient Catholic toad and his wife have a son,

> A little scurvy, purblind-Elf;
> Scarce like a Toad, much less himself.
> Deform'd in Shape, of Pigmy Stature:
> A proud, conceited, peevish Creature.
>
> .   .   .
>
> The stinking Venom; [*sic*] flows around,
> And nauseous Slaver hides the Ground.[1]

[1] Edmund Curll and Elizabeth Thomas (?), *Codrus: Or, The Dunciad Dissected* (London, 1728), p. 12.

Ladies, Ned Ward tells Pope, 'like thee, as they do their Apes, /
Not for thy Wit, but Monkey-shapes'.[1]

His poems are proof that he is envious and spiteful. Pope

> Still brew'd, in Gall, his teizing, trifling Song;
> And spar'd no Malice, though he knew no Wrong:
> Writ, rail'd, and Duncify'd, from Year to Year:
> The Jesuit's Hate inflam'd the Eunuch's Fear.[2]

He longs to be an absolute literary dictator, indeed to be a Pope,
infallible, altering all morality for his own convenience.

> P—'s *Religion*, indeed, allows him to demolish *Hereticks*,
> not only with his *Pen*, but with *Fire and Sword*; and such were
> all those unhappy *Wits* and *Poets*, who were sacrificed to his
> accursed *Popish Principles* . . .[3]

He is, as well, completely ungrateful. He rose to his present
undeserved height with the help of powerful friends whom he
flattered and then cast off and libelled when they were no longer
of use:

> Lost to the Sense of all that's Great or Good,
> Nor with one Spark of Gratitude endu'd.
> Who dares revile the Man whose gen'rous Aid
> First rais'd from Dust th'ungrateful Miscreant's Head,
> Stabs his departing Friend in base Disguise,
> And *Addison* in *Atticus* belies.[4]

The picture that emerges from Popiana is of a man distinguished for his hatred and eagerness to deny.

> . . . *Pope*'s but a specious Knave;
> A Tool to Envy, and Ambition's Slave;
> Link'd with Division, Prejudice and Hate,
> In Anarchy would fain involve the State:
> Of Soul too covetous to sit at Ease;
> And too ill-natur'd any more to please:
> His talent is to cast a Slur on all
> That grace the Court, the Senate, or the Hall.[5]

The metaphor of Satan implicit here was used quite explicitly by

---

[1] Ned Ward, *Apollo's Maggot in his Cups* (London, 1729), A3r.
[2] Leonard Welsted, *Of False Fame* (London, 1732), p. 19.
[3] Jonathan Smedley, *Gulliveriana* (London, 1728), p. xi.
[4] *Mr. P[o]pe's Picture in Miniature* (London, 1743), p. 5.
[5] *Characters* (London, 1739), p. 7.

Dennis: 'By his constant and malicious Lying, and by that Angel Face and Form of his, 'tis plain that he wants nothing but Horns and Tayl, to be the exact Resemblance, both in Shape and Mind, of his Infernal Father.'[1] With a heavy debt to Milton the metaphor underlies a passage in *The Blatant-Beast* (1742):

> If Beauty be the Subject of our Praise,
> A rude, mishapen Lump Contempt must raise.
>   When *Lucifer* with Angels held first Place,
> Seraphic Beauty sparkled in his Face.
> By Pride and Malice tempted to rebel,
> Vengeance pursu'd him to the lowest Hell:
> Not sulph'rous Lakes suffic'd, nor dreary Plains;
> Deformity was join'd t'improve his Pains.
>   Paint then the Person, and expose the Mind,
> Who rails at others, to his own Faults blind. (pp. 3–4)

II

Another group of charges, involving actual biographical details, is of more intrinsic interest. These have done much to complicate the writings of Pope's biography because they are frequently not downright lies but distortions of a truth. How, one is sometimes driven to ask, could one poet manage to be involved in quite so many insanely complicated tangles? Not only did Pope love mystification and devious ways, as everyone knows (the title-page of the 1728 *Dunciad* provides an obvious example), but his enemies published and popularized wildly inaccurate and misleading versions of whatever they could find against him. Since, for example, Giles Jacob had sent Pope the proof sheets of the account of Pope in his *Poetical Register*, it was easy for him to claim later[2] that Pope had by his revisions produced a highly flattering biography of himself.

The obvious falsifications I have not bothered to expose in the bibliography. I have tried there to correct briefly the charges likely to confuse the modern reader, but it will be convenient to

---

[1] John Dennis, *A True Character Of Mr. Pope* (London, 1716), pp. 10–11.
[2] In Dennis's *Remarks Upon . . . the Dunciad* (1729) and *The Mirrour* (1733); the charge also appears in the *Popiad* (1728) and the *Curliad* (1729).

C

look here at the most famous accusations. On almost all of them we could use further new light which does not seem likely to be forthcoming.

The general reader of Pope may be surprised to find that certain poems of Pope which are hardly known today play a large part in Popiana. I suppose few people except specialists are well acquainted with the verse collected in the *Minor Poems* of the Twickenham Edition, but several of these poems appear much more frequently in the attacks than do the *Rape of the Lock* or the *Essay on Man*. 'To Mr John Moore, Author of the celebrated Worm-Powder' was useful, for example, in accusing Pope of indecency, and 'A Roman Catholick Version of the First Psalm' for accusing him of blasphemy and a Popish contempt for Scripture, despite the fact that it is far more reasonable to suppose Pope was parodying the Sternhold and Hopkins version than that he was parodying the psalm itself.[1]

Three Hours after Marriage is another work not, I think, generally read that provoked an extensive attack and became part of the repertory of standard charges. Pope's share in the play, on which he collaborated with Gay and Arbuthnot, is impossible to assess; Gay acknowledged his help and certainly he had a part in it. George Sherburn's admirable article, 'The Fortunes and Misfortunes of *Three Hours after Marriage*',[2] provides the necessary information. The main charges against the play are lewdness and stupidity. That many of the conversations are decidedly suggestive is perfectly true, but obscene it is not, and certainly not dull. It is still an amusing and high-spirited farce, capable of delighting an audience, as was shown in its 1953 production by the players of Wadham College, Oxford. Another charge, that Pope satirized friends and acquaintances in the play, foreshadows the *Dunciad* and subsequent battles. It seems certain that Dr Woodward was meant as Fossile, and several other characters may be identified with some certainty, but I think Sherburn is right in insisting that the claim that the Countess of Winchilsea is satirized in Phoebe Clinket cannot be seriously supported.

[1] See the careful discussion in Ault, pp. 156–62.
[2] George Sherburn, 'The Fortunes and Misfortunes of *Three Hours After Marriage*', MP, XXIV (1926–7), 91–109.

Several years earlier Pope had been awarded a share in *The What D' Ye Call It*, a farce by 'a *small Wit*, and a *clumsey Beau*', as Horneck called it,[1] though, as has been pointed out, there is no evidence Pope had a direct hand in it. Its amusing parodies and the absurdities of its plot were thought ill-natured and scandalous, and Cibber as late as 1742 could refer to 'those polite Pieces, *The What d'ye call it*, and *The Three Hours after Marriage*'.[2]

Pope's relations with Wycherley and Addison provide a popular subject in Popiana. To the discussion in Sherburn's *The Early Career of Alexander Pope* and the chapter on Addison and Pope in Ault's *New Light on Pope* there is little to add here. Gildon in his *Memoirs of Wycherley* (1718) paints for us the standard picture in Popiana of Pope, a ridiculous little provincial, a 'little *Aesopic* sort of an animal in his own cropt Hair, and Dress agreeable to the Forest he came from' (p. 16), following Wycherley around London and using him to gain entrée to the great. The implications are clear: Pope is an *arriviste* with unwarranted pretensions to literary genius but with skill in ingratiating himself and making a reputation. Dennis used this version, and it appears in even cruder form in *Codrus* (1728). A more common charge has it that Pope wrote a poem in praise of his own Pastorals and signed Wycherley's name to it. Dennis first said this in 1711, Gildon repeated it in *A New Rehearsal* (1714) and the *Memoirs of Wycherley* (1718), and it quickly established itself. Pope did revise Wycherley's poem, but he did not write it.[3]

Addison appears in Popiana as the irreproachable genius and generous patron of Pope whom Pope vilely slandered once he was safely dead. The popularity of the charge concerning the Atticus portrait is hardly surprising.[4] What clearer example could one want of Pope the ungrateful and treacherous friend and malevolent satirist than his slandering one of the most virtuous and most

[1] Philip Horneck, *The High-German Doctor*, March 15, 1715.

[2] Colley Cibber, *A Letter From Mr. Cibber, To Mr. Pope* (London, 1742), p. 21.

[3] See *EC* I. 21–3 for the standard charge and *Corr.* I. 50–1 for the refutation Pope was finally driven to make.

[4] It appears, *inter alia*, in *Cythereia* (1723), *The Progress Of Dulness* (1728), *Characters Of The Times* (1728), *Ingratitude: To Mr. Pope* (1733), *Mr. P[o]pe's Picture in Miniature* (1743).

universally admired figures of his age? We now know from the work of Ault and Sherburn that Addison had been behind the attacks on the Homer, that without sneering he had taught the rest to sneer, and that he had been sent the original portrait long before his death.

Pope's Homer provoked the first concerted attack on him, and though the quarrel is of great interest, the charges made are simple. Before the translation appeared, there were two easy lines to take, that Pope wanted to make money and that he knew no Greek.[1] The first one is much the more interesting and is, of course, true, although not in the sense implied by Burnet and Duckett, for example, in *Homerides*. After its appearance one could say that the poem was a pretty thing but not Homer, and, rather oddly, considering its success, that it was selling badly. Lintot's despair over the sales is reported in *The Catholick Poet* (1716), *A Complete Key To the New Farce, call'd Three Hours after Marriage* (1717), and *The Confederates* (1717). In the 'twenties and 'thirties and 'forties the dunces went on repeating how ignorant Pope was of Greek and how much money he had unfairly made, although by now they could also accuse him of having hired drudges to do the *Odyssey* for him.

The accusation so popular throughout the 'thirties that Pope was satirizing the Duke of Chandos as Timon in the *Epistle to Burlington* is fully discussed by F. W. Bateson in *Twick.* III. ii. 170–4.[2] Though the charge has little to support it and much to discredit it, it appealed to the dunces because it was so obviously just what they needed to convert aesthetic embarrassment into moral indignation.

---

[1] Pope was not a great classical scholar, but he was perfectly capable of reading Homer correctly, although, like so many others, he found the prose of someone like Eustathius rather beyond him. Very few howlers in his translations have ever been pointed out.

[2] See also George Sherburn, '"Timon's Villa" and Cannons', *Huntington Library Bulletin*, VIII (1935), 131–52.

IV

To understand the motives behind the pamphlet attacks and the forms that they took, it is necessary to consider their authors. No one generalization about the forty-odd writers can be completely true, and the large number of anonymous attacks makes the problem even more difficult. But if one omits the noble Lord Hervey and Lady Mary, critics of genuine worth such as Gildon and Dennis, and a famous actor-playwright such as Cibber, it is roughly true that the rest of our authors belong to Grub Street. They are the dunces. Even Theobald, though he had acquired much scholarship, was of Grub Street.

If we are to see a little more clearly what that picturesque but vague term 'Grub Street'[1] means in connection with Popiana, we must first be clear as to what it ought not to suggest. The modern reader is in some danger, and I think this may explain his *malaise* before the *Dunciad*, of associating Grub Street with Bohemia. The figure of the starving poet, struggling with his muse in an unheated garret, dunned by bill collectors – Hogarth's *Distressed Poet*, in short – is apt to invoke the wrong stock responses. The reader is apt to admire him as attractively romantic; he may well be a genius; he is certainly a man superior in every way to the uncomprehending bourgeoisie whom he so rightly despises.

But the myth of Bohemia was in Pope's day still to come. We shall never understand the *Dunciad* if we hear Puccini in the background. Grub Street is not the Left Bank, the world of Gérard de Nerval and the *poètes maudits*, complete with garret as romantic symbol and *nostalgie de la boue*. The Grub Street writer was not in full flight from a philistine and materialistic society; he was trying to earn enough money to take his place in it. He was not writing a masterpiece for the happy few and generations yet un-

---

[1] Johnson defined it in his *Dictionary* (1st ed., 1755) as 'Originally the name of a street; near Moorfields in London, much inhabited by writers of small histories, dictionaries, and temporary poems; whence any mean production is called *grubstreet*.'

born, wearing defiantly the neglect and incomprehension of the public as proof of his genius; he was doing his best to catch the public taste and persuade it to buy his books. He was seeking commercial success. He was, in other words, the antithesis of the romantic 'Artist' – a hack writer.

Of the lives and works of the dunces it is probable we know quite enough. The biographical appendix to the Twickenham *Dunciad* gives us the essential facts about their careers. What we know is not very much, to be sure; they remain obscure figures, but any attempt to rescue them from their Limbo, granting that new sources of information could be found, would involve a completely disproportionate effort. As anyone who has ever tried to read them will surely agree, they are just what Pope said they were, thoroughly bad writers. Their real importance for the student of Pope and the Augustan Age is sociological.[1]

The hack writer was a man whose pen was for sale; he was, in Savage's phrase, 'an author to be let'. In the pamphlet of that title Iscariot Hackney explains that after he had managed to get free of Curll for some years,

> He arrested me for several Months Board, brought me back to my Garret, and made me drudge on in my old, dirty Work. 'Twas in his Service that I wrote Obscenity and Profaneness, under the Names of *Pope* and *Swift*. Sometimes I was Mr. *Joseph Gay*, and at others Theory *Burnet*, or *Addison*. I abridg'd Histories and Travels, translated from the *French*, what they never wrote, and was expert at finding out new Titles for old Books. . . . Had Mr. *Oldmixon* and Mr. *Curll* agreed, my assistance had probably been invited into Father *Boheur*'s [*sic*] Logick, and the critical History of *England*.[2]

---

[1] For my discussion here I am particularly indebted to the following: A. S. Collins, *Authorship in the Days of Johnson* (London, 1927); A. R. Humphreys, *The Augustan World, Life and Letters in Eighteenth Century England* (London, 1954); Frank Arthur Mumby, *Publishing and Bookselling* (London, 1949); Harry Ransom, 'The Rewards of Authorship in the Eighteenth Century', *Studies in English, The University of Texas*, XVIII (1938), 47–66; Ian Watt, 'Publishers and Sinners: The Augustan View', *Studies in Bibliography, Papers of the Bibliographical Society of the University of Virginia*, XII (1959), 3–20.

[2] *An Author To Be Lett* (1729), ed. James Sutherland, The Augustan Reprint Society, Publication No. 84 (Los Angeles, 1960), pp. 3–4.

This implies the supremacy of the bookseller. For him the hack worked, writing what he was ordered to write, and getting paid what the bookseller wanted to offer. Not that, necessarily, the Grub Street bookseller was inhuman and thoroughly mean. It is clear, however vague the details remain, that there were far too many men trying to earn a living from writing, and far too few readers, though the reading public was growing slowly. The bookseller, who was after all a business man, did what he could to find work for his writers and probably paid them less than the hacks thought they deserved but about as much as he could and still make a reasonable profit. The Grub Street writer and bookseller were both caught in a classic situation in capitalist economics.

The situation was so acute because there were no alternatives for the struggling writer. He could not set up for himself and publish his own work; this remained difficult throughout the century even for writers of great distinction. Nor were there patrons to whom he could apply – not, at least, very easily. The great days of patronage were ended by 1714. Under Walpole, whatever money was spent was spent for government propaganda. Walpole was interested in political results, not poetry. It is true that patrons continued for some time. Thomson and Young both found patrons, but patronage was no longer an aristocratic fashion, and with the growth of the reading public and the increasing prosperity of the book trade, it became less and less necessary. The unknown writer, then, in Pope's time, was in bondage to the bookseller. The almost inevitable result was the commercialization of literature. The booksellers' race in Book II of the *Dunciad* shows us Pope's awareness of this.

The booksellers, although most of them were interested in publishing good books whenever they could, wanted to sell as many books as possible. The easiest way to this, then as now, was to give the public what it wanted or what it was thought to want: scandal about its betters, secret histories, memoirs, authentic or not as long as they were scabrous, topical libels. The middle class has always enjoyed reading about how dreadfully the great behave, with what flaunting of the laws of God, and what indifference to the proprieties. It enjoyed, and this is more pertinent for

us, being assured by the authors of *Gulliveriana* or *The Twicken-ham Hotch-Potch* that satire (such as *Gulliver's Travels* or the *Dun-ciad*) was effortlessly easy to write and not worth taking seriously. It also enjoyed, as it continues to, histories, digests, and compila-tions of all kinds, giving easy access to information. It was the hack writer's job, sometimes with scissors and paste, and some-times with a flair for the libellous and no scruples about pander-ing to prurience, to furnish the books to order.

It is dangerous to forget this when trying to deal with the ques-tion of why the dunces attacked Pope. What exactly were their motives? The usual answer is that they were replying to Pope's inclusion of them in the *Peri Bathous* and the *Dunciad*, where he had said very damaging things about them. This is true as far as it goes, but it is not a sufficient answer. Almost none of them knew Pope personally or had personal grievances against him, while he, in most cases, had no personal grievances against them. Instead of seeking to explain Pope's use of their names in his satires and their attacks on him entirely in terms of personal spite-fulness and revenge, although in a few instances these undoubt-edly played a part, it is more exact to see the Battle of the Dunces as part of an economic and class war.

The dunces, to begin with a consideration that can never be too much emphasized, attacked Pope because it paid.

> The more we rail, the more bespatter,
> 'Twill make our *Pamphlets* sell the better.[1]

They lived by selling to a market, and one can only presume from the number of pamphlets and publishers involved that Popiana enjoyed sales that made it profitable. Figures are unfortunately wanting. Most of the pamphlets were probably not printed in great numbers. A few ran to several editions, though because of the multiplying of 'editions' in Grub Street to foster sales, this evidence must be used with caution. Still, people bought the attacks and continued to buy them annually until Pope's death.

It did not need much ingenuity to write one; most were short, and the old charges could always be refurbished. There is the following revealing interchange in Fielding's *The Author's Farce* between the bookseller Bookweight and one of his hacks:

[1] *Sawney and Colley* (London, 1742), p. 5.

Bookweight. Fie upon it, gentlemen! What, not at your pens? Do you consider, Mr. Quibble, that it is a fortnight since your letter to a friend in the country was published? Is it not high time for an answer to come out? At this rate, before your answer is printed, your letter will be forgot. I love to keep a controversy up warm. I have had authors who have writ a pamphlet in the morning, answered it in the afternoon, and answered that again at night.

Quibble. Sir, I will be as expeditious as possible: but it is harder to write on this side the question, because it is the wrong side.

Bookweight. Not a jot. So far on the contrary, that I have known some authors choose it as the properest to show their genius.[1]

Pamphlet attacks provided a means of reaching a considerable audience with entertaining scandal about public figures without fear of horsewhipping or assassination, which might be the consequences of attacking the peerage. Profit and personal safety could go hand in hand.

Larger considerations of class and politics are, however, yet more important. The dunces, as a whole, belonged to the lower classes. They represented the commercial element, the small shop-keepers, the part of the population that was, as usual, slowly rising.

Most of these Persons are of very low Parentage, and without any Pretence of Merit, are aspiring to the Rank of Gentlemen,

Savage pointed out very accurately.[2] Nothing in the *Dunciad* has been more misunderstood than Pope's references to the dunces' poverty. It would have been damning indeed if they could have proved that Pope was laughing at a man because he was poor. But Pope was doing nothing of the kind. The dunces' poverty was the visible sign of their pride. They were poor not because they were indifferent to worldly values or because they had

---

[1] Henry Fielding, *The Author's Farce* in *The Complete Works of Henry Fielding*, ed. W. E. Henley, viii (New York, 1902), 218–19.

[2] Savage, A2v.

chosen to follow the evangelical counsel; they were poor because they refused their proper vocations. Savage, in the passage just quoted, continues shrewdly:

> Thus they become ill Oeconomists, Poverty is the Consequence of ill Oeconomy, and dirty Tricks the Consequence of their Poverty. Tho' they are sad Writers, they might have been good Mechanicks; and therefore by endeavouring to shine in Spheres, to which they are unequal, are guilty of depriving the Publick of many that might have been its useful Members ... Had it not been more laudable in Mr. R—m, the Son of an *Undertaker*, to have borne a *Link*, and a *Mourning Staff* in the *long Procession* of a *Funeral*, than to have been frequently *lamenting* the *Burials* of his *miserable, short-lived Libels*? ... Why wou'd not Mr. *Theobald* continue an Attorney? Is not *Word-catching* more serviceable in splitting a Cause, than explaining a fine Poet?[1]

Above all, they did not share the aristocratic ethos. Their spirit was lower middle-class, capitalist, commercial; their spiritual teacher is Defoe. They are concerned with profit, not with the transmission of a cultural tradition, not with holding the mirror up to nature or giving us the abstract and brief chronicles of the time; with getting ahead, selling a product, not with the improvement of English literature by domesticating into it the great writers of Greece and Rome.

In their hatred of Pope, therefore, one detects a powerful infusion of pure class-antagonism. Nothing offends them so much as the thought of Pope's wealth. Far more important to them even than his satire against them is the fact that he has made a fortune by literature and is thus free of the captivity they are enslaved to. That he has done this, at least in part, through a passionate concern for values which simply do not exist in their own world picture, a concern that has made him the spokesman, as Dryden was before him, of order in art, society, and man, simply compounds their antagonism.

To the dunces, for these reasons, Pope appears a betrayer of his own class. Who was this Alexander Pope anyway? The son

---

[1] Savage, A2v–A3v. See the parallel passage in Epictetus quoted in Aubrey Williams, *Pope's 'Dunciad', A Study of its Meaning* (London, 1955), p. 94.

of a farmer or a hatter at best, they said, in an attempt to cut this man down socially. What right had he to a villa at Twickenham, to a comfortable income, and visiting acquaintance with half the peerage? Why should he be accepted on equal terms in households where their own acquaintanceship was among the footmen – and he a Catholic, a Jacobite, legally a pariah, to boot? Furthermore, he had not sold himself to a political party or toadied a patron. Instead, he had beaten the booksellers at their own game. This was what really hurt. That Pope had done it proved that it could be done; the fact that they could not do it too, and knew it, was an ever-present reminder that what he said about them was true: they *had* missed their calling; if a man had the wit and inventiveness, the public to support him was already there. All Pope had had to do was publish an expensive translation of Homer, the proceeds going mostly to himself. And this when he did not even know Greek!

Thus if Pope had never written a line against the men of Grub Street, though they would doubtless have attacked him less often, they could never have approved of him. They were separated from him by two abysses. The first was their attitude toward money. The dunces accepted the Calvinist ethic. With the basic aims of the Walpole administration they were in hearty agreement. Publishers like Curll saw the business man as hero. Pope's views could scarcely have been more different. The *Dunciad* is almost as much a satire on a money society where everything is for sale as is the *Beggar's Opera*. When all the necessary adjustments for animus and vanity have been made, Pope still emerges as one of the great defenders of a society with a moral and cultural centre. In Book IV of the *Dunciad* corruption by money is the last indignity, and in the *Epilogue to the Satires, Dialogue I*, we are reminded of the *Essay on Man*'s vision of love binding the elements into unity; vice binds the world into unity with chains of gold. Pope's attitude to money is complicated, of course, as everyone's is. A moderate income is essential not only to a life of dignity but to the independence which writers must have. Nevertheless neither Balaam, no matter how much money he may make, nor Timon, no matter how much money he may have inherited, will ever belong to Pope's image of the good society.

The second abyss between Pope and the dunces was their attitude toward literature. As I have already suggested, to the dunces and their publishers literature was what sold. One did not in Grub Street consult one's Horace with diurnal hand; one consulted the public. One was not concerned about standards, about a tradition, about works of imagination that might justify an entire civilization. And one could not, as a result, understand Pope's sacerdotal view of literature. One could only regard him as an impostor, who had set himself up as a dictator and proposed to keep all the profits to himself: '*ALEXANDER POPE, Keeper of the* Profound, *Vicar of the* Dunciad, *Blunder-Master-General of* Dramatic *Poetry, Lord Paramount-wou'd-be of* Mount Parnassus...'[1] Quality, craftsmanship, the work well made, were not among the dunces' values. They seem, for the most part, simply unaware of how painstaking Pope's verse is.

Pope's view is again the antithesis of theirs. His standards are absolute and finely discriminated. His verse is the result of thoughtful meditation on the problems of tradition and the individual talent. He forged a distinctive language for his time and purified *les mots de la tribu*, yet he succeeded at the same time in keeping alive within his verse the whole civilizing tradition of the classical heritage.

Whatever his personal failings, Pope saw clearly that a great and civilized literature places a special responsibility on the writer, and he was therefore certain to be troubled by the dunces who acknowledged none. If they were allowed to flourish, and he could see no signs that they were not everywhere succeeding – the Smithfield Muse *had* reached the ear of Kings – was this not chaos come again? Was not the order that he and Swift and all the earlier Augustans cared for doomed? The news-stands of today, Hollywood, television, popular culture in all its forms have taught us so well what uses may be made of literacy in a mass society that we cannot fail to recognize in the apocalypse of Book IV of the *Dunciad* a wild surmise come partly true.

One further way to understand the difference between Pope and the dunces is to invoke the political symbols of Whig and

[1] Sir Butterfly Maggot, pseud., *The Gentleman's Miscellany* (London, 1730), [A2r].

Tory. It is, of course, inaccurate to say that Pope was a Tory, since he was much too concerned to keep himself above the political fight, and it is not true that all the dunces were clearly and officially Whigs. Still the separation into parties corresponds roughly to the realities. Pope moved most in Tory circles. One need only think of his friendships with Swift, Atterbury, and Bolingbroke. He took an active interest in the 'thirties in the Opposition to Walpole, whose method of government he deplored. The parties, as historians remind us, did not exist in anything like their later well-defined forms, but if one thinks roughly of the Tories as representing the interests of the aristocracy, the squirearchy, conservatism and tradition in church and government and economics, then the label of Tory has some meaning for Pope.

The dunces were, on the other hand, decidedly Whiggish. Pope's first difficulties, with the *Pastorals* and the Homer, came from Addison's group at Button's, the Whig coffee house. In the 'thirties some of the dunces were in the pay of Walpole. Praise of Walpole in a pamphlet prepares you for an attack on Pope, whereas if you find a pamphlet attacking Walpole, you can be fairly sure it will not be hostile to Pope. The dunces were hardly in a position to attack political bribery and place-seeking. They were actively trying to profit from these and many, like Welsted and Concanen, succeeded. With the aristocracy, except in so far as it was Whig and could furnish political patronage, the Church (Cooke was the son of a Muggletonian), and the landed interests, they could have no sympathy. They looked to the City, the commercial middle class, and financiers. Where Pope to an extent shared in 'the gloom of the Tory satirists', the dunces were optimistic about progress and suffered from the usual failing of their kind, a totally inadequate sense of evil. No wonder the *Dunciad* and the *Imitations of Horace* seemed to them twisted and perverse. They could explain them only in the terms with which they were familiar: personal malice, revenge, Jacobitism, arrogance.

V

The pamphlet attacks deeply influenced both Pope and his writing. At the beginning of his literary career the unfair preference given to Philips's *Pastorals* in the pages of *The Guardian* over his own must have been disappointing. It was not the entrance into literary life he had dreamed of. But the first major shock must have come later with Dennis's first attack. It is not risking too much to suppose that for psychological effect on Pope it is the most important single attack ever written against him. Pope could hardly have been prepared for it, even with his knowledge of the habits of literary warfare of the time. All he had said about Dennis was,

> But *Appius* reddens at each Word you speak,
> And *stares, Tremendous!* with a *threatning Eye,*
> Like some *fierce Tyrant* in *Old Tapestry!*[1]

There is a flick at Dennis's failed tragedy, at his favourite word, and at his irascible nature. But it is just as important to notice that Pope had aesthetically distanced Dennis. He had turned the unattractive critic into a work of art. Fiercely staring tyrants in tapestry have a grotesque beauty. And they are harmless. They provoke in the spectator not fear but an aesthetic emotion. Nor was there anything offensively original in finding Dennis rather comic. He had been, and continued to be, a natural butt for wits. Eleven years earlier the prologue by Thomas Cheek to Abel Boyer's *Achilles* (1700) had ridiculed him:

> His Muse in Nature's Majesty appears,
> She has no Sounds *Tremendous* to the Ears.[2]

And the author of *A Comparison Between the Two Stages* (1702) had also made fun of him and his favourite adjective.[3]

Dennis was, however, somewhat paranoid. He found attacks on himself in the *Tatler* and *Spectator* whenever they discussed

---

[1] *Essay on Criticism*, ll. 585–7.
[2] Abel Boyer, *Achilles: Or, Iphigenia in Aulis* ... (London, 1700), A4r.
[3] *A Comparison Between the Two Stages, A Late Restoration Book of the Theatre,* ed. Staring B. Wells (Princeton, 1942), pp. 23, 56.

critics.[1] Pope deftly summed up this persecution mania in his *True Narrative of Dr Robert Norris*:

That the said Mr. *John Denn[is]* on the 27th of *March*, 1712. finding on the said Mr. *Lintott's* Counter a Book called an *Essay on Criticism*, just then publish'd, he read a Page or two with much Frowning and Gesticulation, till coming to these two Lines;

> *Some have at first for Wits, then Poets past,*
> *Turn'd Criticks next, and prov'd plain Fools at last.*

He flung down the Book in a terrible Fury, and cried out, *By G— he means Me.*[2]

But even knowing Dennis's sensitivity Pope could hardly have supposed that for several lines of verse he would be attacked in a thirty-page pamphlet which not only criticized his poem in the fiercest way, but attacked its author for his religion and his deformity with wholesale scurrility. Edith Sitwell has pointed out that it is impossible to read the abuse 'without feeling the deepest anger, compassion for its victim, and a kind of horrified pity towards the man who could write such a passage'.[3] It is easy to be sentimental about Pope, and it is absurd to explain satire as a defence-mechanism, but it is relevant in a consideration of Popiana to allow oneself to imagine the anguish with which Pope read this abuse. People with physical defects are notoriously sensitive to references to them, yet for thirty years Pope was to see his shape publicly derided in the vilest way. At the time of Dennis's onslaught he was still in his early twenties. Like most young men in their twenties, he was struggling to appear well before the ladies, to appear a bit of a rake, even, a roistering man about town. These seem normal enough desires, if rather pathetic ones, granted Pope's crazy constitution, but Pope's attackers would see to it that he would be allowed no illusions.

Again, though the young Pope could have had no illusions about the contempt and fear his religion excited in his fellow Englishmen and was not, it is clear, devout, he must have been

---

[1] Before the appearance of the *Essay on Criticism*, Dennis had supposed himself attacked in the *Tatler*, Nos. 29 and 246, and in the *Spectator*, Nos. 40 and 47, and possibly in a few other papers referring to critics (Hooker, II. 440–1).

[2] *Prose*, I. 166.

[3] Edith Sitwell, *Alexander Pope* (Penguin Books, 1948), p. 68.

deeply pained to see the religious convictions and dogmas of his Church turned into a stick to beat him with. The young poet had had a sheltered life. The young are notoriously disposed to believe that they will be treated at least with justice; Pope learned in the most brutal way that justice was the last thing he could expect.

More profound than the abuse of deformity and Catholicism is the revision of Pope's personality that the pamphlets undertook. They presented to the world the portrait of the satirist that we have seen and insisted that it was the full truth about Pope. Pope, of course, knew that it was not a likeness. But his identity was threatened, since all of us construct our concept of self partly from our neighbour's reaction to it.

Pope knew, as he read the pamphlets, that A P—E was not Alexander Pope. Whatever his vanity, he knew he was not a saint (and knew that few people are). He also knew that whatever his personal failings he was not diabolic in malignity, simian in flattery and greed. His actions, if not always blameless nor inspired by pure motives, were not the actions of a Durgen or Codrus or Labeo:

> On, mighty Rhimer, haste new Palms to seize,
> Thy little, envious, angry Genius teize;
> Let thy weak wilful Head, unrein'd by Art,
> Obey the Dictates of thy flatt'ring Heart;
> Divide a busy, fretful Life between
> Smut, Libel, Sing-song, Vanity, and Spleen;
> With long-brew'd Malice warm thy languid Page,
> And urge delirious Nonsense into Rage.[1]

It was only natural that in the face of *this* image he gradually constructed for himself another, that of the Poet of the *Imitations of Horace*: to virtue only and her friends a friend. (No other line more infuriated the dunces, it was for them Pope's ultimate hypocrisy.) This public face may have seemed to its creator *the* basic truth about himself (most of us would say, if pressed, that on the whole, allow a little here, a little more there, we are virtue's friends); at any rate it presented *a* basic truth. It indicated the

---

[1] Leonard Welsted and James Moore Smythe, *One Epistle To Mr. A. Pope* (London, 1730), p. 13.

direction of Pope's ideals and was thus he hoped true. It also presented a good deal of his practice, if we recall the esteem of his friends, his continuing benefactions both in money and service to those he could help (including the aged Dennis), his refusal to be the tool of any party or patron, his dedication to his art and to the values of the civilized imagination. The real Alexander Pope was somewhere between A P—E, the malignant hunchback of the pamphlets, and the Poet of the satires, his ideal self, but he lay a good deal closer to the latter than to the former. It was the realization that Pope was not his literary persona which so shocked his nineteenth-century editors like Elwin. The pamphlet attacks, I think we may conclude, played their part in the construction of this persona.

It also seems certain that they played a part in changing the application of Pope's genius toward the satiric mode. They offered to the poet a provocation and an opportunity, and the opportunity discovered to the poet his own capacity.

To turn to the direct influence that the pamphlets had on Pope's writing, we may distinguish Pope's replies in prose and verse. They are not, to be sure, exactly 'replies'. They are rarely specific refutations, but they are writings clearly occasioned by one or more of the attacks.

Guardian No. 40 is Pope's ironic notice of *The Guardian*'s praise of Philips's *Pastorals*. *The Critical Specimen* is someone's reply to Dennis's first attack; it is far from certain that Pope wrote it, but for completeness here, we may tentatively accept the attribution in Ault's *Prose Works*. *The Narrative of Dr. Robert Norris* is a further reply to Dennis, its immediate occasion being Dennis's *Remarks on Cato*. *The Dignity, Use, and Abuse of Glass-Bottles*, again accepting Ault's shaky attribution, replies to the attacks on Pope in *The Grumbler* and *High-German Doctor*. Then there are the three replies to Curll's offences, *A Full and True Account Of A ... Revenge by Poison*, *On the Body of Mr. Edmund Curll*, *A Further Account Of the most Deplorable Condition Of Mr. Edmund Curll*, and *A Strange but True Relation How Edmund Curll ... was converted from the Christian Religion*. We may include as well *A Clue To the Comedy of the Non-Juror*, in which Pope may or may not have had a hand, inspired by Cibber's offensive play. After this productive period, 1711–18,

D

there are no further prose replies until the *Peri Bathous* in 1728. This is followed by *A Letter to a Noble Lord*, a reply to Hervey, which was not published during Pope's lifetime, and by *A Master Key to Popery*, only recently discovered.[1] Unless we include *A Blast upon Bays*, a reply to Cibber in 1742 and ascribed (wrongly, I suspect) to Pope by T. J. Wise and Ault, these are Pope's only known replies in prose.

The replies in verse are too famous to need dwelling upon. The *Dunciad* in its several forms together with the *Epistle to Arbuthnot* constitute Pope's great answer to the pamphlets. There are references throughout the *Imitations of Horace*, but it is these two poems which preserve allusions to Popiana for us and make an acquaintance with it necessary. A comparison of the above 're-plies' with the following bibliography of attacks will make clear that Pope bore the incessant attacks with remarkable patience. Pope, whatever the dunces said, did not bother to mention in verse or prose a very large number of the pamphlets. He never, it might be pointed out, replied to any of the attacks on the *Iliad* and *Odyssey*, despite their number and vexatiousness. To anyone who tries to read through Popiana year by year, it is Pope's for-bearance and restraint that come to seem remarkable; the image of a poet eager to make every one of his detractors writhe needs serious revision.

There is one specific influence of the pamphlets which should not go unnoticed: their criticisms caused Pope to make several changes in his verse. When he said,

> Did some more sober Critic come abroad?
> If wrong, I smil'd; if right, I kiss'd the rod,[2]

he was being accurate. He did as he had advised in the *Essay on Criticism* and made use of every friend and every foe.[3] Thomas Cooke's *The Comedian*, No. 2, criticized l. 10 of the *Epistle to Bur-lington* and Pope introduced the suggested emendation of 'Rari-ties' to 'Butterflies'. He also in the same poem changed ll. 25 and 127 as a result of criticisms in *A Miscellany On Taste*. The altera-tions he made in the *Essay on Criticism* because of Dennis's objec-tions are well known (and frequently over-emphasized); I have

---

[1] This is printed in *Twick.* III. ii. 175–88.
[2] *Epistle to Arbuthnot*, ll. 157–8.   [3] *Essay on Criticism*, l. 214.

listed them all in my account of the pamphlet. To Concanen's criticisms in *A Supplement To The Profund* (London, 1728) are probably to be ascribed the change in *The Rape of the Lock*, I. 11, and the omission of a couplet after l. 258 in *Eloisa to Abelard*.

How many of the attacks I have listed did Pope know of and read? The *Dunciad* and the *Epistle to Arbuthnot* are sure evidence that Pope had read, and read with care, most of the attacks. His own list of them in Appendix II to the *Dunciad* is almost complete up to 1728 (with several odd omissions of pamphlets there is other evidence he knew). After 1729 he obviously made little effort to keep up the list, but a very high proportion of them find some mention in the final version of the *Dunciad* or in other poems. There is no evidence to prove he knew of a minor item, such as *Malice Defeated*, 1732, but he certainly read a good deal on the Timon scandal. I think it fair to conclude that Pope had read almost all of the attacks here listed.

Outside of the poems and the few comments in the letters, there is little evidence for Pope's reading in Popiana. There are two volumes of miscellaneous poems from Pope's own library in the Dyce Collection, pressmark D.6.c.1–2, but they contain no attacks. The British Museum, however, has four volumes of the attacks originally collected and bound by Pope, pressmark C.116.b.1–4. On a leaf at the beginning of the first volume Pope himself has written: 'Job, Chapt.31. Vers.35. Behold it is my desire, that mine Adversary had written a Book. Surely I would take it on my Shoulder, and bind it as a crown unto me.'

Volume I contains: Dennis's *Reflections Critical and Satyrical*, 1711; his *Remarks Upon . . . Homer*, 1717; and his *A True Character*, 1717; *Aesop At The Bear-Garden*, 1715; *Homerides: Or, A Letter To Mr. Pope*, 1715; *A Complete Key To . . . The What D'Ye Call It*, 1715; *A Complete Key To . . . Three Hours after Marriage*, 1717; *A Letter To Mr. John Gay*, 1717; and *The Confederates*, 1717.

Volume II contains *Sawney*, 1728; *An Essay On The Dunciad*, 1728; *A Supplement To The Profund*, 1728; *Characters Of The Times*, 1728; *A Letter From A Clergyman to his Friend*, 1726 (an attack on Swift, not Pope); and *A Compleat Collection Of all the Verses*, 1728.

Volume III consists entirely of *Gulliveriana*, 1728. Volume IV contains *The Curliad*, 1729; Oldmixon's *An Essay on Criticism*,

1728; Dennis's *Remarks Upon ... the Dunciad*, 1729; Hill's *The Progress of Wit*, 1730; Jacob's *The Mirrour*, 1733; and *An Answer To Mr. Pope's Preface*, 1729. All but the last of these (and *A Letter From A Clergyman*) are mentioned in the *Dunciad*. With the exception of the last volume these all have brief annotations and scorings of passages by Pope himself. But except on Dennis's criticisms of *The Rape of the Lock* and the *Essay on Criticism*, noted in the Twickenham Edition, Pope's jottings are less helpful than the mention of them suggests. I have noted several in my text.

VI

Although the pamphlets are intended simply to abuse Pope, being attacks on a literary figure and his work they are also literary
criticism, however feeble. They offer, once we have made several
large qualifications, some interesting evidence on the contemporary reading of Pope's poetry. To be sure, they are biased. The
great majority are also badly written – so vague, incoherent, and
confused that frequently the meaning of the verse or prose must
simply be guessed at. (This has made the task of giving orderly
résumés in my bibliography exceedingly awkward.) On both
these counts, they are less helpful as unsophisticated contemporary reactions than one could wish. Still, their underlying critical
assumptions and attitudes are reasonably clear and reveal an
approach to literature (based evidently on schoolroom training)
of a sort that we usually forget persisted throughout the Augustan
Age.

Their critical method at its best consists largely in minute attention to every phrase and word. Most of the time it is mere
tedious quibbling, and there is almost never an attempt to see the
poem as a whole, to grasp it as an organic unity.[1] But the assumption behind much of the quibbling is interesting: a perfectly logical consistency, an absolute adherence to the literally true is required in poetry. Concanen was delighted to show that the lord
in the *Epistle to Burlington* could not be at the same time in his
study and advancing over the lawn.[2] Dennis objected to what
Pope had said of wit in the *Essay on Criticism*, l. 503:

Where *wanted*, scorn'd, and envy'd where *acquir'd*.

[1] Bentley's Milton remains the most notorious example of this method
which has certain virtues but dreadful weaknesses. In the nineteenth century
Elwin's savage annotation to the *Essay on Criticism* provides another example.
Mallet's *Of Verbal Criticism: An Epistle To Mr. Pope. Occasioned By Theobald's
Shakespear, and Bentley's Milton* (London, 1733), protested, 'how false, how
vain the *Scholiast's* Art, / Which nor to taste, nor genius has pretence' (p. 4).
This verbal criticism, 'word catching' as the wits called it, treats poetry as it
would the simplest utilitarian denotative prose; it betrays a fatal misunder-
standing of metaphor.

[2] Matthew Concanen, *A Miscellany On Taste* (London, 1732), p. 16.

'... How can Wit be scorn'd where it is not?'[1] (Pope altered both these lines.) Dennis was also concerned to announce that there were no woods near Hampton Court to echo Belinda's cries.[2] (It appears, however, that there were.)[3] He was very much upset by the Temple of Fame in the sky 'contrary to Nature, and to the Eternal Laws of Gravitation'.[4] The author of *The Poet finish'd in Prose* was bothered by the fact that the poet in the *Epistle to Arbuthnot* complained of the dog star in January or February, obviously the relevant date since the poem had been published in one of those months.[5] Whatever else the dunces wanted in verse, they did not want the free play of the imagination.

The dislike of parody to which the pamphlets testify is also interesting. If they can prove that Pope has lifted a passage from another writer with parodic intent, they feel they have scored a hit. The best example of this is the attack on the *What D'Ye Call It* where a long list of sources is given, and the very amusing parody is considered as deliberate and wanton sacrilege on Shakespeare, Rowe, etc. The dunces saw that Pope had lifted a simile from Addison's *Campaign* in the *Dunciad* A, iii. 259–60, and considered it outrageous.[6] Parody, at least when Pope did it, was insult, and not, after all, surprising, coming from the man who had burlesqued Homer. The dunces, of course, chose not to be amused by anything Pope had written, but taking the pamphlets as a whole it is impossible not to conclude that most of them lacked a sense of humour.

Their attitude to imitation is equally simplistic. It was easy for them to accuse Pope of plagiarism since they could show that he had imitated Chaucer, Dryden, Boileau. If they recognized imitation as a serious genre, they chose to forget it when pointing out Pope's indebtedness. Pope is

> The Bard! that first, from *Dryden*'s thrice-glean'd Page,
> Cull'd his low Efforts to Poetic Rage;

---

[1] John Dennis, *Reflections Critical and Satyrical* (London, 1711), p. 20.
[2] John Dennis, *Remarks On Mr. Pope's Rape of the Lock* (London, 1728), p. 17.
[3] See *Twick*. II. 372.
[4] John Dennis, *Remarks Upon Mr. Pope's Translation Of Homer* (London, 1717), p. 51.
[5] *The Poet finish'd in Prose* (London, 1735), pp. 18–19.
[6] James Ralph, *Sawney* (London, 1728), p. xiii.

> Nor pillag'd only that unrival'd Strain,
> But rak'd for Couplets *Chapman* and *Duck-Lane*,
> Has sweat each Cent'ry's Rubbish to explore,
> And plunder'd every Dunce that writ before.[1]

It never occurred to any of his critics to investigate the use that Pope had made of his models and the work he made his borrowings do.

Their attitude to satire is perhaps to us the most interesting yet the most difficult to isolate. To begin with, the dunces, as has been pointed out, did not try to conceive of a poem as a whole. They read the *Dunciad* entirely as a collection of individual passages attacking themselves. They did not see that their attacks on Pope differed in kind from his, although they may have seen that theirs were not so clever. They did not, that is, see that the *Dunciad* was a poem and that though they were indeed its subject they were not its theme. (It may be asking too much to expect the grub to appreciate the amber, but the dunces' failure to read the poem as poem had the most serious critical consequences.) The mis-statements and mis-quotations in the *Dunciad Variorum* they could seize on and triumphantly correct, but they ignored the process by which Pope lifted them out of historical reality and endowed them with a universal significance. The dunces were created for the sake of the poem, as Pope tried to explain.[2] The dunces' quite understandable inability to see things that way meant that they did not respond to the poem except to notice that they were being made ridiculous. All that they could see that Pope was saying was that they were dull. They insisted, in page after page of their replies, proving Pope's point, that they were not. Probably no great poem has ever been so shallowly read.

In so far as they acknowledge the genre of satire at all, it is for them narrowly didactic and has as its end the reformation of vice. It must remain general and never name names:

> Satyr, if justly handled, is of use,
> But real Names turn Satyr to abuse;

---

[1] Leonard Welsted and James Moore Smythe, *One Epistle To Mr. A. Pope* (London, 1730), p. 10.

[2] *Twick*. v. 205.

> Lash Folly in the sharpest terms you can,
> Condemn the Vice, but not expose the Man.[1]

Ward is much concerned with the possibility of retribution for personal satire:

> Pers'nal Reflections, Men of Art must own,
> Cease to be Satyr, and become Lampoon,
> And should against no rival Wit be us'd,
> Except by him that has been first abus'd;
> The meanest Man, when injur'd in his fame,
> Is prone by nature to revenge the same,
> And if unjustly pelted, will, in course,
> Fling back the dirt receiv'd, with greater Force.[2]

More importantly, he betrays here the typical failing of the pamphleteers. If they are willing to admit that in theory general satire aimed at the reformation of society is justifiable, in practice they are quite unable to make any distinction between satire and lampoon. Pope had described this kind of critic,

> Who reads but with a Lust to mis-apply,
> Make Satire a Lampoon, and Fiction, Lye.[3]

Their images for the satirist indicate how they read satire. In *The Metamorphosis* (1728) Pope and Swift are curs who love

> To teize and bite whate'er came next 'em,
> Out of pure Spite, tho' nothing vext 'em;
> To bark, to insult, to run stark wild,
> And foam at Woman, Man, and Child;
> To *foul* and *dirt* each Place they came in,
> And play some Pranks, unfit for naming.   (p. 5)

In *Tom o' Bedlam's Dunciad: Or, Pope, Alexander the Pig* (1729) Pope learns his language from watermen and the wives of Billingsgate. In the dunces' favourite metaphors Pope is a monkey dropping filth, or Aesop's toad that burst with envy.

Part of their blindness to Pope's satiric art comes from their failure to respond to the very elements Pope had so carefully considered and perfected, the diction and versification, the level of style, the careful complicating use of classical epic and satire. Hervey, for example, dismissed the verse of the *Imitations of Horace*

---

[1] Ned Ward, *Durgen* (London, 1729), p. 9.   [2] *Ibid.* pp. 12–13.
[3] *Epistle to Arbuthnot*, ll. 301–2.

by saying that Pope's earlier 'Merit of Versification ... Mr. *Pope* in his late Epistles, and what he calls Satires, has either from Age and Rust entirely lost, or from an Affectation of the *sermo pedestris* chosen to abdicate'.[1] Dennis finds in Pope 'an eternal Monotony'. He has 'neither Judgment nor Numbers, he is neither Poet nor Versifyer, but only an eternal Rhimer ...'[2] Cooke found in the *Dunciad* 'a confusion of Figures, and evident Contradictions to Sense, with a Profusion of Words which mean Nothing, or what they ought not to mean, direct Calumnys, Lewdness, and Prophaneness, and without Wit or Humour ...'[3] In the *Essay on Criticism*, he insisted, 'a nice ear can not distinguish fifty Lines which please'; nothing is more false than the view that Pope is a competent versifier.[4] *Pope Alexander's Supremacy* contains a dull little essay ridiculing Pope's use of alliteration.[5]

Their chief difficulty with satire, however, lies in their refusal to separate the satirist from his persona.

> How strict a Guard then ought the *true* Satyrist to set upon his private Passions! How clear a Head! a Heart how candid, how impartial, how incapable of Injustice! What Integrity of Life, what general Benevolence, what exemplary Virtues ought that happy Man to be master of, who, from such ample Merit, raises himself to an Office of that Trust and Dignity, as that of our Universal Censor?

Cibber exclaimed,[6] and the dunces would agree with their King. The logic of this position leads to a denial of the possibility of satire. Refusing to separate satirist and persona, to them the speaker of the poems was quite simply Pope. The speaker pretended to be honest, devoted to virtue, detached from wealth, a thoroughly admirable and likeable man. But Pope was, they were sure they could prove, a liar and a slanderer, mean, envious, vain, and avaricious. Even the simple fact that a bad man (as they

---

[1] John, Lord Hervey, *A Letter To Mr. C[i]b[e]r* (London, 1742), p. 13.

[2] John Dennis, *Remarks On Mr. Pope's Rape of the Lock* (London, 1728), p. ix.

[3] Thomas Cooke, *Tales, Epistles, Odes, Fables, &c.* (London, 1729), p. 109.

[4] *Ibid.* p. 137.

[5] *Pope Alexander's Supremacy and Infallibility examin'd* (London, 1729), pp. 1–7 (third count).

[6] Colley Cibber, *A Letter From Mr. Cibber, To Mr. Pope* (London, 1742), p. 62.

thought Pope to be) may be moved by good causes escaped them. Since he was bad and his poetry dwelt on virtue, it was all clearly hypocrisy. And the more elaborate Pope's detachment became, the more judicial his air, the more enraged they became. In short, they failed totally to understand the rhetoric of satire. The analogy with several of Pope's nineteenth-century editors and critics is striking.

Hervey in *The Difference Between Verbal and Practical Virtue* (1742), the very title of which underlines his way of reading satire, uses the identical strategy in his attack on Horace:

> His tuneful Lyre when polish'd *Horace* strung,
> And all the Sweets of calm Retirement sung,
> In Practice still his courtly Conduct show'd
> His Joy was Luxury, and Power his God;
> With great *Maecenas* meanly proud to dine,
> And fond to load *Augustus* flatter'd Shrine;
> And whilst he rail'd at *Menas* ill-got Sway,
> His numerous Train that choak'd the *Appian* Way,
> His Talents still to Perfidy apply'd,
> Three Times a Friend and Foe to either Side.
> *Horace* forgot, or hop'd his Readers would,
> His Safety on the same Foundation stood.
> That he who once had own'd his Country's Cause,
> Now kiss'd the Feet that trampled on her Laws. (p. 2)

Satire is versified biography.

This leads to a final point. The dunces testify to a dislike of satire and of wit in general. Welsted's opinion of Horace's satire is less unusual than it appears to be in a superficial view of the Augustan Age: '... though the Satyrs and Epistles are written in a fine spirit, and with great purity of style; yet do they lie more on a level with prose, and are but a better kind of it.'[1]

An earlier battle than the Battle of the Duncs provides an illuminating parallel. The fight between Sir Richard Blackmore and his friends against Dryden and the wits that culminated in

---

[1] Leonard Welsted, 'A Discourse to the Right Honourable Sir Robert Walpole. To which are annexed Proposals for Translating the whole Works of Horace', in *The Works in Verse and Prose of Leonard Welsted*, ed. John Nichols (London, 1787), p. 171.

the *Commendatory* and *Discommendatory Verses* has been shown to be, at least in part, a protest by the City against the corruption of Will's Coffee House and its courtly manners.[1] To the brilliance and indecency of the wits is opposed the sturdy middle-class demand for the sound, the wholesome, and the improving in art. A middle-class ethic that would lead to sentimental comedy and the financially profitable virtue of Pamela is making itself heard. In such a view of life and art, wit can have no place. Satire and wit are, it would seem, aristocratic. Sir Richard Blackmore plainly sees the debate over wit in terms of social classes:

> And hence it is certain, that tho the Gentlemen of a pleasant and witty Turn of Mind often make the industrious Merchant, and grave Persons of all Professions, the Subject of their Raillery, and expose them as stupid Creatures, not supportable in good Company; yet these in their Turn believe they have as great a right, as indeed they have, to reproach the others for want of Industry, good Sense, and regular Oeconomy, much more valuable Talents than those, which any mere Wit can boast of . . .[2]

The same distrust of the imagination and the same tension between classes is behind the Battle of the Dunces. Wit is now associated with irreligion. This explains the dunces' delight in proving that Pope is indecent and blasphemous. The glittering social comedy and verbal richness of the *Rape of the Lock*, for example, does not impress them. They seize instead on what they find its shocking indecencies, hairs less in sight and the puns on 'die'. Curll, of all people, claimed to be shocked by the close of the *Dunciad* because of its overtones of Genesis.[3]

To Grub Street, interested in catering to the tastes of a middle-class public, the wit is no longer an ideal figure. He is obscene and probably an atheist, as Pope's *First Psalm* and *Moore's Worms* made plain. Wit itself is unsound.

---

[1] See Robert M. Krapp, 'Class Analysis of a Literary Controversy', *Science and Society*, x (1946), 80–92, and Richard C. Boys, *Sir Richard Blackmore and the Wits* (University of Michigan, 1949).

[2] Sir Richard Blackmore, 'Essay upon Wit', in *Essays upon Several Subjects*, 1716, reprinted in *Essays on Wit*, ed. Richard C. Boys, The Augustan Reprint Society, Ser. 1, i (May, 1946), pp. 195–6.

[3] Edmund Curll, *A Compleat Key To The Dunciad* (London, 1728), p. 18.

In fine, we live in an Age where Sense, good Sense, and
Nothing but Sense, is required, and nothing else will be
received,

Concanen flatly declared.[1]

To such an audience satire easily appears disquietingly under-
handed, the satiric stance an irritating defence of values to which
their own values are opposed. Satire may even hurt its victims
financially, as James Ralph complained bitterly.[2] If wit is seen
as immodesty, satire, rooted in an older classical and Christian
morality and dedicated to upholding traditional values, is seen
as arrogant, reactionary, and perverse. The logical outcome of
such an attitude to wit and satire is a radical dislike for all of
Pope's works, for the satiric genre in general, and finally for
poetry itself. The dunces agreed with George II who, it will be
remembered, innocently asked, 'Why cannot my subjects write
in prose?'

The following bibliography will, it is hoped, offer abundant
documentation of these uncomprehending attitudes. It should
also illustrate more fully than ever before one aspect of Pope's
contemporary reputation and allow us to judge more accurately
the enemies Pope's verse created for him and the provocations
he himself endured.

[1] Matthew Concanen, The Speculatist (London, 1730), p. 41.
[2] Giles Jacob, The Mirrour (London, 1733), pp. 77–8.

A CHRONOLOGICAL LIST
OF POPIANA

Titles have been greatly shortened; articles and propositions have not been capitalized except initially. Pseudonyms have not been given here. For full information see the bibliography entry. All items not otherwise marked are to be found in the Yale University Library. The following abbreviations should be noted:

California   The University of California Library, Los Angeles, California

Cambridge   The Cambridge University Library, Cambridge, England

Chicago   The University of Chicago Library, Chicago, Illinois

Huntington   The Henry E. Huntington Library and Art Gallery, San Marino, California

Illinois   The University of Illinois Library, Urbana, Illinois

Kansas   The University of Kansas Library, Lawrence, Kansas

Texas   The University of Texas Library, Austin, Texas

E

June 29, 1711 (*Spectator*, June 29, 1711)

Dennis, John. Reflections Critical and Satyrical, Upon A Late Rhapsody, Call'd, An Essay Upon Criticism. By Mr. Dennis. Me Remorsurum petis? Melius non Tangere clamo. Horace. London: Printed for Bernard Lintott, at the Cross Keys between the Two Temple-Gates in Fleetstreet. Price 6d.

8vo in half sheets.

A–E⁴.

[8 pp.], 1–32 pp.

Reprinted in Hooker, I. 396–419, and in W. H. Durham, *Critical Essays of the Eighteenth Century* (New Haven, 1915), pp. 212–53.

Dennis is referred to twice in the *Essay on Criticism*. The first reference is mild, if ironic:

> Discours'd in Terms as just, with Looks as Sage,
> As e'er cou'd D—s, of the Laws o' th' Stage.   (ll. 269–70)

It is the second reference which provoked Dennis:

> 'Twere well might Critics still this freedom take,
> But *Appius* reddens at each Word you speak,
> And *stares*, Tremendous! with a *threatning Eye*,
> Like some *fierce Tyrant* in *Old Tapestry*!   (ll. 584–7)

It is important to keep ll. 584–7 in mind while reading the *Reflections*; one keeps asking oneself what Pope could possibly have said to have so infuriated Dennis.

WORKS: A. *Pastorals*; B. *Essay on Criticism*.

CHARGES: 1. Pope deformed; 2. Pope a Jacobite; 3. Pope, under Wycherley's name, wrote verses in praise of himself; 4. Pope attempting to undermine Dryden's reputation.

The Preface gives us Dennis's version of his motives for writing the *Reflections*:

> ... I had not publish'd the following Letter, but had suffer'd his Readers to have hugg'd themselves in the Approbation of a Pamphlet so very undeserving, if I had not found things in it that have provok'd my Scorn, tho' not my Indignation. For I not only found myself attack'd without any manner of Provocation on my side, and attack'd in my Person, instead of my Writ-

1

ings, by one who is wholly a Stranger to me, and at a time when all the World knew that I was persecuted by Fortune; I not only saw that this was attempted in a clandestine manner with the utmost Falshood and Calumny, but found that all this was done by a little affected Hypocrite, who had nothing in his mouth at the same time but *Truth, Candor, Friendship, good Nature, Humanity,* and *Magnanimity.* (A3r)

He will, he promises us, 'make amends for the Ill-nature of my Criticism, by the Allurements of my *Satyr*' (A4r).

The *Reflections* themselves are written in the form of a letter addressed to an imaginary 'Mr. — at Sunning-Hill, Berks.' The point of the address is that Sunning-Hill is not far from Binfield (Durham, p. 416). Dennis is writing the letter to say that in his opinion the anonymous *Essay on Criticism* was written by 'some young, or some raw Author' (p. 1). The pamphlet derives what little organization it has from the reasons Dennis gives for this opinion. Unless otherwise indicated all my quotations from the *Essay on Criticism* are taken from the first edition as given in *Twick.* I, whose line numbering I have everywhere followed.

B   First, Pope

discovers in every Page a Sufficiency that is far beyond his little Ability; and hath rashly undertaken a Task which is infinitely above his Force ... There is nothing more wrong, more low, or more incorrect than this Rhapsody upon Criticism. (pp. 1–2)

Secondly, While this little Author struts and affects the Dictatorian Air, he plainly shews that at the same time he is under the Rod; and that while he pretends to give Laws to others, he is himself a pedantick Slave to Authority and Opinion ... (p. 2)

He gives as an example, ll. 15–16,

Let such teach others who themselves excell,
And *censure freely* who have *written well.*

This, Dennis says, insinuates,

that they alone are fit to be Criticks who have shewn themselves great Poets. (p. 2)

Although it is true that many good critics have been great poets, as, for example, Horace and Boileau, it is undeniable that there are great critics who were not poets – Aristotle, Quintilian, Bossu, Dacier.

Thirdly, Pope has

borrow'd both from Living and Dead, and particularly from the Authors of the two famous Essays upon Poetry and Translated Verse [Roscommon and Mulgrave]; but so borrow'd, that

he seems to have the very Reverse of *Midas*'s noble Faculty.
(p. 6)

In Pope's hands, he goes on, the finest gold turns immediately to lead.
Dennis's fourth point is potentially more dangerous:

> A fourth thing that shews him a young man, is the not know-
> ing his own mind, and his frequent Contradictions of himself.
> His Title seems to promise an Essay upon Criticism in general,
> which afterwards dwindles to an Essay upon Criticism in Poetry.
> And after all, he is all along giving Rules, such as they are, for
> Writing rather than Judging. (p. 6)

He then accuses Pope of saying in ll. 88–9 that the Rules are nothing
but Nature, but in ll. 130–3 that they are two different things, and
then in ll. 139–40 that they are the same (pp. 6–7). Dennis refuses to
allow Pope to answer that it was Virgil who thought at first that
Nature and the Rules were distinct; that would be for Pope to parade
his own wisdom while talking of Virgil's ignorance (p. 7). This extraordinary argument is not untypical of Dennis's logic throughout.

Dennis's fifth proof has an attractive simplicity:

> A fifth sign of his being a young Author is his being almost
> perpetually in the wrong. (p. 7)

Finally, the pretence of reasonableness is dropped entirely:

> ... As there is a great deal of Venom in this little Gentleman's
> Temper, Nature has very wisely corrected it with a great deal
> of Dulness ... As there is no Creature in Nature so venomous,
> there is nothing so stupid and so impotent as a hunch-back'd
> Toad; and a Man must be very quiet and very passive, and
> stand still to let him fasten his Teeth and his Claws, or be sur-
> priz'd sleeping by him, before that Animal can have any power
> to hurt him. (p. 26)

He inaugurates one of the favourite charges in Popiana – that Pope
was a Jacobite. Referring to ll. 536–53, to the couplet on the Dutch
Pope later omitted after l. 545, and to l. 162,

> (As *Kings* dispense with *Laws* Themselves have made)

he says,

> King *Charles* the Second was too much a Libertine, and too
> much an Encourager of Wit for him; King *William* the Third
> was too much a *Socinian*. But tho' he has without Mercy con-
> demn'd the Reigns of the foremention'd Monarchs, he is gra-
> ciously pleas'd to pass over in silence that which comes between
> them ... We find what that is which so happily reconcil'd him
> to it, and that was the Dispensing Pow'r, which was set on foot

in order to introduce and to establish Popery, and to make it the National Religion. Now I humbly conceive that he who Libels our Confederates, must be by Politicks a *Jacobite*; and he who Libels all the Protestant Kings that we have had in this Island these threescore Years, and who justifies the Dispensing Pow'r so long after we are free'd from it, a Pow'r which as was hinted above was set on foot on purpose to introduce Popery: He who justifies this when he lyes under the Tye of no Necessity, nor ev'n Conveniency to approve of it, must, I humbly conceive, derive his Religion from St. *Omer's*, as he seems to have done his Humanity and his Criticism; and is, I suppose, politickly setting up for Poet-Laureat against the coming over of the Pretender . . .
(p. 27)

His last paragraph begins with a combination of sheer abuse and threat:

ABI   And now if you have a mind to enquire between *Sunning-Hill* and *Ockingham*, for a young, squab, short Gentleman, with the forementioned Qualifications, an eternal Writer of Amorous Pastoral Madrigals, and the very Bow of the God of Love, you will soon be directed to him. And pray as soon as you have taken a Survey of him, tell me whether he is a proper Author to make personal Reflections on others; and tell him if he does not like my Person, 'tis because he is an ungrateful Creature, since his Conscience tells him, that I have been always infinitely delighted with his: So delighted, that I have lately drawn a very graphical Picture of it; but I believe I shall keep the *Dutch* Piece from ever seeing the Light, as a certain old Gentleman in *Windsor-Forest* would have done by the Original, if he durst have been half as impartial to his own Draught as I have been to mine. This little Author may extol the Ancients as much and as long as he pleases, but he has reason to thank the good Gods that he was born a Modern. For had he been born of *Graecian* Parents, and his Father by consequence had by Law had the absolute Disposal of him, his Life had been no longer than that of one of his Poems, the Life of half a day. (p. 29)

Hooker, I. 531, points out that Dennis apparently did not keep to his good intention of suppressing the 'very graphical Picture'. In a letter to the *Spectator*, dated October 23, 1711, he said he enclosed in the same cover a 'character' of a wretch who had insulted and affronted him; this is probably the 'very graphical Picture', which may also have been the basis for a *True Character*, 1716, q.v.

3   Dennis also mentions towards the end of the *Reflections* another
charge that would be often repeated – that Pope had written a poem
in his own praise and signed Wycherley's name to it. The little gentleman, he says,

> has writ a Panegyrick upon himself! Which Panegyrick if it was
> now writ with Judgment, yet was it publish'd with Discretion,
> for it was publish'd in Mr. *W*[ycherley]'s Name; so that by this
> wise Proceeding he had the Benefit of the Encomium, and Mr.
> *W*[ycherley] had the Scandal of the Poetry ... (pp. 29–30)

The verses first appeared in *Poetical Miscellanies: The Sixth Part*, 1709,
p. 253 (Ault, p. 116, n.1). Pope was so annoyed by the lie that he had
written them that he took pains to refute the accusation in a note to
a letter from Wycherley. See *EC* 1. 21–3 for the verses and the standard
charge, and *Corr.* 1. 50–1 for the refutation.

He has as well a malicious picture of Pope and Wycherley together;
their friendship became a favourite target in Popiana.

> It has been observ'd that of late Years a certain Spectre exactly
> in the shape of that little Gentleman, has haunted a certain
> ancient Wit, and has been by the People of *Covent-Garden* styl'd
> his evil Genius. For it hath been extremely remarkable, that
> while that Spectre hath haunted that ancient Wit, he has never
> been able to write or talk like himself ... (pp. 28–9)

4   He makes one charge that is, as far as I know, unique, that Pope
was attempting to undermine the reputation of Dryden. He finds
ll. 335–6 a libel upon Dryden since Dryden was a great coiner of
words (p. 16) and says later, *à propos* of ll. 458–9,

> Now Mr. *Dryden* is dead, he commends him with the rest of the
> World. But if this little Gentleman had been his Contemporary
> thirty Years ago, why then I can tell a very damn'd shape that
> Pride and Malice, and Folly would have appear'd in against
> Mr. *Dryden*. (p. 28)

As Hooker points out in a note to this passage (Hooker, II. 530), this
idea grew in Dennis's mind and on June 4, 1715, he wrote a letter to
Tonson on Pope's conspiracy to undermine Dryden's reputation. This
curious letter is reprinted in Hooker, II. 399–401.

It is in the context of this virulence that Dennis's few sensible criticisms must be read. (In three pages, pp. 26–8, he calls Pope 'little'
five times.) Besides the abuse, there is a feature of the pamphlet to
which insufficient attention has been drawn. Dennis is attempting a
detailed examination of Pope's text. Yet his transcription of the text
is unusually faulty. The eighteenth century hardly made a fetish of

textual accuracy; it would be absurd to condemn Dennis by modern scholarly standards. The point is, rather, that while employing a method which examined every word and held Pope strictly accountable for detail, Dennis displays an indifference to the accuracy of the lines he quotes so cavalier that the seriousness of the whole undertaking is compromised. Since few poets have revised their verse with more minute attention and more unceasingly than Pope, I think we can suppose that he was distressed to find that his critics would set down for examination mangled versions of his lines. Dennis was careless in his quotations throughout his attacks on Pope but never again quite so careless. Nor, judging from the collations I have made of the quotations from Pope in the rest of Popiana, were any of the other attackers.

Statistics may seem pretentious, but a few may be helpful. Dennis quotes 106 lines of verse from the *Essay on Criticism*, not counting lines he quotes more than once. In all, there are 32 different quotations. In these, Dennis makes 104 errors; only three quotations, or six lines, appear exactly as Pope wrote them. The vast majority of these errors are in punctuation, capitalization, and spelling, and for these (and Pope's habits of italicization and use of large and small capitals) there are frequent departures in all of the attacks. But Dennis also makes a total of thirteen verbal errors, not all of which have been corrected by his editors. I give a list of these in the order in which they appear in the pamphlet, giving Dennis's version first, then the reading of the first edition, which I have here taken from Griffith 2, then the name of the editor (if any) who has corrected the error:

1. l. 16   censure others] censure freely *Durham*
2. l. 102 Handmaid, proud] Handmaid prov'd *Hooker*
3. l. 139 and just Esteem,] a just Esteem; *Hooker*
4. l. 72   next to all] must to all *Durham*
5. l. 80   hath bless'd] has blest
6. l. 83   others, are] other's Aid,
7. l. 83   others, and] other's Aid,
8. l. 296 Ornament] Ornaments
9. l. 56   a Soul where memory ne'r] the Soul while Memory
   Durham
10. l. 124 Study day and night,] Study, and Delight,
11. l. 678 Judgment,] Sentence,
12. l. 539 The Wits] Nay Wits
13. l. 539 Pensions, but] Pensions, and

At least one of these errors, that in l. 102, explains part of Dennis's objection. He had quoted ll. 100–4 as,

> The gen'rous Critick fann'd the Poet's Fire,
> And taught the World with Reason to admire;
> Then Criticism, the Muses Handmaid, proud
> To dress her Charms, and make her more belov'd:
> But following Wits from that Intention stray'd.

His comment is,

> Never was any thing more obscure and confus'd than the fore-
> going Rhimes ... (p. 5)

He is referring to the whole passage, but his destruction of the syntax of ll. 102–3 really does make the passage confused. Dennis's version of l. 56,

> Thus in a Soul where memory ne'r prevails,

for

> Thus in the *Soul* while *Memory* prevails,

alters the meaning completely, and makes even harder to understand his contention that ll. 56–7 contradict ll. 76–9 (pp. 10–11).

Every writer who has discussed Dennis's pamphlet has pointed out that Pope changed a number of lines in his poems as a result of Dennis's criticisms. This is perfectly true, but unless the facts are carefully stated, a very misleading impression is given. The number of changes that Pope made in his poem makes accurate figures difficult to arrive at, but help may be found in R. H. Griffith's essay, 'Pope Editing Pope', *University of Texas, Studies in English*, 1944, pp. 5–108. Ignoring changes made in successive recensions and comparing solely Griffith 8 with Griffith 590, one sees that Pope added four couplets, removed four couplets, and altered 81 other lines. Eighty-nine lines, then, were altered. Of these alterations, only six can safely be attributed to Dennis's remarks. See Pope's Manuscript Memoranda on the poem where several of Dennis's objections are referred to, *Twick.* i, Appendix B, 482–4.

I shall give first the six changes in the poem that may safely be attributed to Dennis.

Ll. 62–3 had read,

> Not only bounded to *peculiar Arts*,
> But ev'n in *those*, confin'd to *single Parts*.

Dennis commented,

> What a wretched narrow Soul hath this Essayer? And what a thoughtless one—when *Homer*, whom he mentions so often in this Essay, had as admirable a Talent for Pleasantry, as he had a Genius equal to the most exalted Poetry? To come to the *Romans*, *Horace* is famous both for Elevaion [*sic*] and Pleasantry. (p. 9)

Pope altered l. 63, beginning with Griffith 8, to,
> But oft in *those*, confin'd to *single Parts*.

Ll. 80–1 had read:
> There are whom Heav'n has blest with store of Wit,
> Yet want as much again to manage it.

Dennis quoted this twice on one page (the first time reading *hath* for *has*, making the line more awkward) and commented,
> By the way what rare Numbers are here? Would not one swear that this Youngster had espous'd some antiquated Muse, who had sued out a Divorce upon the account of Impotence from some superannuated Sinner; and who having been pox'd by her former Spouse, has got the Gout in her decrepit Age, which makes her hobble so damnably ... (p. 11)

Pope, postponing action, as Griffith notes, until 1744, altered this in Griffith 590 to,
> Some, to whom Heav'n in wit has been profuse,
> Want as much more, to turn it to its use.

Ll. 82–3 had read,
> For *Wit* and *Judgment* ever are at strife,
> Tho' meant each other's Aid, like *Man* and *Wife*.

Dennis commented,
> What a Devil, Mr. *Bays*, they cannot be at strife sure, after they are parted, after Wit has made an Elopement, or has been barbarously forsaken by Judgment, or turn'd to separate maintenance! Much less can they be at strife when they never came together, which is the Case in the Essay. (p. 12)

Pope altered the line in Griffith 590 to,
> For Wit and Judgment often are at strife.

Pope, however, ignored Dennis's further objection to the whole thought of the couplet.

Ll. 500–3 had read,
> What is this *Wit* that does our Cares employ?
> The *Owner's Wife*, that *other Men* enjoy,
> The more his *Trouble* as the more *admir'd*;
> Where *wanted*, scorn'd, and envy'd where *acquir'd*.

Dennis had asked,
> ... How can Wit be scorn'd where it is not? Is not this a Figure frequently employ'd in *Hibernian* Land? The Person who wants this Wit may indeed be scorn'd; but such a Contempt declares the Honour that the Contemner has for Wit. (pp. 20–1)

Pope altered the third line four times, the fourth line twice, ending
with, in Griffith 590,

> Then most our *Trouble* still when most *admir'd*,
> And still the more we *give*, the more *requir'd*.

See *Twick.* I, Appendix B, 483.

Ll. 546–7 had read,

> Then *first* the *Belgian Morals* were extoll'd;
> We their *Religion* had, and they our *Gold*.

Dennis had commented,

> I find then that in the compass of one Page . . . he has Libell'd
> two Monarchs and two Nations. The two Monarchs are King
> *Charles* and King *William*: The two Nations are the *Dutch* and
> our own. The *Dutch* we are told are a parcel of Sharpers, and
> we are downright Bubbles and Fools. (p. 27)

Pope omitted this couplet, beginning with Griffith 413.

Ll. 566–7 had read,

> Be *silent* always when you *doubt* your Sense;
> *Speak* when you're *sure*, yet speak with *Diffidence*.

Dennis commented,

> Now I should think that when a man is sure, 'tis his Duty to speak
> with a modest Assurance; since in doing otherwise he betrays
> the Truth, especially when he speaks to those who are guided
> more by Imagination than they are by Judgment . . . (pp. 21–2)

Pope altered l. 567, beginning with Griffith 8, to,

> And *speak*, tho' *sure*, with *seeming Diffidence*.

See *Twick.* I, Appendix B, 483.

Three other alterations may possibly be due to Dennis, although
the evidence seems very doubtful.

Ll. 130–1 had read,

> When first great *Maro* in his boundless Mind
> A Work, t' outlast immortal *Rome* design'd,
> Perhaps he seem'd *above* the Critick's Law,
> And but from *Nature's Fountains* scorn'd to draw.

Dennis objected to this and the lines following,

> . . . Who acquainted him with that noble Particularity of *Virgil's*
> Life, that he designed to write his *Aeneis* without Art? Had he it
> from ancient or modern Authors, or does he owe it to a noble
> Effort of his own sagacious Soul? . . . But, secondly, what does
> he mean by *Maro's* designing a Work to outlast immortal *Rome*?
> Does he pretend to put that Figure, call'd a Bull upon *Virgil*?
> (pp. 7–8)

F

From Griffith 8 to and including Griffith 582, ll. 130–1 read,

> When first young *Maro* sung of *Kings* and *Wars*,
> Ere warning *Phoebus* touch'd his trembling Ears.

But in Griffith 590 Pope changed them back to the original reading, except for keeping the revision of *young* for *great*:

> When first young *Maro* in his boundless Mind
> A Work t' outlast immortal *Rome* design'd.

Pope wished to avoid the 'bull' that Dennis had objected to (see Pope to Caryll, June 25, 1711, *Corr.* I. 121), and then decided to restore it. The change to *young* may possibly glance at Dennis's objection, since it offers an excuse for Virgil's ignorance. See *Twick.* I, Appendix B, 483.

A couplet which appeared following l. 648 had read,

> Not only *Nature* did his Laws obey,
> But *Fancy's* boundless Empire own'd his Sway.

Dennis commented,

> The Expression in the first Verse is not only absurd, but blasphemous. The Laws of Nature are unalterable and indispensable but by God himself . . . (p. 22)

Pope omitted this couplet beginning with Griffith 8, perhaps because it contained the expletive *did*. See *Twick.* I. 313, n.

Pope's Manuscript Memoranda, *Twick.* I, Appendix B, 484, also suggest that he attempted, possibly as the result of Dennis's criticism, another version of l. 483,

> And such as *Chaucer* is, shall *Dryden* be.

Dennis had insisted that Dryden 'whatever alteration happens to the Language, can never be like to *Chaucer*' (p. 20). For the same objection see Welsted, *Epistles, Odes*, 1724.

Several alterations attributed by H. G. Paul, *John Dennis, His Life and Criticism* (New York, 1911), p. 88, to the effect of Dennis's criticisms have nothing, I think, to do with Dennis. Paul cites ll. 179–80, misquoting in l. 179 *best* for Pope's *but*,

> Those are but *Stratagems* which *Errors* seem,
> Nor is it *Homer Nods*, but *We* that *Dream*.

Dennis had objected that this was a 'presumptuous Contradiction' of Horace's 'Aliquando bonus dormitat Homerus', and of Roscommon (p. 15). Pope's change of *are but* to *oft are* from Griffith 8 on does nothing to answer Dennis.

Paul also gives ll. 74–5 which had read,

> That *Art* is best which most resembles *Her*,
> Which still *presides*, yet never does *Appear*.

Dennis's only criticism was that the lines were trite, 'as much as to
say, *Artis* [*sic*] *est celare artem*' (p. 10), and he could make the same
objection to the revision which first appeared in Griffith 79,

> *Art* from that Fund each *just Supply* provides,
> Works *without Show*, and *without Pomp* presides.

Pope's motive may have been the removal of the expletive *does* (*Twick.*
I. 247, n.).

April 6, 1714 (*Evening Post*, April 6, 1714)

[Gildon, Charles.] A New Rehearsal, Or Bays the Younger. Con-
taining an Examen of The Ambitious Step-mother. Tamerlane,
The Biter, Fair Penitent, Royal Convert, Ulysses, and Jane
Shore. All Written by N. Rowe Esq;. Also A Word or Two upon
Mr. Pope's Rape of the Lock. To which is prefix'd, a Preface in
Vindication of Criticism in General, by the late Earl of Shafts-
bury. Why is he Honour'd with a Poet's Name, / Who neither
knows, nor wou'd observe a Rule? Roscommon. London:
Printed for J. Roberts in Warwick-Lane, MDCCXIV. (Price
1 s.)

12mo.
A–D¹², E⁶, F².
[22 pp.], 1–88 pp.

On May 14, 1715 (*Post Boy*, May 14, 1715), this was reissued with
a new title-page and the addition of eight pages ('Some Remarks on
the Tragedy of the Lady Jane Gray', which contains no Pope references) as:

Remarks On Mr. Rowe's Tragedy Of The Lady Jane Gray, And
All his other Plays. Viz. The Ambitious Step-Mother, Tamer-
lane, The Biter, The Fair Penitent, The Royal Convert, Ulysses,
Jane Shore. With some Observations upon, I. Mr. Smith's
Phaedra and Hippolytus. II. Mr. Philips's Distress'd Mother.
III. Mr. Addison's Cato. IV. Mr. Pope's Rape of the Lock, &c.
To which is prefix'd, A Prefatory Discourse in Defence of Criti-
cism in general. Collected from the Works of the late Earl of

Shaftsbury. The Second Edition. London, Printed for J. Roberts, near the Oxford-Arms in Warwick-Lane, 1715. Price 1 s.

12mo.

A in five leaves, A in eleven leaves, B–D^{12}, E^6, F^2.

[2 pp.], 5–12 pp., [20 pp.], 1–88 pp.

The Bodleian copy has an additional leaf at the beginning – the half-title, 'Remarks On Mr. Rowe's Plays'.

A 'Second Edition' of this was advertised in the *Weekly Packet*, July 2, 1715, as 'just publish'd'. Since the 'Second Edition' is ambiguous, I cannot be sure whether the copy of the *Remarks* I have described is the one referred to in the May or in the July advertisement.

Pope had published the enlarged version of *The Rape of the Lock* in March and had signed the *Iliad* agreement with Bernard Lintot on March 23. *A New Rehearsal* was clearly prompted by these and constitutes the first attack on both *The Rape of the Lock* and the *Iliad*. Pope had, so far as is known, done nothing to offend Gildon personally. For Gildon's earlier attacks on Pope in the *British Mercury* see Jean Honoré, 'Charles Gildon rédacteur du *British Mercury* (1711–1712): Les attaques contre Pope, Swift, et les wits', *Etudes Anglaises*, xv (1962), 347–64. Straus thinks Pope was correct in *A Full and True Account* (*Prose*, I. 263) in claiming that Curll was the publisher (Straus, p. 231).

WORKS: A. *Imitations of English Poets. Waller. On a Fan* (doubtful; the reference may be to Gay's *The Fan*); B. *Essay on Criticism*; C. *Rape of the Lock*; D. *Iliad*.

CHARGES: 1. Pope a conceited and empty versifier; 2. Pope ignorant of Greek; 3. Pope skilled in making a reputation; 4. *Rape of the Lock* indecent; 5. Machinery in *Rape of the Lock* inserted after poem was written; 6. Pope wrote verses in his own praise under Wycherley's name; 7. Pope writing a play on Lady Jane Gray.

This is a critical essay half-heartedly put into dramatic form. Far more space is given to the criticism of Rowe indicated by the title-page than to Pope, although the latter is much the liveliest figure in the play. On the identification of Sir Indolent Easie with Charles Montagu, Lord Halifax, see G. L. Anderson, 'Lord Halifax in Gildon's *New Rehearsal*', *PQ*, xxxiii (1954), 423–6, and on the identification of Freeman and Truewit with Addison and Steele see Malcolm Goldstein, 'Gildon's *New Rehearsal* Again', *PQ*, xxxvi (1957), 511–12. The play owes little but the title to Buckingham.

In Act I, Truewit, just arrived from the country, is greeted by his
friend Freeman at the Rose Tavern, Covent-Garden; they condemn
the modern poets and dramatists as insipid, unnatural, and dull. Sir
Indolent Easie, who admires whatever is successful, enters and says
he has left Sawny Dapper (Pope) below who will be glad to see Freeman 'when he has despatch'd some Booksellers who teize him for
Copy' (p. 8). (*Sawney*, a frequent name for Pope in Popiana, is 'a Scot-
tish local variant of Sandy, short for Alexander' [*OED sub* Sawney].)

1   Dapper, who is listed in the cast of characters as 'A young Poet of
the Modern stamp, an easy Versifyer, Conceited and a Contemner
secretly of all others' (A1 IV), is described by Freeman as 'one of the
most Empty and most Conceited of the whole Tribe', but Sir Indolent
insists that Sawny 'has a very pretty Genius, is very Harmonious, and
Writes a great many fine things, ask the Ladies else' (p. 8). The rest
of the act, which closes with the entrance of Dapper, is a severe dissection of *The Ambitious Stepmother*, with, however, no personal abuse of
Bayes (Rowe).

In Act II attention is for the first time centred on Dapper who tells
them how he has gained a reputation:

3   I appear'd first in the Character of a *Critic in Terrorem* to the
Reigning Wits of the Time, that they shou'd the more easily
admit me into their Number: But then for their Encouragement,
I writ in Rhime, and faith, to say Truth, as to Matter, not so far
above them, as to make them fear that I shou'd not fall down to
their Level. (p. 39)

He would teach them 'the Art of raising a Name by Poetry, without
any' (p. 41), if he did not have the Greek poets on his hands now for
a translation.

2   Sir Ind. 'Foregad *Sawny*, I did not know that you understood
Greek; nay, I must needs say, thou art a pretty Industrious
Young Fellow.

           Dap. Why, Sir *Indolent*, if I did not understand *Greek*, what of
that; I hope a Man may translate a *Greek* Author without
understanding *Greek* . . . (p. 41)

3   Continuing with his art of getting a reputation, he advises them to
chuse some odd out of the way Subject, some Trifle or other that
wou'd surprize the Common Reader that any thing cou'd be
written upon it, as a *Fan, a Lock of Hair*, or the like. (p. 42)

4   . . . Besides the newness of the Verse, you must have a new
manner of Address; you must make the Ladies speak Bawdy,
no matter whether they are Women of Honour or not; and then

you must dedicate your Poem to the Ladies themselves. Thus a Friend of mine has lately, with admirable Address, made Arabella *F[er]m[o]r* prefer the Locks of her Poll, to her Locks of another more sacred and secret Part.

> Oh! hadst thou Cruel! been content to seize
> Hairs less in Sight—*or any Hairs* but these.

But this is likewise a Complement to those Parts of the Lady, to let the World know that the Lady had *Hairs* elsewhere, which she valu'd less.

> Nor fear'd the chief th' unequal Fight to try,
> Who sought no more than on his Foe to Die.

Admirable Good again, you know what Dying is on a fair Lady Sir *Indolent* ... But then, Sir, the *Machinary* of this Poem is admirably contrivd to convey a luscious Hint to the Ladies, by letting them know, that their Nocturnal Pollutions are a Reward of their Chastity, and that when they Dream of the Raptures of Love, they are immortalizing a *Silph* as that Ingenious and Facetious Author sweetly intimates in his Epistle Dedicatory... (pp. 43–4)

c5   Truewit objects that the poets of antiquity founded their poems on the machinery, but that the new way of writing is to insert the machinery after the poem is not only written but published. Dapper replies that he cares nothing for what the old authors did (pp. 44–5).

6   He explains that he wrote

> a Copy of Verses in my own Praise ...; then I put the Name of a Celebrated Old Author to it, but the Devil of it was, tho' that Author was of an Establish'd Reputation for *Wit*, yet he was remarkable for an ill Versification, so that my Stile discover'd me; and indeed, when I heard them prais'd, I cou'd not help owning to my Friends, that I writ them my self. (p. 45)

7   After drinking a toast to the lock least in sight, Dapper tells them that the poet who sang the lock is 'Writing a Play of the Lady *Jane Grey*. The Protestant Poet writes a Play on a Popish Whore, and the Popish Poet is to write one on the Protestant Queen' (p. 48).

The charge of indecency in *The Rape of the Lock* was to recur frequently (on the attack on *The Rape of the Lock* here see Bond, pp. 75–6), as was Pope's alleged ignorance of Greek. Pope pointed out in the *Dunciad* (*Twick.* v. 45) that *Lady Jane Grey* 'afterwards proved to be Mr. Row's'. On Pope's friendship with Rowe see Ault, pp. 128–55. For the Wycherley charge see Dennis's *Reflections Critical and Satyrical*, 1117.

April 7, 1714 (*Evening Post*, April 6, 1714)

[Oldmixon, John.] Poems And Translations. By Several Hands. To which is Added, The Hospital of Fools; A Dialogue; By the Late William Walsh, Esq; Dulces ante omnia Musae. Virg. London: Printed for J. Pemberton, at the Buck and Sun against St. Dunstan's Church in Fleet-street. MDCCXIV.

Half-title: Poems And Translations, &c.

8vo.

A⁸, a², B–H⁸, I in seven leaves, K–T⁸, (a)⁸, (b)⁶.

[4 pp.], [i]–vi, i–v, [vi–xiv], 1–120, [121–2], 123–282, [1]–26 pp., [27–8] book-list.

Case 277.

The dedication is signed 'J. Oldmixon' (A5v).

This contains one Pope attack, a ten-line epigram, p. 245, under the title 'Advice to Mr. Pope, On his intended Translation of Homer's Iliads', the same title being used in the table of contents. John Hughes was the author, as was revealed by the inclusion of it in his *Poems On Several Occasions. With Some Select Essays In Prose* (London, 1735), II. 90, reprinted in Anderson, *Works of the British Poets* (Edinburgh, 1793), VII. 314.

Oldmixon's Miscellany was much advertised in the newspapers; 'The 5th Edition' was advertised on August 10, 1714, in the *Post Boy* with the epigram on Pope named as one of its attractions. Case gives a second edition, 277 (b), which I have not seen.

WORK: A. *Iliad*.

CHARGE: 1. Pope undertook *Iliad* to make money.

I quote the last lines of this sneer at the money Pope would make from the *Iliad*:

> If *Britain* his translated Song wou'd hear,
> First take the Gold—then charm the list'ning Ear,
> So shall thy Father *Homer* smile to see
> His Pension pay'd, tho' late, and pay'd to Thee.   (p. 245)

Oldmixon also printed in this miscellany 'Two or Three; or a Receipt to make a Cuckold'. See *Twick.* VI. 105 for his ironic apology in the preface for including this poem of Pope's, whose printing 'stands near, if not at, the very beginning of his lifelong quarrel with Curll and of his persistent animosity to Oldmixon'.

August 15, 1714 (*Post Boy*, August 3, 1714)

[Lacy, John.] The Steeleids, Or, The Tryal of Wit. A Poem, In Three Cantos: By John Lacy, Esq;. Quo propius stes, Te Capiat magis. Then will I say, swell'd with Poetick Rage, / 'Tis I, John Lacy, have Reform'd the Age. London: Printed, and Sold by J. Morphew, near Stationers-Hall. 1714.

8vo in half-sheets.

A–H⁴. B2 is incorrectly signed B3; G is misbound as G1, G4, G3, G2.

[8 pp.], 1–14, [15–16], 17–38, [39–41], 42–53, [54–6] pp.

WORKS: A. *Windsor Forest*; B. *Temple of Fame*.

CHARGE: 1. Pope deformed.

This is an obvious imitation in three cantos in heroic couplets, each canto provided with 'Notes truly Bentleian' (p. 14), of Pope's *Temple of Fame*. It is an attack on Steele and the Whigs and mentions Pope only incidentally. The poem is supposed to be written by Lacy's ancestor. In Canto II the poet travels to the Court of Fame which turns out to be 'Whig-Fame' or Rumour. The Pope reference comes here:

AB   In yon fam'd Forest, where the Vulgar Eye
      Does naught but Trees, and Streams, and Deer descry,
                    ·   ·   ·
      Three Worlds in little, ⁴Curious *P—pe* enjoys,
      And there, to rise in *Fame*, in Rapture lies.

                    ·   ·   ·
      P—p's [*sic*] Directions strictly we pursu'd,
      To the Mid-Forest, where this *Palace* stood.   (pp. 21–2)

The only sting is in the note:

⁴ Note, to my Honour, in the Line which runs thus,
        Three Worlds in Little Curious *P—pe* Enjoys.

I   The Epithet *Curious* was invented by me... In the Original it ran thus,
        Three Worlds in Little, little *P—pe* Enjoys.
... *P—pe*'s Name being *Alexander*, *a Little Man*, my Ancestor has describ'd him as a Second *Little Alexander the Great*, in the Realms of *Poesy*; But that being a *Pun* and too trivial ... I blotted it out...
(pp. [39–40])

September, 1714 (*Monthly Catalogue*)

A Farther Hue and Cry After Dr. Sw[if]t. Being A Collection of Curious Pieces found since his Departure. Price 6d.

8vo in half-sheets.

Five unsigned leaves, в⁴, c², a⁴, в in three leaves.

[6 pp.], 5–20, 1–13 pp., [14] blank.

Case 273.

A made-up miscellany: only the title-page has been printed expressly for this collection. The collection consists of two pamphlets, each of which contains two poems: *A Genuine Epistle from M[atthe]w P[rio]r, Esq; at Paris,* and *An Ode To The Pretender,* the title-page of this second pamphlet having been removed (Case 273).

[A Farther Hue and Cry after Dr. Swift.]

Another edition, lacking title-page, and with a different edition of the second pamphlet, the collation of which is as follows:
в–c⁴, c².

1–13, [14–16], 17–19 pp., [20] blank.

Case 273 (b). Yale's copy is misbound.

A Farther Hue and Cry After Dr. Sw[if]t. Being a Collection of Curious Pieces found since his Departure. Viz. I. A Genuine Epistle from M[atthe]w P[rio]r, Esq; at Paris, to the Revd Dr. J[onatha]n Sw[if]t at Windsor. II. Smut's Epitaph. III. A Letter to Sir Patrick Lawless, late the Pretender's Nuncio. IV. An Ode to the Pretender, written by several Hands in Greenwich Park. V. Earl Mortimer's Fall. A Fragment. Publish'd from the Original Manuscripts, By Timothy Brocade, Esq; Late Author of the Examiner. —Tempora mutantur, O Hominum! O Mores! The Second Edition. London: Printed for A. Boulter. MDCCXIV. Price 6d.

Half-title: A Farther Hue and Cry After Dr. Sw[if]t. Being A Collection of Curious Pieces found since his Departure. Price 6d.

8vo in half-sheets.

One unsigned leaf, a–b⁴, a⁴, b³.

[4 pp.], 3–16, 1–13 pp., [14] blank.

Case 273 (c).

WORK: A. *Windsor Forest.*

CHARGE: 1. Pope a Jacobite.

'An Ode To The Pretender. Inscrib'd to Mr. Lesley and Mr. Pope' (pp. 1–10, second count, in Case 273 and 273 (c); pp. 1–13, second count, in Case 273 (b)), besides its title, contains one Pope reference in an ironic eulogy of the Pretender. (The text is the same in all three editions.)

> And if the Youth's Conversion don't offend
> A while, O *Pope,* thy daring Genius lend.
> O could I Transubstantiate my Lays,
> And make them thine, to Sing the Heroe's Praise,
> Aloft I'd Soar, and Celebrate my Theme,
> In Lines as soft as soft ¹*Loddona's* Stream.

> ¹ See *Windsor-Forest,* a Poem (p. 2; p. 3 in Case 273 (b)).

December 10, 1714

[Horneck, Philip.] The High-German Doctor, With many Additions and Alterations. To which is added, a large Explanatory Index. In Two Volumns [*sic*]. Vol. I. —Ridentem dicere Verum Quid vetat? Hor. London Printed, and Sold by J. Roberts, near the Oxford-Arms in Warwick-Lane, 1719.

The High-German Doctor. To which is added, a large Appendix, With An Explanatory Index. Vol. II. London Printed, and Sold by J. Roberts, near the Oxford-Arms in Warwick-Lane, 1719.

12mo.

Vol. I: One unsigned leaf, B–P¹², Q⁴.
          [2 pp.], 1–344 pp. Pages 41, 45, 102, and 162 are misnumbered as 31, 54, 210, and 164.

Vol. II: A–O¹².
          [2 pp.], 1–271, [272–4], 275–304, [305–32] pp., [2 pp.] blank. Pages 177, 192, and 209 are misnumbered 771, 292, and 229.

Vol. I extends from No. 1, May 4, 1714, to No. 50, October 19–22, 1714; Vol. II from No. 1, October 22–6, 1714, to No. 50, April 30–

May 12, 1715. In 1720 a second edition of Vol. 1 only appeared with the title-page as in 1719 above, except for the imprint: London Printed, and Sold by the Booksellers of London and Westminster. 1720. The errors in pagination are corrected.

Lowndes aptly characterizes *The High-German Doctor* as 'a tissue of nonsense and political abuse'. The title is explained in the explanatory index as 'an Ostentatious Quack, or Pretender to Physick' (I. 295). For Philip Horneck see *Twick.* v. 445.

WORKS: A. Prologue to *Cato*; B. *Iliad*.

CHARGE: I. Pope a Roman Catholic.

I   In the issue of December 10, 1714, 'honest *Parnassus Bernard* [*Lintot*], of *Fleet-street*' visits the doctor with a copy of the *Iliad* to which the doctor is a subscriber. Bernard states,

> we have been Nine Months debating about the first Word of the Book, whether we should express Μηνιν by the *English* Word *Rage* or *Wrath*: the last Letters from St. *Omers* say, it should be rather Zeal, because *Achilles* took pet at his being disappointed of a Wench. (II. 65)

Cambridge is for 'Honey-Pot', Oxford for 'the Absolute Will and Pleasure of Prince *Achilles*'; the doctor, whose opinion Bernard promises to stand by, suggests 'Church' which would 'please abundance of People, without any manner of Signification' (II. 65–6).

I   The doctor wonders how Bernard could have supposed

> a *Lion* could translate *Homer* . . . But I don't blame thee, a *Prologue* writ with an old *Roman* Spirit, and as much modern *Roman*, Bigottry conceal'd, first deceiv'd a noted *Bard* about this Town [Addison?], and well may'st thou be impos'd on in such good Company. (II. 66–7)

Ault, p. 104, thinks that it may have been this attack which led Pope to announce on December 25 and during the next two weeks that the translation of the first four books of the *Iliad* which was to have been published 'by the Beginning of May next . . . shall be deliver'd two Months sooner than the Time promis'd'.

March 7, 1715 (*The Grumbler*, March 3, 1715)

[Burnet, Thomas, and Duckett, George.] Homerides: Or, A Letter To Mr. Pope, Occasion'd by his intended Translation of Homer. By Sir Iliad Doggrel. [4 lines of Greek, *Iliad* II. 216–19, from the portrait of Thersites] London: Printed by W. Wilkins, and sold by J. Roberts in Warwick-Lane, 1715. (Price Six-Pence)

Half-title: Homerides: Or, A Letter To Mr. Pope.

8vo in half-sheets.
[A]–C⁴, D in three leaves.
[4 pp.], [5]–30 pp.

The above is the Yale copy; the British Museum copy lacks the half-title, but has D4, which is blank. The Bodleian has two copies, one with half-title but missing D4, one with both half-title and D4. The Cambridge University Library copy has both half-title and D4. My quotations are taken from this 'edition'.

May 30, 1715 (Ault, p. 105)

Homerides: Or, A Letter To Mr. Pope, Occasion'd by his intended Translation of Homer. By Sir Iliad Doggrel. [4 lines of Greek, as above] The Second Edition, Amended and Enlarged. Printed by W. Wilkins, and sold by J. Roberts in Warwick-Lane, 1715. [Price Four-Pence.]

8vo.
A in seven leaves, B⁴.
[2 pp.], [5]–23 pp., [24] blank.

This is the British Museum copy. Sherburn, p. 135, says that this pamphlet 'proved to be not a second edition but a new attack. Two pages jeer at Pope's audacity and eagerness for cash; the rest contain mainly doggerel specimens of passages from various books of the *Iliad*.' He mentions as well the inclusion of Duckett's 'An Epilogue for Punch to speak'. All of these are, however, to be found in the 'first edition' above from which the 'second edition', in the copy I have examined, differs in no important respect. Did Sherburn see another text of the March 7 pamphlet? No indication of difference in the text between the two 'editions' I have listed is given in David Nichol Smith's biblio-

graphy of Burnet and Duckett in *Letters of Thomas Burnet. Homerides: Or, A Letter To Mr. Pope*, 1715, is not to be confused with *Homerides: Or, Homer's First Book Moderniz'd*, 1716, q.v.

The pamphlet is signed only 'Iliad Doggrell' (p. 30), but Burnet's letters to Duckett make the authorship certain. The pamphlet was originally to have been called 'The Hump Conference', and in his first reference to it, in a letter of December 25, 1714, Burnet supposes that it 'will be in great forwardness' (*Letters of Thomas Burnet*, p. 77). On February 2, 1715, he writes that he expects to be able 'to put the *Conference* out just a fortnight before his first Volume [i.e. Pope's *Iliad*], when all the Town will be full of Expectation . . .' (*ibid*. p. 80). And then in a letter of February 19, 1715, he says:

> As to our *Specimen*, I shewd great part of it to Mr. Addison who advised me in two things, first to convert the Dialogue into a Narrative Letter, and secondly to strike out all the Reflections upon the poor fellow's person; all this I have done, but his Homer is so speedily to appear, that I cannot have time to wait for your second Approbation, but have put the Press to work already, and with all the haste I shall make *mine* won't be published above a week before his. The Title of it, I have altered much for the better, and it is *Homerides* or a Letter to Mr Pope on his Intended Translation of Homer, by *Sir Iliad Doggrell*; and that Pope may see I coud be sharp on his Person if I woud, I have placed the Greek Sentence at the head, but have not translated it; and so much for Homer. (*Ibid*. p. 81)

After it had appeared, he wrote in a letter of March 26, 1715,

> I can assure you *Homerides*, notwithstanding your anger at it, is universally approved, and although much of the Humour is lost by the Exchange, yet I woud not have printed the *Hump Conference* for any money. For *Pope* as he is a fellow of a Contemptible figure is the object of the Town's Pity; and all they blame in *Homerides* is the motto. What then woud they have done if the whole *Hump Conference*? [*sic*] I will acknowledge to you that I believe you guess right, that Addison did this out of no manner of good will to me; but till you give me some farther Reasons, I shall think I was wise in following his Advice. (*Ibid*. p. 85)

It is thus clear that both Burnet and Duckett wrote it, that the earlier version, the 'Hump Conference', contained personal abuse, and that Addison was responsible for the toning-down of the offensive pamphlet.

The Puppet-Show Epilogue is reprinted in slightly different form in Curll's *A Compleat Key To The Dunciad*, 1728, q.v.

WORK: A. *Iliad.*

CHARGES: 1. Pope greedy for money; 2. Pope a Catholic.

He begins by warning Pope:

> 'Tis indeed somewhat bold, and almost prodigious, for a single Man to undertake a Work, which not all the Poets of our Island durst jointly attempt, and it is what no Man of an Inferior Genius to Mr *Pope* cou'd even have thought of. But *jacta est alea*, it is too late to disswade you, by demonstrating the Madness of your Project. No! not only your attending Subscribers, whose Expectations have been raised in Proportion to what their Pockets have been drained of, but even the industrious, prudent *Bernard* [*Lintot*], who has advanced no small Sum of Money for the Copy, require the Performance of your Articles. (pp. [5]–6)

Since it is now too late to stop Pope, all he can do is give him 'all the Assistance imaginable in this great Time of Need'.

> There are indeed but two Things to be considered in every Heroick Poem; first, how to *write* the Poem, secondly, how to make it *sell.*

A I

> The Latter of these being without dispute the main and principal Thing about which you and *Bernard* are concern'd, I shall begin with that. (p. 6)

He will use his friendship with Robin Powell, puppet-showman at Bath, to get him to do a puppet-show of the Siege of Troy. Powell is a favourite of the Beaux and Ladies, 'And, I suppose, 'tis only for such as them, who do not understand the *Greek*, that you design your Translation' (p. 7). A Copy of Pope's Proposals for Subscribers may be kept lying open in Powell's room at Bath. He then gives 'an *Epilogue*, which *Punch* shall speak by way of a Recommendation to *Homer*, after the *Puppet-show* is ended'.

> Genteels, I come to wish you Joy,
> Of a much better Tale of *Troy.*

A I

> Ours was but scanty, light and short,
> And made to yield the Audience Sport:
> *Homer* has this at length related.
> Do you not wish he were Translated?

·   ·   ·

How *Troy* held out ten Years and more,
And all for one poor batter'd Whore;
How all the Heroes had their Misses,
But one sly Sinner called *Ulysses*.

. . .

All this and more, will *Homer* say.
Is he not worth Translating, pray?
I speak without a Fee, or Bribe,
Here's Pen and Ink—good Sirs, subscribe,
Six Guineas each at least, I hope,
Adds me—'tis done by Master *Pope*.   (pp. 7–8)

He would not have Pope imitate Dryden or Ogilby or 'any of those Translators, that pin themselves down to the Sense of their Author', but rather Cotton 'who in his *Heroi-Comical* Translation of *Virgil*, has never baulk'd a Jest, because it was not in the Original. And your Task in this Case will be exceedingly easy; for any Translation must of it self be a Burlesque upon *Homer*' (p. 9).

The rest of the pamphlet consists of 'translations' of Homer intended to serve Pope as models, or supposed literal renderings to convince him of the need for modernization.

He is not sure that Pope will want to use his version of lines from *Iliad* z:

But *Saturn*'s Son in the mean Season,
From *Glaucus* stole away his Reason,
Who changed with *Diomede* (O Ass!)
His Arms of Gold, for his of Brass;

Now the great Objection I have to these Lines, is an Apprehension that I have, lest your Subscribers should take this to be the State of the Case between you and them; and imagine that you have changed away your *Brass* for their *Gold*. (p. 29)

There are several anti-Catholic sneers; e.g., he wants a prayer to the Muses changed into a prayer to St Ursula and the eleven thousand virgins. 'This will be something surprisingly new' (p. 14).

March 10, 1715 (*Post Boy*, March 8–10, 1715)

Preston, Mr. [pseud.] Aesop At The Bear-Garden: A Vision. By Mr. Preston. In Imitation of the Temple of Fame, a Vision, By Mr. Pope. London: Sold by John Morphew near Stationers-Hall. 1715.

Half-title: Aesop At The Bear-Garden. Price Six Pence.

8vo in half-sheets.

[A]–E⁴.

[8 pp.], 9–38 pp., [2 pp.] blank.

Bond 40.

Since Mr Preston, according to a note on p. 34, was 'bear marshal' at Hockley in the Hole, this attack was published pseudonymously. It was published, apparently, as part of the Homer campaign by the wits at Buttons; Pope's advertisement of December 1714 giving March 1, 1715, as the date for the appearance of the first volume of the Homer may have led to the appearance of this in early March (Sherburn, p. 136).

WORKS: A. *Temple of Fame*; B. *Iliad* advertisement.

A   The 'Advertisement' ([A3]r and v) parodies Pope's advertisement before *The Temple of Fame* and charges Pope with plagiarism from *Hudibras* ([A]3 and 4 are badly cropped at the outer margin in the Yale copy; I have silently supplied several missing letters):

> Mr. *Pope* owns he took his Hint from *Chaucer*, and I own I took mine from Mr. *Pope*. What his Design may be, I cannot say, but mine, I must acknowledge, is to get Money from the Bookseller. For the particular Thoughts, I further acknowledge I consulted *Hudibras*, who I take to be the greatest Master of Bear-baiting that ever the World produc'd. Whether Mr. *Pope* consulted him or not, 'tis hard to judge; but he that will look into *Hudibras*, *Pag. 113, l. 45*. [see *Hudibras*, ed. A. R. Waller (Cambridge, 1905), pp. 106–7] and compare his Description of Fame with Mr. *Pope*'s Temple of Fame, will be apt to conclude that never Two good Wits jump'd more exactly. This is an Acknowledgment I could not omit, because a Concealment of this Nature, as Mr. Pope very excellently expresses it, I look upon to be utterly below the Dignity of an Author. ([A3]r and v)

The note following this is clearly a burlesque of Pope's *Iliad* advertisement:

B   The first Book of *Tom Thumb*, transform'd from the original
Nonsense into *Greek* Heroicks, is so near finished, that the
Undertaker hopes to be able to deliver it to the Subscribers by
the first of *April* next. ([A4]r)

Gentlemen and Ladies who have not yet done so are urged to pay in
their subscription money, and an 'N.B.' adds that there will be 'fine
cuts, and learned Annotations' ([A4]r and v).

A   The poem itself does not try to imitate very closely the structure of
The Temple of Fame. The poet falls asleep and dreams that he is hurried
through the air to the bear garden at Hockley in the Hole where he
hears the voice of Hudibras describe fame. Preston gives his ancestry
and praises the sport of bear-baiting. Two butcher's boys quarrel over
their bear dogs and start to fight. The crowd takes sides, but 'One
that's yclip'd my Lord, / By some call'd *Aesop*, the more ancient Word'
(p. 19) urges them to stop and promises them that if they will follow
him he will show them the wonders of the Temple of Fame. ('Aesop'
is possibly meant for Pope.) But the fight grows general, the dogs
break loose and then the bear. Preston praises the heroes who finally
capture the dogs and promises them a reward. Then the dreamer is
snatched away to where he can see a fair structure, *'Its site uncertain
if in Earth or Air'* (p. 28), surrounded by a huge crowd of poets, 'But
few, exceeding few, of them were good' (p. 28). At the top in a silver
car he sees Homer, Virgil, Pindar, Horace, and Ovid. He sees a poet
he knows (clearly Pope) 'who pretends to teach, and please Mankind'
(p. 29), who recites a parody of ll. 436–41 in *The Temple of Fame*:

> *As on the smooth Expance of Chrystal Lakes,*
> *The sinking Stone at first a Circle makes;*
> So from a House of Office o'er a Lake,
> A T—d falls down, and does a Circle make.
> *The trembling Surface by the Motion stir'd*
> *Spreads in a second Circle, then a third;*
> *Wide and more wide the Excrements advance;*
> *Fill all the watry Place, and to the Margin dance.*   (p. 30)

A voice banishes this 'vain Youth' (p. 31):

> *How vain that second Life in others Breath,*
> *Th' Estate that Wits inherit after Death;*
> For which I'm sure thou well deserv'st the Bays,
> Did ever wretched Nonsense merit Praise.   (p. 32)

   The major satiric device of the poem consists in describing the low
life of a bear garden frequently in the very words Pope had used to
describe the Temple of Fame, consists that is, in a mock-heroic re-

duction. The first two lines, for example, in the description of the boards and rails of the bear garden carved over with initials,

> *Inscriptions here of various Names I view'd,*
> *The greater Part by hostile Time subdu'd;*
> For as the Planks and Posts of Deal decay,
> So must these Names of Heroe's wast away,   (p. 11)

are ll. 31–2 of Pope's poem. Pope's 'Intellectual Scene' in l. 10 of his poem is forced into the context of,

> And there the sturdy Butchers in a Ring,
> Leading their four-leg'd Champions in a String.
> Whilst I this INTELLECTUAL SCENE survey.   (p. 10)

Sometimes the criticism becomes explicit, as in the speech of Preston to the heroes who have captured the dogs, borrowed from *The Temple of Fame*, ll. 324–5, 378, which concludes with an objection taken by up Elwin (*EC* I. 221, n.):

> *Nor with bare Justice shall your Act be crown'd,*
> (Said he) *but high above Desert renown'd.*
> *At this the youthful Train their Scorn exprest,*
> To hear such Nonsense in gay Language drest.   (p. 26)

The notes, too, occasionally reinforce the satire. The note, for example, to the third line in the following typical passage,

> *Hockley-i'th'-Hole* shall suffer no Decay,
> When *Zembla's beauteous Rocks* shall melt away.
> And that *bright Mountain of Eternal Snow,*
> Shall thaw, and drown the Country all below.
> When *Pope's* stupendious Pile of Snow and Ice,
> Shall tumble from it's slip'ry Precipice,   (p. 17)

reads:

> These are Mr. *Pope's* own Words, [ll. 57–8] and he must account for them, or no body. 'Tis a good full-mouth'd Verse, I own; but between Mr. *Pope* and I, 'tis hardly possible to put more Nonsence in one single Line. (p. 35)

And the note to,

> *And up the* WINDS *triumphant swell the Note,*
> *So soft, tho' high, so loud, and yet so clear,*   (p. 19)

objects,

> This I own to be insufferable Nonsense; but since I have Mr. *Pope's* Authority for it [ll. 373–4], whose Words they are, I think I ought not to make further Enlargements. (p. 36)

Pope included the scatological simile in the *Dunciad* A, ii. 373–6.

March 15, 1715

The High-German Doctor. See December 10, 1714.

WORK: A. *What D'Ye Call It.*

In the issue of March 15, 1715, Horneck apologizes for breaking off a
farce begun in the preceding number by saying that he did not want
to tire his audience

A   with a dull *what d'ye call it,* tho' that, I find, cannot Miscarry
under the Auspicies of a *small Wit,* and a *clumsey Beau.* (II. 186)

March 17, 1715

[Burnet, Thomas.] Numb. IV. The Grumbler. By Squire Gizzard. To be continued Weekly. There is a Machiavelian Plot, /
Though every Nare olfact it not. Hudibras. Thursday, March 17.
1715. [At foot of first column] (Price Two-pence. [At end] London: Printed by W. Wilkins, at the Dolphin in Little-Britain;
and Sold by R. Burleigh, in Amen-Corner. Where Advertisements are taken in.

Folio half-sheet, printed on both sides in double columns. Dated and
signed on verso 'March 8th. 1715. Aaron Gizzard.'

The Grumbler appeared every Thursday from February 24 to April 14
(Nos. 1–8), and thereafter twice a week, on Tuesdays and Fridays,
from Tuesday, April 19, to Friday, July 15, 1715 (Nos. 9–34) (*Letters
of Thomas Burnet,* p. 302). No. 4 is missing from the Bodleian collection
but is to be found at Harvard.

WORK: A. *What D'Ye Call It.*

CHARGE: 1. Pope a Catholic (and a Jacobite?).

The author on visiting his family last Saturday found them all 'grum-
bling out their Censures on the New *Farce,* intitled the What-d'ye call
it' (r). Omitting their assignment to members of the family, the following are the main objections:

     . . . saying of Prayers and going to Church, were made Subjects
of Laughter, in the *Soldier's Lamentation,* when he was preparing
to be shot . . . (r)

1   There is very probably a plot in the farce:

> ... For besides the Ghosts of deceased Soldiers, which were
> maliciously raised to move the People's Resentments, against
> the Men that formerly were clamoured at, *as delighting in War*,
> the Author makes a Jest of the Dangers of Popery, when he says,
> Beware of *Papishes*, and learn to Knit.   (v)

The author is guilty of a crime in trying to ridicule an Act of Parliament, the Press Act (r and v).

He has also violated the Laws of Parnassus. The dying soldier 'rather inclines you to pity his Circumstances, than to be diverted with his Language'. The handkerchief in *Othello* is 'a Joke as old as *Westminster-Abby* [*sic*]'. And the author has

> found out a new and happy Secret, which makes Burlesque for
> ever after an easy Task, which is, writing infinitely worse than
> those you intend to ridicule. (v)

April 2, or earlier, 1715 (*Evening Post*, March 31–April 2, 1715, 'Just Published')

[Theobald, Lewis, and Griffin, Benjamin.] A Complete Key To the last New Farce The What D'Ye Call It. To Which is prefix'd a Hypercritical Preface on the Nature of Burlesque, and the Poets Design. — Ut nec pes, nec Caput, uni / Reddatur formae—Hor. The best Actors in the World, either for Tragedy, Comedy, History, Pastoral, Pastorical-Comical-Historical-Pastoral, Tragical-Historical, Tragical-Comical-Historical-Pastoral, Scene undividable, or Poem unlimited: Seneca cannot be too heavy, nor Plautus too light; for the Law of Wit, and the Liberty; These are the only Men! Polon. in Hamlet. London; Printed for James Roberts at the Oxford Arms in Warwick-lane. 1715. Price 6d.

8vo in half-sheets.

A–E⁴.

[8 pp.], 1–32 pp.

Pope in a note to his *Letters* in 1735 said that this pamphlet 'was written by one *Griffin* a Player, assisted by *Lewis Theobald*' (*Corr.* 1. 288, n.8); he added a similar note to the *Dunciad* (*Twick.* v. 207, n.5). Jones, pp.

16–17, accepts the attribution to Theobald. Why Theobald should have attacked Pope at this period is, however, unknown. On Benjamin Griffin, an actor in the Lincoln's Inn Fields company, see the article in the *DNB* and Leo Hughes, *A Century of English Farce* (Princeton, 1956), pp. 186–8.

Charles Kerby-Miller in *Memoirs of the Extraordinary Life, Works, and Discoveries of Martinus Scriblerus*, ed. Charles Kerby-Miller (New Haven, 1950), pp. 43–5, argues unconvincingly for Pope's and Gay's authorship of this *Key*. He objects that Theobald and Griffin would have had only two weeks to prepare and publish the *Key*. But pamphlets were usually done very quickly and this one is not an elaborate composition, but almost entirely a series of parallel quotations. He also argues that though some of the sources are obvious and others far-fetched, a score or so 'are specific identifications which only a person endowed with an unusual knowledge and patience could have discovered and still another score are so esoteric and slanted in their application that it does not seem possible for a person who did not know what was intended to have discovered the original passages' (p. 44). Without knowing exactly which identifications he has in mind, it is impossible to argue, but surely the great majority of the identifications are not 'original passages' but rough parallels. Theobald and Griffin would have been familiar with dramatic literature. It may be pointed out that very few of Pope's attributions of Popiana can be proved to be wrong.

The What D'Ye Call It had been produced at Drury Lane on February 23, 1715; it was published March 19, 1715, and passed through six editions in Gay's lifetime. (My quotations are taken from the first edition.) The farce was acted 28 times the first two seasons, and there was scarcely a year without a revival down to 1750 (Irving, pp. 114–15). There are good discussions of the play in F. W. Bateson, *English Comic Drama, 1700–1750* (Oxford, 1929), pp. 81–7, and in Frederick S. Boas, *An Introduction to Eighteenth-Century Drama, 1700–1780* (Oxford, 1953), pp. 170–5.

WORKS: A. *Guardian No. 40* (?); B. *What D'Ye Call It.*

The Preface (A2r–A4v) clearly implies that Pope collaborated with Gay:

> I own, that I despise the Composition horribly, and look on it as the most unnatural, ill-affected Wit that the Age has produc'd. But we could expect nothing less from the baseness of a busy Pen, which is now attacking all the Reputations that rais'd

its won, and skreens it self behind a borrow'd Name. For give
me leave to Quote *Virgil* for once; and I think I may say of the
skreening Friend,

—Nihil ille nec ausus

Nec potuit;—

But this *malevolent Critick* fights, like *little Teucer,* behind the shield
of *impenetrable Stupidity.* (A2v–A3r)

A   There is a probable allusion to Pope's *Guardian No. 40.* (Sherburn,
p. 138, n.1, suggests it may be an allusion to the *Key to the Lock,* but
this does not seem to have been published until later in April; see
Prose, I. lxxiv.)

However you lovely Yoak-mates, Joint Fathers of a poor Jest,
your equally laborious Commentators, who have endeavour'd
to trace your Allusions, hope for your Pardon and Patronage
... A late *gentle* Author, famous for his *Madrigalls,* took the
pains to comment upon his own Writings; and this Farce, having an equal right to his Esteem, ought at least to be favour'd
with the same Indulgence. (A4r and v)

B   The preface also expresses the writers' solemn disapproval of parody.
Unlike *The Rehearsal, The What D' Ye Call It*

seems rather to be a Banter on the solemn stile of Tragedy in
general, than a Satyr upon faulty Passages of our Poets ... The
Application of a fine well-work'd Passion to a mean Object certainly makes it Ridiculous; and the Pomp of Words only more
exposes the Sentiment. This is in short but barely making a
Parodie, to which the best Writings are capable of being debas'd;
and the most moving Passages in all the Antients, with a moderate share of Wit, may by this means be sunk into Contempt.

(A3v–A4r)

The *Key* itself simply goes through the play page by page, identifying with comments the passages parodied.

Behold how low you have reduc'd a Maid,   (p. 10)

is called 'an invidious Parodie' (p. 5) of

Behold how low, you have reduc'd a Queen,

from *The Distressed Mother.* They comment on Peascod's farewell to
Filbert,

The Solemnity of parting with dying Friends, which has so
often drawn Tears in the Tragedies of *Oroonoko, Othello, Anthony,*
&c. is here made a Subject of Merriment. (p. 18)

For Peascod's

—When I am dead—you'll bind my Grave with Wicker (p. 27)

they suggest several parallels and conclude that it reflects on these,
        Or on any thing else, in short, of this kind; so fond are these
Farce Writers of triumphing over an Audience's Compassion in
being touch'd at Distress, and proclaiming their own Insensi-
bility. (p. 24)

Any echo of Shakespeare meets with stern disapproval. In their
examination of the most amusing moment in the farce, their critical
method is seen at its most inept:

> II. Countryman.—Repent thine Ill,
> And Pray in this good Book.—
> [*Gives him a Book.*
> Peascod.   —I will, I will.
> Lend me thy Handkercher—*The Pilgrim's Pro-*
>   [*Reads and weeps.*
> (I cannot see for Tears) *Pro- Progress*—Oh!
> —*The Pilgrim's Progress—Eighth—Edi-ti-on*
> *Lon-don—Prin-ted—for—Ni-cho-las Bod-ding-ton:*
> *With new Ad-di-tions never made before*
> —Oh! 'tis so moving, I can read no more.   (p. 20)

They first object to the abuse of Othello's bidding Desdemona to
pray, and then find that, 'These Lines are the most unjust Abuse of
the Famous *Cato*' (p. 16). They claim that the authors first planned
to parody Addison's

>   It must be so,—*Plato*, thou reason'st well

as,

>   —*Bunyan*, thou reason'st well

but found this 'so flagrant, that they expected it would entail the
Curse of an Audience, and for that reason grew more Modest' (p. 16)

> Were the Author of this Tragedy but half as subject to Jea-
> lousy as Mr *Dennis* the Critick, he would in this Quotation find
> more than one occasion of Affront. The *Eighth* Edition of the
> *Pilgrims Progress* is taken notice of, insinuating that *Cato* has just
> as often visited the Press ... (p. 17)

The malice implied here is reinforced by their noting a parallel to
Jane Shore and adding, 'This is reckoned only fair Play, for Wits always
are free with their *Friends*' (p. 15). (*The What D'Ye Call It* was first
produced with *Jane Shore*, and Rowe seems never to have objected to
the farce.)

Their do occasionally approve of some of the parody, and the
sudden reprieval of Peascod they find

> exposes the too sudden and unprepar'd *Peripetias* in most *Trage-*

dies. If this had been the Conduct of the *Farce Writers* throughout their *Scenes*, their Design, instead of deserving Censure, would have merited Applause. (p. 26)

They end by assuring the reader that they have taken care 'to mark the most flagrant [allusions] at length' (p. 31).

Although most of their parallels seem roughly right, a few are totally unconvincing. It is hard to believe that the aunt and grandmother are meant to mimic the Duchess of York in *Richard III* (p. 4), and the parallel they find to Dennis's *Appius and Virginia* (p. 23) is so slight as to suggest malice on the part of the authors.

Gay and Pope mention the *Key* with amusement in their letter to Caryll, April, 1715 (*Corr.* I. 288–9).

April 23, 1715

The High-German Doctor. See December 10, 1714.

WORK: A. *What D'Ye Call It.*

CHARGE: I. Pope a Jacobite.

In the issue of April 23, 1715, Horneck hopes for his reader's attention to an entertainment,

AI   especially since Farces of *Popes* and *Pretender's* have taken such a Run alate. (II. 240)

These three attacks of Horneck were answered by Pope, if we may assume his authorship, in the *Sermon on Glass-Bottles*, where Horneck is clearly referred to in the Preface – a print of the German Doctor has 'brought in far more Money than wou'd be given for the real Author of a Paper under the same Title, were he slash'd, season'd, and serv'd up in a *Ragoo*' (*Prose*, I. 206–7). He is also probably referred to in 'And it is not in the Nature of a true *German* to neglect a true Bottle-Man', 'since Two [bottles] at any Time make a *Doctor*' (*ibid.*), and in the reference to German Mum (*ibid.* 219; for this last reference cf. the reference to Mum in *The High German Doctor*, September 10, 1714, I. 221). He makes his appearance in the *Dunciad* A, III. 146, where the note calls the paper 'Billingsgate'.

May 6, 1715

[Burnet, Thomas.] Numb. XIV. The Grumbler. By Squire Gizzard. Ne tamen ignores ubi sim venalis, & erres / Urbe vagus totâ; me duce certus eris. Mart. From Tuesday May 3. to Friday May 6. 1715. [At foot of first column] (Price Two-Pence.) [At end imprint as for No. IV, March 17.]

Folio half-sheet, printed on both sides in double columns.

WORKS: A. *Temple of Fame*; B. *Key to the Lock*.

CHARGES: 1. Pope praises his own verse; 2. Pope wrote *A Key to the Lock* and *A Complete Key To The What D'Ye Call It*.

'The inferior Class of Writers' is addicted to 'catching at Applause and Admiration' (r).

AI
> Let the unwary take warning from a Poet, who not long ago raised a *Temple of Fame* to himself, which was no sooner finished, than it fell to the Ground, and buried the Architect under its Ruins. (r)

After Burnet has gone on to describe the methods little wits take to make their books sell – false names, misleading title-pages, etc. – he adds,

12
> Another obliges the World with a *Key* to his own *Lock*, in which the *Wards* are all false: Under the borrowed Shape of an Apothecary, he modestly takes an opportunity to commend the Smoothness of his own Verses, and to publish a Sale of Six Thousand of his Books. The same Arch Wag, a little before this, gave us a *Compleat Key* to his *Farce*. I think it proper to advize him and his Journey-Man, to play no more Pranks of this kind; if they do, I have a *Master-Key* now under the File, with which I shall be able to unlock all their Secrets from the Beginning. (v)

September 17, 1715 (*Post Boy*, September 15–17, 1715)

[Harris, John.] A Treatise Upon The Modes: Or, A Farewell To French Kicks. Est Modus in Rebus. The Modes depend upon Sense. London: Printed for J. Roberts, at the Oxford Arms in Warwick-Lane. 1715.

Half-title: A Treatise Upon The Modes. Price One Shilling.

8vo.

Two unsigned leaves, A⁴, B–E⁸.

[4 pp.], i–viii, 1–64 pp.

Attributed by Rawlinson to John Harris, afterwards Bishop of Llandaff; this attribution is confirmed by the inscription in D. N. Smith's own copy (*Letters of Thomas Burnet*, p. 260). For Harris see *Twick.* IV. 364.

WORKS: A. *Essay on Criticism* (?); B. *Rape of the Lock* (?).

CHARGE: 1. Pope plagiarized from Boileau.

ABI   This foolish attack on all things French contains possibly two quite incidental references to Pope. Plagiarism is hinted at between 'a certain Poet of this Nation, and a *French* Poet, call'd *Despreaux*' (p. 40). If aimed at Pope, Harris had in mind the *Essay on Criticism* and *The Rape of the Lock*.

The other reference is puzzling:

> That *British* Poet, whom I mention'd before, as animated with the spirit of *Despreaux*, was, about three Years ago (as it is said) carry'd before a Justice, for riding in a Full-bottom'd Wig: The Country imagining that he had kill'd a Man, and had not Time to Undress. (p. 44)

A marginal note reads 'Tale of the *British* Despreaux', and would seem to connect the anecdote with Pope.

May 19, 1716 (*Post-Man*, May 19, 1716)

State Poems. Viz. I. Verses upon the Sickness and Recovery of the Right Honourable Robert Walpole, Esq; By N. Rowe, Esq; &c. II. The Three Patriots. III. The Ramble between Belinda a Demy-Prude, and Cloe a Court-Coquette. In Imitation of Fontaine. IV. An Epilogue written for the New Comedy, call'd the Drummer, but not spoke. V. The Worms. A Satire. By Mr. Pope. London: Printed for J. Roberts near the Oxford Arms in Warwick Lane. 1716. Where may be had, Mr. Pope's Court Poems. Price 6d.

Half-title: State Poems By The most Eminent Hands. Price Six Pence.

8vo in half-sheets.

Two unsigned leaves, B–D⁴, E².

[4 pp.], 1–28 pp.

Griffith 55.

Case 292.

This book was later included in *Court Poems, Part II*, 1717 (Case 295 (2) [a]), which in turn was included in *The Ladies Miscellany*, 1718 (Griffith 97; Case 306). I have seen *Court Poems, Part II* only as included in *The Ladies Miscellany*; for the lengthy description of the latter, see Case 306.

'An Epilogue written for the late celebrated New Play called the Drummer, but not spoke' (pp. 20–3) is the only Popiana here.

CHARGE: 1. Pope a Jacobite.

This discarded prologue to Addison's unsuccessful comedy *The Drummer* which began its brief run on March 10, 1716, involved Pope in its satire of Jacobite fears of meteors and of the recent displays of aurora borealis (Sherburn, p. 160).

1
> A very POPE (I'm told) may be afraid,
> And tremble at the Monsters, which he made.
> From dark mishapen ¹Clouds of many a Dye.
> A different Object rose to every Eye:
> And the same Vapour, as your Fancies ran,
> Appear'd a *Monarch*, or a *Warming-Pan*.
>
> ¹ The late *Meteor* (p. 21).

'The last verse quoted refers to scandalous gossip – kept alive by Hanoverians – to the effect that the Pretender was not of royal birth, but had been smuggled into the queen's chamber in a warming-pan, and presented as a new-born, royal heir' (Sherburn, p. 161, n.1).

May 29, 1716 (*Post-Man*, May 26–9, 1716)

[Burnet, Thomas, and Duckett, George.] Homerides: Or, Homer's First Book Moderniz'd. By Sir Iliad Doggrel. Nostra Poetantes producunt saecula multos. Anon. London, Printed for R. Burleigh in Amen-Corner. M.DCC. XVI.

12mo in half-sheets.

[A]–C⁶, D in five leaves.

[2 pp.], iii–vi, 7–45 pp., [46] advertisement.

Bond 46.

The Yale copy above is heavily cropped at the bottom. 'Price 6d.'
appears after the date on the title-page in the British Museum copy.
This has been cut away in the Yale copy, as have all the signatures
for A. The British Museum copy lacks D6; the Bodleian copy has D6.

Achilles Dissected, 1733, pp. 14–15, quotes from the Preface of
Homerides, pp. iv–v; also quoted, with several minor changes, are p. 15,
ll. 1–8, and pp. 16–19, ll. 637–96.

The first reference to this second *Homerides* pamphlet is in a letter from
Burnet to Duckett of December 14, 1715: 'Your Translation of
Homer's first Iliad, I beg you would send me, and I will look it over
with a friend who is no small judge of those affairs' (*Letters of Thomas
Burnet*, p. 95). In his letter of May 3, 1716, he writes that he has 'with
a good deal of satisfaction read through and in some places corrected
your Homer's first Book; Dr. Garth and I went over it together, and
the Doctor was very much delighted with the Performance. I have
furbished up a short Preface and laid the whole in Darby's hands to
come out assoon [*sic*] as possible . . .' (*Ibid.* p. 96).

Burnet's letter of June 1, 1716, is so valuable a testimony to Addison's share in these attacks on the Homer that it may be quoted at
length. David Nichol Smith observes that it shows that Burnet had
not met Pope before:

> I have sent you here above half a dozen of your *Homerides*, and
> if you should dislike the Preface I have put to it, or be displeased
> with the Compliment made in it to Mr Pope, I must wholly lay
> the blame upon my friends in Town, for I was not at all pleased
> with either one or the other. Only the Compliment to him
> seemed proper, because that Addison and the rest of the Rhim-
> ing Gang have dropt their Resentment against the *Lordlike Man*.
> The few Corrections I have made, I fancy you your self will
> approve of, I am assure [*sic*] I altered nothing upon the bare
> strength [*sic*] of my own Judgment, and what I have done is
> but very little. It has often made me smile at the pitifull soul of
> the Man, when I have seen Addison caressing Pope, whom at
> the same Time he hates worse than Belzeebub [*sic*] and by whom
> he has been more than once lampooned. For my part Garth
> made Mr Pope and my self dine together, and would have us

friends and Acquaintance; and to speak it is an illnatured little false Dog, but he does not want for a great deal of very diverting Satyrical Wit. (*Ibid.* p. 99)

The statement in *Achilles Dissected*, p. 14, that the preface to this second *Homerides* is by Duckett is, on this evidence, incorrect.

WORK: A. *Iliad.*

CHARGE: I. Pope a Catholic.

The 'complimentary' Preface (pp. iii–vi) signed, p. vi, 'Valeas', is not quite straightforward:

A   I CONFESS, When I publish'd my Letter to Mr. *Pope*, in which I advis'd him to brush up the old-fashion'd *Greek* Bard, and give him the *English* Air as well as Tongue; I was apprehensive that my Counsel was come too late, and that the Gentleman had already gone through several Books, wherein he had kept to the Sense of his Author, without modernizing him in the least. This Fear of mine appear'd soon after to be very well grounded; for the aforemention'd Poet has been so careful of doing justice to his Original, that he has nothing in his whole Poem that is not *Homer's*, but the Language. And I think one may say of his Translation, as one wou'd of a Copy by *Titian* of one of his own Pictures, That nothing can be better, but the Original.

(pp. iv–v)

But since Pope has not followed his advice, he feels himself bound to show the public that his method 'was not impracticable, and would have been entertaining' (p. v). The burlesque version of the first book of the *Iliad* in 808 lines of Hudibrastic couplets which follows has several borrowings almost verbatim from the 1715 *Homerides*: ll. 259–70 are taken from 1715, p. 10; ll. 51–6 from 1715, p. 33; l. 304 from 1715, p. 11. Except for the implied mockery of serious translation the only allusion to Pope in the verse is the heavy-handed satire on Catholic doctrine and practice:

I
            In nine days time (O horrid Story!)
            They'ad almost fill'd up Purgatory.   (ll. 87–8)

          ' 'Tis not the want of *Ave-maries*,
          Masses and Beads, and such Vagaries;
          But 'tis cause *Aggy* made a Jest
          Of our old Mumpsimus the Priest.'   (ll. 141–4)

May 31, 1716 (*Flying Post*, May 31, 1716)

[Oldmixon, John.] The Catholick Poet; Or, Protestant Barnaby's Sorrowful Lamentation: An Excellent New Ballad. To the Tune of, Which no body can deny. [At top of p. 3, under a double rule] To all Gentlemen, Authors, Translators, or Translating Poets, who are Protestants, and well affected to the present Establishment in the most Illustrious House of Hanover. The humble Petition of Barnaby Bernard Lintott, Living at the Sign of the Cross-Keys between the Two Temple Gates in Fleet-street. [At bottom of p. 6 under a single rule] London: Printed for J. Morphew, J. Roberts, R. Burleigh, J. Baker, and S. Popping; and sold by all the Booksellers in England, Dominion of Wales, and Town of Berwick upon Tweed. 1716. (Price Three-pence.)

Folio.
Three unsigned leaves.
1–6 pp.

Pope attributed this to 'Mrs. *Centlivre* and others' (*Twick.* v. 207); he mistakenly dates it 1715, and says in one place that it came out before the Homer had appeared (*Twick.* v. 125, n.), and in another, before he had begun it (*Twick.* v. 146, n.). Curll commented in *The Curliad*, 1729, p. 27, 'In the Note upon this Verse, Mrs *Centlivre* is said to have *writ a Ballad* against Mr. *Pope's* Homer *before he begun* it. The *Fact* is *true*, but the *Person* on whom it is charged, is falsely accused. The Ballad, here referred to, being wrote by Mr. *Oldmixon*.' 'Pope accepted Oldmixon's authorship of the ballad, but never ceased to attribute it to Mrs. Centlivre as well' (*Twick.* v. 125).

WORKS: A. *Rape of the Lock*; B. *What D'Ye Call It*; C. *Iliad*.

CHARGES: 1. The bad sale of the *Iliad* has hurt Lintot financially; 2. Pope deformed; 3. Pope a Catholic and Jacobite; 4. Pope a Tory spy; 5. Pope has written for both the *Guardian* and the *Examiner*; 6. Pope ignorant of Greek.

The Ballad, of thirteen stanzas sung by Pope and Lintot, charges Pope with both bawdry and the failure of the *Iliad*. It opens:

ABC   My Song is of *SAWNY*, The Poet of *Windsor*,
1 2 3   Whose *HOMER* will sell, when the *Devil is blind*, Sir;
         And the *Hump* is *before* him, that now is *behind*, Sir;
           Which no Body can deny.

His *Muse* fed with Sack:[1] Growing warmer, and warmer,
He *Ravish'd a Lock* from the pretty *Bell. Fermor,*
And thought with vile *Smut* to have charmed, the *Charmer;*
    Which, &c.

On the Stage *Collier* fell, long ago, and did maul it;
He cares not for that, he's more Bawdy than all yet,
Ev'n *Horner* Would blush at his Lewd *What d'ye call it;*
    Which, &c.

When he [Pope] has undone thee [Lintot], his Muse will be
    jaded,
And grinning he'll cry, thou hast traded, and traded,
But never did'st know what was *Greek* for a *Spade* yet;
    Which, &c.

From Learned and Simple, from Goers and Comers,
From *Oxford,* and *Cambridge,* from *Rome* and St. *Omers,*
A Thousand Subscriptions I got for my *HOMERS;*
    Which, &c.

[1] Mr. *Pope's* Breakfast is Sop and Sack (pp. 1–2).

Lintot replies to Pope that his Homers are nothing but waste paper
on his hands.

'Tis a Lye by the Mass, cries the *Catholick* Poet,
To the Wall will I stick thee, – Quo' *Bernard,* aye do it;
I'm a *Protestant,* Z—ds, and I'll make you to know it;
    Which, &c.   (p. 2)

The prose *Petition,* pp. 3–5, continues the attacks on the Homer and
Catholicism. Lintot explains that he purchased the copy of Pope's
translation of the *Iliad,* of which the first two volumes have appeared.

... The *First* Volume met with but very little Encouragement,
and the *Second* is likely to meet with much less ... When he
[Pope] began this Work, he told your *Petitioner* he should have
great helps, and the Design indeed seem'd prosperous by the
Wits of the Town declaring in his Favour; but this true *Catholick,*
after he had got a Number of Subscriptions, by the Recomen-
dation of our *Protestant Authors,* who are Men of Honour; he
immediately betray'd all their private Conversation to the Late
Ministry, and at the same time wrote GUARDIANS and EX-
AMINERS, for which Reasons these Gentlemen have very justly forsaken him, and all the Books lye upon my Hands. (pp. 4–5)

There is the standard charge that Pope knew no Greek and was
assisted by Broome and Fenton.

c6   . . . Mr. *Pope* doth not understand *Greek* thoroughly, for he never
was at any University, nor ever learn'd that Language till he
undertook to translate *HOMER*, (being first litterally render'd
for him, by two Young *Oxford* Dabs, one lately ordain'd, and the
other a Smatterer in Physick.) All your *Petitioner's* Hopes, were,
that this Copy would have been an Estate to his only Son here-
after, but he was amaz'd in *Easter*-Holydays, that no Subscribers
came for their Books, and rather chose to loose their first Pay-
ment than go any farther . . . (p. 5)

Lintot's son discovers that Pope has mistranslated [I. 3] 'Plutonia
Regna' as 'Pluto's Reign' instead of 'Pluto's Realms', as Tickell had
correctly done, that Pope has wounded Achilles whom Homer had
made invulnerable and

c3   in another Place [I. 126], he makes *Homer* say, *that the Priest can
pardon Sins*, which is downright *Popery*. Upon which your *Petitioner*, could not forbear crying out, Z—nds *This Papish Dog has
ruin'd me, he has translated HOMER for the Use of the PRE-
TENDER* . . . (p. 5)

In a postscript Lintot adds Pope's 'Verses To be prefix'd before Bernard Lintot's New Miscellany' (*Twick*. VI. 82–5). The note to them,
Mr. *Pope* writ these Verses before he had undertaken to translate *Homer*, [the poem was first printed anonymously in Lintot's
Miscellany, 1712] and your Petitioner took the Complement so
kindly, that he was resolv'd upon any Terms to be Mr. *Pope's*
Bookseller, (p. 6)

attempts with no evidence at all to strengthen the impression that
Lintot was, or ought to have been, offended by the verses.

May 31, 1716 (*Flying Post*, May 31, 1716)

[Dennis, John.] A True Character Of Mr. Pope, And His
Writings. In a Letter to a Friend. A Lump Deform'd and Shape-
less was he Born, / Begot in Love's Despight, and Nature's
Scorn. Roch. Aw'd by no Shame, by no Respect controul'd, / In
Scandal busie, in Reproaches bold: / Spleen to Mankind his
envious Heart possest, / And much he hated All, but most the
Best. Pope's Homer. Vol. I. Book 2. London: Printed for S.
Popping at the Black Raven in Pater-Noster-Row. 1716. Price 3d.

8vo in half-sheets.

[A]⁴–B⁴, one leaf.

[2 pp.], 3–18 pp.

The above is the British Museum copy; Yale's copy lacks the title-page.

The British Museum has a copy of the second edition, 1717, 'in preparing which there is no reason to suppose that Dennis played any part' (Hooker, II. 458). The title-page is lacking.

Drop-title: A True Character of Mr. Pope. The Second Edition.

8vo in half-sheets.

B⁴.

1–8 pp.

Reprinted in Hooker, II. 103–8.

Curll in *The Curliad*, 1729, p. 4, promised that a new edition would appear shortly, but I have not discovered evidence that this was published.

A True Character was issued under the imprint of Sarah Popping who was sometimes a front for Edmund Curll. Both *A True Character* and *The Catholick Poet* were published on the same day and are clearly part of Curll's programme of revenge for the emetic and *A Full and True Account* (Hooker, II. 457).

As Pope noted in the *Dunciad* (*Twick.* v. 25, n.), Curll in the first edition of his *Key to the Dunciad*, 1728, p. 10, stated that Gildon wrote *A True Character*. According to Pope, Curll dropped this assertion 'in the subsequent editions'; it appears, however, in the second edition of the *Key*, although not in the third. In *The Curliad* Curll, pp. 4, 7–8, insisted that Dennis alone had written it. Pope gave it to Dennis and Gildon and in the *Dunciad* ascribed quotations from it sometimes to one, sometimes to the other, and sometimes to both.

Dennis's authorship may be taken as certain. Sherburn, p. 178, pointed out that it was done 'Denisissime', and Hooker includes it in his *Critical Works of John Dennis* with a summary of the reasons for the ascription (II. 458). A fuller examination of the authorship may be found in his article, 'Pope and Dennis', *ELH*, VII (1940), 188–98, an unsatisfactory defence of Dennis's conduct in his quarrel with Pope.

It is clear that Dennis, after his introductory paragraph, is transcribing, pp. 4–6, the 'Character' which he had received 'from another Hand'. He concludes his quotation, 'This was the Character, which my Friend gave . . .' (p. 6). It is obviously the presence of the

H

'Character' which led Pope to believe in a dual authorship. Curll's statement in his *Key* that Gildon wrote *A True Character* and his shifty explanation of this statement in *The Curliad* suggest that Pope was right in associating Gildon somehow with *A True Character*, and although Dennis insisted that he had never written 'so much as one Line, that was afterwards printed, in Concert with any one Man whatsoever' (*Remarks Upon . . . the Dunciad*, 1729, p. 50), he did not say he had never quoted from anyone, as Hooker pointed out (Hooker, II. 458). Gildon, then, seems a likely candidate for the 'other hand'.

There are other more difficult problems. To whom is the letter addressed? All we know is that the correspondent sent Dennis the 'Libel', which was in the form of an imitation of Horace, and that Pope had tried 'to expose [him] in a *Billingsgate* Libel' at the same time that the friend was doing Pope a favour at Pope's 'own earnest Desire' (p. 6). Can we take Dennis literally here? The correspondent may be imaginary, a literary device, as in many other Popiana pamphlets. If we read the favour ironically, it might be possible to identify the correspondent with Edmund Curll; the favour could be the publication of the *Court Poems*, and the '*Billingsgate* Libel' *A Full and True Account Of A . . . Revenge by Poison*. There is, however, no evidence that Dennis would address a letter to Curll in this tone.

The provocation of the pamphlet also remains unclear. The only immediate provocation it mentions is the libellous Imitation of Horace. Unfortunately, this Imitation of Horace has never been identified. It may be the missing Imitation which Pope told Spence he had done 'several years ago, and in quite a different manner' of the first satire of the first book of Horace (*Twick.* IV. xxvi).

There is one curious point. One of the reasons for ascribing *A True Character* to Dennis is its quotations from *Hudibras*, a favourite poem of Dennis's which he quoted frequently. The 'Character' contains a four-line quotation from *Hudibras* on which, after identifying, Hooker comments, 'Dennis is apparently quoting from memory' (Hooker, II. 459). But if Dennis is not the author of the enclosed 'Character', how could he be quoting several lines of verse embedded in it from memory?

WORKS: A. *Pastorals*; B. *Essay on Criticism*; C. *Windsor Forest*; D. Prologue to *Cato*; E. *Guardian No. 40*; F. *Ode on St. Cecilia's Day*; G. *Rape of the Lock*; H. *Temple of Fame*; J. *Iliad*; K. *Worms*.

CHARGES: 1. Pope deformed; 2. Pope a Whig and Tory, a writer of *Guardians* and *Examiners*; 3. Pope a Roman Catholic and Jacobite;

4. Pope urged Lintot to publish Dennis's *Remarks upon Cato*; 5. Pope published *A Letter from the Facetious Doctor Andrew Tripe*; 6. Pope has lately published five or six libels in prose.

The pamphlet opens:

> I Have read over the *Libel*, which I received from you the Day before Yesterday. Yesterday I received the same from another Hand, with this Character of the Secret Author of so much stupid Calumny. (p. 3)

He then gives the 'character', of which the following is typical:

> 'Tis *says he*, a very little but very comprehensive Creature, in whom all Contradictions meet, and all Contrarieties are reconcil'd; when at one and the same time, like the Ancient *Centaurs*, he is a Beast and a Man, a Whig and a Tory, a virulent *Papist* and yet forsooth, a Pillar of the Church of *England*, a Writer at one and the same time, of *GUARDIANS* and of *EXAMINERS*, an assertor of Liberty and of the Dispensing Power of Kings; a Rhimester without Judgment or Reason, and a Critick without Common Sense; a Jesuitical Professor of Truth, a base and a foul Pretender to Candour; a Barbarous Wretch, who is perpetually boasting of Humanity and Good Nature, a lurking way-laying Coward, and a Stabber in the Dark; who is always pretending to Magnanimity, and to sum up all Villains in one, a Traytor-Friend, one who has betrayed all Mankind ...
>
> He is a Professor of the worst Religion, which he laughs at, and yet has most inviolably observ'd the most execrable Maxim in it, *That no Faith is to be kept with Hereticks*. (pp. 4–5)

Dennis resumes:

> This was the Character, which my Friend gave of the Author of this miserable Libel, which immediately made me apprehend that it was the very same Person, who endeavour'd to expose you in a *Billingsgate* Libel, at the very time that you were doing him a Favour at his own earnest Desire, who attempted to undermine Mr. *PHILIPS* in one of his *Guardians*, at the same time that the *Crocodile* smil'd on him, embrac'd him, and called him Friend, who wrote a Prologue in praise of *CATO*, and teaz'd *Lintott* to publish Remarks upon it; who at the same time, that he openly extoll'd Sir *Richard Steele* in the highest manner, secretly publish'd the Infamous Libel of Dr. *Andrew Tripe* upon him; who, as he is in Shape a *Monkey*, is so in his every Action: in his senseless Chattering, and his merry Grimaces, in his doing hour-

ly Mischief and hiding himself, in the variety of his Ridiculous Postures, and his continual Shiftings, from Place to Place, from Persons to Persons, from Thing to Thing. But whenever he Scribbles, he is emphatically a *Monkey*, in his awkward servile Imitations. For in all his Productions, he has been an *Imitator*, from his Imitation of *VIRGILS Bucolicks*, to this present Imitation of *HORACE*.—His *Pastorals* were writ in Imitation of *VIRGIL*,—His *Rape of the Lock* of *BOILEAU*,—His *Essay on Criticism*, of the present Duke of *Buckingham*, and of my Lord *Roscommon*,—His *Windsor-Forest* of Sir *John Denham*,—His *Ode upon St. Caecilia* of Mr. *Dryden*, and—His *Temple of Fame*, of *CHAUCER*. (pp. 6–7)

Sherburn, p. 105, points out that there is no evidence other than this accusation by Dennis that Pope teased Lintot into publishing the *Remarks on Cato*. 'The Infamous Libel of Dr. *Andrew Tripe*' is *A Letter from the Facetious Doctor Andrew Tripe, at Bath, to the Venerable Nestor Ironside*, published apparently about the middle of February 1714 and certainly not by Pope; it has been variously ascribed to Swift, Wagstaffe, Arbuthnot, and the Scriblerus Club (Hooker, II. 459). Dennis continues with an extraordinary justification of his pamphlet:

K I   But if any one appears to be concern'd at our Upbraiding him with his Natural Deformity, which did not come by his own Fault, but seems to be the Curse of God upon him; we desire that Person to consider, that this little Monster has upbraided People with their Calamities and their Diseasies [*sic*], and Calamities and Diseases, which are either false or past, or which he himself gave them by adminstring Poison to them ...

... The Deformity of this Libeller, is Visible, Present, Unalterable, and Peculiar to himself. 'Tis the mark of God and Nature upon him, to give us warning that we should hold no Society with him, as a Creature not of our Original, nor of our Species. And they who have refus'd to take this Warning which God and Nature have given them, and have in spight of it, by a Senseless Presumption, ventur'd to be familiar with him, have severely suffer'd for it, by his Perfidiousness. They tell me, he has been lately pleas'd to say, *That 'tis Doubtful if the Race of Men are the Offspring of Adam or of the Devil*[1]. But if 'tis doubtful as to the Race of Men, 'tis certain at least, that his Original is not from *Adam*, but from the *Divel*. By his constant and malicious Lying, and by that Angel Face and Form of his, 'tis plain that he wants nothing but Horns and Tayl, to be the exact Resem-

blance, both in Shape and Mind, of his Infernal Father. Thus, Sir, I return you Truth for Slander, and a just Satire for an Extravagant Libel, which is therefore ridiculously call'd an Imitation of *Horace* ...

¹The *WORMS*, a Satire, stanza 4 (pp. 9-11).

Of all present-day libellers,

6

the present Imitator is the most Impudent, and the most Incorrigible, who has lately pester'd and plagu'd the World with Five or Six Scandalous Libels, in Prose, that are all of them at once so Stupid, and so Malicious, that Men of Sense are Doubtful, if they should attribute them to the Libellers Native Idiotism, or to Accidental Madness. (p. 15)

These five or six scandalous libels present a problem. Hooker conjectures that they probably refer to *The Narrative of Dr. Norris*, which ridicules Dennis, *Guardian No. 40*, on Philips, *A Letter from the Facetious Dr. Andrew Tripe*, which ridicules Steele, and *A Full and True Account Of A Horrid and Barbarous Revenge*, ridiculing Curll. Possibly *The Critical Specimen* should be included. None of these quite deserves the characterization Dennis offers.

Dennis then attacks the Homer:

J

I know nothing for which he is so ill Qualified as he is for Judging, unless it be for Translating *HOMER*. He has neither Taste nor Judgment, but is, if you will pardon a Quibble, the very necessity of *Parnassus*; for he has none of the Poetical Laws; or if he has the Letter of any, He has it without the Spirit ... The *Preface* is full of gross Errours, and he has shewn himself in it, a Dogmatical, Ignorant, Impudent Second-Hand Critick. As for the *Poem*, however he may cry up *HOMER* for being every where a *Graecian-Trumpeter* in the Original, I can see no *Trumpeter* in the *Translator*, but the King of *Spains's* ...

As for what they call his *Verses*, he has, like Mr. *Bayes*, got a notable knack of Rhimeing and Writing smooth Verse, but without either Genius or Good Sense, or any tolerable Knowledge of *English*, as I believe I shall shew plainly, when I come to the rest of his Imitations. As for his Translation of *HOMER*, I could never borrow it, till this very Day, and design to read it over to Morrow; so that shortly you may expect to hear more of it. I will only tell you beforehand, that *HOMER* seems to me to be untranslatable in any Modern Language. (pp. 16-17)

November 22, 1716 (*St James's Post*, November 23, 1716)

Baker, J., Kt., [pseud. ?] A Letter From Sir J— B— to Mr. P—, upon Publishing of a Paper, intituled, God's Revenge against Punning; shewing the Miserable Fates of Persons addicted to this Crying Sin, in Court and Town. By J. Baker Kt. [At bottom of p. 2] London, Printed for J. Baker and T. Warner at the Black-Boy in Paternoster-Row. 1716. (Price Two Pence.)

A folio half-sheet, printed on both sides, and paged 1–2.

Both authorship and contents are puzzling. This is clearly a reply to *God's Revenge Against Punning*, signed 'J. Baker, Knight', published on November 7, 1716, and ascribed to Pope by Norman Ault with impressive evidence (*Prose*, I. cx–cxiv). Pope also fathered on 'James Baker, Knt.' one of the congratulatory poems he prefixed to the second edition of *A Key to the Lock*. But 'James Baker, Knight' escapes identification. He is not the bookseller J. Baker, whose Christian name was John, but there seems to have been a James Baker connected with the publication of the *St. James's Journal* and the *Whitehall Evening Journal*, probably referred to in *Gulliveriana*, 1728, p. 10, as 'Sir James Baker, Knight, Chief-Journalist of Great Britain' (*Twick.* VI. 136; cf. VI. 191). Ault thinks Curll may have had something to do with the publication of the present letter (*Prose*, I. cxii).

It is hard to know how to read the letter. It is just possible that it is not an attack on Pope at all, but a continuation of the hoax begun with *God's Revenge Against Punning* and continued in *An Heroi-Comical Epistle . . . In Defence of the most Ancient Art of Punning*. It is impossible to take several passages seriously; on the other hand, it contains the grossest abuse, abuse it is impossible to imagine being written by any friend of Pope.

WORKS: A. *Worms*; B. *First Psalm*; C. *God's Revenge Against Punning*.

CHARGES: 1. Pope deformed; 2. *Iliad* subscription a cheat; 3. Pope blasphemous and malicious.

C   The *Letter* opens by accusing Pope of being the author of *God's Revenge Against Punning*. He continues,

B1   Whence this Rancour came into thy Heart, I know not how to imagine, unless it be that thou naturally enviest a Person of an erect Figure and a manly Aspect. Be that as it will, I wonder not that after having father'd a bawdy Psalm on King *David*, thou

shouldst wound the Order of Knighthood through my sides...

(p. 1)

But then he goes on to say, surely comically, that every one knows that the men abused in the lampoon are 'the shortest Men in the two Kingdoms', which is sufficient proof that he, Baker, did not write it. He threatens Pope unpleasantly:

2

3

... We who heretofore (to make Fools subscribe to thy Writings) used to extol thee to the skies, shall continue so to do, but —in a Blanket. It avails nothing to publish thy Works under a borrow'd Name, which are as easy to be distinguish'd as thy Person. Thy Inkhorn overflows with Blasphemy, and thy Pen is always scratching thy Neighbour: for by many of thy late Productions thou seemest to have taken an aversion both to God and Man [an allusion to the *Worms*]. Tho many allow thee to be a Witty Vermine ... thy Mind is so tetter'd with Envy and an Itch after Fame, that thou canst neither rest thy self nor let any body else be at quiet for thee. (p. 2)

He refers to Curll's emetic, but adds,

I my self am not unacquainted with the Barbarity of these Emeticks: they are dangerous to the Constitution when often repeated, especially upon an empty Stomach. (p. 2)

Then a cascade of abuse:

... I look upon Thee to be no better than the Fart of a *Jesuit*. But if thou continuest to run a-muck at Mankind, it will be no more harm to knock thee on the head than a Pole-cat. For my own part, if thou persistest to abuse me or any Human Form, I will level thy Hump, and break every crooked Bone in thy Body ... (p. 2)

January 22, 1717 (*Evening Post*, January 22, 1717)

The Drury-Lane Monster. Humbly Inscrib'd To the Old Woman in Hand Alley. —Geminentur Tigribus Agni. Hor. Yet no Man lards salt Pork with Orange-Peel, / Or garnishes his Lamb with Spitscock Eel.

Folio broadside, printed on recto only. At the bottom is the imprint: 'Printed for J. Roberts in Warwick-Lane. [Price Two-pence.]'

This undated, anonymous broadside appeared the day after the publication of *Three Hours after Marriage*.

CHARGES: 1. Pope writes bawdry and blasphemy; 2. Pope ignorant of Greek.

WORKS: A. *Iliad*; B. *Three Hours after Marriage*.

The 30 lines of verse open:

B
> Near the Hundreds of *Drury* a Monster was shown
> For five Days together, the Talk of the Town,
> What Species it was, or what was its Frame,
> Whether Human or Brute, or whence it first came,
> It puzzl'd the Criticks of *Gresham* to tell,
> 'Till Doctor *W*[*oo*]*dward* to dissecting it, fell.

The authors, he discovers, 'In *Tripple-Alliance* united to Jest', and he proceeds to identify Pope, Gay, and Arbuthnot:

A I 2
> Each Parent is seen in each odd sort of Feature.
> By his Crump, and his Paunch, and his Belly reclining,
> By Bawdy and Blasphemy, Hand in Hand joining,
> The first of them dealt in a Greek kind of Metre,
> Tho' he ne'er saw the Language and knew not a Letter;
> (For *English* translated from *French* is much better.)

January 24, 1717 (*Evening Post*, January 24, 1717)

A Satyr Upon The Present Times. Qui quid sit pulchrum, quid turpe, quid utile, quid noti, / Plenius ac melius chrysippo, & crantore dicunt. Hor. The busy Statesman with a sneering Look, / A forc'd Grimace, or low obsequious Bow, / Will work himself into a Prince's Counsel; / Whilst others, whose Ambition carries them / To seek Renown Abroad, where Honour's got, / To fight their Monarch's and their Country's Cause; / Shall fall a Sacrifice to him. London: Printed, and Sold by J. Morphew, near Stationers-Hall. M DCC XVII. Price Four Pence.

8vo in half-sheets.
Two unsigned leaves, B–C⁴.
[4 pp.], [5]–19 pp., [20] blank.

WORK: A. *Three Hours after Marriage.*

In an attack on bad plays in the Land of Nonsense, there is a single reference to *Three Hours after Marriage*:

A
> But we are always pleas'd without a Cause;
> We know no Reason A[ddiso]n goes down,
> Or P[op]e, or R[ow]e should bear away the Crown. (p. 16)

February 2, 1717 (*Evening Post*, February 2, 1717)

Parker, E., Philomath, [pseud.] A Complete Key To the New Farce, call'd Three Hours after Marriage. With an Account of the Authors. By E. Parker, Philomath. Why on these Authors shou'd the Criticks fall? / They've writ a Farce, but shown no Wit at all. / The Play is damn'd, and Gay wou'd fain evade it, / He cries Damn Pope and Arbuthnott who made it; / But the Fools-Cap that on the Stage was thrown, / They take by Turns, and wear it as their own. Prol. London: Printed, and Sold by E. Berrington, at the Cross-Keys near Essex-Street, without Temple-Bar. 1717. (Price Six Pence.)

8vo in half-sheets.
A⁴, B in three leaves.
[2 pp.], 3–14 pp.
The ironic dedication 'To Mr. Lintott' (p. 3) is signed 'E. Parker'.

'Curll seems to have had some share in this pamphlet, which he advertises in one of his lists, and which is included in his *Miscellanies upon Several Subjects*, 1719' (Straus, p. 248). The Yale copy of *Miscellanies upon Several Subjects*, 1719, contains only Francis Chute's *The Petticoat*. This pamphlet is reprinted in *Three Hours after Marriage*, ed. Richard Morton and William M. Peterson, Lake Erie College Studies, Vol. 1 (Painesville, Ohio, 1961), pp. 70–7.

WORKS: A. *Iliad;* B. *Three Hours after Marriage.*

CHARGES: 1. *Three Hours after Marriage* sold badly; 2. Pope, Gay, and Arbuthnot have satirized their acquaintance; 3. Pope is touching up Cibber's *Cid*; 4. Pope taught Gay the art of rhyming; 5. *Iliad* has sold badly; 6. *Three Hours after Marriage* largely plagiarized.

A hastily written pamphlet giving brief comments on passages in each act. The Pope references are not especially abusive, but his share in the play is insisted on, and, therefore, the criticisms of the play reflect upon him.

The author identifies the two friends mentioned in the 'Advertisement' Gay prefixed to the first edition of the play as

B 1   Mr. *Pope*, and Dr. *Arbuthnott*, who constantly attended the Rehearsal of this *Surprizing* Performance, and both came in *Conjunction* on Monday the 21st Day of *January* 1716–17 [the day the play was published], between the Hours of Eleven and Twelve of the Clock, in the Forenoon, to Mr. *Lintott's*, to enquire how it Sold; but to their great *Mortification*, and his *Misfortune*, found poor *Barnaby* in a Melancholly Posture, scratching his Head, and not one Customer in the Shop. (pp. 4–5)

To show the play's lewdness he quotes from Act II, calling it 'This Vile Obscenity' (p. 10) (I quote from the first edition of the play),

> *Clinket.* Ah, dear Uncle! How do the *Platonicks* and *Cartesians* differ?
>
> *Fossile.* The *Platonicks* are for Idea's, the *Cartesians* for Matter and Motion. (p. 51)

Among other passages he finds obscene, he quotes at length the scene in Act III in which the mummy and crocodile embrace Townley, which elicits from him ironic comment on polite dialogue and 'fine *Entendre* and *Humour*' (p. 13). He claims that Gay has given out that it was this scene which caused Ladies of Honour to raise 'Four Hundred Guineas, to divide between him and his Partners, as some small Encouragement for them to proceed in their *Dramaticall Studies*' (p. 13).

B 2   The implication in his useful identification of characters is that the authors are maliciously satirizing their acquaintance. Fossile is identified as Dr Woodward, Mrs Townley as 'the Wife of another Eminent Physician', the Countess of Hippokekoana as 'the Dutchess of M[on-mout]h' (pp. 5–7). Phoebe Clinket 'is design'd to Ridicule the Countess of W[i]n[chils]ea ... This *Punning* Character was drawn by Pope ...' (p. 5).

3   '*Plotwell's* fathering *Clinket's* Play, is levell'd at *Cibber* ...' (p. 8), and Pope is said to have taken Cibber's adaptation of Corneille's *Le Cid* in order to touch it up, 'the Diction being somewhat *obnubilated*' (p. 8). '*Ximena: or, The Heroick Daughter*, Cibber's adaptation, first appeared at Drury Lane in 1712, was revived in 1718, and was published in octavo in 1719. Was *Ximena* as produced in 1718 a revised

play? The printed text nowhere gives evidence of Pope's hand' (Malcolm Goldstein, *Pope and the Augustan Stage* [Stanford, 1958], p. 28). See also Pope's reference in the *Dunciad* B, i. 250, n.

4   After Gay left the service of the Duchess of Monmouth, Pope 'took him to learn the *Art of Rimeing*, and *Gay* is now nam'd the *Jabberer*' (p. 7).

5   The Homer is also brought in. The author quotes a passage from Act I, written, he says, by Pope, in which Fossile complains that his house 'is haunted by Broken Booksellers' and comments in a note,

> In reading this Passage *Bernard* could not refrain from Tears, to think that *Pope* should bring him into the *Farce* as a Broken Bookseller, after having receiv'd so many Pounds of his Money; and with some Concern, thus broke forth to his Wife and only Son, *This ungrateful Man! If ever I should do otherways than well, it is oweing to his* HOMER *by G—d.* (p. 6)

6   His charges of plagiarism are muddled. That the letters sent to Fossile are taken from Molière's *The Imaginary Cuckold* and the water of virginity from *The Changeling* (pp. 9–10) may pass. But he also claims that Dr Lubomirski is taken from a farce or Spanish comedy called *The Anatomist* (p. 9), and concludes his *Key* by saying that the play is 'all stole from the *Theatre Italien*, call'd, *The Mummies of Aegypt*' (p. 14). Leo Hughes in *A Century of English Farce* (Princeton, 1956), pp. 140, 150, n., says that all that *Three Hours after Marriage* has in common with *The Anatomist* is a doctor and all that it has in common with Regnard and Dufresny's *Momies d'Egypte* in *Le Théâtre Italien de Gherardi* is a man posing as a mummy. The most thorough discussion of the play's sources is to be found in *Three Hours after Marriage*, ed. Richard Morton and William M. Peterson, Lake Erie College Studies, Vol. I (Painesville, Ohio, 1961), pp. vi–x.

February 28, 1717 (?) (*Evening Post*, February 28, 1717)

Dennis, John. Remarks Upon Mr. Pope's Translation Of Homer. With Two Letters concerning Windsor Forest, and the Temple of Fame. By Mr. Dennis. —Suus quoique attributus est error; / Sed non videmus manticae quod in tergo est. Catull. London, Printed for E. Curll, in Fleet-street. MDCCXVII.

8vo in half-sheets.

One unsigned leaf, A⁴, b², B–M⁴, N².

[14 pp.], [1]–38, [39]–44, [45]–74, [75]–92 pp.

Reprinted in Hooker, II. 115–58. The *Remarks* were reprinted with omissions and alterations in *The Popiad*, 1728, pp. [1]–16. Practically all of the 'Observations on The Temple of Fame', except for the Latin and Italian quotations, is reprinted in *The Progress Of Dulness*, 1728. A passage on the English neglect of genius is quoted in *The Twickenham Hotch-Potch*, 1728, pp. ii–vi.

Ault, p. 21, summarizes the publication history. Curll first announced the pamphlet in *The Post-Man*, Tuesday, February 26, 1717, and, as 'This Day is publish'd', in *The Daily Courant*, Thursday, February 28, and *Evening Post*, February 26–8. But according to an advertisement, which Ault reprints, in *The Flying Post* of the following Tuesday, March 5, something seems to have happened between the 26th and the 28th. According to the advertisement, Pope on the 27th got hold of the *Remarks* and gave orders to Lintot to buy up the whole impression. If any such thing occurred – it is difficult to see what good it would have done Pope other than give him a few days' respite – Curll would seem to have taken the money and rushed another 'impression' through, as he is able to advertise in an evening paper, *The Evening Post*, March 2–5, on the same day, 'This Day is publish'd, Mr. Dennis's Remarks . . .' Two days later, in *The Post Boy*, March 5–7, it is advertised as 'Just publish'd'.

In December, 1714, Dennis composed his remarks on *Windsor Forest* in a letter to Barton Booth. In 1715, apparently, he wrote the observations on *The Temple of Fame* in the form of a personal letter, probably shortly after the poem's appearance on February 1 (Hooker, II. 461). In his article, 'Pope and Dennis', *ELH*, VII (1940), 188–98, Hooker from evidence in Dennis's letters dates the remarks on Homer between September 20, 1716, and February 1, 1717. Provoked by Theobald's attack on him in *The Censor* of January 5, 1717, and by *Three Hours after Marriage*, Dennis published the remarks on Homer, adding to them the old letters on *Windsor Forest*, *The Temple of Fame*, a preface, a postscript, and a few pages on *The Censor*. Hooker is, however, unable to offer any evidence to support his contention that the remarks on the Homer were not intended for publication and were privately circulated among Dennis's friends.

WORKS: A. *Windsor Forest*; B. *Rape of the Lock*; C. *Temple of Fame*; D. *Iliad*; E. *First Psalm*.

CHARGES: 1. Pope a Roman Catholic and Jacobite; 2. Pope bawdy.

In the preface, Dennis, with painful lack of self-knowledge, justifies his criticism:

> I esteem it to be one of the greatest Misfortunes of my Life, that I have been so often forc'd to be engag'd in Disputes of this Nature with my Contemporaries. I can safely affirm, that I never attack'd any of their Writings, unless I was provok'd to it, and unless they had Success abundantly beyond their Merit . . .
> (A1r)

In his examination of their work, he has, however, borne no malice to the authors, and would 'do them any manner of Service that lay in [his] little Power' (A1r). This moderation he does not extend to Pope:

1
> . . . I regard him as an Enemy, not so much to me, as to my KING, to my COUNTRY, to my RELIGION, and to that LIBERTY which has been the sole Felicity of my Life. (A1v)

Pope has gained power with his reputation and must be exposed:

> . . . I look upon it to be my Duty to all These, to pull the *Lyon*'s Skin from this Little *Ass*, which Popular Error has thrown round him, and show him in his natural Shape and Size, in spight of all his Malice, a quiet, harmless Animal . . . (A2r)

That Pope has been popular is no wonder, since bad writers have always been so,

»1
> but that Protestants, that Lovers of Liberty, and of their Country, should encourage him at this extraordinary rate, to suborn Old HOMER to propagate his ridiculous Arbitrary and Popish Doctrines . . . This, I must confess, is to me a Prodigy . . . (b2r)

D   In the *Remarks* themselves Dennis's judgment of the *Iliad* is quite without shading:

> . . . there is in this Translation neither the Justness of the Original, even where the Original is just; nor any Beauty of Language, nor any Variety of Numbers. Instead of the Justness of the Original, there is in this Translation Absurdity and Extravagance. Instead of the beautiful Language of the Original, there is in the Translation Solecism and barbarous English.
> (p. 10)

Fortunately, he explains the basis for his objections more precisely than usual: Homer had the advantages of the language in which he wrote; he had available several ways of making his language poetical, by the use of compounds, dialects, purely poetic words, changing endings, contractions and lengthenings, etc. But his translator has

but one way of rendering his Diction Poetical; and that is, the frequent Use of Figures, and above all Figures of Metaphors . . . Now in the late Translation of HOMER, there are, modestly speaking, Twenty Lines where there is no Figure, for One that is Figurative; and, consequently, there are Twenty Prosaick Lines, for One that is Poetical. (p. 11)

His conclusion may fairly be said to summarize most of the objections to the Homer: 'In short, the HOMER which LINTOTT prints, does not talk like HOMER, but like POPE . . .' (p. 12).

He will prove his point, he says, by taking the same two similes from Book II that *The Censor* had taken. He then quotes, with minor departures in spelling and punctuation, from Griffith 42 (which I follow here), II. 109–16:

> The sceptred Rulers lead; the following Host
> Pour'd forth in Millions, darkens all the Coast.
> As from some Rocky Cleft the Shepherd sees
> Clust'ring in Heaps on Heaps the driving Bees,
> Rolling, and black'ning, Swarms succeeding Swarms,
> With deeper Murmurs and more hoarse Alarms;
> Dusky they spread, a close-embody'd Crowd,
> And o'er the Vale descends the living Cloud.

Dennis objects to 'Pour'd forth in Millions'. Homer in this very book tells us that the Grecians are not more than 100,000.

> Never human Army yet consisted of Millions. No Place upon Earth can contain such Numbers congregated, but what at the same time will starve them. (p. 13)

Hooker, II. 465, calls this 'mere cavilling', but does not seem to know that in the 1720 edition, Griffith 122, Pope altered the line to

> Pour'd forth by Thousands, darkens all the Coast.

Pope, we may presume, thought Dennis's argument had some weight.

He objects further that bees cannot drive and cluster at the same time, that only one swarm of bees can come from one cleft of a rock, that while bees are a 'close-embody'd Crowd' they cannot spread, that a 'close-embody'd Crowd' is tautological, that to descend 'over' is barbarous; the preposition must be 'to', 'into', 'on', or 'upon' (pp. 13–15).

He then quotes II. 249:

> Murmuring they move, as when old *Ocean* roars,

and asks,

> Now did ever any Mortal before compare a *Murmur* to a *Roar*?
> (p. 16)

As an example of Pope's Jacobitism, he quotes, p. 18, 1. 249–50:

> And hence to all our Host it shall be known,
> That Kings are subject to the Gods alone.

Saying very sensibly that one may object as unfair to his culling passages here and there, he proceeds to take up the first hundred or so lines of Book 1 to see how many errors Pope has been guilty of. (He misnumbers ll. 87–8 and l. 118; these errors are not noticed in Hooker. In l. 144 he gives 'fill'd my Arms' for the 1715, 1720 'blest my Arms'.)

He objects in l. 3 to 'Reign'.

> *Reign* signifies the Duration of Imperial Power with one or more particular Person: But here it is made to signify *Place* ...

(pp. 21–2)

On l. 12,

> And heap'd the Camp with Mountains of the Dead,

he objects that Homer tells us the bodies were burnt.

> Besides, to *heap the Camp*, does not seem to me to be *English*, and *to heap the Camp with Mountains*, is vilely low, and monstrously absurd. A Heap is infinitely less than a Mountain ... (p. 23)

On l. 44,

> Or doom'd to deck the Bed she once enjoy'd,

he objects that the line is contrary to Homer's modesty, and attempts to refute Pope's note on the line. He strays from the task to raise the issue of bawdiness in Pope, with the usual examples:

But 'tis no Wonder that this Translator, who in his *Rape of the Lock*, could not forbear putting Bawdy into the Mouth of his own Patroness, should put something like it into the Mouth of HOMER ... For, notwithstanding his Jesuitical Advertisement, it was He who burlesqu'd the *First Psalm* of DAVID. In that Jesuitical Advertisement, he does not deny it, but would appear to deny it ... 'Tis apparent to me, that that *Psalm* was burlesqu'd by a Popish Rhymester. Let Rhyming Persons, who have been brought up Protestants, be otherwise what they will; let them be Rakes, let them be Scoundrels, let them be Atheists; yet Education has made an invincible Impression on them in behalf of the Sacred Writings. But a Popish Rhymester has been brought up with a Contempt for those Sacred Writings in the Language which he understands ... Mr. POPE, I suppose, endeavour'd to make a Jest of God Almighty, out of a Spirit of Revenge and Retaliation, because God Almighty has made a Jest of him. (pp. 26–8)

For Pope's 'Jesuitical Advertisement' in the *Post-Man* of July 28–31, 1716, see Ault, p. 158.

Ll. 125–6,

I
> Perhaps, with added Sacrifice and Pray'r,
> The Priest may pardon, and the God may spare,

provoke Dennis's habitual anti-Catholic prejudices:

> HOMER makes CALCHAS say nothing of the *Priest's Pardoning.*
> HOMER was an honest old Pagan, of a Religion much less absurd,
> and much less an Imposition upon the Understandings of Man-
> kind, than Popery. For the Heathens who taught, That one
> God could beget another, and afterwards devour him, would
> never have swallowed that monstrous Absurdity, of a Mortal's
> making a God, and swallowing him down at a Mouthful.
>
> (p. 34)

He concludes with general remarks on the versification and, astonish-
ing in Dennis, who was famous for his hatred of them, a pun (see
Dunciad A, i. 61), and a pun he seems to have been so pleased with
that he used it in two other Pope attacks (in *Remarks On Mr. Pope's
Rape of the Lock,* 1728, ix, and *Remarks Upon . . . the Dunciad,* 1729,
p. 54):

> . . . instead of a pleasing Variety of Numbers, there is nothing
> but a perpetual Identity of Sound, an eternal Monotony. The
> Trumpet of HOMER, with its loud and its various Notes, is
> dwindled in POPE's Lips to a Jew's-Trump. The *Pegasus* of this
> little Gentleman, is not the Steed that HOMER rode; but a blind,
> stumbling *Kentish* Post-Horse, which neither walks, nor trots,
> nor paces, nor runs; but is upon an eternal *Canterbury,* and often
> stumbles, and often falls. (p. 36)

A
The 'Observations upon Windsor Forest, To Mr. B. B.', pp. [39]–
44, dated, p. [39], '*Decemb.* 18. 1714', are slight and unimportant. He
opens by finding Pope's poem 'a wretched Rhapsody, not worthy the
Observation of a Man of Sense' (p. [39]), and says he will use it only
to display the beauties of Denham's *Cooper's Hill.* And this is what he
does do. His only real criticism of Pope's poem is that there is in it
nothing peculiar to Windsor-Forest; the objects presented are 'for the
most part trivial and trifling' (p. 40).

> . . . There is no manner of Design, nor any Artful and Beautiful
> Disposition of Parts. Whereas Sir JOHN has both an Admirable
> Design, and a Beautiful Disposition of Parts. (p. 40)

C
The 'Observations Upon The Temple of Fame', pp. [45]–74, constitute the most ridiculous lapse in Dennis's criticism of Pope. Not only

are the objections so outrageous that many are comic, but he does not
seem to have realized that Pope was imitating Chaucer, despite Pope's
clear announcement of this in the 'Advertisement' placed before the
poem. Dennis afterwards recognized his error. (For his text Dennis
may have used the first edition, Griffith 36, or the second, Griffith 45.
His transcription is as careless as usual: in l. 373 he gives *Wind* for
Winds, and in l. 374 *So soft, so high*, for *So soft, tho* [second edition, *tho'*]
high.)

Pope, Dennis says, thinks that calling his poem a vision will excuse
every extravagance (p. 45).

> But a true Vision is acknowledg'd by all to be a Divine Inspira-
> tion, and therefore can have nothing in it inconsistent and in-
> congruous ... And as a true Vision can have nothing possible
> in it, that is wild and incoherent, so the fictitious ones which are
> invented in Imitation of them, must resemble them in their
> Reasonableness, and their Consistency. (p. 46)

His objection to the temple's situation delights the reader of Freud
with its neo-classic rule for dreams:

> Now, Sir, I would fain know from you, if this Image of a Temple
> built on a Rock of Ice, self-suspended in the Air, be not so wild,
> and so extravagant, that 'tis not only unworthy of a Vision, but
> even of the Dream of a Man in Health ... This Image of the
> *Temple of Fame*, is contrary to Nature, and to the Eternal Laws
> of Gravitation ... (p. 51)

Pope has marked in his own copy, 'what no dream ought to be'. Of
ll. 13–18, where Pope is following Chaucer, Dennis remarks that the
poet might see the ocean but certainly not mountains, rocks, wastes,
forest, even ships and single trees (p. 49). And why the difficulty of
ascent in ll. 27–8, again from Chaucer, when a vast multitude are
admitted and among them the idlest and laziest (pp. 53–4)?

He quotes ll. 83–92 and finds the ideas 'foolishly rash and impudent'
(p. 56). Dr Johnson approved of his comment:

> For *Trees starting from their Roots*, a *Mountain rolling into a Wall*,
> and a *Town rising like an Exhalation*, are Things that are not to
> be shown in Sculpture. (p. 56)

Or on l. 87,

> Methinks I could give a good deal, to see that Sculptor, who
> should pretend to carve an Eccho. (p. 57)

Hooker notes, ii. 467, that 'Pope's blunder is a departure from
Chaucer'. It is not, for a reader less obstinately literal than Dennis,
quite a blunder. See Bateson's remarks, *Twick.* ii. 239.

I

Fame's trumpets Dennis thinks Pope has borrowed from *Hudibras*. His notion of fame Dennis finds confused and inconsistent. Virgil and Ovid meant 'rumour' by 'fame'. But Pope seems to mean '*Renown*, or a *fair* and a *great Reputation*' (p. 58), and yet he also confounds her with Slander and Rumour.

He objects that 'this Monster, without Justice, and without Discernment' is

> made the absolute Mistress of the Muses; who have been hitherto always esteem'd the Righteous and Discerning Dispensers of Fame, and Bestowers of Immortality. (pp. 62–3)

Her inconsistent conduct bothers Dennis, and he quarrels with it for several pages. Why are there statues of warriors within her temple when she banishes other warriors? Why does she accept the petitions of some and deny those of others? He admits that you may say

> that this is the Way of the World, which blames some, and applauds others, for the very same Qualities: To this I reply, that this is absolutely false; that Persons indeed with the same Qualities, are some applauded, and others blam'd by the World; but then they appear in very different Lights; and the World is far from taking them to have the same Qualities. (p. 68)

Dennis's point here I find obscure.

He has several fundamental objections to the structure. Pope has destroyed the unity of his design by shifting the scene and deserting the Temple of Fame for the Temple of Rumour (p. 48); Pope has marked in his own copy here, 'Chaucer'. It was also wrong of Pope to make himself an actor in the Temple of Rumour (pp. 73–4).

The Postscript, pp. [75]–92, discusses and quarrels with Mme Dacier's opinion that Agamemnon had a passion for Chryseis and adds more on the proper meaning of *murmur*.

March 1, 1717 (*St James's Post*, March 1, 1717)

Drub, Timothy [pseud.] A Letter To Mr. John Gay, Concerning His late Farce, Entituled, A Comedy. Nunc satis est dixisse, Ego mira Poemata / pango. Hor. This I am sure of, that the Skill Apollo has given all his Physicians is not sufficient to cure the Madness of his Poets. John Gay, or one of his Two Friends.

London, Printed: And Sold by J. Roberts in Warwick-Lane.
MDCCXVII. Price Six Pence.

8vo in half-sheets.
A⁴, a² ('Dedication' inserted between A1 and A2), B–D⁴, E².
[6 pp.], 3–35 pp., [36] blank.

WORKS: A. *Rape of the Lock*; B. *Three Hours after Marriage*.

CHARGES: 1. Pope made Gay fight his battle with Cibber for him;
2. Pope and Arbuthnot too cowardly to own their share in *Three Hours
after Marriage*.

The pamphlet opens with a dedication signed 'Timothy Drub' to
Wilks, Cibber, and Booth which clearly implies that Pope and Arbuthnot collaborated with Gay. By performing the farce, the actors
exposed it more effectively than could anything written against it.

1 He gives in a dialogue between Momus and Maevius an account of
the quarrel with Cibber in which Momus [Pope] urges Maevius [Gay]
to fight Cibber while Momus retires to his club to await the news of
Maevius' success. '... It is a sad thing to fall into the Hands of a
Boxing-Bard ...' (a2v)

The text proper recurs to the charge of Pope's collaboration:

2 ... I rather think this Issue from the United Powers of a *Triumvirate* of Authors more resembles the old Fable of the three
Heathen Gods, who clubbed their Urine in a Hide to produce
one dirty, nasty Bantling ... I tell you plainly what I think of
your Friends in the Dark, that their Assistance is no manner of
Honour either to them or you, and so they have taken Care to
stand behind the Curtain, while you only are exposed upon the
Stage. The greatest *Doctor* and the greatest *Wit* might be so far
mistaken as to imagine a Town, very much depraved in its Taste,
might come into any extravagant Whimsy of theirs; but then
they were wise enough to retreat betimes ... (p. 7)

The moral of the play is offensive – that 'half the *Husbands* are *Fools*,
and half their *Wives Whores* and so between both one Part at least of
the Nation is *bastardized*' (p. 11).

The stage directions in the scene between Fossile, Sarsnett, Townley, and Ptisan are absurd (p. 15), as is the scene in which five letters
are delivered; Mrs Townley would never be so foolish as to allow herself to be addressed by five persons one hour after marriage (pp. 17–
18).

The play attacks the clergy, the Book of Common Prayer, the Old and New Testaments, and the genealogy of Christ. This charge of profanity has a splendid inclusiveness, but is supported by examples like,

In the Name of Beelzebub! (p. 21)

and Sir Tremendous's,

There is not in all this *Sodom* of Ignorance *Ten righteous Critics*.
(p. 21)

It is the lewdness he illustrates at loving length. Of the dialogue between Mrs Clinket and Sir Tremendous at the beginning of Act II he says,

... the Character both of *Fossile* and Mrs. *Clinket* are directly obscene, only with this difference, that one talks Bawdy in *Terms*, and the other in *Metaphors* ... I pass over a whole *Dunghill* of this Ribaldry ... (p. 24)

The Platonic–Cartesian passage quoted in *A Complete Key*, 1717, is 'one of the bluntest Pieces of Smut that I ever saw ... This is bringing the very *Act* before our Eyes, and speaking home to the very point of Lewdness' (p. 28).

He adds the curious detail, unsubstantiated elsewhere, that when he saw the play for the second time, the actors left out 'a considerable load of Obscenity and Prophaneness' (p. 8).

A propos of Mrs. Townley's 'I could forgive thee, if thou hadst poison'd my *Father*, debauch'd my *Sister*, kill'd my *Lap-Dog* ...' (p. 16), he insists on Pope's authorship:

A

Now methinks if a Man may presume to be as wise as Doctor *Possum*, and guess from Similitudes of Features, who this Bratt belongs to, one would suspect this Author of

Men, Monkies, Lap-Dogs, Parrots, perish all!

It is not impossible for to trace several other Passages that have a strange Resemblance of that Parent; but perhaps, *John*, you made use of them under the Notion, that *all things were Common among Friends*. (pp. 16–17)

March 7, 1717 (*Post-Man*, March 7, 1717)

[Welsted, Leonard.] Palaemon To Caelia, at Bath; Or, The Triumvirate. London, Printed: And Sold by J. Roberts near the Oxford-Arms in Warwick-Lane. 1717.

Folio.

[A]–c², D in one leaf.

[2 pp.], 3–14 pp.

There was a second edition, March 13, 1717 (*Daily Courant*, March 13, 1717). The British Museum's copy and the Bodleian's copy are the same as the first edition, except for 'The Second Edition' on the title-page before the imprint.

Reprinted in *The Works, in Verse and Prose, Of Leonard Welsted*, ed. John Nichols (London, 1787), pp. 36–44.

WORKS: A. *What D'Ye Call It*; B. *Iliad* (?); C. *First Psalm*; D. *God's Revenge Against Punning*; E. *Three Hours after Marriage*.

CHARGES: 1. Pope collaborated in *The Wife of Bath*, and other Gay plays.

Palaemon writing the news of the town to Caelia complains that the arts are now counterfeit:

> The Province of Delight two Bards invade,
> With mock Astrology and Emp'ric Aid:
> No Satyr starts, no Humour, or Intrigue,
> But still we owe it to this Triple League.   (p. 5)

He tells the story of the emetic given by the Triumvirs to Curll who in the midst of his suffering addresses Pope:

E

> 'Sarcastic Youth, said he, I give thee leave
> In artless low Obscenities to shine:
> The fertile Realms of Drury shall be thine:
> Design with deep Contrivance plotless Plays,
> And teem with Comets which no Wonder raise;
> Be still Licentious, and still teaze the Age
> With feeble Malice, and with hectic Rage.'   (p. 7)

Palaemon then relates a conversation with friends on Wit and its decline.

D

> O Rage! to persecute unhappy Puns!
> Burlesqu'd you see the tuneful *Hebrew's* Strain,
> And *David* is both Bard and Saint in vain.   (pp. 9–10)

The conversation turns to the theatre where the Triumvirs are busy. Sir Fopling would, apparently, involve Pope and Arbuthnot in *The Wife of Bath* as well as in *The What D'Ye Call It.*

I

> Crown'd by *the Wife of B——th*, with thundering Fame;
> To see their first Essay, the House was full;
> None fear'd a Secret to make *Chaucer* dull:

This damn'd, absurder Projects they disclose,
And raise preposterous Mirth from human Woes:
From generous Minds th' Unhappy claim Relief,
And Virtue sees a Dignity in Grief;
But they, with Sport unknown to human Breast,
Laugh in Distresses, and in Horrors jest.   (p. 10)

Bruce thinks this too severe, but admits he can least commend their
last attempt, *Three Hours*.

E

That Play, retorted Fopling, was so lewd,
Ev'n Bullies blush'd, and Beaux astonish'd stood;
But gentle Widows with soft Maids prevail,
And kindly save the Alligator's Tail.   (p. 11)

Sir Harry praises Garth, Philips, and Tickell:

B?

Like *Titian*'s finish'd work is *T*[*ickel*]*l*'s song,
The colouring beauteous, and the figures strong:
Ev'n *P—pe*, (I speak the Judgement of his Foes)
The Sweets of Rhime and easy Measures knows.   (p. 11)

But Sir Fopling disagrees about Pope:

He wants the Spirit, and informing Flame,
Which breathes Divine, and gives a Poet's Name:
His Verse the Mind to Indolence may sooth;
The Strain is even, and the Numbers smooth;
But 'tis all level Plain; no Mountains rise,
No startling Line, that's pregnant with Surprize.
                                          (pp. 11–12)

March 26, 1717 (*Evening Post*, March 26, 1717)

[Blackmore, Sir Richard.] Essays Upon Several Subjects. By Sir
Richard Blackmore, Kt. M.D. and Fellow of the College of Phy-
sicians in London. Vol. II. London: Printed by W. Wilkins, for
A. Bettesworth, at the Red Lyon in Pater-Noster-Row; and J.
Pemberton, at the Buck and Sun against St. Dunstan's Church
in Fleetstreet. 1717.

8vo.
A⁸, a–c⁸, B–Z⁸, Aa–Ff⁸.
[2 pp.], iii–xli, [5 pp.], 3–446 pp., [2 pp.], recto: Errata; verso blank.

Volume I published in 1716 does not concern us. Volume II contains two incidental attacks on Pope.

WORKS: A. *Three Hours after Marriage*; B. *First Psalm*.

CHARGE: 1. Pope obscene and profane.

... A New Comedy has been acted, so empty of Wit and Sense, and so redundant in shameless Immorality, that perhaps no Dramatick Representation did ever so much disgrace the Stage or affront a *British* Audience. The Author and his two Friends, who, as he affirms, gave him their Assistance, and therefore must have approv'd this obscene Piece, have not only discover'd their own vitiated Judgment, but with an arrogant Assurance have taken it for granted that the Nation has the same degenerate and corrupt Taste; I cannot therefore but take Notice with Satisfaction, that the people have asserted their Honour and vindicated their Capacity and Discernment by expressing universally their Contempt and Detestation of that Performance; and it is to be hoped, that after the Publick Mortification which these Conspirators against Vertue and Decency have receiv'd, our Comick Poets will desist from such audacious Attempts on the good Sense of the Audience...

Sure such Poets impudently presume, that they shall bring the modest Sex to bear anything, and by imposing on their vertuous and unaffected Simplicity, make them sit out a whole Play with steady and unblushing Serenity, which the Men, notwithstanding their firmer Complexion, on the Account of its unsufferable Lewdness, would universally nauseate and detest.

But should these Persons be permitted to employ their licentious and profane Pens, till they have destroy'd all just Taste, disgrac'd Vertue, and brought Immorality into publick Esteem and universal Practice, at which they seem to direct their Aim, by what Means will the Church maintain the Veneration of her Altars, or the Civil Magistrate the Force of his Authority? (pp. xlvii–l)

I cannot but here take notice, that one of these Champions of Vice is the reputed Author of a detestable Paper, that has lately been handed about in Manuscript, and now appears in Print, in which the godless Author has burlesqu'd the *First Psalm* of *David* in so obscene and profane a manner, that perhaps no Age ever saw such an insolent affront offer'd to the establish'd Re-

ligion of their Country, and this, good Heaven! with Impunity.
A sad Demonstration this, of the low Ebb to which the *British*
Vertue is reduc'd in these degenerate Times.

Quoted by Curll in his *A Compleat Key to the Dunciad*, 1728, 1st ed.,
pp. 18–19; 2nd and 3rd eds., pp. 19–20.

March 30, 1717 (*Evening Post*, March 30, 1717)

[Breval, John Durant.] The Confederates: A Farce. By Mr. Gay.
Rumpantur ut ilia Codro. These are the Wags, who boldly did
adventure / To club a Farce by Tripartite Indenture! / But, let
'em share their Dividend of Praise, / And wear their own Fools'
Cap, instead of Bays. Prol. to the Sultaness. London: Printed for
R. Burleigh, in Amen-Corner. 1717. [Price 1 s.]

8vo in half-sheets.
A⁴, b in three leaves, B–F⁴.
[14 pp.], [1]–40 pp.

The Dedication and 'To the Reader' are both signed 'Joseph Gay'
A3r, A4r). See *Dunciad* A, ii. 120, n. On the verso of the title-page to
The Curliad, 1729, Curll advertises 'The Confederates, a Farce. For
The Use of Messieurs *Pope, Arbuthnot,* and Gay. Price 1 *s.*' but I do not
know of any copy with a 1729 imprint.

The verse on the title-page is taken from Charles Johnson, *The
Sultaness*, 1717, q.v. *The Confederates* is reprinted in *Three Hours after
Marriage*, ed. Richard Morton and William M. Peterson, Lake Erie
College Studies, Vol. 1 (Painesville, Ohio, 1961), pp. 78–100.

WORKS: A. *Windsor Forest*; B. *Rape of the Lock*; C. *Temple of Fame*;
D. *Iliad*; E. *Worms*; F. *Three Hours after Marriage*; G. *Court Ballad*.

CHARGES: 1. Pope deformed; 2. Pope let Gay fight Cibber for him;
3. *Three Hours after Marriage* a dismal failure the first night; 4. Pope,
Gay, and Arbuthnot packed the house the succeeding nights; 5. Pope
offered insincerely to revise Cibber's *Cid*; 6. *Iliad* sales a failure;
7. Pope wrote the *Court Ballad* to thank the ladies-in-waiting for send-
ing money to save *Three Hours after Marriage*.

This is a play in which Pope, Gay, and Arbuthnot appear, purporting
to give a true account of the first night failure of *Three Hours after*

Marriage and its rescue by a present of gold from three ladies. Pope is made largely responsible for the play.

The Prologue announces that though the play will not show mummies or crocodiles, we will see 'One *Strange Monster*', i.e. Pope,

> On whom Dame Nature nothing good bestow'd,
> In *Form*, a *Monkey*; but for *Spite*, a *Toad*.   (b2v–b3r)

The first scene, in a room in the Rose-Tavern, opens with Pope *solus* and Arbuthnot listening at the door.

> Thus in the *Zenith* of my Vogue I Reign,
> And bless th' Abundance of my fertile Vein;
> My pointed Satire aim alike at All,
> (Foe to Mankind) and scatter round my Gall:
> With poyson'd Quill, I keep the World in Awe,
> And from My Self my own THERSITES draw.
> This very Night, with Modern Strokes of Wit,
> I charm the *Boxes*, and divert the *Pit*;
> Safe from the Cudgel, stand secure of Praise;
> Mine is the Credit, be the Danger[1] Gay's.

> [1] Because he Father'd the Play, and has since stood Mr. *Cibber's* Drub for it (pp. [1]–2).

Arbuthnot quarrels with Pope who says that Arbuthnot is responsible only for the part of Fossile (p. 3) and warns him not to go too far:

> Thou might'st thy Rashness, but too late, repent:
> In my keen Satires handed thro' the Town,
> With Shame and Madness, hang thy self, or drown.
> Nor Button's[1] Wits from my Lampoons are free,
> And Thou, and BLACKMORE are but *Worms* to me.

> [1] He ridicul'd the Wits of *Button's*, in a Satire call'd *The Worms* (pp. 4–5).

Arbuthnot threatens to break the neck of the 'Vain Pigmy' like a second Aesop (p. 5), but they mend their quarrel and Gay enters with the news that their play was hissed. The theatre was so crowded, he tells Pope, 'Scarce for a Mouse, or You, had Room been found' (p. 8),

> But soon a Murmur in the *Pit* began,
> And thence all round the *Theatre* it ran;
> The Noise increasing as along it mov'd,
> Nor Wit, nor Humour, could their Rage appease,
> *Clinket* and *Plotwell* strove in vain to please;
> Each smutty Phrase, and ev'ry cutting Line,
> Was thrown away, and lost, like Pearls on Swine:

> Some Females only (to the good old Cause
> True Friends, I ween) gave Tokens of Applause. (p. 9)

Pope exclaims:

D
> Have I for this, ye Gods! for this, been crown'd
> So Young with Lawrel, and so long Renown'd?
> Make Lords and Ladies to my Works subscribe,
> Now to be damn'd by such a noisy Tribe? (p. 10)

4 They decide to try to pack the house, and a note insists, 'It is well known they did so' (p. 11). They arrange to meet at Lintot's, while Gay is sent off to soothe Mrs Oldfield and Mrs Bicknell.

In Scene II, both actresses refuse to play again. Gay promises Mrs Bicknell the aid of Pope:

> If you have Male or Female Foes,
> These *Sawney* shall lampoon, I'll challenge Those. (p. 20)

But both actresses insist on being bribed with money.

5 In Scene III at Lintot's house, Cibber is found with Pope, Arbuthnot, and Lintot. Pope, to placate Cibber who is complaining that he has never been so jeered at, offers to revise Cibber's translation of Corneille's *Le Cid*, but as soon as Cibber is gone, Pope says:

> Damn'd Blockhead! not to see so plain a Bite!
> I mend his Play!—I will as soon go fight. (p. 29)

(For this charge see *A Complete Key To ... Three Hours*, 1717.)

When Gay enters with the news that they must pay Mrs Bicknell and Mrs Oldfield if they are to perform again, Pope, complaining in an aside that if only 'that cursed Homer' had sold well, he might have squeezed some money from Lintot, tries unsuccessfully to get money from the bookseller. Pope says,

ABC
> Ungrateful Man! *Fame*'s *Temple*, call to mind,
> My *Forest*, *Rape*, and *Satires on Mankind*;
> Think, how by These thou hast increas'd thy Store,

but Lintot replies,

D 6
> Look on your HOMER, there, behind the Door.
> Thou little dream'st what Crowds I daily see,
> That call for TICKELL, and that spurn at Thee!
> Neglected there, your Prince of Poets lyes,
> By DENNIS justly damn'd, and kept for Pyes.
> Alas! his Outside I enrich in vain,
> And by the Gilding, Custom hope to gain ...
> But your fam'd Heroes, with their warlike Bands,
> Grace the same Shelf where OGILBY now stands,
> And rot on mine, or on Subscribers Hands. (p. 32)

Then a footman enters with a letter and a purse of gold from
>   Three Ladies known full well;
>   Their Names are G[RIFFI]N, B[ELLENDE]NE, L[E]P[EL]L.
>   (p. 34)

The letter expresses their appreciation of the play's smutty jests
'hook'd in with won'drous Art' (p. 35) and begs the authors to accept
the gold. Pope promises to record their names which, the note adds,
'he did in the *Court Ballad* presently after' (p. 36).

The play ends with an Epilogue apologizing for the lack of smut,
and 'A Congratulatory Poem Inscribed to Mr. Gay, on his Valour
and Success behind Drury-Lane Scenes':

> POPE finds the Pen, and GAY the Sword;
> And may for SATIRE, and for COURAGE,
> B'esteem'd the Champions of our Age.
> 'Tis true, they had a damn'd Miscarriage,
> In their THREE HOURS AFTER MARRIAGE.   (p. 40)

March, 1717 (*Monthly Catalogue*, March, 1717)

Johnson, Charles. The Sultaness: A Tragedy. As it is Acted at
the Theatre-Royal In Drury-Lane, By His Majesty's Servants.
By Mr. Johnson. London: Printed by W. Wilkins, for J. Brown,
at the Black Swan without Temple-Bar; W. Hinchliffe, at
Dryden's-Head under, and J. Walthoe, Jun. against, the Royal-
Exchange in Cornhill. M DCC XVII. (Price One Shilling Six-
Pence.)

8vo in half-sheets.
[A]–H⁴.
Frontispiece, [6 pp.], [1]–55 pp., [56] blank.

The British Museum has the second edition; it is the same as the first
except for 'The Second Edition' on the title-page before the imprint.

The Sultaness was first performed at Drury Lane on February 25,
1717 (Allardyce Nicoll, *A History of English Drama, 1660–1900*, 3rd ed.
(Cambridge, 1952), II. 339).

WORK: A. *Three Hours after Marriage.*

CHARGE: 1. Pope collaborated on *Three Hours after Marriage.*

Only the 'Prologue. Spoke by Mr. Wilks' concerns us. After explaining that the play is owing to Racine [to *Bajazet*], he concludes,

A

> At least, 'tis hop'd, he'll meet a kinder Fate,
> Who strives some *Standard* Author to translate,
> Than they, who give you, without once repenting,
> Long-labour'd Nonsense of their own inventing.
> Such Wags have been, who boldly durst adventure
> To Club a Farce by Tripartite-Indenture:
> But, let them share their Dividend of Praise,
> And their own *Fools-Cap* wear, instead of Bays.   (A3r)

1717

[Jacob, [Giles. The Rape of the Smock. An Heroi-Comical Poem. In Two Books. London: Printed for R. Burleigh, in Amen-Corner. 1717. [Price 1 s.]

8vo in half-sheets.
Four unsigned leaves, B–F⁴. C2 is unsigned.
Frontispiece, [6 pp.], [1]–39 pp., [40] Curll book-list.
Case 303.

The book was later incorporated in *The Ladies Miscellany*, 1718, Case 306. For the collation of *The Ladies Miscellany*, see Case.

The Rape of the Smock. An Heroi-Comical Poem. In Two Books. By Mr. Jacob. The Second Edition. London: Printed for H. Curll, over-against Catherine-street in the Strand. 1727. Price 1s.

8vo in half-sheets.
A–E⁴. A3 misprinted A2.
[8 pp.], [1]–11, [12–13], 14–26, [27], 28–30, [31], 32 pp.
Case 303 (b).

This edition was later incorporated in *The Altar of Love*, 1727, Case 340. Yale's copy of *The Altar of Love* is Griffith 183, is much shorter than Case 340, and does not include *The Rape of the Smock*. It may, however, be found in the Bodleian copy of *The Altar of Love*, 1727, and again in the Bodleian copy of *The Altar of Love* ... *The Third Edition* ... *M.DCC.XXXI.*

The Rape of the Smock. An Heroi-Comical Poem. By Mr. Jacob. The Third Edition. With other Miscellanies. London: Printed for E. Curll, at Pope's Head, in Rose-Street, Covent-Garden, 1736. Price One Shilling.

Case 303 (c).

I have not seen a copy. See Case for collation.

WORKS: A. *Rape of the Lock*; B. *Three Hours after Marriage.*

B   The Preface contains a hit at *Three Hours after Marriage*:

> But now I think on't, why should a poor *Author* be at the Trouble of making an Apology for writing upon a SMOCK, when the BEAUTIES of this Age, look upon it as a Want of Good Breeding, to Blush at a harmless *Double Entendre*; and I have seen, not long since, a *Front-Box* sit so *Unconcern'd* at the *smuttiest Performance*,[1] that a *Stranger* would have been apt to question, whether there were One *Natural Complexion* among them All ...

> [1] That stupid Farce, called *Three Hours after Marriage* ([A4]r).

The footnote was omitted in the second edition and 'Performance' altered to 'Comedy'.

A   There is only one direct reference to Pope in the poem which is 'a kind of prurient burlesque "In Two Books" of the original version in two cantos of *The Rape of the Lock*' (Ault, p. 168):

> Let OZELL sing the *Bucket*, POPE the *Lock*.   (p. 2)

According to Pope, John Ozell in *The Weekly Medley*, September 20, 1729, claimed that because Jacob had mentioned Ozell's *Rape of the Bucket* 'in the same Breath with *Pope*'s ... the little Gentleman had like to run mad' (*Twick.* v. 198).

January 2, 1718 (*Post-Man*, January 2, 1718)

Cibber, Colley. The Non-Juror. A Comedy. As it is Acted at the Theatre-Royal, By His Majesty's Servants. Written by Mr. Cibber. —Pulchra Laverna / Da mihi fallere; da Justum, Sanctumq; videri, / Noctem Peccatis, & Fraudibus objice Nubem. Hor. London: Printed for B. Lintot, at the Cross-Keys in Fleet-street. MDCCXVIII.

8vo.

A in six leaves, B–F⁸.

[2 pp.], i–vi, [vii–x], 1–76, [77] Epilogue, [78–80] Lintot book-list.

There were five editions within the year. I have examined only the first and third (advertised in *The St. James's Evening Post*, January 4, 1718, as 'just published'). There were, as well, editions in 1719, 1721, 1736, 1746, 1759, and 1760. See *CBEL* and Dudley Miles, 'A Forgotten Hit: *The Non-Juror*', *SP*, XVI (1919), 68, n., 69, n.

WORKS: A. *Rape of the Lock*; B. *Iliad*; C. *Eloisa to Abelard*.

CHARGE: 1. Pope a Jacobite and Roman Catholic.

Cibber, in this very anti-Catholic play, an adaptation of *Tartuffe* now directed against non-jurors, introduces three clear references to Pope's works. Only the last one can be thought disparaging.

A   In Act I, Maria, the coquette, taking a book from the table, reads aloud *The Rape of the Lock*, ii. 9–14, 17–18, lines which describe her own character (pp. 7–8).

B   In Act II, Maria hands the book she has entered with to her maid saying, 'Here take this odious *Homer*, and lay him up again, he tires me.' What follows makes it clear that she is reading him in translation (p. 29).

In Act V, the evil Dr Wolf, exposed at the end as a Popish priest, enters with a book and says to his host's wife, Lady Woodvil, whom he is attempting to seduce,

C   I had just dipt into poor *Eloisas* Passion for *Abelard*; It is indeed a piteous Conflict! How Terrible! How Penitent a Sense she shews of Guilty Pleasures past, and fruitless Pains to shut them from her Memory ... O! think then, what I endure for you, such are my Pains ... (p. 67)

It is just possible that this last is a reference to Hughes's prose translation, but much more probable that it is a reference to Pope's *Eloisa to Abelard* published six months previously (Ault, p. 310). Cibber's use of Pope's poem in his villain's attempt to justify his illicit love seems particularly disingenuous.

These three allusions, not very meaningful in themselves, were
I   probably meant to suggest that Pope's verse would be popular in homes disaffected to Hanoverian interests and to remind the audience or reader that Pope himself was a Catholic and, all too probably, like Dr Wolf, a Jacobite. See William M. Peterson, 'Pope and Cibber's *The Non-Juror*', *MLN*, LXX (1955), 332–5. Pope replied to Cibber's very successful play in *A Clue To the Comedy of the Non-Juror*, 1718.

April 10, 1718 (*Post Boy*, April 10, 1718)

[Gildon, Charles.] Memoirs Of the Life Of William Wycherley, Esq; With a Character of his Writings. By the Right Honourable George, Lord Lansdowne. To which are added, Some Familiar Letters, Written by Mr. Wycherley, and a True Copy of his Last Will and Testament. London: Printed for E. Curll, at the Dial and Bible over against St. Dunstan's Church in Fleet-street, 1718. Price One Shilling.

8vo in half-sheets.
One leaf unsigned, A–E⁴, F², [F2 missing, probably blank].
[2 pp.], 1–42 pp. Catchwords omitted on pp. 31 and 38.
F2 is also missing in the Bodleian copy.

WORK: A. *Pastorals*.

CHARGES: 1. Pope flattered Walsh and Wycherley; 2. Pope's father a rustic; 3. Pope wrote verses in his own praise under Wycherley's name.

The 'Life' of Wycherley is only a brief sketch, much padded with digressions on the avarice of the age, the sad want of patrons, the neglect of genius. It contains one fierce attack on Pope, of some length:

About this time [i.e. 1704] there came to Town, and to *Will's*, one *Pope*, a little diminuitive [*sic*] Creature, who had got a sort of Knack in smooth Vercification [*sic*], and with it was for setting up for a Wit and a Poet. But unknown as he was, furnish'd with a very good Assurance, and a Plausible, at least Cringing Way of Insinuation, first got acquainted with that Ingenious Gentleman and excellent Critick Mr. *Walsh*, who was pleas'd to bear with his Impertinence, and suffer his Company sometimes to divert himself either with his Figure or forward Ignorance. For a Man of Wit may find an agreeable Diversion in the Company of a pretending Fool sometimes, provided that the Interviews are short and seldome ...

From this Acquaintance he advances to that of Mr. *Wycherley*, then disgusted with the Wits; him he follows, attends and cringes to in all Places, and at all Times, and makes his Courtly Reflections on such as he found not very much in his good Graces.

I remember I was once to wait on Mr. *Wycherley*, and found in his Chamber this little *Aesopic* sort of an animal in his own cropt Hair, and Dress agreeable to the Forest he came from. I

confess the Gentleman was very silent all my stay there, and scarce utter'd three Words on any Subject we talk'd of, nor cou'd I guess at what sort of Creature he was ... I thought indeed he might be some Tenant's Son of his, who might make his Court for continuance in his Lease on the Decease of his Rustick Parent [Pope's father had recently died], but was sufficiently surpriz'd, when Mr. *Wycherley* afterwards told me he was Poetically inclin'd, and writ tolerably smooth Verses.

Not long after this I found a Copy of Verses of Mr. *Wycherley*'s to him, on his *Pastorals*, which happening to please some of the Town, this young Gentleman's Vanity of being Author of them destroy'd his other Vanity of being perused by so considerable a Person, for he was pleas'd to own, that he writ them himself tho' in his own Praise. (pp. 15–17)

Gildon had first mentioned the charge about Wycherley's verses on Pope in *The New Rehearsal*, 1714.

December 4, 1718 (*Post Boy*, December 4, 1718)

[Jacob, Giles.] The Poetical Register: Or, The Lives and Characters Of The English Dramatic Poets. With An Account Of Their Writings. London: Printed for E. Curll, in Fleetstreet. MDCCXIX.

8vo.
A⁸, a⁴, B–Y⁸, z⁴, Aa⁴, Bb².
Frontispiece, [2 pp.], [i]–vii, [viii] blank, [ix–xx], [1]–280, [281], 282–302, [303], 304–34, misnumbered 433, [335–56] pp.

The second volume, not Popiana, *An Historical Account Of The Lives And Writings Of Our most Considerable English Poets*, appeared in 1720. Volume I was issued again in 1723 together with Volume II:

January 17, 1723 (Straus, p. 272)

The Poetical Register: Or, The Lives and Characters Of All The English Poets. With an Account of their Writings. Adorned with curious Sculptures, engraven by the best Masters. Poets have an undoubted Right to claim, / If not the greatest, the most lasting

Name. Congreve. Vol. I. London: Printed, and Sold by A. Bettesworth, W. Taylor, and J. Batley, in Paternoster-Row; J. Wyat and C. Rivington, in St. Paul's Churchyard; E. Bell and W. Meadows, in Cornhill, and J. Pemberton and J. Hooke in Fleetstreet. 1723.

Collation as in 1719, but with A4 and A5 missing (pp. iii–vi). The British Museum copy, shelfmark 1066.9.18, contains A4 and A5 and an additional Z4, 'The Poetical Register Continued'. There was another edition in 1724 which I have not seen (Griffith 146).

WORK: A. *Three Hours after Marriage.*

A   In the account of John Gay, *Three Hours after Marriage* is said to have 'some extraordinary Scenes in it; which seem'd to trespass on Female Modesty' (p. 115).

    In the account of Joseph Gay, Gay is said to be the author of *The Confederates*, a Farce 'written to expose the Obscenity and false Pretence to Wit, in a Comedy call'd, *Three Hours after Marriage.* In which, Three mighty Bards their Forces join'd;[1] and in whose Praise were spoke the following Lines, at the Theatre Royal, by Mr. *Wilks.*' [The four lines from the Prologue to *The Sultaness*, quoted on the title-page of *The Confederates* follow.]

    Pope showed his annoyance at these remarks in his reference to them in the *Dunciad* (*Twick.* v. 164, n.).

    Jacob sent Pope the proofs of the account of Pope included in *An Historical Account*, 1720, pp. 145–52 (see Griffith 123, 142, 146). '... This fact was afterwards perverted by Curll and others into a statement that he had written the life himself' (*Twick.* v. 199, n.1). See *A Compleat Collection Of all the Verses*, 1728; *The Popiad*, 1728; *The Curliad*, 1729; Dennis's *Remarks Upon ... the Dunciad*, 1729; *The Mirrour*, 1733. Griffith thinks it not impossible Pope wrote the sketch of his life and work and highly probable he at least revised it (Griffith 123).

---

[1] Mr. *John Gay*, Mr. *Pope*, and Dr. *Arbuthnott* (p. 289).

K

1718

Hill, Aaron. The Northern-Star. A Poem. Written by Mr. Hill. London: Printed for E. Berington at the Cross-Keys near Essex-street End in the Strand, and J. Morphew near Stationers-Hall. MDCCXVIII. Price One Shilling.

Folio.

[A]–E², E², second count.

[4 pp.], 1–17, [18] blank, 19–20 pp.

The Preface, [A2r and v], alone concerns us.

WORKS: A. *Essay on Criticism*; B. *Windsor Forest*.

CHARGE: 1. Pope through envy found Hill's *Northern Star* politically dangerous.

1   Hill had, apparently through Lintot, asked Pope's opinion of *The Northern Star*. Lintot, according to Hill, reported to him that Pope thought 'Printing any thing in Praise of the *Czar* of *Russia* wou'd be receiv'd as a Satyr on the Government' ([A2r]).

Hill cannot conceive,

A   how so whimsical an Objection cou'd come into a Head, so well stor'd with Judgment, as we are to conclude Yours to be, from Your *Essay on Criticism*. ([A2r])

He assures Pope that his esteem for his genius as a poet is hardly exceeded by his contempt for Pope's vanity.

... Mr. *Dennis*, for whose Skill in Judging I profess an Esteem, has assured us, that you are a Kind of *Foe* to every Body but Your-self, and on that Foundation, supports his rough Attempt *to pull the Lyon's Skin from a certain little Ass* he there mentions, and I fear he means You, Sir. ([A2r])

Even if the Czar were Britain's enemy, his merits would be no less shining. Hill deplores the flattery of English poets to whom every woman is a nymph, every King, Augustus; Virgil's praise of Italy is falsehood and flattery applied to *Great Britain*. Hill reflects directly on *Windsor Forest*:

B   ... our Highway-Poets, whose utmost Reach of Skill is a *Poor Imitation*, forget that they make *Themselves* contemptible, instead of ornamenting their Subject, when Peace in *our* Climate is dress'd in her *Olives*, when *Pan* fills our Woods, and *Tritons* our Seas; and our Shepherds sit *Piping*, like the Swains of *Arcadia*. ([A2v])

In the Preface to *The Creation*, 1720 (reprinted in The Augustan Reprint Society, Series 4, March, 1949, ed. Gretchen Graf Pahl), Hill apologized for this 'angry and inconsiderate Preface'; Pope was entirely guiltless of his charge (p. [1]). See Hill's letter to Pope [1720], and Pope's reply, March 2 [1719/20], *Corr.* II. 35–7.

1718

Gildon, Charles. The Complete Art of Poetry. In Six Parts. I. Of the Nature, Use, Excellence, Rise and Progress of Poetry, &c. II. Of the Use and Necessity of Rules in Poetry. III. Of the Manners, Rules, and Art of Composing Epigrams, Pastorals, Ode, &c. IV. Of Tragedy and Comedy, how to draw the Plot, and form the Characters of both. V. The Rules of the Epic or Narrative Poem. Of the Poetic Diction or Language, and of English Numbers. VI. A Collection of the most beautiful Descriptions, Similes, Allusions, &c. from Spenser, and our best English Poets, as well Ancient as Modern, with above Ten Thousand Verses, not to be found in any Performance of this Kind. Shakespeariana; or the most beautiful Topicks, Descriptions, and Similes that occur throughout all Shakespeare's Plays. By Charles Gildon, Gent. Why is He honour'd with a Poet's name, / Who neither knows, nor wou'd observe a Rule? Roscom. Volume I. London: Printed for Charles Rivington, at the Bible and Crown in St. Paul's Church-yard. MDCCXVIII. Price 6s.

12mo.

a⁸, A in eleven leaves, A5 signed B5; B–P¹², Q⁴.

[16 pp.], iii–xv, 16–25, [26], 27–303, [304–5], 306–62 pp., [6 pp.]

Volume II does not concern us. It is simply an anthology of short selections from the poets arranged under headings from 'Abbot' to 'Zones'. There is no Popiana. The entries from Pope are noticed in Griffith 92.

WORKS: A. *Pastorals*; B. Homer.

Laudon, the chief speaker in these didactic dialogues, asks for news of the controversy over the rival translations of Homer:

B   Why Faith (answered I) the Controversy as yet remains undecided: *Will*'s *Coffee-House* gives it to the four Books, *Button*'s
to the one. For my part ... I must say this of Mr. *Tickel*'s, that
he seems to have enter'd into the Soul of *Homer*: You are sure,
at least, of having some Taste of the Genius and Manner of the
Poet, when you read his Version; for there seems to be a Mascu-
line Strength, both in his Expression and Numbers, and the
Native Simplicity of that Old Father of Verse is not embarrass'd
with any modern Turns and Embellishing Softnesses. Mr. *Pope*
has indeed all the Softness and Harmony of the *Lydian* Measures,
as I may call them; but whether he comes up to the Majesty and
Variety of his Author, I dare not determine.

It is not indeed to be supposed, that any Modern Tongue can
come up to that of *Greece* ...; but I know that a Master of the
English Numbers is capable of giving a wonderful Variety of
Cadence, of which a vulgar smooth Versifyer has not the least
Knowledge... *Dryden*, who was the greatest Master of *English*
Versification we have yet known, was perfectly acquainted with
the agreeable Secret of diversifying his Numbers. I can't help
observing, That some of the zealous Partizans of the subscrib'd
Translation, express a mighty Astonishment at the Notes it is
set out with; but alas! That is only the Labour of the Hand, a
meer Transcript from Authors who have gone before, and give
not the least Addition to the Merit of the Translation. (xii–xiii)

Tickell's translation is thus clearly preferred. That Gildon's mild
praise of Pope's versification is really no compliment at all is apparent
from several other passages where Gildon claims,

Smoothness of Verse is now become so common, that it loses the
Name of a distinguishing Perfection; for 'tis a difficult Matter
to find an Ear so unharmonious, as not to fall into Sounds that
flow into easie Numbers. (ix)

This *Smoothness* of *Versification* is now so common, that it has
swallow'd up all the more substantial Graces of Poetry; and it
is as difficult now to find the meanest *Scribbler* of the Times,
without this Quality, as to meet in them the *Genius* and *Essence*
of *Poesy*. (p. 83)

Laudon is disinclined to find Pope a poet:

But granting all this (said *Laudon*) nay, granting that the Trans-
lation it self is good; yet can't I discover how that can make a
Poet. We find none arriv'd at that Title among the *Greeks* and
Romans, by any profess'd Translation... (xv)

Gildon's dislike of Pope is evident in several other ways: although he refers to Roscommon and Sheffield frequently he never mentions Pope's *Essay on Criticism*, and he claims that Ambrose Philips 'beyond Controversy' makes a third with Theocritus and Virgil in pastoral A poetry: 'all tolerable Judges give him the first Place among the Moderns.' (p. 157)

1719

[Morrice, Bezaleel.] Three Satires. Most Humbly Inscribed and Recommended to that Little Gentleman, of Great Vanity, who has just published, A Fourth Volume of Homer. To which is added, A Character of the Nuns. A Satire. —Ridentem dicere verum / Quid vetat? —Horace. London: Printed for J. Roberts in Warwick-Lane. 1719. (Price Six-pence.)

Half-title: Three Satires Inscrib'd to Mr Pope.

8vo in half-sheets.
[A]–c⁴, d³.
[4 pp.], [5]–10, [11]–15, [16] blank, [17]–21, [22] blank, [23]–29 pp., [30] blank.

Called by Pope 'Satires on the Translators of Homer, Mr. *P.* and Mr. *T.* Anon. [*Bez. Morris*]' and dated by him 1717 (*Twick.* v. 208).

Morrice's authorship is shown by the inclusion of the first satire here, 'On The English Translations of Homer' in *An Epistle To Mr. Welsted*, 1721, the dedication to which is signed 'Bezaleel Morrice'.

WORK: A. *Iliad*.

Satire III, 'An Epistle To Homer', and Satire IV, 'A Character Of The Nuns' (a nasty little poem on the amours of nuns), are not Popiana.
  Satire I, 'On The English Translations of Homer' (pp. [5]–10), was later expanded from 78 to 100 lines and included in *An Epistle To Mr. Welsted*, 1721, q.v., and again expanded for *On The English Translations of Homer*, 1733, q.v.
  Satire II, 'To Mr. T[i]ck[e]ll, on the first Appearance of Mr. P[o]pe's Proposals for Printing by Subscription, his Version of Homer's Iliad' (pp. [11]–15), is mostly devoted to abuse of Tickell; the abuse of Pope is by the way:

A

Sing joyful *Iö Peans*! ancient wit
Shall not to *modern confidence* submit.
Great *P*[o]*pe* has to the combat *Homer* dar'd,
Already see the *champion* is prepar'd!
In martial pomp, hark! to the *lists* he comes,
Hight *Lintott*'s shop, *subscriptions* are the *drums*.
The *beaus*, and *criticks*, judges of the field,
How soon do's the poor baffled *ancient* yeild!

(pp. [11]–12)

1719

[Dacier, Anne Lefebvre.] L'Iliade D'Homere, Traduite En
François, Avec Des Remarques. Par Madame Dacier. Tome
Premier. Seconde Edition Reveüe, corrigée & augmentée. Avec
Quelques Reflexions sur la Preface Angloise de M. Pope. A Paris,
Aux dêpens de Rigaud Directeur de l'Imprimerie Royale.
M.DCCXIX. Avec Privilege Du Roy.

A work in three volumes; only the third volume concerns us. Title-
page as for the first volume, but omitting everything from 'augmentée'
to 'A Paris.' I have seen only microfilm of the copy in the Bibliothèque
Nationale, Paris.

12mo.
Two unsigned leaves, A–Z^{12}, Aa–Dd^{12}, Ee^{10}, *^{8}.
[4 pp.], [1]–664, [4 pp.] Privilege du Roy, [16 pp.] Reflexions.

This is the second edition of Mme Dacier's translation in which the
'Reflexions' (the only Popiana) first appeared. For an account of this
attack see the English translation, *Remarks Upon Mr. Pope's Account of
Homer*, 1724.

For later editions see the Bibliothèque Nationale, Paris, *Catalogue
des livres imprimés*. Of these I have examined only the Bodleian copy
of the 1741 edition where the 'Reflexions', unpaged, follow the title-
page of Vol. 1 (*^{8}).

August 22, 1720 (*Daily Post*, August 22, 1720)

An Answer To Duke upon Duke, &c.

Folio.

Two leaves unsigned.

[1]–4 pp.

Musical score and first two verses on p. [1].

The *Daily Post* advertisement referred to gives 'An Answer to Duke upon Duke. With a Key, set to Musick by the same Hand ... Printed for A. Moore ... Price 3d.'

WORKS: A. *Iliad*; B. *Duke upon Duke*.

CHARGES: I. Pope a Roman Catholic; 2. Pope deformed.

An attack upon Pope in 41 ballad stanzas as sole author of *Duke upon Duke*. For Pope's poem see *Twick*. VI. 217–24, and for what little is known of it, Ault, pp. 186–94. Since almost nothing is known of the circumstances of the poem, the answer to it is very obscure, but the attack on Pope is plain.

B

2

I. Thou *POPE*; oh *Popery* burning hot,
 For none but *Papists* wou'd,
 Enter into a cursed Plot
 'Gainst *Protestant* so good.

II. For this have I, O Libeller,
 As 'twill be made appear,
 For the Succession kept a stir,
 And *Speech'd* it Year to Year.

III. For this, thine *Homer* have I bought,
 All thy smart Things on *Curle*?
 With a Sham *Dukedom* set at nought,
 Who thought to be an E—l.

 .   .   .

V. Take heed thou Satan's crooked Rib,
 For, though not Tall, I'm strait;
 That thou, like me, not bilk thy Crib,
 Like me, repent too late.

VI. Since in *Greek* Poet it is Writ,
 Which thou'st not *turn'd* amiss;
 Hector sometimes had's lucky hit,
 Achilles sometimes his.

(pp. [1]–2)

1720 (Irving, p. 161)

John Shuttle, And His Wife Mary. London Printed: And Sold by S. Baker, at the Black-Boy and Crown in Pater-Noster-Row. [Price Four-Pence.]

12mo in half-sheets.
A–B⁶, C⁴.
[2 pp.], 3–32 pp.

WORKS: A. *Iliad*; B. *Three Hours after Marriage*.

Most of this small pamphlet is humorous and political, but the conversation between Jeremiah Shuttle, who is the author; John Shuttle, his cousin; and Mr Brisk turns for several pages on the quarrel between the Ancients and the Moderns. When John asserts the superiority of the Moderns, Brisk agrees and says,

A   There's Mr. *Pope*, what a fine Poem has he made out of the Works of an old blind Ballad-Singer? *Homer* owes him more than to his own Genius; and the Immortality of his Name, if it does prove immortal, will be more due to the Translator than to the Original. (p. 21)

B   Could Aristophanes, Terence, or Plautus write a comedy equal to *Three Hours after Marriage*? (p. 22).

That these passages are to be read ironically is made clear by the comparisons that follow of Tom Durfey's odes to Horace's and Sir James Baker to Martial, and, even more clearly, by the bitterly ironic praise of Swift (p. 23).

May, 1721 (Sherburn, p. 294)

[Morley, Richard.] The Life Of the late Celebrated Mrs. Elizabeth Wisebourn, Vulgarly call'd Mother Wybourn; Containing Secret Memoirs of several Ladies of the first Q—y, who held an Assembly at her House; Together with her Last Will and Testament. By Anodyne Tanner, M.D. Author of the P—c—l Sch—e, &c. and One of her Physicians in Ordinary. Post funera Virtus. London: Printed for A. Moore, near St. Paul's. (Price One Shilling.)

8vo in half-sheets.

A- G⁴, H in three leaves.

[2 pp.], [iii]–vii, [viii] blank, [1]–50, [51], 52–4 pp.

There is also at Yale a 'Second Edition', with a new title-page, inserting 'The Second Edition.' after 'Virtus.'

This is ascribed to Dick Morley in Savage's *An Author To Be Let*, 1729, A3r and p. 3.

WORKS: A. *First Psalm*; B. *Verses to the Memory of an Unfortunate Lady*.

CHARGES: 1. Pope deformed; 2. Pope is the lover of the Duchess of Buckinghamshire; 3. A young woman, forced into a convent, committed suicide for love of Pope; 4. Pope was Gay's tutor.

This grossly anti-Catholic pamphlet, quite properly classified by the Sterling Library as Erotica, gives Pope a mistress named 'Monavaria' whom Sherburn would identify as the Duchess of Buckinghamshire (Sherburn, 295). The pamphlet pretends to give an account of the life of the famous bawd, 'Mother Wisebourn', and of the select society of either sex who came to her house 'for each other's *Recreation* and *mutual Solace*' (p. 15). One member, Monavaria, natural born, her impotent husband dead, has taken a doctor as a lover.

2   The *Doctor*'s only Rival, if (which is much doubted) he has really any, is a Poet, who is as eminent for his Person as his *Genius*; his *Form* is the best *Index* of his *Mind*; nor can the Drawings of Sir *Godfrey Kneller*, or *Dahl*, give one so just an Idea of the former, as *that it self* does of the latter: If *Monavaria* does now and then scatter some of her Favours upon him, it must be only to appease the *Manes* of her Husband; he was his *Friend* when he was living, and therefore ought to be considered as his *Representative* now he is dead. (p. 33)

That Pope is the poet is put beyond doubt by the other charge made:

3   Perhaps it would be thought an Injustice to her Memory, to pass over, unspoke of, so shining an Ornament of this Society as that Lady once was, who stabb'd her self in the Nunnery, into which she was forc'd by the *Cruelty* of her *Relations*, for the Love of Mr. *P[o]pe*, whom I have already mention'd in the Account of *Monovaria* and the *Doctor*; as he himself relates it in a Poem of his, under the Title of *Verses to the Memory of an unfortunate Lady*: However, the Cause of her Death, I will venture to say, almost atones for the Sin of it; his *Person* is as amiable as his *Muse*, and certainly not to be seen by *any of the Sex* without some fatal Effect;

especially if big with Child, as this Lady was before she enter'd
into a Vow for the *Conservation* of her Chastity. (p. 44)

There is also a hit at the *First Psalm*: one glance at Cangia, another
member of the society,

A   and she *will dissolve* (as Mr. P[o]*pe*, in his intended *New Version*,
          ['an excellent Specimen of which he has publish'd already,'
          added in the second edition] happily expresses it) *like Snow upon
          the Mountains of* Bether. (p. 16)

4   Pope is called Gay's tutor and it is hinted (p. 30) that they both had
a share in an insipid three-quatrain poem printed on p. 29.

1721

[Morrice, Bezaleel.] An Epistle To Mr. Welsted; And A Satyre
on the English Translations of Homer. Parturiunt Montes—Hor.
To which is added, An Essay towards an Encomium on the true
Merit of Homer. London: Printed, and Sold by Tho. Bickerton,
at the Crown in Pater-Noster-Row. 1721. (Price Six-Pence.)

8vo in half-sheets.
Three unsigned leaves, B–C⁴, D in three leaves.
[4 pp.], [7]–11, [12–15], 16–23, [24–7], 28–30 pp.
The dedication to Prior is signed (p. [3]) 'Bezaleel Morrice'.

The above is the Yale copy. The British Museum copy has the half-
title: 'An Epistle To Mr. Welsted. And A Satyre On the English
Translations of Homer'.

The pamphlet contains three poems: 'An Epistle To Mr. Welsted',
pp. [7]–11; 'On The British Translations Of Homer: A Satyre', pp.
[15]–23; 'A [*sic*] Essay On The Character of Homer', pp. [27]–30.
Only the second is Popiana. It is an expansion to 100 lines of the 76-
line 'Satire I. On The English Translations of Homer', in *Three Satires*,
1719. It was again expanded for *On The English Translations Of Homer*,
1733, q.v.

WORK: A. *Iliad.*

Morrice feels disdain and rage when he sees a trivial author who
pleases the crowd with fashionable rhymes rashly dare 'the mightiest
Work' (p. 16).

A
> And Justice from a weak Attempt like thine,
> Oh *Pope*! can its transcendant Author find?
> In whose capacious, whose prodigious Mind,
> Conduct and Force their utmost Aid impart,
> And shew the whole Extent of human Wit, and Art! (p. 17)

But it is vain to censure the pride of modern wits who

> ... all Things rightly, but themselves, will know;
> All Things industriously attempt, when Pay
> (Their noble Guide) prepares the chosen Way.   (p. 18)

He criticizes in turn Chapman, Ogilby, and Hobbes, but returns to Pope, his chief target:

> Smart *Pope* comes now—yet not so stern as these;
> He proves more kind; treats him with Grace and Ease;
> And makes him spruce, the *Beaus* and *Belles* to please;
> So gentle female Habits, heretofore
> Renown'd *Achilles* and *Alcides* wore.   (p. 20)

The metaphor suddenly changes to a horse:

> Th' immortal Steed from his triumphant Race
> Is led, and taught a pretty modish Pace,
> With Bells he gingles, do's with Harness shine,
> Is something sprightly, in Appearance fine.   (p. 21)

How can 'choice Judges of the *British* Kind' (p. 21) approve such work? He concludes that adequate translation is impossible and that the attempt to translate is a sign of pride. Who are we 'to cope with such stupendious Things'? (p. 23).

1721

Smedley, Jonathan. Poems On Several Occasions. Liberius si / Dixero quid, seu forte jocosius, hoc mihi jure, / Cum Venia, dabis—Hor. London: Printed by S. Richardson, for the Author. MDCCXXI.

8vo.

Seven unsigned leaves, the third leaf, the Dedication, signed A4, B–M8. [4 pp.], [vii]–xv, [xvi] blank, [1]–176 pp., page 90 misnumbered 09.

WORKS: A. *First Psalm*; B. *Three Hours after Marriage*.

The volume contains several attacks on Swift, some mild praise of Pope (p. 110), and one attack on Pope and his friends in 'Cloe to Mr. Tickell, Occasioned By His Avignon-Letter', a poem of 76 lines, pp. 81–5:

> How long shall *Dulness*, dreaming God! sustain,
> In this fair Island, his inglorious Reign?
>
> . . .
>
> See! how his awful Godhead does dispence
> At *Child*'s, and *Will*'s, his solid Influence!
> How! willy-whisps *P[op]e*'s Senses quite astray;
> And sheds his whole collected Force on *G[a]y*!
> How puzzles pert *Ar[buthno]t*'s Learned Head;
> Who, tho' to *Recipe*'s and Pulses bred,
> His former Studies, dozing, new reverses,
> Writes Madrigals, Crack [*sic*] Puns, and Clubs for Farces.
>
> (pp. 83–4)

He then apostrophizes Addison and bids him rise to convince the world,

>   that *George*'s Reign
> Is not condemn'd to Folly, and to Gain.
> Thus each Alloy disclos'd, by thy pure Ore,
> Bombast shall pass for Sterling Wit no more.
> Nor David's Poetry, inspir'd, sublime,
> Obscenely shock in barbarous, doggrel Rhime.
>
> (pp. 84–5)

'Cloe to Mr. Tickell' was reprinted, pp. 246–50, in:

April 17, 1729 (*Daily Post*, April 17, 1729)

Miscellaneous Poems, By Several Hands: Particularly The D— of W—n, Sir Samuel Garth, Dean S—, Mr. John Hughes, Mr. Thomson, Mrs C—r. Publish'd By Mr. Ralph. London: Printed by C. Ackers, for W. Meadows at the Angel in Cornhill; J. Batley at the Dove in Pater-noster-Row; T. Cox at the Lamb under the Royal-Exchange; S. Billinsley at the Judge's Head in Chancery-Lane; R. Hett at the Bible and Crown in the Poultry near Cheapside; and J. Gray at the Cross-Keys in the Poultry. MDCCXXIX.

British Museum.

Smedley published it under his own name, pp. 81–5, in:

Poems on Several Occasions. —Liberius si Dixero quid, seu forte jocosius, hoc mihi, jure, / Cum venia dabis. Hor. By Jonathan Smedley, Dean of Clogher. London: Printed in the Year M.DCC.XXX. Price 1s.6d.

British Museum.

April, 1723 (Griffith, 139)

Cythereia: Or, New Poems Upon Love and Intrigue. Viz. [19 names in two columns.] Res est Solliciti plena timoris Amor. Ovid. London: Printed for E. Curll, over-against Catharine-street in the Strand; and T. Payne, near Stationers-Hall. M.DCC. XXIII. Price 1s. 6d.

Half-title: Cythereia: Or, New Poems Upon Love and Intrigue.

8vo in half-sheets.
One unsigned leaf, B–D⁴, D⁴, F–P⁴.
[2 pp.], [1]–112 pp.

The half-title, missing in the Yale copy, and the title-page from 'Stationers-' on, the remaining words having been cut away from the Yale copy, are given from Griffith 139.
Griffith 139.
Case 327.

According to Case, *Cythereia* was later made a part of *The Altar of Love*, 1727 (Case 340); the Yale copy of the latter, however, does not correspond to Case 340 and does not contain the 'Answer'. Neither the Bodleian copy of the 1727 edition nor of the 'Third Edition', 1731, contains it.
    This volume which prints Pope's 'Verses Occasioned by Mr. Tickell's Translation of the First Iliad of Homer' (see *Twick.* VI. 142–5) also prints an 'Answer to the foregoing Verses; Presented to the Countess of Warwick', pp. 92–4, listed on the title-page in the list of nineteen titles as 'XIII. Answer; By Mr. M.' Curll in *The Curliad*, 1729, p. 6, said,

> . . . *Pope*'s *Libel* upon Mr. *Addison* was *first* published by Mr. *John Markland*, of St. *Peter*'s College in *Cambridge*, with an *Answer* thereto, in a Pamphlet, intitled, *Cythereia* . . .

The 'Answer', however, is by Thomas Tickell, not by 'John Mark-

land'. In the bibliography of Thomas Tickell in Richard Eustace Tickell, *Thomas Tickell and the Eighteenth Century Poets* (London, 1931), this 'Answer' is No. 31, pp. 193–4. R. E. Tickell there explains that there is a manuscript copy of the verses in the Worcester College Library in the handwriting of George Clarke, giving Tickell as the author. He points out that Curll only stated that the lines were published by Markland, not that they were written by him and that Curll was wrong in his identification of Markland: the only Markland of St Peter's College, Cambridge, was Jeremiah Markland.

The 'Answer' was reprinted in *The Progress Of Dulness*, 1728, pp. 30–1, where it is signed 'J. Markland'. Nichols in his *Literary Anecdotes*, IV. 314, reprinted the 'Answer' and attributed it to Jeremiah Markland, IV. 273–4, n. The 'Answer' is also reprinted in *Notes and Queries*, Ser. 2, II, 243.

WORK: A. Atticus portrait.

The 40-line 'Answer' turns Pope's own poem against him:

A
    When soft Expressions covert-Malice hide,
    And pitying Satire cloaks o'er-weening Pride;
    When Ironies reverst right Virtue show,
    And point which Way true Merit we may know:
    When Self-conceit just hints indignant Rage,
    Shewing its wary Caution to engage;
    In mazy Wonder we astonish'd stand,
    Perceive the Stroke, but miss th'emittent Hand.

    So the skill'd Snarler pens his angry Lines,
    Grins lowly fawning, biting as he whines;
    Traducing with false Friendship's formal Face,
    And Scandalizing with the Mouth of Praise:
    Shews his Intention, but his Weakness too,
    And what he would, yet what he dare not do. (pp. 92–3)

February 8, 1724 (*Post Boy*, February 8, 1723 [*sic*])

Dacier, Anne Lefebvre. Madame Dacier's Remarks Upon Mr. Pope's Account of Homer, Prefixed To his Translation of the Iliad. Made English from the French, By Mr. Parnell. Sound

Judgment is the Ground of Writing well. Hor. London: Printed
for E. Curll, over against Catherine-street in the Strand.
M.DCC. XXIV. (Price 6d.)

8vo in half-sheets.
Two unsigned leaves, B–C⁴, D².
[2 pp.], iii–iv, 1–18 pp., [19–20] Curll book-list.

A translation of the 'Reflexions' in her *Iliade* . . . *Traduite En François*,
1719, q.v.

The dedication to Sir Richard Steele (pp. iii–iv) is signed 'T. Parnell', who is not Pope's friend, and is possibly a Curll invention.

Reprinted in *The Popiad*, 1728, pp. [26]–32, and in *Mr. Pope's Literary Correspondence, Volume the Fifth*, 1737, pp. 136–46.

WORK: A. Preface to the *Iliad*.

CHARGE: 1. Pope plagiarized from Mme Dacier.

> Upon the finishing of the *second Edition* of my Translation of
> Homer, and on the same Day the last Sheet was brought me
> from the Press to correct, a particular Friend of mine sent me a
> Translation of part of Mr. *Pope's* Preface prefixed to his Version
> of the Iliad into *English* Verse. As I do not understand that Lan-
> guage, I cannot form any Judgment of his Performance, tho' I
> have heard much of it. I am indeed willing to believe that the
> Praises it has met with are not unmerited . . . (pp. 1–2)

But she finds in Pope's Preface that

> . . . nothing is more overstrained or more false ['rien n'est plus
> outré ni plus faux' in the French of 1719] than the Images in
> which his Imagination has represented Homer . . . (p. 3)

She objects particularly to Pope's images of Homer as a 'wild Para-
dise', 'a copious Nursery', and a 'mighty Tree' (see the reprinting of
the first edition of Pope's Preface in *Prose*, I. 224, 243).

> What! is *Homer's* Poem then, according to Mr. *Pope*, a confused
> Heap of Beauties, without Order or Symmetry, a Plat [*sic*]
> whereon nothing but Seeds, nor nothing perfect or formed is to
> be found . . . The most inveterate Enemies to *Homer* never said any
> thing more injurious, or more unjust, against that Poet. (p. 4)

The following is typical of her refutations:

> . . . The Iliad is so far from being a wild Paradise, that it is the
> most regular Garden, and laid out with more Symmetry than
> any ever was. Monsieur *le Nostre*, who was the first Man of the

World in his Art, never observed in his Gardens a more perfect or more admirable Symmetry, than *Homer* ... (pp. 5–6)

She defends herself against Pope's criticism of her own preface where she is said to have found 'these antient Times so much the finer, as they the less resemble our Own' (p. 9; *Prose*, I. 239). She meant, she explains carefully, only their simplicity, not their cruelty, concubinage, etc.

> I own I did not expect to find myself attacked by Mr. *Pope*, in a Preface wherein I might have expected some small Token of Acknowledgment, or at least some slight Approbation; for having been so happy as to think on several Things in the manner he himself does, especially on the Manners of the Antients ... (p. 11)

She quotes several passages she believes paralleled in Pope's Preface. A note added by the Curll translator argues a much stronger view of the resemblances. Since Mme Dacier's preface was written long before Pope's, she is

I
> very modest, when he uses her own Words, to say that she was happy in having *thought* as he did; tho' it is plain that he borrowed of this *Thought* from her ... (p. 12, n.)

She also corrects what she believes to be several errors of Pope's – his statement that Homer invented the fable he used, and his interpretation of Aristotle's 'manners'. She closes with not very lively irony on the great benefits one might expect in political matters from the man who can reform Homer, would he turn his talents to them.

Pope complained about the French text of these remarks in a letter to Buckley, February 12 [1722/3]. Sherburn points out that, 'With his intimate friend Atterbury in the Tower Pope would not relish remarks connecting him with politics' (*Corr.* II. 157, n.2).

March 25, 1724 (*Daily Post*, March 23, 1724)

Welsted, Leonard. Epistles, Odes, &c. Written on Several Subjects. With A Translation of Longinus's Treatise on the Sublime. By Mr. Welsted. To which is prefix'd, A Dissertation concerning the Perfection of the English Language, the State of Poetry, &c. —Juvat immemorata ferentem / Ingenuis oculisq; legi manibusque teneri. Hor. London: Printed for J. Walthoe, over-against

the Royal Exchange in Cornhill; and J. Peele, at Locke's Head in Pater-noster Row. MDCCXXIV.

8vo.

A⁸, a–c⁸, ʙ–ɪ⁸, ᴋ⁴, ʟ–ʀ⁸, s⁴.

[2 pp.], [iii]–lxiv, [1]–255 pp., [256] blank.

There was a second edition without the translation of Longinus:

Epistles, Odes, &c. Written on Several Subjects: With A Dissertation Concerning the Perfection of the English Language, the State of Poetry, &c. By Mr. Welsted. —Juvat immemorata ferentem / Ingenuis oculisq; legi manibusque teneri. Hor. The Second Edition. London: Printed for J. Walthoe, over-against the Royal Exchange in Cornhill; and J. Peele, at Locke's Head in Pater-noster Row. M DCC XXV.

12mo in half-sheets.

A–N⁶.

[2 pp.], [iii]–lii, [1]–101 pp., [102] blank, [103] book-list, [104] blank.

The 'Dissertation' has been reprinted in *Critical Essays of the Eighteenth Century*, 1700–25, ed. Willard Higley Durham (New Haven, 1915), pp. 355–95, where the Pope passage appears on pp. 359–60, and in *Eighteenth-Century Critical Essays*, ed. Scott Elledge (Ithaca, 1961), 2 vols., I. 320–48, where the Pope passage appears on p. 323. Elledge silently corrects Welsted's quotation from the *Essay on Criticism*.

ᴡᴏʀᴋ: A. *Essay on Criticism*, l. 483.

The 'Dissertation' refers to the

A   vulgar Error, *viz*, that our Language will continue to go on from one Refinement to another, and pass through perpetual Variations and Improvements, till in Time the *English*, we now speak, is become as obsolete and unintelligible as that of *Chaucer*, and so on, as long as we are a People; this is what one of our Poets laid down some Years ago as an undoubted Maxim,
> And what now *Chaucer* is, shall *Dryden* be.

But whoever this Writer is, he certainly judg'd the Matter wrong ... (p. x, 1st ed.; pp. viii–ix, 2nd ed.)

The anonymous author of *Characters Of The Times*, 1728, thought that Welsted would have been spared Pope's abuse if he had not, in his 'Dissertation', 'happen'd to cite a low and false Line from Mr. *P[o]pe* for the meer Purpose of refuting it, without seeming to know, or care

L

who was the Author of it' (p. 24). See also Pope's quotation from the 'Dissertation' in *Twick.* v. 26.

September, 1724 (*Monthly Chronicle*, August–September, 1724)

[Haywood, Elizabeth.] Memoirs Of a Certain Island Adjacent to the Kingdom of Utopia. Written by a Celebrated Author of that Country. Now translated into English. London, Printed, and Sold by the Booksellers of London and Westminster. M.DCC.XXV.

Half-title: Memoirs Of a Certain Island Adjacent to the Kingdom of Utopia.

8vo.
Two unsigned leaves, B–T⁸, U in two leaves.
[4 pp.], 1–290, [2 pp.] blank.

This is the Bodleian copy. Volume II does not concern us, except for the Key, inserted after the title-page in Volume II, pp. 1–4.

A new edition of Vol. I was issued with Vol. II, advertised in *The Evening Post*, October 26, 1725. I have not seen a copy. Yale has a copy of the 'Second Edition', March 5, 1726 (*Mist's Weekly Journal*, March 5, 1726):

Title-page as in the first edition, adding after 'English', 'Vol. I. The Second Edition.' and dated M.DCC.XXVI.

8vo.
One leaf unsigned, B–T⁸, U in three leaves.
[2 pp.], 1–294 pp.

Volume II again does not concern us. Vol. I has the Key, pp. 291–4. In the Bodleian copy of the 'Second Edition' the Key is inserted after the title-page of Vol. I.

CHARGES: 1. Martha Blount dissolute and shameless; 2. Pope her lover (?).

12   The first of the tales in this scandalous book is the 'Story of the Enchanted Well', i.e., the South Sea Bubble, pp. 7–13. Among the de-

votees of the well is Marthalia, identified in the Key as Mrs. Bl[oun]t, 'the most dissolute and shameless of her Sex' (p. 12). She has 'at last married an old Servant of the Necromancer's [identified in the Key as C[rag]gs]—he languishes under an incurable Disease, and she has the Management of his Affairs, and is by this means become a Woman of Consequence ...' (p. 12).

> ... there are some who of late have severely repented trusting themselves in her Embraces, and cursed the artificial Sweets and Perfumes, which hindred them from discovering those Scents, that would have been infallible Warnings of what they might expect in such polluted Sheets. (p. 13)

Sherburn, p. 296, wonders whether Pope is intended as the 'old Servant'.

May, 1725 (*Monthly Catalogue*)

[Cooke, Thomas.] The Battle Of The Poets. An Heroick Poem. In Two Cantos. Bella per Aenios plus quam Civilia Campos / Canimus. Lucan. London: Printed for J. Roberts in Warwick-Lane. MDCCXXV.

Folio.

[A]–E².

[2 pp.], [3]–20 pp.

Teerink 1199 lists a Dublin reprint in 1731, but I have not located a copy.

An offensive poem, not because it contains any special abuse of Pope, but because it ranks him among the minor poetasters of the day and has him lose the battle to Ambrose Philips. (Cooke's critical sense was defective.) This is not to be confused with the longer and much more abusive version included in Cooke's *Tales, Epistles, Odes, Fables, &c*, 1729, q.v. See Carter R. Bishop, 'Alexander Pope and "The Battle of the Poets"', *West Virginia University Studies*, I. *Philological Papers* (1936), 19–27. E. L. Steeves in *The Art of Sinking in Poetry*, ed. Edna Leake Steeves (New York, 1952), p. 151, wrongly states, as does Teerink, that Swift is attacked in the 1725 version. This version is reprinted in *The Bays Miscellany*, 1730, q.v.

WORKS: A. *Windsor Forest*; B. *Rape of the Lock*; C. Homer; D. Pope's edition of Shakespeare.

Apollo decrees a battle on Windsor Forest to settle the discord among the poets. Pope, a general, and his troops are first described:

AB

> First on the Plain a mighty General came,
> In Merit great, but greater far in Fame,
> In shining Arms advanc'd, and POPE his Name.
> A pond'rous Helm he wore, adorn'd with Care,
> And for the Plume *Belinda*'s ravish'd Hair.
> Arm'd at all Points the Warrior took the Field,
> With *Windsor*'s Forest painted on his Shield. (p. 5)

Among his troops are Wesley and Fenton, and three captains, Trapp, Cibber, and Gay, 'Heading a Thousand Witlings of a Day' (p. 5). Pope warns his men:

> Beware of WELSTED, in the warring Throng,
> Wise as *Ulysses*, and as *Ajax* strong;
> Avoid his Arm, nor too presumptuous be,
> For he's a Victim worthy only me.
> Or should you PHILIPS in the Battle spy,
> 'Tis Death to meet him, and 'tis wise to fly.
> *Belinda* be the word; and when I nod,
> Review your Forces, and invoke the God. (p. 6)

Hill is enraged when a messenger from Pope bids him and his troops leave the field. Welsted, who heads an army composed of Amhurst and Jacob, among others, is given the most flattering description:

> Himself a Godlike Chief, deriv'd from *Jove*,
> Whom much *Apollo*, and the *Muses*, love. (p. 8)

After Welsted's troops defeat Hill and his men, they see Pope's army approach.

> Forward he [Welsted] sprung to meet th' approaching Foe,
> Eager his great Antagonist to know. (p. 10)

Pope and Welsted engage in single combat, but the approach of night leaves the outcome of the battle doubtful.

In Canto II Dennis at night searches the field for spoils.

> Odious of late to each Pretender grown,
> But to the Wise his hoary Judgment's known. (p. 13)

He enters Welsted's camp where he wounds Welsted's 'Dissertation concerning the Perfection of the English Language', and then enters Pope's camp.

> To FENTON's Charms he was excessive kind,
> One of an hundred Lines he left behind. (p. 15)

Next he turns to Pope,

> By whom he saw the deathless *Grecian* lye;
> And *Shakespear* stood, stupend'ous Ruins, by.
> Oh! mercenary Bard, the Critic cry'd,
> For lesser Faults than these have Thousands dy'd;
> Too dire an Instance of what Gold can do,
> That thy own Country-man must suffer too!
> Too weighty are thy Crimes for me to bear.
> He spoke, and left the guilty Volumes there.
> But in his other Works, what Beauties shine!
> While sweetest Music dwells in ev'ry Line;
> These he admir'd, on these he stamp'd his Praise,
> And bad them live to brighten future Days.   (pp. 15–16)

As Dennis is leaving the field he sees one who 'was, or seem'd, a Spy' (p. 16), Savage, who is removing the body of a fallen friend; on Savage, Dennis promises, the world will soon begin to smile (p. 17).

In the final battle Tickell appears in Addison's helmet, but is stripped as an impostor by Philips, who overcomes everyone except Welsted and Pope. Welsted is bidden by Apollo to leave and promised that 'equal Honours shall e're long be thine' (p. 20); Pope is rescued by 'the lovely Nymphs of *Windsor*'s Plain / Whom he had sung in his immortal Strain' (p. 20). Philips wins the laurel crown.

November 11, 1725 (*Post Boy*, November 11, 1725)

[Macky, Spring, tr.] The Adventures Of Pomponius. Part. II. Containing I. The entire History of Prince Relosan. II. Characters of the Court-Ladies and Lords. III. The Jerbian War, its Progress and Conclusion. IV. The Chronicle of the Chevalier Sotermelles. V. An Account of the Regiment of the Cap. VI. The deplorable Catastrophe of Prince Jonas. London: Printed for E. Curll in the Strand. MDCCXXVI Price 2s. 6d.

12mo in half-sheets.
A^2, B^6–N^6, O^4.
[2 pp.], 3–4, 1–131, [132] blank, [133–4], 135–52 pp.

This is the Bodleian copy; the British Museum copy lacks N and O. The Bodleian copy is bound with the first part of this scabrous novel which has as its title-page: 'The Adventures of Pomponius, A Roman Knight: Or, The History of Our Times. Made English from the Rome Edition of the French Original, By Mr. Macky. London; Printed for E. Curll, over-against Catherine Street in the Strand. M.DCC.XXVI.' Both the Bodleian and *BM Cat.* attribute this to 'Labadie'.

The Bibliothèque Nationale, Paris, *Catalogue des livres imprimés*, gives the author as 'Labadie religieux convers de la congrégation de S. Maur' and adds 'Attribué à Labadie et revu par l'abbé Prevost'. The *BM Cat.* lists several other translations of Macky's.

WORKS: A. Pope's edition of Shakespeare; B. *Odyssey*.

The 'Clavis' (pp. 3–4) lists, p. 4, 'Pope, *a Digression concerning him, by the Translator* p. 28'. The passage is as follows:

AB   As a Parallel to this Management of Authors by *Cabal*, may be mentioned that late Jobb of Journey-Work, the Translation of Homer's ODYSSEY, *Undertaken* by Mr. POPE: Or, his mutilated Edition of the Works of the immortal *Shakespeare*, wherein indeed, he frankly owns—*He has only performed the Duty of a* dull Editor. *See*, his Preface. For *both* those wretched Performances, a large Subscription has been carried on, purely through the sycophantick Meanness of the *Undertaker*, who crawls under the *Toilet* of every *Court-Lady*; and, with venal Praises, flatters every brocaded *Fop* of *Distinction*. (p. 28)

December 23, 1725 (Straus, p. 277)

[Pope, Thomas?] The Stamford Toasts: Or Panegyrical Characters Of The Fair-Ones, Inhabiting the good Town of Stamford in Lincolnshire. With Some other Poetical Amusements. By Mr. Pope; not the Undertaker. Nihil immane est: Odiumque perit, / Cum jussit amor:—Sen. Hippolyt.—Ubi non est pudor, / Nec cura juris, sanctitas, pietas, fides: / Instabile regnum est.—Sen. Thyestes. London: Printed for the Author; and Sold by E. Curll in the Strand; J. Jackson near St. James's-House; and E. Palmer and W. Thompson at Stamford. 1726. (Price One Shilling).

8vo in half-sheets.

A², B–G⁴, H².

[4 pp.], 1–52 pp.

'To The Reader' (A2r and v) is signed at the end 'Tho. Pope' and dated 'Peterborough, October 5. 1725' (A2v). The catalogue of the Yale Library questions whether 'Tho. Pope' is not a pseudonym.

WORKS: A. *Odyssey.*

A   The only attack on Pope, indeed the only reference to him at all, is the use of his name and 'undertaker' on the title-page. Pope's use of 'undertaker' in the translation of the *Odyssey* is clearly hit at. See Sherburn, pp. 263–4.

January, 1726 (*Monthly Catalogue*)

Cooke, Thomas. The Bath. A tale. Addressed to His Grace the Duke of Montague. By Mr. Cooke. To which is added, The Scandalous Chronicle: Or, Ballad of characters. Written for the Use of the Poets, and proper to be sung at their next session. Dublin, Reprinted in the Year 1726.

12mo.

Six unsigned leaves.

[2 pp.], 3–12 pp.; the British Museum copy is heavily cropped and pagination is visible only for p. 3.

Only 'The Scandalous Chronicle, &c. To the Tune of, To all you Ladies now at Land, &c' (drop-title, [p. 9]), pp. [9–12], is Popiana. Yale has a copy of *The Bath*, 1726, with a London imprint, but it does not contain 'The Scandalous Chronicle'.

WORK: A. *Odyssey.*

In the thirteen stanzas of 'The Scandalous Chronicle' Flash, a beau and poet, and Lucia express their love for each other before going to a play. Pope appears only in the third stanza:

> E'er I forsake my *Flash,* (said she)
> *Johnson* shall grow refin'd;

> Pert *Cibber* his own *Errors* see,
>   And to new Plays prove kind;
> *Brome* be no more a Drudge esteem'd,
> Nor *Pope* an undertaker deem'd,
>   *With a fa, la, &c.*

Welsted, Theobald, Morrice, Bond, and Cooke are also mentioned.

March, 1726 (*Monthly Catalogue*)

Theobald, Lewis. Shakespeare restored: Or, A Specimen Of The Many Errors, As Well Committed, as Unamended, by Mr. Pope In his Late Edition of this Poet. Designed Not only to correct the said Edition, but to restore the True Reading of Shakespeare in all the Editions ever yet publish'd. By Mr. Theobald. —Laniatum Corpore toto / Deiphobum vidi & lacerum crudeliter Ora, / Ora, manusque ambas, —Virg. London: Printed for R. Francklin under Tom's, J. Woodman and D. Lyon under Will's, Covent-Garden, and C. Davis in Hatton-Garden. M.DCC. XXVI.

4to.
A in three leaves, B–z⁴, Aa–Cc⁴, Dd in one leaf.
[6 pp.], [i]–viii, [1]–132, [133]–94 pp.; p. 54 misnumbered p. 55 and vice versa.

Yale has a copy identical with the above but with the imprint: 'Printed for R. Francklin and T. Woodman in Russel-Street, Covent Garden, Charles Davis in Hatton-Garden, and S. Chapman in Pall-Mall. M.DCC.XXVI'. I have not seen the second edition, 1740 (Jones, p. 351).

WORK: A. Pope's edition of Shakespeare.

For a full account see Jones, pp. 61–99.
    This 'attack', if such it can be called, never descends to the purely personal and is never abusive, but the title-page suggests its offensiveness. Theobald, as Johnson remarked, 'detected his [Pope's] deficiencies with all the insolence of victory' (*Lives of the English Poets*, ed. George Birkbeck Hill (Oxford, 1905), III. 138).
    Theobald is careful to include praise of Pope:

I have so great an Esteem for Mr. *Pope*, and so high an Opinion of his Genius and Excellencies, that I beg to be excused from
the least Intention of derogating from his Merits, in this Attempt
to restore the true Reading of SHAKESPEARE. Tho' I confess a
Veneration, almost rising to Idolatry, for the Writings of this
inimitable Poet, I would be very loth even to do *him* Justice at
the Expence of *that other* Gentleman's Character. (p. iii)

He makes quite clear, however, what he thinks of Pope's edition.
Having selected *Hamlet* for his examination here, he says,

If *HAMLET* has its Faults, so has every other of the Plays; and I
therefore only offer it as a Precedent of the same Errors, which,
every body will be convinced before I have done, possess every
Volume and every Play in this Impression. (p. vii)

The character of Theobald's book, consisting as it does of an examination of the text of *Hamlet* (pp. [1]–132) and an appendix discussing other plays (pp. [133]–94), makes summary impossible. See
the discussion in Sherburn, pp. 244–7; Thomas R. Lounsbury, *The
Text of Shakespeare* (New York, 1906), pp. 155–75 (highly prejudiced);
and James Sutherland, ' "The Dull Duty of an Editor" ', *RES*, xxi
(1945), 202–15. Several examples of Theobald's insulting remarks
must suffice here.

Pope had read *Hamlet*, i. v. 77, as,

　　　　　Unhouzzled, unanointed, unanel'd,

and defined 'unanointed' as 'without extream unction', and 'unanel'd' as 'no knell rung' (p. 52).

I am very much afraid (and as apt to believe I shall prove it,
to the Satisfaction of every Judge, before this Note is ended;)
that this Passage is neither rightly read, nor, as it is read, rightly
explained throughout. (p. 52)

Theobald first corrects 'unhouzzled' to 'unhousel'd'.

This, however, is but a trivial Slip, in comparison with the next
that offers it self. I don't pretend to know what *Glossaries* Mr.
POPE may have consulted, and trusts to; but whose soever they
are, I am sure their Comment is very *singular* upon the Word I
am about to mention. (p. 53)

He then demonstrates that 'unanel'd' means 'not having the extream
Unction' (p. 53). He further corrects Pope's 'unanointed' to 'dis-
appointed', meaning 'unabsolv'd' (p. 54, misnumbered p. 55).

Pope had read *Hamlet*, iii. iv. 92,

　　　　　In the rank sweat of an incestuous bed.

If we go back, however, to the second *folio* Edition (which is one

of those collated by the *Editor*) we have there a *various Reading*,
of which he is not pleased to take the least Notice, tho' as I verily
believe, it restores us the Poet's own Word. (p. 104)

He then alters Pope's 'incestuous' to 'enseamed' (p. 104).

September 24, 1726 (*Evening Post*, September 24, 1726)

Whartoniana: Or, Miscellanies, In Verse and Prose By The
Wharton Family, And Several other Persons of Distinction.
Never before Published. Volume I. London: Printed in the Year,
1727. (Price 5s.)

12mo.
Two unsigned leaves, A–B⁴, two leaves, the first signed K3, c–Q⁶, R⁴.
[4 pp.], [i]–vii, [viii] book-list, [1]–84, [8 pp.], [93]–156, [2 pp.],
159–85 pp., [3 pp.]

The Dedication, A1–4, is signed, A4r, and dated, 'E. Curll. Sep 9.
1726.' There is a second volume, but only the first contains any Popiana, a single item entitled 'To Mr. Pope, on his second Subscription
for Homer'.

WORK: A. *Odyssey*.

CHARGES: 1. Pope venal; 2. Pope a faithless friend.

A1   Your *Pen* with MARLBOROUGH's *Sword* is much the same,
      He *fought*, you *write*, for *Profit*, more than *Fame*:
      His *Eagles* after Grants and *Pensions* flew,
      And all your *Laurels* from *Subscriptions* grew:
2   His *Friendship* too, like yours, was *false*, and *feign'd*,
      No longer *lasting* than his Ends were *gain'd*:
      Thus then at once, *we* both your Deeds *rehearse*,
      Gold was his *God* of *War*, your *God* of *Verse*.   (p. 144)

January 12, 1727 (*Evening Post*, January 12, 1727)

[Haywood, Eliza?] Memoirs Of The Court of Lilliput. Written by Captain Gulliver. Containing an Account of the Intrigues, and some other particular Transactions of that Nation, omitted in the two Volumes of his Travels. Published by Lucas Bennet, with a Preface, shewing how these Papers fell into his hands. London: Printed for J. Roberts, near the Oxford-Arms in Warwick-Lane. M.DCC.XXVII. (Price 2s.)

8vo in half-sheets.

A–X⁴.

[2 pp.], [iii]–viii, 1–159 pp., [160] blank.

A second edition was advertised in *The Evening Post*, February 7, 1727. Teerink, 1221, lists as well a Dublin edition, 1727. I have located neither.

Pope in the *Dunciad* (*Twick*. v. 208) attributed this to Mrs Haywood, but Whicher, pp. 119–20, finds it quite different from her other works, and does not believe it is hers. 'The Publisher to the Reader' is signed, p. viii, 'Lucas Bennet', probably a pseudonym, since Bennet claims to be a childhood friend of Gulliver.

CHARGES: 1. Pope deformed and impotent; 2. Pope a plagiarist.

In Chapter 1 Gulliver is attempting to reassure Clefgarin, a Maid of Honour, with whom he frequently talks alone.

> And besides, the inequality of our Stature rightly consider'd, ought to be for us as full a Security from Slander, as that between Mr. *P—pe*, and those *great* Ladies who do nothing without him; admit him to their Closets, their Bed-sides, consult him in the choice of their Servants, their Garments, and make no scruple of putting them on or off before him: Every body knows they are Women of strict Virtue, and he a harmless Creature, who has neither the Will, nor Power of doing any farther Mischief than with his Pen, and that he seldom draws, but in defence of their Beauty; or to second their Revenge against some presuming Prude, who boasts a Superiority of Charms: or in privately transcribing and passing for his own, the elaborate Studies of some more learned Genius. (pp. 16–17)

1727 (?)

Gulliver Decypher'd: Or Remarks On a late Book, intitled, Travels Into Several Remote Nations of the World. By Capt. Lemuel Gulliver. Vindicating The Reverend Dean on whom it is maliciously Father'd. With Some probable Conjectures concerning the Real Author. Sit mihi fas audita loqui: sit numine vestro / Pandere res alta terra & caligine mersas. Virg. Aen. 6. London: Printed for J. Roberts near the Oxford Arms in Warwick Lane: And Sold by the Booksellers of London and Westminster. (Price 1s.)

8vo in half-sheets.
Two unsigned leaves, a⁴, B–G⁴, one unsigned leaf.
[2 pp.], v–xii, [xiii–xiv], 1–49 pp., [50] blank.

This is Teerink 1216. The copy I have used is *BM* C116 b2(1), Pope's own copy with annotations in his hand. Pope has marked with an 'X' in the margin many of the passages referring to himself or to Swift, Arbuthnot, and Gay. I have also examined the Bodleian copy, Godwyn Pamphlets 1398, which lacks G4 and the last leaf. There is a second edition in the Bodleian; the title-page is the same except for 'To which is prefix'd a Prefatory Discourse concerning Decyphering. The Second Edition, with a complete Key' added after 'Author'. It is the same printing, the first two leaves having been removed and a double leaf inserted bearing the new title-page and the Key. The Key lists Pope four times and makes the references to him certain.

WORKS: A. Homer; B. *First Psalm*; C. *What D' Ye Call It*; D. *Three Hours after Marriage*.

CHARGES: 1. Pope ignorant of Greek; 2. Pope blasphemous; 3. Pope obscene.

Much of this pamphlet is devoted to 'proving' that Swift could not have written *Gulliver's Travels*. There is an account of Pope's friendship with Arbuthnot and Gay and of the Homer, marked by Pope with X's and several underscorings.

A1   The next Person our physician [Arbuthnot] grew intimate with, was a little deformed cross-grained fellow, but very ingenious and witty, and in great favour with the *Chief Secretary*. His talent was Rhyming, and 'tis said he raised a great fortune by turning an old Collection of Ballads into the language of the Country,

tho' some are so malicious as to say, that he did not really understand them himself, but got certain Druids to explain them, and
so put them off for his own; this Wight, who they named *Peter*
[Pope], had an intimate friend [Gay], a very harmonious fellow,
and an excellent Bagpipe player, to which he us'd to set sonnets
of his own making in the Pastoral kind; he was the freed man of
a certain Lady of great Quality, who had given him his liberty
for several good Services; and her Ladyship being after troubled
with fits of the Mother, had often occasion for Dr. *Johnny*, who
then being in vogue, no body could be modishly sick without
him. You may be sure sympathy of Disposition and so favourable an opportunity soon made an intimate Friendship between
Peter, his friend, and our witty Doctor; accordingly they made
an Alliance offensive and defensive between each other. The
Doctor was to cry them up at Court, and in return *Peter* was to
make *Lyricks* in *his* praise, and his Friend was frequently to persuade his Lady that she was sick, in order to promote *his* Business. Thus they went on prosperously thriving like Jesuits...

(pp. 3–4)

He quotes a couplet (from *The Confederates*, q.v.) referring to *Three
Hours after Marriage*,

These are the *Wags*, who boldly did adventure,
To club a Farce by *Tripartite* Indenture.   (p. 1)

And he tells us later that Pope, Gay, and Arbuthnot, to revenge their
injuries together,

produced a kind of Satyr or Stage-performance, called by the
moderns a FArce.

Here each Party, had a fine Opportunity of being reveng'd
of their several adversaries; *Peter* [Pope] abused the Witlings of
the Town, for not having Sense enough to taste his Mock-
Heroicks and his Friend's Pastorals ... (p. 7)

There is an ironic reference to *The What D' Ye Call It*:

... there are more Fools than People of Judgment in the World;
therefore a famous poet [Pope] was certainly in the right, when
giving an Account why—*What-d'y'call it* was hiss'd off the Stage,
—*D—n them*, said he, *they have not Wit enough to take it*; for really
the Farce was allow'd to be a very *uncommon* Performance.

(pp. 44–5)

He mentions the *First Psalm*:

He [Swift] had an excellent Knack of composing merry Odes
upon Matters of State, and of burlesquing the Hymns that were

dedicated to their Deities; tho' some Writers attribute these rather to his Friend *Peter* [Pope], since more consistent with his Character as a Ballad-singer, and as not being of the Pontifical College, tho' he professed himself to be one of that Sect, whose way of Worship was most absurd and superstitious ... (p. 16)

He quotes loosely from *Gulliver's Travels*, Book II, Chapter I, the passage, 'This made me reflect upon the fair skins of our English ladies, who appear so beautiful to us, only because they are of our own size ...' and says in a note,

3   The common Opinion is, That most of this Part of the Work is *Peter*'s, from the Touches of Obscenity that are frequently met with; and particularly in the foregoing Passage. (p. 32)

March 16, 1728 (*Monthly Chronicle*)

[Oldmixon, John.] An Essay on Criticism; As it regards Design, Thought, and Expression, In Prose and Verse. By the Author of the Critical History of England. London: Printed for J. Pemberton, at the Golden-Buck in Fleet-Street. MDCCXXVIII. 1s. 6d.

8vo.
One unsigned leaf, B⁸–G⁸.
[2 pp.], 1–94 pp., [95–6] blank.

The *Essay* was included in:

May 21, 1728 (*Monthly Chronicle*)

The Critical History of England, Ecclesiastical and Civil: Wherein The Errors of the Monkish Writers, and others before the Reformation, are Expos'd and Corrected. As are also the Deficiency and Partiality Of Later Historians. And particularly Notice is taken of The History of the Grand Rebellion, And Mr. Echard's History of England. With Remarks on some Objections made to Bishop Burnet's History of his Times, and the Characters of Archdeacon Echard's Authors. Also an Explanation of a Passage in the Bishop's History relating to King William, which has generally been misunderstood. The Third Edition Corrected

and Improved. To which is added, An Essay on Criticism; as it regards Design, Thought, and Expression, in Prose and Verse. London: Printed for J. Pemberton, at the Buck and Sun against St. Dunstan's Church in Fleetstreet. MDCCXXVIII.

8vo.

a⁸, one unsigned leaf [title-page], b–f⁸, g in seven leaves, b–y⁸ [b3 second count incorrectly signed a3].

[4 pp.], i–xi, [xii], [2 pp.], 1–94, 1–309 pp., [310] blank, [4 pp.] book-list.

This is the copy in the Cambridge University Library. The second volume does not concern us. The *Essay* occupies b⁸–g⁷, and has its own title-page as in the separate edition above, but omitting 'is. 6d.' The separate printing is reproduced in *An Essay on Criticism*, ed. R. J. Madden, c.s.b., The Augustan Reprint Society, Nos. 107–8 (Los Angeles, 1964).

WORKS: A. *Essay on Criticism*; B. Homer.

In this long and rambling essay there are several incidental hits at Pope.

After discussing briefly Horace's, Roscommon's, and Buckingham's arts of poetry, Oldmixon says:

> I dare not say any Thing of the last *Essay on Criticism* in Verse, but that if any more curious Reader has discovered in it something new, which is not in *Dryden's Prefaces, Dedications*, and his *Essay* on *Dramatick Poetry*, not to mention the *French* Criticks, I should be very glad to have the Benefit of the Discovery.
>
> (p. 2)

Oldmixon has several objections to the diction of Pope's prose in the Homer:

> I take *brisk* in our Tongue to be to *lively*, as *pert* is to *witty*: But I cannot depend on my own Judgement; the Translator of *Homer* having used *Briskness* in the same Sense as Doctor *Felton* uses it: *Heaven and Earth became engaged in the Subject, by which it rises to a great Importance, and is hastened forward into the briskest Scenes of Action.* If that Author could bear the least Objection to any Thing that belongs to him, I would ask the Reader whether he does not fancy there is some Affectation in the Expression.
>
> (p. 57)

A little later he warns that people are apt to

> mistake Affectation for Beauty, and I wonder the Translator of

Homer should give them the least Countenance by his Example; for I am very much deceiv'd if there is a more affected Period in the *English* Tongue than what follows: *Nothing is more lively and* Picturesque *than the* Attitude *of* Patroclus *is describ'd in* [*sic*]; *The* Pathetick *of his Speech is finely contrasted by the* Fierte *of* Achilles. [*Iliad*, XVI. Note on the opening lines.] Again, *there's something inexpressibly* riant *in the* Compartments of *Achilles*'s Shield.

(pp. 72–3)

He is careful to observe, however,

I do not insinuate any thing to depreciate the Translator of *Homer*'s excellent Performance, which, as I have observ'd, has the Merit of the most pure and harmonious Diction and Versification; but to hint a little of the Confusion of our Taste . . .

(p. 69)

He repeated, more strongly, his objections in *The Arts of Logick And Rhetorick*, 1728, q.v.

April 18, 1728 (*Monthly Chronicle*)

A Collection Of Several Curious Pieces Lately Inserted in the Daily Journal. Containing, I. Observations on some of the Articles that have been published several Times in the News-Papers, for the Encouragement of Voluntier Sailors. II. The Letter to the Author of the Daily Journal of March 18. signed Philo-Mauri, relating to the third Volume of Mr. Pope's Miscellanies. III. The Letter of Friday March 29. with Animadversions on Mr. Pope's Project of erecting a Council of Six; togegether [*sic*] with the Character of Thersites in his Translations of Homer. IV. On the same Subject, animadverting on Pope and Company for the Licences taken by that Partnership both on the Living and Dead Moderns. V. The Monkey: Being the excellent Letter of April 9. of a Tenth Species of Profundity, omitted, through Bashfulness, by the Doctor. With the much admired Satire, intitled, The Devil's Last Game. VI. The Twickenham Auction: Or, An Hypercritical Collection of Beauties scatter'd up and down the Rape of the Lock, Windsor Forest, and other celebrated Pieces of a certain inexorable Critic. VII. A Copy of

Verses, said to be omitted, by Accident, in the last New Miscellany. VIII. The Letter from the Honest Sailor of Woolwich, in Relation to the Debate now depending about Encouraging that Brave and Useful Body of Men, the Sailors of Great Britain. IX. The Competition: Or, Rival Opera's. A Song. With the Notes prefix'd. X. A Receipt for a Running-Frush, in the Foot of a Horse. In a Letter to a Friend. XI. The List of the Royal Navy of Great Britain, as inserted in the Daily Journal of April 8. With some necessary Alterations, occasion'd by the Arrival of Part of Sir Charles Wager's Squadron from the Coasts of Spain, &c. Collected and Republished on Occasion of the great Demand made for the respective Papers in which they were originally inserted, and which are now no where else to be met with. London, Printed for T. Warner, at the Black-Boy in Pater-Noster-Row; J. Jackson, near St. James's; N. Blandford, at Charing-Cross; and H. Whitridge, at the Royal-Exchange. 1728. (Price Six-Pence.)

Folio.

One unsigned leaf, B–D², E in one leaf.

[2 pp.], [3]–16 pp., p. 15 misnumbered 13.

Nos. II, III, IV, VI, and VII attack Pope. All but No. VII Pope attributed to James Moore Smythe. No. VII is by Aaron Hill (*Twick.* v. 209). It has been suggested that Pope himself was the author of No. II (*Twick.* v. 209; but see Ault, pp. 200–1). Nos. II–VII are reprinted in *A Compleat Collection*, 1728, q.v.

WORKS: A. Epigram on *Cato*; B. Pope–Swift *Miscellanies*.

CHARGES: I. Pope plagiarized from Moore Smythe; 2. Pope plagiarized from Rowe; 3. Pope and Swift satirized Bishop Burnet; 4. Pope deformed.

The letter of March 18 (No. II) signed 'Philo-Mauri' (p. 4) accuses Pope of plagiarizing lines from James Moore Smythe's *The Rival Modes*, a charge which Pope refutes in the *Dunciad* (*Twick.* v. 33–4).

> Upon reading the third Volume of *Pope's* Miscellanies, I found five Lines, which I thought excellent; and happening to praise them afterwards in a mix'd Company, a Gentleman present, immediately produced a modern Comedy, publish'd last Year, where were the same Verses, almost to a Tittle. I was a good

M

Deal out of Countenance, to find that I had been so eloquent in praise of a Felony ... The Lines are these ...

> A *Youth* of *Frolicks*, and *Old Age* of *Cards*;
> *Fair* to *no Purpose*, *artful* to *no End*;
> *Young* without *Lovers*; *old* without a *Friend*:
> A *Fop*, their *Passion*; but their *Prize*, a *Sot*;
> *Alive*, ridiculous; and *dead*, forgot!

But my Confusion was vastly aggravated, when the same Gentleman, pursuing his Triumph, turned me to the Discourse at the Head of the Third Volume, where the Author of these admirable Lines is ingeniously liken'd to a Frog in Poetry ...

(p. 4)

Pope had granted Moore Smythe permission to use the six lines (which later became ll. 243–8 in *Of the Characters of Women*) in Act II of his play *The Rival Modes*, 1727, which Pope presumably saw in manuscript. He afterwards withdrew permission a month before the play was acted or printed, but Moore Smythe insisted on keeping them. Pope published them himself a year later in *To Mrs. M.B. on her Birth-Day* in *Miscellanies. The Last Volume*. For this poem's very complicated bibliography see *Twick*. VI. 246–7 and Ault, 365–6. Other scraps of verse are quoted by Moore Smythe in his play without any attribution, but Pope may reasonably have thought that there was a difference between quoting printed sources without acknowledgement and quoting from an unpublished poem (Ault, 200–1). Griffith, 1 [139], suggests that Pope may have withdrawn his permission on learning that Theobald had written the Prologue for Moore Smythe's play. The charge was repeated in *A Compleat Collection*, 1728.

The letter of March 29 (No. III) is sufficiently described on the title-page.

AB2   The letter of April 3 (No. IV) signed Philo-Ditto (p. 6) charges Pope and Swift with

> publicly taking to themselves an *Epigram* of the late Mr. *Rowe's*, singly upon the Merit of putting one low and foolish Word into the Title of that *Epigram* ... (p. 6)

The reference is to the 'Epigram on Cato', the authorship of which is uncertain; the word inserted is 'P—st' (*Twick*. VI. 99–100).

B3   *The Memoirs of a Parish Clerk* is called 'a very dull and unjust Abuse of an excellent Person, who wrote in Defence of our Religion and Constitution, and who has been dead many Years [Bishop Burnet]' (p. 6). Pope refuted this charge in the *Dunciad* (*Twick*. v. 34). On this letter see *Dunciad* A, ii. 46, n.

In the letter of April 16 (No. vii), Hill's 'A Copy of Verses, said to be omitted, by Accident, in the Last New Miscellany', the devil complains to the guardian angel that though he had been promised a free hand, Pope is tempting the whole world into virtue. The sting is in the angel's reply:

4
> Never fear, cry'd the Angel,—my Promise once given,
> You are safe, for *this Time*, from the Outguards of Heaven;
> *Pope* is *gelt*, in his Youth, for his Countrymen's Crimes,
> And his Lustre dim'd down, to the *Dusk* of the Times:
> God sent *Pain*, and *Impertinence*, Wit to controul,
> Gave the *Devil* his Body, and bid *Swift* take his Soul.   (p. 7)

The letter of April 5 (No. vi), 'The Twickenham Auction', consists of phrases from Pope's verse displayed as curiosities in a collection on view at Twickenham, e.g.

> 7. Adamantine Lungs—*as good as new.*
> 8. A Vermilion Prore—*Dutch.* [*Iliad* ii. 778]

This letter is used in *Durgen*, 1728, pp. 25–7, q.v. It is quoted by Geoffrey Tillotson in his *Augustan Studies* (London, 1961), pp. 83–4.

May 11, 1728 (*Monthly Chronicle*)

[Cooke, Thomas, and Mottley, John.] Penelope, A Dramatic Opera, As it is Acted at the New Theatre In The Hay-Market. London: Printed, and Sold by Tho. Green, at the Corner of Spring-Garden, near Charing-Cross, and Charles Davis, in Pater-noster.Row. 1728. [Price 1s. 6d.

8vo in half-sheets.
Four unsigned leaves, fifteen leaves of music score, c–g⁴, h in three leaves. g2 misnumbered 'f2'.
[38 pp.], [17]–60 pp., [61] Epilogue, [62] blank.

Cooke collaborated with John Mottley. *Penelope* was first performed at the Little Theatre in the Haymarket, May 8, 1728 (Allardyce Nicoll, *A History of English Drama, 1660–1900*, 3rd ed. [Cambridge, 1952], ii. 346).

WORK: A. *Odyssey*.

A   In the 'Preface', in the course of defending his transformation of the story into farce and opera, Cooke attacks Pope:

> ... the *English* Translator of the Eighteenth Book of the *Odyssey* says, *it may be thought that* HOMER *is the Father of another Kind of Poetry, I mean the Farce*. We hope it will not be thought Matter of great Wonder, that a Farce should be extracted from *Homer*, since so considerable a Person as his Translator has made him Parent of that sort of Writing. It may not be unworthy our Enquiry into the Reasons which might induce him to be of this Opinion. Perhaps he thought it farcical that any Woman should be sayed to preserve her Chastity for such a Length of Time; or that such a Number of Princes as her Wooers, would for so many Years make such Fools of themselves. He may possibly think *Ulysses* himself, at his Return, made a Figure a little below Comedy; and indeed we cannot help concuring with his Sentiments, when we read the following Lines.
>
> > Propt on a Staff a Beggar old and bare,
> > In Rags dishonest, flutt'ring with the Air.
> >
> > POPE [*Odyssey*, XVII. 228–9]
>
> We should be very glad to know whether he or his Rags were dishonest, poor King! (second unsigned leaf, r and v).

See Pope's note to *Dunciad* A, i. 68.

May 13, 1728 (*Monthly Chronicle*)

D'Anvers, Caleb [pseud.] The Twickenham Hotch-Potch, For the Use of the Rev. Dr. Swift, Alexander Pope, Esq; and Company. Being A Sequel To The Beggars Opera, &c. Containing, I. The State of Poetry, and Fate of Poets, in the Reign of King Charles the IId. II. Seriosities and Comicalities, by Peter Henning, a Dutchman. III. Two Dozen of Infallible Maxims, for Court and City. IV. The Present War among Authors, viz. Swift, Pope, Theobald, Rolli, Voltaire, Parson B—dy, and Mr. Ozell. V. The Rival Actresses, viz. Mrs. O—d, Mrs. P—r, Mrs. B—h, Miss Y—ger, and Miss Polly Peachum. VI. A Poetical Catalogue of Polly Peachum's Gallants. VII. An Epistle from Signora F—na to a Lady. VIII. A True Copy of Polly Peachum's Opera.

Also, her Panegyrick. Written by Caleb D'Anvers. Puissant Pom-
pey planted Phrygian-Powers, / And topsy-turvy turn'd the
Tyrian-Towers. Lee's Art of Rising in Poetry. London: Printed
for J. Roberts in Warwick-Lane. 1728. (Price One Shilling)

8vo in half-sheets.
One leaf unsigned. B–H⁴, I², K in one leaf.
[2 pp.], [i]–vii, [viii] blank, [1]–2, [3]–54 pp.
Teerink 1286.

Not likely to be by Nicholas Amhurst, editor of *The Craftsman* whose
pseudonym was 'Caleb D'Anvers'. Straus, p. 286, lists this as a Curll
publication.

WORKS: A. Pope's edition of Shakespeare; B. Pope–Swift *Miscellanies*.

CHARGE: 1. Pope a Catholic.

A   Mostly concerned with Gay and *The Beggar's Opera*, the pamphlet
reprints, pp. 26–34, Theobald's letter to *Mist's Weekly Journal*, April
27, 1728, under the title 'Pope Corrected, Not Amended'. Theobald
here argues that,

> In my Attempts to restore *Shakespeare*, I had laid open some
> Defects of *his* Edition . . . But to set any Thing right, after Mr.
> *Pope* had adjusted the Whole, was a Presumption not to be for-
> given! (p. 26)

Nevertheless he may have stimulated Pope to strive for

> some Degree of *Accuracy* in his next Edition of that Poet, which
> we are to have in a few months: And then we shall see whether
> we owed the Errors of the former Edition to *Indiligence*, or his
> *Inexperience* in the Author. And as my *Remarks* upon the whole
> Works of *Shakespeare* shall closely attend upon the Publication of
> his Edition, I will venture to promise, without Arrogance, that
> I will then give about *five hundred* more fair *Emendations*, that shall
> escape *him* and all his *Assistants*. (p. 34)

Theobald reveals, however, total insensitivity to the problem of integrity of style which engages the true writer and so qualifies himself
for enrolment among the Dunces. In defending himself against the
criticism in the *Peri Bathous* of three passages from *The Double Falsehood*, he proceeds to justify each figure largely on the authority of
similar images and expressions in Shakespeare.

Theobald's letter is reprinted in *A Compleat Collection Of all the Verses
* . . . , 1728, pp. 40–8.

B 1   Item I of the title-page has an attack on Pope and his friends, 'an impertinent *Scotch*-Quack, A Profligate *Irish*-Dean, The Lacquey of a Superanuated Dutchess, and a little virulent Papist' (p. vi).

> Their own *Example*, strengthens all their *Law*,
> They are, *Themselves*, the *Bathos* that they *draw.*   (p. vii)

B   Item II has its own title-page, at the foot of which is a glance at the Pope–Swift preface to the *Miscellanies*.

> This Piece is Genuine, though I must honestly own, it is made publick without the Consent either of Mr. *Alexander Pope*, or Mr. Dean *Swift.* (p. [1])

A   Item IV is one of the 'Two Dozen of Useful Maxims':

> Fierce is the present *War* among Authors, *viz. Swift* has maul'd *Theobald*, but *Theobald* has maul'd *Pope.* (p. 4)

May 28, 1728 (*Monthly Chronicle*)

[Curll, Edmund.] A Compleat Key To The Dunciad. How easily Two Wits agree, / One finds the Poem; One the Key. London, Printed for A. Dodd. 1728. (Price 6d.)

8vo.

A⁸, B in three leaves.

[2 pp.], [iii]–vi, [7]–22 pp.

There were two other editions. (See next entry.)

Curll's *The Curliad*, 1729, which he signed, establishes his authorship of the *Key*. For his text of the *Dunciad* he probably used either 1728a or 1728b, since his reading of A, i. 86, is not that of 1728c, and his readings of A, ii. 170, and A, ii. 230, are not those of 1728d.

WORKS: A. *Rape of the Lock*; B. *First Psalm*; C. *Homer*; D. *Dunciad.*

CHARGES: 1. Pope uses Scripture blasphemously; 2. Pope equivocated over his authorship of the *First Psalm*.

D   'To the Public' (pp. [iii]–vi) on 'The Publisher to the Reader' claims that Pope 'is both the *Publisher* and Author of this Patch-Work Medley' (p. iv), and ridicules the assertion that the poem took six years of the author's life:

> ... He must be a very great *DUNCE*, who, from a Plan so extensive, could not have raised a much nobler Structure in Six Days. (p. iv)

He argues that Pope has mangled for his purposes the closing quotation from La Bruyère (pp. v–vi).

Since the information offered by the *Key* has been put to the best possible use in Mr Sutherland's edition of the *Dunciad*, I shall attempt here only to offer a few of the more interesting comments relevant to Popiana and to summarize Curll's efforts.

His principal endeavour is to supply the names that are indicated in 1728 only by letters and asterisks. He is remarkably successful. He does not attempt to fill up the following names; I supply in parentheses the names that Pope (in some cases not quite certainly) intended and note whether Curll offered an identification in the *Key*'s second edition a week later.

i. 244	(Heidegger) Given in the second edition
ii. 118	(Breval, Besaleel, Bond)
ii. 136	(Dunton) Given, incorrectly, in the second edition as 'Dennis'
ii. 195	(Rolli) Given in the second edition
ii. 286	1728 a–f (Diaper) Given in the second edition
ii. 287	(Roome and Whatley) Given, incorrectly, in the second edition as 'Edward Young and Thomas Newcome'
ii. 380	(James Pitt?)
ii. 381	*T—s* (Travers)
ii. 382	(Motteux)
iii. 98, n.	(Apelles)
iii. 138	(Ward)
iii. 145	(Mrs Haywood and Mrs Thomas?) 'Mrs. Haywood' given correctly in the second edition where 'Trotter' is given for 'Thomas'
iii. 299	(Peers and Potentates in *EC* MS) Given in the second edition as 'Kings and Princesses'
iii. 180	(Hearne) Given in the second edition

He also misidentifies the following. I give first Curll's guess, and, in parentheses, the correct identification.

i. 126	Brome (Blome) Corrected in the second edition
i. 250	Bond and Higgons (Banks and Howard) Howard corrected in the second edition
ii. 155	Mrs. Mary Hearne (Mrs Hayward)
ii. 283	Walter Harte (Aaron Hill) 'Others say, this is a Compliment to *Aaron Hill*, Esq;'
ii. 293	Woodward (Welsted)
ii. 338	George Herbert (Hoadley or Henley) Corrected in the

second edition where Hoadley and Henley are both suggested

ii. 382   Shippen (Selkirk may possibly have been intended)
iii. 16   Dennis (Shadwell)
iii. 146   Milbourne (Mitchell)
iii. 188   Blackmore (Henry Baker) Corrected in the second edition

It is evident from this that Curll guessed correctly the large majority of names. He was ideally placed, of course, to understand references to Grub-street, but his success would suggest that the 1728 *Dunciad* was not quite so impossibly obscure as is often assumed by the modern reader.

Amusingly enough, Curll would alter the 'Glad chains' of A, i. 86, to 'Gold Chains' (p. 8). This emendation might have offered Pope sufficient excuse for his Scriblerian note without the necessity of producing the 'Gold chains' edition, Griffith 200, if Mr Sutherland's guess about this edition is correct (*Twick.* v. 3). Curll omitted this remark from the second edition.

There is very little direct abuse of Pope; Curll is too busy annotating. He does mistake Brome for Blome in A, i. 126, oddly because it is '*Bl*—' in all editions Curll could have used, but he takes the opportunity to attack the Homer:

C   This last Poetical Ecclesiastic, likewise dug deep in *Eustathius*'s Commentaries, &c to supply Mr. *Pope* with critical Notes for his *Iliad* of *Homer*. And was also one of the Journey-men employed by Mr. *Pope*, as *Undertaker-General*, in Translating the *Odyssey*.
(p. 9)

His main charge against Pope is the blasphemous use of Scripture. He adduces A, i. 47–8, and calls 'Let there be darkness' (A, iii. 337, 1728 a–f)

A 1   a Blasphemous Ridicule ... Mr. *Pope* was at this once before, in his *Rape of the Locke* [III. 46]. (p. 18)

He quotes, p. 19, from Blackmore's *Essays*, II, 1717, pp. 269–70, q.v., and explains about the publication of the *First Psalm*:

B 2   This profane Version of the *First Psalm*, was handed about by Mr. *Pope* in the *Lent*-Season, and printed from an Original Copy in his own hand Writing. He put out an Advertisement in the *Post-Man* offering *Throe* [*sic*] Guineas reward to discover the Person who sent it to the Press, but this was only an evasive Feint, for Mrs. *Burleigh* in *Amen-Corner*, was the Publisher of it, and was ready to produce the Manuscript under his own hand,

but neither He, nor any one for Him, ever paid the *Premium*, or said one word more about it when he found it could be proved upon him. (p. 19)

The pamphlet adds a 'Postscript' which reprints, pp. 20–2 (freely adapted), the Puppet-Show Epilogue from *Homerides*, 1715, and ends with Curll's warning:

> ... this Poem is to mimic a *Weather-Glass* and vary every Impression as the Author's Malice *Increases* to one, or *abates* to *Another*. (p. 22)

June 4, 1728 (*Evening Post*, June 4, 1728)

[Curll, Edmund.] A Compleat Key To The Dunciad. With a Character of Mr. Pope's Profane Writings. By Sir Richard Blackmore Kt. M.D. The Second Edition. How easily Two Wits agree, / One finds the Satire; One the Key. London, Printed for E. Curll in the Strand. 1728 (Price 6d.) Where may be had, The Dunciad. (Price 1s.)

8vo.

A⁸, B⁴.

[2 pp.], [iii]–vi, [7]–22 pp., [23–4] book-list.

CHARGE: 1. Pope bribed by the Duchess of Buckinghamshire to write a satire against Ward in the pillory.

Curll's important changes and additions I have recorded above. Several new errors may be noted here; I give in parentheses the correct identification:

ii. 136   Dennis (Dunton)
ii. 140   Titus Oates (Tutchin) Curll had given Tutchin in the first edition
ii. 287   Edward Young and Thomas Newcome (Roome and Whatley)
iii. 145   Mrs. Trotter (Mrs Thomas)

He also alters the first edition guess at ii. 141, 'Roper', to 'Ridpath'; Pope in 1729 included them both.

The note on A, iii. 26,

> As thick as eggs at *W—d* in Pillory,

had read in the first edition of the *Key*:

Who had not one thrown at him, having committed no other
Crime than Writing a merry Burlesque Poem ...

In the second edition the note is altered to,

I   Against whom Mr. *Pope* wrote a Satire, to please a certain
Duchess, while he was under his Punishment; the greatest Act
of Barbarity. (p. 16)

Pope used this in his 1729 note, and Edward Ward took up the charge
in *Durgen*, 1729.

The Blackmore 'Character' of the title-page is the quotation from
his *Essays*, II, 1717, as in the first edition, here on pp. 19–20.

The book-list at the end is obviously part of the attack, including
Pope's letters to Cromwell, the *Court Poems*, etc.

There was a third edition:

July 2, 1728 (Straus, p. 286)

[Curll, Edmund.] A Compleat Key To The Dunciad. With A
Character of Mr. Pope's Profane Writings. By Sir Richard
Blackmore Kt. M.D. The Third Edition. How easily Two Wits
agree, / One finds the Satire; One the Key. London, Printed
for E. Curll in the Strand. 1728. (Price 6 d.) Where may be had,
The Dunciad, The Progress of Dulness, and The Popiad. (Price
1 s. Each)

8vo.
A⁸, B⁴.
[2 pp.], [iii]–vi, [7]–22 pp., [2 pp.] book-list.

This is the Bodleian copy. The third edition contains only one change
of any importance from the second: Woolston in iii. 149 has been
changed to Whiston.

June 1, 1728 (*London Evening Post*, June 1, 1728)

A Popp upon Pope: Or a True and Faithful Account Of a late
Horrid and Barbarous Whipping, Committed on the Body of
A. Pope, a Poet, as he was innocently walking in Ham-Walks,
near the River of Thames, meditating Verses for the Good of the
Publick. Supposed to have been done by Two evil dispos'd Per-

sons, out of Spite and Revenge, for a harmless Lampoon which the said Poet had writ upon them. London: Printed for A. Moore, near St. Paul's. 1728.

Folio.

Three unsigned leaves.

[2 pp.], 3–5 pp., [6] blank.

Reprinted in *The Popiad*, 1728, pp. 5–7, and in *Gulliveriana*, 1728, pp. 321–3, with minor changes. 'There is no evidence now available to show who had written it, but Pope believed it to be Lady Mary's, and so it was reported in *The Grub-street Journal*, No. 20' (*Twick.* IV. xvi–xvii). See also Halsband, p. 135. Pope, surprisingly enough, omitted this pamphlet from his list of attacks in Appendix II to the *Dunciad*.

WORK: A. *Dunciad*.

CHARGE: I. Pope deformed.

The offensiveness of this famous attack lies in its carefully pious tone and in the pleasure with which the author indulges in his compensatory fantasy of Pope's humiliation. It begins with irreproachable sentiments:

There is nothing so lamentable as to behold the Excesses to which an unchristian Spirit of Revenge is but too apt to hurry Mankind, when they have not the mild Disposition of the Gospel before their Eyes ... Therefore, how much soever Papists may be mistaken in their Opinions, we ought not to give them bodily Persecutions or ill Usage, but leave them to the Laws of the Land; for altho' mistaken, they are still some sort of Christians.

O! that this pious Consideration could have withheld the Hands of two Protestant Gentlemen from offering opprobrious Violence to the Body of Mr. *Pope*; which, however, we hope will be no Reflection on the Protestant Religion abroad. (p. 3)

The author then arrives at the delightful scene:

The Barbarous Fact was as follows:

Last *Thursday*, being a pleasant Evening, Mr. *A. Pope*, a great Poet (as we are inform'd) was walking in *Ham-Walks*, meditating Verses for the Publick Good, when two Gentlemen came up to him, (whose Names we cannot certainly learn) and knowing him perfectly well, partly by his Back, and partly by his Face, walk'd a Turn or two with him; when, entring into a Conversation (as we hear on the *Dunciad*, a pretty Poem of the said Poet's writing) on a sudden, one of the Gentlemen hoisted poor Master

Pope the Poet on his back, whilst the other drew out, from under his Coat, a long Birchen Rod, (as we are inform'd, made out of a Stable Broom) and with the said long Rod, did, with great Violence and unmerciful Hand, strike Master *Pope* so hard upon his naked Posteriors, that he voided large Quantities of Blood, which being yellow, one Doctor *A*[*rbuthno*]*t* his Physician, has since affirm'd, had a great Proportion of Gall mix'd with it, which occasion'd the said Colour. (pp. 3–4)

They left him 'weltring in his own yellow Blood'. 'Mrs. *B*[*lount*] a good charitable Woman, and near Neighbour of Master *Pope*'s at *Twickenham*' happening to come by, she

took him up in her Apron, and buttoning up his Breeches, carried him to the Water-side, where she got a Boat to convey him home. (p. 4)

Since then, he has been greatly disordered; he raves and calls for pen, ink, and paper.

The account is rounded off with a blasphemy. It is impossible not to compassionate Pope's case, 'but we cannot too much admire the Wisdom of Providence, which brings this Man to the Lash, whose wanton Wit has been lashing of others' (p. 5). May Pope make proper use of his senses, when he has recovered them and say with David '*It's good for me that I have been afflicted*' (p. 5).

Pope felt himself forced to deny the incident in an advertisement in *The Daily Post*, June 14, 1728, reprinted in *The Popiad*, 1728, p. [8], from which I quote:

Whereas there has been a scandalous Paper cried about the Streets, under the Title of, *A* Popp *upon* Pope, insinuating, that I was whipped in *Ham-Walks*, on *Thursday* last. This is to give Notice, that I did not stir out of my House at *Twickenham* all that Day, and the same is a malicious and ill-grounded Report. *A.P.*

June 12, 1728 (*Monthly Chronicle*)

A Compleat Collection Of all the Verses, Essays, Letters and Advertisements, Which Have been occasioned by the Publication of Three Volumes of Miscellanies, by Pope and Company. To which is added an Exact List of the Lords, Ladies, Gentlemen and others, who have been abused in those Volumes. With a large

Dedication to the Author of the Dunciad, containing some Animadversions upon that Extraordinary Performance. Thee, great Scriblerus, Malice still inspires, / And with cold Venom damps the Poet's Fires: / A snarling Elf, who breaks the Critick's Trust, / With Spleen condemns, and always is unjust; / Whose own Example best explains his Laws, / And is himself the vast Profund he draws. London; Printed for A. Moore, near St. Paul's. M.DCC. XXVIII. (Price One Shilling.)

8vo in half-sheets.
Frontispiece, A⁴, a⁴, B–G⁴, H².
Frontispiece, [2 pp.], iii–xv, [xvi] blank, 1–52 pp.
Case 350, Teerink 1284.

The frontispiece shows Pope on crutches, his legs and feet those of a satyr, standing on a pillar made of The Profund, Miscellanies, Pope's Shakespeare, and his Homer; there are four owls, two on each side of Pope, and a monkey at the base of the pillar; over Pope's head is a motto, 'Hic Est Quem Quaeris. Mart.' See Wimsatt, pp. 362–3.

With the addition of a preface 'To The Author Of The Dunciad' (pp. iii–xv) and a concluding advertisement (pp. 51–2), this reprints the following contributions to newspapers. For Pope's ascriptions see *Twick.* v. 209–10. The page numbers refer to *A Compleat Collection*. The six items marked '*' from the *Daily Journal* had been printed earlier in *A Collection Of Several Curious Pieces*, 1728, q.v. The items marked '†' were reprinted in *Gulliveriana*, 1728.

   † *British Journal*, November 25, 1727, pp. 1–6. By Matthew Concanen who reprinted it in *The Speculatist*, 1730, pp. 260–5; *Gulliveriana*, pp. 294–9.
   * *Daily Journal*, March 18, 1728, pp. 6–7, signed 'Philo-Mauri'. Ascribed by Pope to Moore Smythe.
   Whitehall Evening Post, March 21, 1728, p. 8.
   London Evening Post, March 21, 1728, pp. 8–10, enclosing a letter 'To the Author of the *Daily Journal*', signed 'Philalethes'.
   London Evening Post, March 26, 1728, pp. 10–11, signed 'Philalethes'.
  *† *Daily Journal*, March 29, 1728, pp. 11–13. Ascribed by Pope to Moore Smythe; *Gulliveriana*, pp. 285–7.
   † *Mist's Weekly Journal*, March 30, 1728, 'An Essay on the Arts of a Poet's Sinking in Reputation; being a Supplement to the Art of Sinking in Poetry', pp. 13–19. Ascribed by Pope

to Theobald. See Jones, p. 352; *Gulliveriana*, pp. 299–306.

* *Daily Journal*, April 3, 1728, pp. 19–21, signed 'Philo-Ditto'. Ascribed by Pope to Moore Smythe.

† *Flying Post*, April 4, 1728, pp. 21–2; *Gulliveriana*, pp. 267–8. *London Evening Post*, April 4, 1728, pp. 23–4, signed 'Philalethes'.

*† *Daily Journal*, April 5, 1728, pp. 24–5. Ascribed by Pope to Moore Smythe. Reprinted and dated April 6 in *Gulliveriana*, 1728, pp. 287–8, and quoted in *Durgen*, 1728.

† *Flying Post*, April 6, 1728, pp. 25–7. Ascribed by Pope to Oldmixon; *Gulliveriana*, pp. 268–70.

Daily Journal, April 8, 1728, p. 27.

The Senator, April 9, 1728, p. 28. Ascribed by Pope to Roome.

*† *Daily Journal*, April 9, 1728, including 'The Devil's Last Game, A Satire', pp. 28–30; *Gulliveriana*, pp. 270–4.

† *Flying Post*, April 13, 1728, pp. 31–3. Ascribed by Pope to Oldmixon; reprinted in part in *Gulliveriana*, pp. 289–90.

*† *Daily Journal*, April 16, 1728, 'A Copy of Verses, said to be omitted, by Accident, in the Last New Miscellany', pp. 33–4; *Gulliveriana*, pp. 275–7.

Daily Journal, April 23, 1728, pp. 34–8. Ascribed by Pope to 'J[ohn] D[ennis], &c', then to 'Tho. Cooke, D[ennis], etc.'

† *Flying Post*, April 23, 1728, pp. 38–9; *Gulliveriana*, pp. 277–9.

Mist's Weekly Journal, April 27, 1728, pp. 40–8, signed 'Lew. Theobald'. First reprinted in *The Twickenham Hotch-Potch*, 1728, q.v.

† *Daily Journal*, May 11, 1728, a letter from 'A.B.' enclosing another letter, pp. 48–51, which Pope ascribed to Dennis. Hooker, II. ix, thinks the attribution 'has a very high degree of probability', and reprints the letter, II. 416–17; *Gulliveriana*, pp. 291–4.

WORKS: A. *Pastorals*; B. *Messiah*; C. 'Prologue Design'd for Mr. Durfy's last Play'; D. *Rape of the Lock*; E. *Temple of Fame*; F. *What D' Ye Call It*; G. Homer; H. Pope's edition of Shakespeare; J. Pope–Swift *Miscellanies*.

CHARGES: 1. Pope a plagiarist; 2. Pope did not acknowledge Broome and Fenton's collaboration; 3. Pope attacked Congreve; 4. Pope a Jacobite; 5. Pope foisted off old publications as new in the *Miscellanies*.

The Preface, which Pope ascribed to Concanen (*Twick.* V. 210), addressed to Pope is abusive:

I Address this Collection to you, upon a presumption that you are not the little Gentleman, who sets his Name to the *Profund*. A Presumption I must indeed own to be but slightly grounded, since I have no better Authority for it than your own Word: However, my Wishes incline me to believe it, because I wou'd chuse to have a Correspondence of this kind, or indeed any Dealings, with any body rather than him. I look upon him to be a dangerous Creature to have any Friendship or Intimacy with; and I think whoever you are, if you be not Mr. *A. P—E*, you have a fair chance of being an honester and a worthier Man.

(pp. iii–iv)

The more important of these repetitious attacks may conveniently be classified under the charges they make.

Writers in *The London Evening Post*, April 4, 1728 (they give their initials as 'J.H. J.C. L.S. J.E.', but I cannot identify them), accuse Pope of plagiarism by claiming,

1. That the Authors have been heard to confess, that an *Epigram* on *Handel* and *Bononcini*, printed in the last Volume of Miscellanies, *did not belong to any of them*. [See *Twick*. VI. 447.]

2. That the *Ode on the Longitude* has been for many Years, and in our Hearing, frequently own'd, and sung, by a Reverend Clergyman. [See *Twick*. VI. 415.]

3. That the *Prologue* to Mr. *Durfey's* last Play was written at *Button's* in a publick Room, *by several Hands*. [See *Twick*. VI. 101–2.]

4. That the *Eclogue* on the *Messiah* so long printed as Mr. *Pope's*, was at its first Appearance in the *Spectator* publickly claim'd by a Gentleman of *St. John's College, Cambridge*, (now a Reverend Clergyman also.)

5. That the same learned Person hath divers Times acknowledg'd himself to have had no small part in the Translation of *Homer's Iliad*, which passes wholly for Mr. *Pope's*; and that several Witnesses can be produced from *White's* and *St. James's*, who know Mr. *Ger—* to have had a considerable Share in the said *Iliad*, and in the *Rape of the Lock*. (p. 23)

'Philalethes' in the enclosed letter sent to *The London Evening Post*, March 21, 1728, repeats the charge that Pope stole the lines in *The Rival Modes* from Moore Smythe (see *A Collection Of Several Curious Pieces*, 1728), but adds that *Memoirs of a Parish Clerk* has to his knowledge been owned by 'Mr. *S—* in several Companies' more than two years ago (p. 9).

Dennis's letter enclosed to *The Daily Journal*, May 11, 1728, makes sweeping charges of inept imitation:

AEF
> Tho' I have not for several Years read *Chaucer*'s *Temple of Fame*, yet I am well enough acquainted with his Character, to know that he has too much Genius, and too much good Sense to have committed many Absurdities; whereas the *Temple of Fame*, writ by the *Pantomimical A. P—E* is one long chain of Blunders and Boggisms, and one continued Absurdity.
>
> All the World knows how very much he falls short of *Ambrose Philips* in *Pastorals*; but in the *Drama*, he is *below* even *Tom Durfey*. The *Marriage-Hater match'd*, and the *Boarding-School*, tho' but indifferent Performances, are yet ten times better Dramatical Pieces than the whimsical *What d'ye call it*. (p. 50)

G   On the Homer, *The Flying Post*, April 13, 1728, included 32 lines 'On one of the Admirers of that Translation, who said, *There was a great deal of Wit in* Homer',

> For what are you in Love with *Homer*? speak,
> And own the Wit is *English*, and not *Greek*.
> If Greek t'had been, I shou'd have look'd about
> To know how *P—* or you cou'd find it out.   (p. 32)

His translation of the Thersites passage is criticized in *The Daily Journal*, April 23, 1728, and a new translation of it promised. Cooke's authorship of this letter seems certain; cf. 'The Episode of Thersites' in Cooke's *Tales, Epistles*, 1729.

More mistranslations are noted in 'An Essay on the Arts of a Poet's Sinking in Reputation', *Mist's Weekly Journal*, March 30, 1728, and Pope is charged with unacknowledged collaboration:

G2
> Now as Gain or Profit, is to be the main Object of his Studies, it might be no bad Expedient, if he should *undertake* a Book in his *own* Name by *Subscription*, and get a great part of it done by *Assistants*: Tho' I should not advise this Experiment too often, lest any of the *extraneous* Parts should unhappily *ascend* to the *Sublime* . . . (p. 16)

H   The same essay recommends that anyone interested in sinking in reputation ought to

> lay out some of his Faculties upon *publishing* such Authors as he has least studied, and are most liable to miscarry under his *Mismanagmeent*: In *revising* which, let him forget even to *discharge the dull Duty of an Editor*; and shew such a *Velocity of Judgment* in the Execution, as may, without any Strain, be mistaken for *Ignorance*. (p. 15)

J   The essay has also some interesting objections to the diction of the
Peri Bathous:

> ... Let his Expressions depart from known *Idiom,* and common
> Understanding, so that he may talk of—[1]*referring exactly the Mold*;
> —of [2]*applying his whole Time upon*;—and that, [3]*nothing is of equal
> Consequence, as*—In short, let his Happiness be to invert the Order
> of Nature; and not to imagine that particular Words must be
> confined to explain particular Things and Ideas. In the *Vege-
> table* World, let him esteem *Weeds* beyond *Flowers,* and there-
> fore call [4]*Flowers the lowest of Vegetables*: In *Dramatics,* let him call
> the *Intermedes* of a Play, its [5]*Interludes*; In *Painting,* a [6]*Toad* or a
> *Small-Pox, Still Life*; and in *Musick,* the [7]*Stops* of an Organ, its
> *Registers.*

[1] *Art of Sinking*, p. 44.   [2] *Id.* p. 73.   [3] *Id.* p. 76.   [4] *Id.* p. 63.
[5] *Id.* p. 90.   [6] *Id.* p. 25.   [7] *Id.* p. 75 (p. 17).

3   Pope and Swift are twice accused of attacking Congreve. Concanen
in *The British Journal,* November 25, 1727, claims they attacked Congreve on p. 9 of the *Miscellanies* 'whom they can have no reason to be
angry with, except that he excels them ...' (p. 3). ['*Nonum prematur
in Annum,* is a good Rule for all Writers, but chiefly for Writers of
Characters; because it may happen to those who vent Praise or Censure too precipitately, as it did to an eminent *English* Poet, who celebrated a young Nobleman for erecting *Dryden's* Monument, upon a
Promise which his Lordship forgot, till it was done by another' (*Miscellanies in Prose and Verse, Volume the First,* 1728, p. 9). The reference
seems to be to Congreve's praise of the Duke of Newcastle for having
ordered a monument to Dryden's memory ('Preface to Dryden's
Dramatick Works', *The Complete Works of William Congreve,* ed. Montague Summers [London, 1923], IV. 181). Newcastle's promise came
to nothing; it was the Duke of Buckingham (Lord Mulgrave) who
finally erected the monument (*ibid.* IV. 220). See also *Twick.* IV. 113,
n., for Halifax's unfulfilled promise to erect a monument for Dryden.]
     The writer in *The Daily Journal,* April 23, 1728, claims that in the
fifth chapter of the *Peri Bathous,* 'A Footman speaking like a Philosopher; and a fine Gentleman like a Scholar' satirizes Jeremy and
Valentine in *Love for Love,* and that Pope

> slily aims at his Friend *Congreve,* a Gentleman that has never run
> into an Abuse of other Authors. (p. 36)

'Nothing in the relations between Pope and Congreve indicates that
any strain upon their friendship resulted from Pope's criticisms of the

N

dramatic improprieties of that play, if, indeed, the reference actually is to Congreve. The statement seems doubtfully reliable' (*The Art of Sinking in Poetry*, ed. Edna Leake Steeves [New York, 1952], p. 103).

4   Pope and Swift are Jacobites. Swift has,

> pick'd up in his Travels, a decrepid, diminutive *Lilliputian* Poet, whom he has plac'd by his Side on the Throne of Wit; an Empire to which they have just as much Right as their dear King at *Bologna* has to his Majesty's ... (*Flying Post*, April 4, 1728, p. 22)

J5   Concanen in *The British Journal*, November 25, 1727, complains that when he looked over the *Miscellanies* and discovered,

> that much the greatest part of them had been already printed in one Volume, Octavo, and that all the rest were either very common in single Pamphlets, or in old Collections, and compared all this with the Greatness of the Price those Books bore, I began to fancy that it was some Bookseller's Fraud upon the Publick ... (pp. 1–2)

J   The concluding advertisement gives a list of some of the most considerable persons abused in the *Miscellanies*, a list which opens with 'ALMIGHTY GOD, The King, The Queen, His Late Majesty, *Both Houses of Parliament*' and continues from Shakespeare to Garth, Addison, Welsted, Tickell, and Dennis (pp. 51–2).

June 15, 1728 (*St. James's Evening Post*, June 15, 1728)

[Bond, William.] The Progress Of Dulness. By an Eminent Hand. Which will serve for an Explanation of the Dunciad. Nought but Himself can be his Parallel. Theob. Dulness o'er all possess'd her antient Right, / Daughter of Chaos and eternal Night: / Fate in their Dotage this fair Ideot gave, / Gross as her Sire, and as her Mother grave, / Laborious, heavy, busy, bold, and blind, / She rul'd, in native Anarchy the Mind. Dunc. London: Printed in the Year M.DCC. XXVIII. (Price One Shilling.)

8vo in half-sheets.
Two unsigned leaves, B–E⁴, F².
[4 pp.], 1–8, [9]–34 pp., [35–6] book-list.

A 'New Edition', which I have not located, was advertised in the *St. James's Evening Post*, June 25, 1728. The title poem is also included in

The Supernatural Philosopher; or the Mysteries of Magick in all its Branches, clearly Unfolded . . . in the History of . . . Duncan Campbell . . . The Second Edition, which appeared June 20, 1728 (Straus, p. 286). It may be found in the British Museum *sub* Bond, William; I have not seen a copy. William J. Thoms reprints the title poem in *Notes and Queries*, Ser. 2, II, 201–3.

Curll in *The Curliad*, 1729, pp. 24–5, suggests that 'H. Stanhope' is a pseudonym here for William Bond. See *Twick.* v. 41, n., and 430.

The first duodecimo edition of the *Dunciad* and newspaper advertisements of the poem had carried an announcement, 'Speedily will be Published, The Progress of Dulness . . .' Pope was apparently suggesting that the poem of that title he was supposed to be working on had not yet appeared. The present pamphlet is Curll's attempt to capitalize on the title (*Twick.* v. xxi–xxii).

WORKS: A. *Windsor Forest*; B. *Temple of Fame*; C. *Rape of the Lock*; D. Atticus portrait; E. Pope's edition of Shakespeare; F. *Dunciad*.

The title poem, pp. 1–8, signed, p. 8, 'H. Stanhope', and dated June 6, 1720, chiefly in praise of Duncan Campbell, attacks Pope:

> *Pope* first descended from a *Monkish* Race,
> Cheapens the Charms of Art, and daubs her Face;
> From *Gabalis*, his Mushroom Fictions rise,
> Lop off his *Sylphs*—and his *Belinda* dies.   (p. 2)

There is the inevitable reference to IV. 175–6:

> Some guard an Upper, some a *Lower* Lock: . . .
> The curling Honours of her Head they seize,
> *Hairs less in sight, or any Hairs* they please.   (p. 2)

and a bald charge of immorality:

> But less by Comedies and lewd Romances,
> Are ruin'd, less by *French* lascivious Dances,
> Than by such Rhimer's Masqueraded Fancies.   (p. 3)

Windsor Forest is '*Pope*'s String of Verses . . . without any Connection' (p. 6, n.):

> In *Windsor-Forest*, if some trifling Grace,
> Gives, at first Blush, the whole a pleasing Face,
> 'Tis *Wit*, 'tis true; but then 'tis *Common Place.*
> The *Landscape-Writer*, branches out a *Wood*,
> Then digging hard for't, finds a *Silver Flood.*   (p. 6)

There follow under the title 'Observations On Windsor Forest, The Temple of Fame, And The Rape of the Lock, &c' (p. [9]), and making up most of the pamphlet, reprintings of Dennis's letter on

Windsor Forest (pp. [9]–12), his letter on *The Temple of Fame* (pp. 12–29), and a few sentences from a letter on *The Rape of the Lock* (p. 29). See his *Remarks Upon Mr. Pope's Translation Of Homer*, 1717, and *Remarks On Mr. Pope's Rape of the Lock*, 1728.

D   Under the title 'Verses Presented to the Countess of Warwick. Occasioned by Mr. Pope's impudent Satire on Mr. Addison' the reply to the Atticus portrait is reprinted (pp. 30–1) and signed 'J. Markland'. See *Cythereia*, 1723.

F   'Duncidiana. Verses to be inserted in the next Edition Of The Dunciad' consists of twelve lines on Vulcan and Thersites, comparing Pope to the latter (p. 32).

E   On p. 33 are four lines entitled 'The Evidence summ'd up', beginning,

> Nor Rhimer is *Theobald*, nor Critic is *Pope*.

June 26, 1728 (*Monthly Chronicle*)

[Ralph, James.] Sawney. An Heroic Poem. Occasion'd by the Dunciad. Together With A Critique on that Poem address'd to Mr. T[heobal]d, Mr. M[oo]r, Mr. Eu[sde]n, &c. If Thou beest He — But O how fall'n! How chang'd! Milton. Now Farce and Epic get a jumbled Race. Dunciad. London: Printed; and Sold by J. Roberts in Warwick-Lane. 1728. (Price One Shilling.)

8vo in half-sheets.
One unsigned leaf, A⁴, a⁴, B–G⁴. A2 incorrectly signed a2.
[2 pp.], [i]–xvi, [1]–45 pp., [46–8] blank.

On Ralph see *Twick.* v. 165 and Robert W. Kenny, 'James Ralph: An Eighteenth-Century Philadelphian in Grub Street', *Pennsylvania Magazine of History and Biography*, LXIV (1940), 218–42.

WORKS: A. *Essay on Criticism*; B. *Windsor Forest*; C. *Rape of the Lock*; D. *Dunciad*; E. Pope's edition of Shakespeare; F. Homer.

CHARGES: 1. Pope deceived the public with his edition of Shakespeare and his *Odyssey*; 2. Pope a plagiarist.

The dedication (pp. [i]–xvi), whose title 'To The Gentlemen Scandaliz'd In The Dunciad, An Essay on the Profund' sufficiently ex-

plains the genesis of *Sawney*, contains the usual general indictment of the *Dunciad*:

D

> ... the whole Piece is so notoriously full of Pride, Insolence, Beastliness, Malice, Prophaneness, Conceits, Absurdities, and Extravagance, that 'tis almost impossible to form a regular Notion of it ... (p. iii)

Like Curll in his *Key*, he is annoyed by Pope's ironic remark that six years were spent in the composition of the *Dunciad*:

> ... It looks like no very great Compliment to the *Authors* Sense, or Good nature, to have employ'd so large a Part of Life, in a Piece of unjustifiable *Satyr* ... (p. iv)

A, i. 48, 'Who hunger, and who thirst, for scribling sake', is dismissed as profanity (pp. viii–ix), and he comments on A, ii. 25–6,

> But now, so Anne and Piety ordain,
> A Church collects the saints of Drury-lane.
>
> ... One would almost imagine, they had declar'd open War with every thing that was good and sacred; and waited only for Opportunities of acting accordingly. (p. xi)

There is the usual charge that Pope was ridiculing poverty, 'as if the want of a Dinner made a Man a Fool, or Riches and good Sence only kept company' (p. vii).

He is bothered by A, i. 31–2,

> Here in one bed two shiv'ring sisters lye,
> The cave of Poverty and Poetry.
>
> ... The two shivering *Sisters* must be the Sister Caves of *Poverty* and *Poetry*, which would be but an odd sort of Couple to lye in one Bed together; or the Bed, and Cave of *Poverty* and *Poetry* must be the same, and the two Sisters the Lord knows who.
>
> (p. viii)

Pope used Ralph's criticism in his note on the lines.

Of the difficult lines, A, iii. 191–4, 1728a–f,

> Round him, each *Science* by its modern type
> Stands known; *Divinity* with box and pipe,
> And proud *Philosophy* with breeches tore,
> And *English Musick* with a dismal score:
> While happier *Hist'ry* with her comrade *Ale*,
> Sooths the sad series of her tedious tale,

he says obscurely,

> Can any Lines be more execrably dull? more stupidly nonsensical? the amount of the whole is this; that smoaking makes a *Parson*, and ragged Breeches a *Philosopher*; that *English Musick*

is ridiculous for its dismal *Score*, and *History* remarkable for drinking *Ale* ... (p. vi)

See *Twick*. v. 469.

The literary borrowings in the poem he considers deliberately offensive. The parody of Addison's lines (A, iii. 259–60) rouses him to:

even Mr. *Addison*'s incomparable Simile of the *Angel* in the *Campaign* ... is sneer'd at ... concluding a Rant of unintelligible Fustian, and most sublime Nonsense. (p. xiii)

Pope has made fun of the dunces' personal appearances, and is therefore to expect the same usage from them:

... He who burlesques any Oddness in a particular Person, ought to be contented when his own is expos'd: And as 'tis apparent, that one Man's *ruful Length of Face* is lampoon'd in the second Book, and another's in the third, the Truth can't be disputed. (p. xii)

He must have had in mind A, ii. 134, and A, iii. 146, 1728a–f.

Sawney is in blank verse, although since rhyme is 'the very best Recommendation of *Sawney*'s Writings' (p. ix), Pope is given rhyme to speak in the poem 'that his Sentiments mayn't loose the Advantage they so apparently want; tho' 'tis wholly ungrateful to my self ...' (p. x). The opening lines are the best in the poem:

> SAWNEY, a mimick Sage of huge Renown,
> To *Twick'nham* Bow'rs retir'd, enjoys his Wealth,
> His Malice and his Muse: In Grottos cool,
> And cover'd Arbours dreams his Hours away.   (p. [1])

Pope's well-received offer to translate the *Odyssey* and edit Shakespeare provides the slight action of the poem.

EFI
> A Bite! He whispers to himself and grins
> At the Deceit: Then, to his *Twick'nham* Haunts,
> Revokes his dissipated Friends, and vaunts
> The purpos'd Fraud:—'My learned Sons, he cries,
> From hence your Fortunes, with your Fame shall rise;
> The stupid Crowd so much admires our Strain,
> That all we breath, and all we speak is Gain,
> Th' *Odyssey* now demands our future Toil,
> And *Shakespear*'s Muse, the Glory of our Isle!
> To you the Labour wholly I resign,
> And but one half of the Reward be mine;
> And sure that's due for my protecting Name,
> Source of the Toil and Builder of its Fame!   (pp. 17–18)

When the books are published, the fraud is discovered to the loss of

Sawney's immense reputation. Shakespeare finds a champion in
Theobald; when Sawney reads Theobald, he sends in haste for
Hounslow [Gay], 'a trifling empty Fop / Who only father'd SAWNEY's
third rate Wit' (p. 20), and Shameless [Swift], 'a gay, lewd, swearing Priest' (p. 20). Swift calls for pen and ink to write a fierce attack;
Gay, however, cautions him that to please they must observe the
humour of the town, and they summon Fraud and Envy to visit the
Goddess Fancy to obtain her aid. Fancy refuses, but Swift insists that
they can do without her and proposes a lampoon on Theobald.

> SAWNEY, and *Hounslow* lend their needful Aid,
> One turn'd the Humour, and one smooth'd the Verse.
>
> (p. 41)

It is clearly implied that Swift did the major work on the *Dunciad*;
this explains the dedication's assumption that the *Dunciad* had more
than one author. The result sells well, but everyone is horrified at the
insolence and malice, Sawney's shrine is destroyed, and in anger and
vexation, he 'takes a final Leap, / Into the vast *Profund* ...' (p. 44).

C   The earlier part of the poem consists of a series of charges of pla-
giarisms. Pope has, for example, borrowed from Garth and Boileau in
The Rape of the Lock, and from Denham in *Windsor Forest*. His general
attitude may be seen in his treatment of the *Essay on Criticism*:

2
> Hemh! he begins, attend ye Criticks, hear
> Ye Poets what by him the *God* ordains.
> ' 'Tis hard to say if greater want of Skill
> 'Appear in writing, or in *stealing* ill.'   (p. 8)

His objection to the Homer is chiefly to Pope's use of the couplet:

F
> ... could the Wretch, in Rhime, pretend
> To give us *Homer*, plain, majestick, great,
> When *Milton*, his distinguish'd Son, who knew
> His inmost soul, despis'd the *Lydian* Airs,
> And, with a Grandeur equal to his Theme,
> Delighted *Albion*'s Sons?
>
> (p. 13)

June 27, 1728 (*Whitehall Evening-Post*, June 27, 1728)

An Essay On The Dunciad[.] An Heroick Poem. Some judge of
Authors Names, not Works, and then / Nor praise nor blame the
Writings, but the Men. Pope's Essay on Criticism. 'Tis best some-

times your Censure to restrain, / And charitably let the Dull be vain: / Your Silence there, is better than your Spite; / For who can Rail as long as they can Write? Ibid. London: Printed for J. Roberts, near the Oxford-Arms in Warwick-Lane. MDCCXXVIII.

Half-title: An Essay On The Dunciad (Price Six-Pence.)

8vo in half-sheets.
A–C⁴, D².
[4 pp.], [5]–27 pp., [28] blank.

WORK: A. *Dunciad*.

CHARGES: 1. Untrue that Pope has been constantly libelled for the past two months; 2. *Dunciad* too ill-natured and inferior poetically to be by Pope; 3. Pope guilty of blasphemy, and disloyalty to the Crown; 4. Pope ungrateful to Broome; 5. Pope a rich man.

A 1   To the declaration in 'The Publisher to the Reader' that, for these two months past, the town has been persecuted with pamphlets and libels against Pope (*Twick*. v. 202), the writer replies:

> ... a forg'd Thing, and something untrue: We know very well what Mr. *Theobalds* published in relation to Mr. POPE; but I believe every other Mouth has been silent, except it was in his Praise. (p. 9)

Pope paraphrased this, *Twick*. v. 210.

2   He insists ingeniously that Pope could not have written the *Dunciad*:

> But certain I am, that Piece was never the Employment of a Gentleman, and much less of Mr. POPE, upon whom the World is pleas'd to father it. I am sure he has too much good Nature to engage in any such Matter ... Is it consistent with Mr. POPE'S Character, to lay aside all Candor and Decency, and turn Lampooner? (p. 7)

The style is inferior:

> I must own, the Author, whoever he is, has aim'd at something of an Imitation of Mr. POPE'S way of Writing, which is only peculiar to himself: I can't say quite throughout, but here and there you may trace some Glimmerings of his Fancy, and some Structure of his Verse. (p. 8)

He says of 'Keen, hollow winds howl thro' the bleak recess' (A, i. 29),

> This I must own is a very good Imitation ... yet one may easily discern the Bristol-Stone from the Diamond. (p. 10)

'Sleepless themselves to give their readers sleep' (A, i. 92), he finds a
pun unworthy of Pope (p. 11), and he comments on ' "God save King
Tibbald!" Grubstreet alleys roar' (A, i. 256),

> That's downright *Grubstreet*, ... I fancy if Mr. POPE had
> handled that Thought, he'd have made something better of it.
> (p. 15)

But he obviously enjoys the race in Book II, points out the Nisus
Euryalus parallel, and admires the diving game.

3   Of 'A Church collects the saints of Drury-lane' (A, ii. 26) he says:

> Here's Blasphemy and Disloyalty to the highest Degree ...
> that Queen ANNE built the New Church in the *Strand* on pur-
> pose for the Reception of all the Strumpets of *Drury-Lane*, whom
> he is pleas'd to call by the Name of SAINTS. (p. 17)

He criticizes Curll, however, for having found 'Let there be darkness'
(A, iii. 337, *1728a–f*) blasphemous in his *Compleat Key*, 1728:

> ... for my part I see nothing in it: sure a Man may embelish
> his Poem with a little Scripture-Language now and then, or it's
> very hard. (p. 25)

4   He misreads 'Broome' for 'Blome' in

> A Gothic Vatican! of Greece and Rome
> Well-purg'd, and worthy *W*[*esle*]*y*, *W*[*att*]*s*, and *Bl*[*ome*],
> (A, i. 125–6)

as Curll had done in his *Compleat Key*:

> Why the Author should change these Names to *Withers*,
> *Quarles*, and *Blome*, I can't imagine, unless (if the true Author
> be Mr. POPE, which I am very unwilling to believe) he was con-
> scious of the wrong he had done that worthy Gentleman, who
> dug so deep for him in *Eustathius*, and supply'd him with almost
> all the Critical Notes for his Iliad in *Homer*; beside the Employ-
> ment he follow'd, as Journeyman to Mr. POPE, in translating
> the *Odyssey*. (p. 13)

But although Pope in 1728 did change '*W—y*, *W—s*' to '*W—s*, *Q—s*',
the '*Bl—*' ('Blome' in 1729) remained; Broome had never appeared
in the passage.

5   In a hit at Pope's wealth, he objects to the inclusion of Lintot in a
satire on Grub Street since Lintot has published the poems of Pope,

> who I believe has as little to do with the Cave of Poverty, as any
> of the Fraternity. (p. 12)

June 29, 1728 (*Evening Post*, June 29, 1728)

An Essay Upon The Taste and Writings Of The Present Times, But With A more particular View to Political and Dramatick Writings. Occasion'd by a late Volume of Miscellanies By A. Pope, Esq; and Dr. Swift. Inscrib'd to the Right Honourable Sir Robert Walpole. By a Gentleman of C[hri]st C[hurc]h, Oxon. O Shame, where is thy Blush! Hamlet. Who rich in Spleen, tho' meanly poor of Spirit, / Wou'd raise false Fame by crushing real Merit. W—t—d. London: Printed for J. Roberts near the Oxford-Arms in Warwick-Lane. 1728. (Price 1s.)

8vo in half-sheets.
A–G⁴, H².
[8 pp.], [1]–46, [47]–52 pp.
Teerink 1289.

Pope asked Fortescue to ask Sir Robert Walpole the name of the author, but seems never to have learned it (*Corr*. III. 11–12).

WORKS: A. *Iliad*; B. Atticus portrait; C. Pope's edition of Shakespeare; D. *Odyssey*; E. Pope–Swift *Miscellanies*; F. *Dunciad*.

CHARGES: 1. Pope patched up his translation of the *Odyssey* with other men's work; 2. Pope a tyrant.

Now that the heat of the battle over the *Miscellanies* is over the writer hopes he may achieve impartiality. Most of the remarks on the *Miscellanies* were scurrilous or mere quibbling.

ABC

DFI

  Yet how unjust and severe soever the Treatment those two Gentlemen have lately receiv'd, may seem, I fear their Behaviour of late Years has been such as will scarce deserve even the Pity of understanding Men. The Publick might, perhaps, have forgiven Mr. *Pope*'s patching up a Translation from different Hands, which he himself had promis'd them, or bartering an imperfect Edition of *Shakespear* for plentiful Subscriptions (and some other Disappointments of that Nature); this they would have patiently suffer'd, and thought their Pardon due to that great Genius, which once gave them the *Iliad*: But when, instead of clearing the Way of Fame, he maliciously busieth himself in spurning back others,

  When being grown too fond to rule alone,
  Bears, like the *Turk*, no Brother near the Throne,

in libelling the whole Body of the most perfect Writers of the Nation; might it not be well expected that they would have so little Command of their Passion, as to return him his own Usage?

(p. 3)

Pope, in the decline of his powers, has, like a tyrant, tried to crush other writers:

2   The poor Gentleman had long found himself upon the Decline, his Strength failing him, his Credit and Reputation sinking; in short, he was just setting in the Poetical Hemisphere, when he resolves to make one last Push for all, and vainly endeavours to evade his Fall by levelling others with himself. (pp. 4–5)

In his consideration of the *Miscellanies* he finds that 'the Scheme of the Essay upon the *Bathos*, is very ingeniously calculated for a comprehensive Libel, and that a happy and uncommon Vein of Scurrility runs through every Part of it ...' (p. 9). He objects to the distortion of the quotations from Addison and counters by ridiculing

D   those inimitable Pieces of Finesse in his [Pope's] *Odyssey*; such as this Description of the shutting of a Door,

The Door reclor'd;

The Bolt, obedient to the silken Cord,
To the strong Staple's inmost Depth restor'd,
Secur'd the Valves.

(p. 12)

He returns in 'A Scheme For Raising an Hospital For Decay'd Poets', pp. [47]–52, to the idea of Pope's tyranny in his decline. The decay of an author may be discovered by his attempt 'to make his Fall undistinguish'd, by levelling all others with himself ...' (p. 51).

c   Having found from the continued scandalous Libels which Mr. *Pope* had been publishing for these Six Months past, that without special Care the poor Gentleman wou'd be entirely lost, I apply'd to his Friends Mr. *Gay*, and Dr. *Swift*, to desire that he might be confin'd ...

After I had long represented to them the Inconveniences arising to the Publick from his *walking Abroad*, they at last, with Tears, consented to his Confinement at *Twickenham*, till such Time as the Hospital be finish'd.

Therefore seeing whatever Attacks this poor unfortunate Gentleman has, since the beginning of his Delirium, made upon the Reputations of our best Writers, have all prov'd entirely harmless; it is desir'd, that laying aside all Animosities, they immediately send their Pictures and most perfect Writings to *Twickenham*, that they may there ease the unhappy Prisoner, by being *burnt* in *Effigy*. (p. 52)

July 2, 1728 (*St. James's Evening Post*, July 2, 1728)

[Curll, Edmund.] The Popiad. Bella plusquam Civilia – Lucan. His own Example strengthens all his Laws, / He is Himself the Bathos that He draws. Ess. on Crit. London: Printed in the Year M.DCC.XXVIII. (Price One Shilling.)

12mo.

A–E⁴.

[2 pp.], 3–7, [8], [1]–16, [17], 18–25, [26], 27–32 pp.

Attributed to Curll by Pope in *Twick.* v. 210. Straus accepts the attribution (Straus, p. 286). *The Evening Post*, July 18, 1728, advertises 'a new Impression'.

WORKS: A. *Iliad* (Dennis and Dacier attacks reprinted); B. *Dunciad*.

CHARGES: 1. Pope wrote the flattering account of himself in Jacob's *Poetical Register*; 2. Pope whipped in Ham-Walks (*A Popp upon Pope*, 1728, reprinted).

Another miscellaneous collection of reprinted material, in which only the brief 'Conclusion' is original.

1   'Mr. Pope's Account of Himself, transmitted to Giles Jacob, Esq; to whom he subscribed two Guineas to be enrolled in his Lives of the Poets, though in the Dunciad, he is now pleased to stile this Gentleman,—Blunderbuss of Law', pp. 3–4, gives a brief, innocuous passage on Pope from Jacob's *Poetical Register*; the point in printing it lay in the title. Jacob accused Pope of having so altered the account of himself in the proofs Jacob had sent him that, in effect, Pope had written his own praise. See *The Poetical Register*, 1719.

2   'A Popp upon Pope' reprinted, pp. 5–7, with several small changes. Pope's denial of the incident in *The Daily Post*, June 14, 1728, is reprinted here on p. [8].

A   'The Popiad', pp. [1]–16, consists entirely of Dennis's *Remarks Upon Mr. Pope's Translation Of Homer*, 1717, abridged and slightly altered, with no indication of source or authorship. It begins with Theobald's praise of Pope in *The Censor*, but softens Dennis's abuse of Theobald.

The 'Postscript', pp. [17]–25, is the 'Postscript' to Dennis's *Remarks*, similarly unacknowledged and again with slight alterations and omissions (notably, Dennis's admission of error in line numbering).

A   'Madame Dacier's Reflections upon Mr. Pope's Account of Homer, in his Preface to the Iliad. Dacier and Dennis in One Cause unite, /

And prove that Pope can nor Translate, nor Write', pp. [26]–32, is a reprinting, with small changes, of *Madame Dacier's Remarks*, 1724.

B   The 'Conclusion', p. 32, is only a few lines in prose beginning:

> The most partial *Popeling*, or *Dunciadier*, cannot but allow, upon an impartial Perusal of what Mr. *Dennis*, and Madam *Dacier* have herein advanced, that, the present Residence of the *Goddess* of *Dullness* is at *Twickenham*.

July 18, 1728 (*Monthly Chronicle*)

[Smedley, Jonathan.] The Metamorphosis: A Poem. Shewing The Change of Scriblerus into Snarlerus: Or, The Canine Appetite: Demonstrated In the Persons of P—pe and Sw—t. —'Tis fit / The Biter, sometimes, shou'd be bit. Vet. MS. London: Printed for A. Moore, near St. Paul's. MDCCXXVIII. (Price 6d.)

Folio.
A–B².
[2 pp.], 3–8 pp.
Teerink 1285.

Attributed to Smedley by Pope in *Twick.* V. 210.

WORKS: A. *Peri Bathous*; B. *Dunciad*.

CHARGE: 1. Pope and Swift spiteful and fond of dirt.

Pope and Swift in this thoroughly unpleasant production are transformed into dogs by Jove and subjected by the dunces to torments which Smedley lingers over.

Jove calls on his publisher friend *B*[*enjamin*] *M*[*ot*]*te* (publisher of the Pope–Swift *Miscellanies*), who tells him that the booksellers are grown,

> Witty and rich! beyond our Hope,
> Between an *Irish* Dean and *P*—!   (p. 4)

Jove, however, assures him that Swift's and Pope's shapes of a Parson and an Ape are mere phantoms. Never before had Jove formed creatures similar to them, and he is now resolved to fix their natures once for all by turning them into snarling dogs. The change is hardly for the better:

I

And ever after, 'twas their Drift
(A *Spaniel P—p-e*; a *Mastiff Sw—t*)
To teize and bite whate'er came next 'em,
But of pure Spite, tho' nothing vext 'em;
To bark, to insult, to run stark wild,
And foam at Woman, Man, and Child;
To *foul* and *dirt* each Place they came in,
And play some Pranks, unfit for naming.   (p. 5)

The neighbours having vainly tried threats decide to put the curs 'To *Thorough Discipline*' (p. 5).

First, *M[oor]e* began their *Nails* to pare,
And cut close to the very *Hair*.
But *E[usde]n*, of a bloody Mind,
To *Cut their Throats* was more inclin'd;
Yet said; No, Hang't; Hence come the Wrongs,
And so, He whip't out both their Tongues.
Cu[rl]l next advanc'd and full of Spight,
Swore, that they never more shou'd bite;
And, falling to his Work, like mad,
He kick'd out every Tooth they had.
But *Lin[to]t*, frighted with the Gore,
Which stream'd, in Floods, along the Floor,
To stop the *Flow*, and wash their Mouth,
Piss'd, plentifully upon both.
Swearing, that while he cou'd make *Water*,
P—e n'er shou'd want such *saline Matter*.
   Well done! quoth *D[enn]is*: But of all
Ye do, be sure, *Let out their Gall*;
Deprive the *Currs* of what makes *Ink*;
And then we'll thrash 'em, till they stink.
   With that, *Len W[elste]d*, wondrous keen
Levell'd his Penknife at their Spleen;
And, with *Loud Laugh*, cry'd, *Here 'tis*!
(Ev'n Twittering, till he 'gan to piss)
No more, I warrant ye; no! ne'er, O!
Shall they make me their *Grub-street Hero*.   (pp. 6–7)

Cooke insists that the thing to do is to turn the dogs' brains. Concanen, taking up the suggestion, makes from some lines of Cooke and other poets (but not a word by Lady Mary, since that would destroy the compound) a snuff which works so effectively that the dogs now lie drivelling harmlessly in the chimney corner (p. 8).

July 18, 1728 (*Monthly Chronicle*)

Dennis, John. Remarks On Mr. Pope's Rape of the Lock. In Several Letters to a Friend. With a Preface, Occasion'd by the late Treatise on the Profund, and the Dunciad. By Mr. Dennis. London, Printed for J. Roberts, at the Oxford Arms in Warwick-Lane. 1728 Price 1s.

8vo.

A–D⁸, E⁴.

[2 pp.], iii–xvi, 1–48, 33–40 pp. (an error in pagination only; there is no break in the text or signatures).

After the Preface (pp. iii–xvi) the text is divided into seven letters only the first four of which are dated: I. May 1. 1714; II. May 3. 1714; III. May 8. 1714; IV. May 9. 1714.

Reprinted in Hooker, II. 322–52.

WORK: A. *Rape of the Lock*.

Dennis in the preface explains that the following remarks on the *Rape of the Lock* were written 'towards the latter End of the Reign of Queen Anne' (p. iii) but that,

> I took care to keep back the ensuing Treatise purposely *in Terrorem*; which had so good an Effect, that he endeavour'd for a time to counterfeit Humility and a sincere Repentance: And about that Time I receiv'd a Letter from him, which I have still by me, in which he acknowledg'd his Offences past, and express'd an hypocritical Sorrow for them.
>
> But no sooner did he believe that Time had caus'd these Things to be forgot, than he relaps'd into ten times the Folly and the Madness that ever he had shewn before. (p. iv)

Is the letter, Pope to Dennis, May 3, 1721. *Corr.* II. 75–6? He cannot even find Pope a competent versifier; he accuses him of

> an eternal Monotony. His *Pegasus* is nothing but a batter'd *Kentish* Jade, that neither ambles, nor paces, nor trots, nor runs, but is always upon the *Canterbury* ... So that having neither Judgment nor Numbers, he is neither Poet nor Versifyer, but only an eternal Rhimer, a little conceited incorrigible Creature, that like the Frog in the Fable, swells and is angry because he is not allow'd to be as great as the Ox. (p. ix)

Dennis had used the pun on 'Canterbury' earlier in his *Remarks Upon*

... *Homer*, 1717, p. 36. He tells the story of *Cato* and his own attack upon it, which he retold, more circumstantially, a year later in his *Remarks Upon ... the Dunciad*, 1729, q.v.

Twick. II, Appendix D, pp. 392–9, reprints Pope's annotations in his own copy of Dennis's *Remarks* with numerous quotations from the latter. I have not attempted to repeat this information here, only to supplement it, and to give objections not annotated by Pope.

Letter I indicates the absolute humourlessness with which Dennis approaches the poem. He finds that the faults begin on the title-page:

> What can this Author mean by creating in his Readers an Expectation of Pleasantry, when there is not so much as one Jest in his Book? (p. 2)

For his objection to 'heroi-comical' see Appendix D, (b), and for his first objections to the machinery, Appendix D, (a) and (c). In the rest of the letter he ridicules the Rosicrucians.

Letter II insists,

> The *Rape of the Lock* is a very *empty Trifle*, without any *Solidity* or *sensible Meaning*; whereas the *Lutrin* is only a *Trifle* in *Appearance*, but under that Appearance carries a very grave and very important Instruction ... (pp. 6–7)

Dennis defines the moral of *Le Lutrin* (see Appendix D, [d]. [e]); the poem is only made to appear a trifle 'otherwise it would not have been suffer'd in a bigotted Popish Country' (p. 8). He is perfectly sure no such case can be made out for the *Rape of the Lock*:

> But you know very well, Sir, that there is not the least Shadow of a Moral or Fable in the *Rape*. (p. 9)

Pope's intention is to raise mirth, but mirth 'is chiefly to be rais'd by the *Incidents*' (p. 10). And there are none such in the *Rape of the Lock* Appendix D, [f]).

Letter III proposes to deal with the characters and the machines, though it is really 'largely an argument against cosmetics' (Appendix D, [g]). In *Le Lutrin* character is well marked.

> But there is no such Thing as a Character in the *Rape of the Lock*. *Belinda* who appears most in it, is a Chimera, and not a Character. (p. 11)

Pope represents Belinda first as beautiful in i. 13–14.

> And yet in the latter End of this very *Canto* he makes her owe the greater Part of her Beauty to her Toilette. (p. 12)

And he quotes i. 129–34, 139–44. Even the lock, as iv. 97–102 proves, is not shewn so desirable for its native Beauty, as for the constant Artifice employ'd about it. (p. 12)

He sums up his basic objection thus:

> ... Her *counterfeit Charms* can please none who have a Taste of
> *Nature* ... (p. 13)

He then quotes Tibullus, Horace, Terence, and Tasso to show that
they all preferred beauty unadorned and negligent (pp. 13–16).

His second major objection is that Pope represents, as in ii. 11, 15,
Belinda as 'a fine, modest, *well-bred* Lady' (p. 16);

> And yet in the very next *Canto* she appears an arrant Ramp and
> a Tomrigg ... (p. 16)

And he quotes iii. 99–100.

> Must not this be the legitimate Offspring of *Stentor*, to make such
> a Noise as that? The Nymph was within Doors, and she must
> set up her Throat at a hellish Rate, to make the Woods (where,
> by the by, there are none) and the Canals reply to it. (p. 17)

On these objections, see Appendix D, (g), (h).

He has another objection to her character. Pope shows her not only
as beautiful and well-bred but as virtuous, too, as in ii. 11.

> And yet in the latter End of the fourth *Canto* she talks like an
> errant *Suburbian* ... (p. 18)

And he quotes iv. 175–6.

In Letter IV Dennis treats of the machines. He lays down that the
best modern heroic poets (1) take their machines from the religion of
their country; (2) make them allegorical; (3) oppose them to one
another; (4) show 'a just Subordination among them, and a just Proportion between their Functions' (p. 24).

In the *Rape of the Lock*, however,

> His Machines contradict the Doctrines of the Christian Reli-
> gion, contradict all sound Morality; there is no allegorical and
> sensible Meaning in them; and for these Reasons they give no
> Instruction, make no Impression at all upon the Mind of a sen-
> sible Reader. (p. 24)

His basic objection is quite clear:

> They do not in the least influence that Action; they neither pre-
> vent the Danger of *Belinda*, nor promote it, nor retard it, unless,
> perhaps, it may be said, for one Moment, which is ridiculous.
> (p. 24)

Appendix D, (i), makes this more precise. On Dennis's potentially
serious objection here, Ian Jack observes, 'Pope might have defended
himself by citing Le Bossu's distinction between machines which re-
quire "*Human Probability*" and those to which "*Divine Probability*" only
is proper. (Sect. VII.) The latter class, he rules, "should be so disen-

o

gaged from the Action, that one might subtract them from it, without destroying the Action." The sylphs appear to conform precisely to the requirements of the class of machines to which "*Divine Probability*" only is appropriate' (Ian Jack, *Augustan Satire, Intention and Idiom in English Poetry*, 1660–1750 [Oxford, 1952], p. 82, n.4). There is also (his third rule) no just subordination.

> *Ariel* summons them together, and talks to them as if he were their Emperor. (p. 25)

His further objection to Ariel's speech is given in Appendix D, (j). He makes still another objection to Ariel:

> ... he who calls himself their Chief, is only the Keeper of a vile *Iseland Cur*, and has not so much as the Intendance of the Lady's *Favourite Lock*, which is the Subject of the Poem? But that is entrusted to an inferior Spirit, contrary to all manner of Judgment and Decorum. (pp. 26–7)

The machines 'are infinitely less considerable than the *human Persons*, which is without Precedent'. Dennis's refusal to see the mock heroic is painfully obvious; of Ariel's speech, he says,

> ... After he has talk'd to them of *black Omens* and *dire Disasters* that threaten his Heroine, these Bugbears dwindle to the breaking a Piece of *China*, the staining a *Petticoat*, the losing a *Necklace*, a *Fan*, or a Bottle of *Sal Volatile* ... (p. 27)

The spirits Pope intends to be benign are malignant, and vice versa. He intends the sylphs to be beneficent and the gnomes malignant, yet the sylphs promote female vanity, and the gnomes mortify it. And vanity is 'the Cause of most of the Misfortunes which are incident to Humanity' (p. 29). The final defect he finds is that the machines are not drawn from a single system. See Appendix D, (k).

Letter v examines the sentiments in Cantos i–iii. Pope, he notices, proposes to sing a general, not a particular, action, unlike Homer and Virgil, and he asks assistance from Belinda, not from the Muse. The imitation of Virgil in i. 55 is unlucky. In Virgil the passage is appropriate, but

> the Passage in the *Rape* shocks the fundamental Doctrines of the Christian Religion, and is therefore a most absurd Imitation.
> (p. 34)

His objection to the 'New Stratagems' of iii. 120 is typically inane:

> Now what was this *new Stratagem*, or these *new Stratagems*? Why, the Baron comes *behind Belinda* as she was drinking her Coffee, and, snap, off goes the *Lock*. Now if this was the *new Stratagem*, what in the Name of *Impertinence* could be the *old one*? (p. 37)

Letter VI examines the sentiments in Cantos iv and v. He first objects to Umbriel's journey; see Appendix D, (m). He continues by objecting to Pope making Ill-Nature the handmaid of Spleen in iv. 25–7.

> *Ill-Nature* may with some Colour be said to be the *Mother* of *Spleen*, but she can never be call'd her *Maid*, without shocking common Sense. The *Nature* of a Man must be *coeval* to the *Man*, and must far *precede* any Thing that the world calls *Spleen* in him.
>   (p. 43)

Affectation is also out of place; it can never have anything to do with spleen.

> *Spleen* is the *Mother* of *Passion*, which is *Nature*; *Affectation* is the *Child* of *Tranquillity*, and for the most part is nothing but *counterfeit Passion*. (p. 43)

For his objection to v. 45–52 see Appendix D, (n). His final objections in this letter are to the puns.

> *Puns* bear the same Proportion to *Thought*, that *Bubbles* hold to *Bodies*, and may justly be compared to those gaudy Bladders which Children make with Soap; which, tho' they please their weak Capacities with a momentary Glittering, yet are but just beheld, and vanish into Air. (p. 47)

He quotes v. 75–8 and comments,

> Now what sensible Meaning can this have, unless he takes her for a *Russian*, who is to grow passionately fond of him by the extraordinary Gallantry of a lusty Bastinado? (p. 48)

As another example he quotes v. 97–8 and v. 99–102 for which see Appendix D, (o). Of the same nature as the puns are the 'Banters in Rhyme' throughout:

> ... For by placing something important in the Beginning of a Period, and making something very trifling follow it, he seems to take pains to bring *something* into a Conjunction Copulative with *nothing*, in order to beget *nothing*. (p. 33)

His example is ii. 101–10.

Letter VII examines only the first twelve lines of the poem. The first two lines of the poem Dennis claims are wrong syntax.

> ... For here the Verb Active *sing* has no Accusative Case depending on it; as the Nominative Case is without a Verb in the Beginning of the Prologue to *Cato*, which Prologue was writ by the same little whimsical Gentleman. (p. 36)

See Appendix D, (p).

To what does 'Goddess' in l. 7 refer? By its usual meaning it refers to Muse,

but according to Grammar and Construction, it relates to *Belinda*, because she was mention'd last, and she is the inspiring Person. (p. 36)

'Compel' in l. 7 is a botch for the sake of rhyme. 'Induce' or 'provoke' would be correct.

The Word *compel* supposes the Baron to be a Beast, and not a free Agent. (p. 37)

July 20, 1728 (*St. James's Evening Post*, July 20, 1728)

[Oldmixon, John.] The Arts of Logick And Rhetorick, Illustrated By Examples taken out of the best Authors, Antient and Modern, In all the Polite Languages. Interpreted and Explain'd By that Learned and Judicious Critick, Father Bouhours. To which are added, Parallel Quotations Out of the Most Eminent English Authors in Verse and Prose: Wherein the like Observations are made on their Beauties and Blemishes, in all the various Kinds of Thought and Expression. As all is Darkness when the Fancy's bad; / So without Judgment Fancy is but mad. D. of Bucks. London: Printed for John Clark and Richard Hett, John Pemberton, Richard Ford, and John Gray. M.DCC.XXVIII.

8vo.
A⁸, a⁸, B–P⁸, *P⁴, Q–Z⁸, Aa–Ee⁸, Ff².
[2 pp.], [iii]–xxxii, 1–232, 225–418 pp., [16 pp.] index, [2 pp.] book-list.
The dedication to Dodington (pp. [iii]–xvi) is signed (p. xvi) 'J. Oldmixon'.

Teerink 1291.

WORKS: A. *Essay on Criticism*; B. Homer; C. *Peri Bathous*.

This very free version of Bouhours's *La Manière de bien penser dans les ouvrages d'esprit*, with editorial comment and generous examples supplied by Oldmixon, contains several attacks on the diction of the Homer.

Oldmixon apologizes at length for translating 'Naiveté', 'Naivety', and not by 'Simplicity'.

B   Shou'd I have made use of the Word *Simplicity* instead of *Naivety*,

what a Conception cou'd the Reader have had of it, after having
read this in Mr. *Pope*'s Notes on His *Homer*? *Simplicity is our
Word of Disguise for a shameful unpoetical Neglect of Expression*; by
which he assures us, that we do not know what the *Simple* in
Style is, and by which he more certainly seems not to know it
himself: For *Simplicity* is some of the Perfection of Thought and
Expression ... But I think what follows has no Parallel, in any
Tongue, for a Babel of Languages: *Nothing is more lively and picturesque, than the Attitude* Patroclus *is here describ'd in. The Pathetick
of the Speech is finely contraverted by the* Fierté *of that of* Achilles.
Notes on *Homer*. [*Iliad*. XVI. Note on the opening lines.] Which
in plain *English* is, *Nothing is more lively and picture like* or picturish
than the Posture Patroclus *is here describ'd in. The* Tenderness *of this
Speech, being a fine* Opposition *to the* Fierceness *of that of* Achilles.
                                                    (pp. 146–7)
And when the Translator of *Homer* tells us the Field of Battle
was *ensanguin'd*, though there is nothing less *abstruse* and *new* than
bloody Plains, speaking of War, yet he has here spoilt two good
Languages, *English* and *French*, to adorn his Poetry with an *out
of the way* Word. The nearest Word in *French* to it is *Sanguinaire*,
or blood-thirsty; and there is no other Foundation for this new
Invention of his. (p. 414)
Besides *ensanguin'd*, we have *Picturesque, Riant, Fierte, Comparte-
mens, Traits, &c.* without the least Necessity for it, as good *English*
all as are his Political Principles and Religion. (p. 415)
Several lines from the Homer are given as examples of false figures.
To illustrate an obscurity which is 'somewhat a-kin' to the Galimatias,
or complete obscurity, he quotes, p. 367,
          Slow rolls the Chariot o'er the following Tide.
                                            [*Iliad*. XXIV. 897]
To illustrate obscurity caused by the exigencies of metre, he quotes,
          If Chance a swelling Brook his Passage stay,
          Eyes the rough Waves.   [*Iliad*. V. 736–7]
He points out that 'brook' is a monosyllable, 'river' a dissyllable.
     The *rough Waves* of a Brook are either not very intelligible, or
     they are very ridiculous. (p. 367)
     The Translator of *Homer* does not always *shine so peculiarly nice*
     as in those fine *French* Words before mention'd: He sometimes is
     very homely in his Expression and Sentiment; as when he speaks
     of his Hero as of a Hogshead of Ale, and instead of describing
     him as a Poet, tells us he will *gage him* like an Exciseman. This

delicate Author has written a *rhiming Essay on Criticism*, and made himself merry with his Brethren, in a notable Treatise call'd the *Art of Sinking*, to which he and his Partner, *S—t*, have contributed more than all the rest of their Contemporary Writers, if *Trifling* and *Grimace* are not in the high Parts of Writing. (p. 416)

August 8, 1728 (*St. James's Evening Post*, August 8, 1728)

The Female Dunciad. Containing I. A faithful Account of the Intrigues, Gallantries and Amours of Alexander Pope, of Twickenham, Esq; Written by Himself. II. A Satire upon the Court-Lords and Ladies. Written also by him in the year 1717. III. A single Instance of his Repentance. IV. The New, Surprising Metamorphosis: or, Mr. Pope turn'd into a Stinging-Nettle; being a Familiar Epistle from a Gentleman in Town to a Lady in the Country. Occasion'd by reading the Dunciad. V. Irish Artifice; or, The History of Clarina. A Novel. By Mrs. Eliza Haywood. VI. Female Worthies. By the Bishop of Peterborough. The whole being a Continuation of the Twickenham Hotch-Potch. London: Printed for T. Read, in White-Fryers; and Sold by the Booksellers of London and Westminster. M.DCC. XXVIII. Price 1s.

8vo in half-sheets.
a⁴, A–F⁴.
[2 pp.], [iii]–vii, [viii] blank, 1–48 pp.

Straus, p. 286, would make Curll responsible for this, as did Pope (*Twick.* v. 210).

WORKS: A. *Worms*; B. *First Psalm*; C. Letters to Cromwell; D. *Dunciad*.

CHARGES: 1. Pope sexually dissolute and blasphemous; 2. Pope's father a bankrupt.

The opening section, pp. [iii]–vii, under the title 'The Female Dunciad' gives us 'Female Biography' in a list of famous English women, briefly identified, from the Bishop of Peterborough's *Register and Chronicle Ecclesiastical and Civil*. We then turn to Pope:

And as we have thus far survey'd it [female conduct] on the Side

of *Virtue*, let us now see what Advances it is like to make in a *vicious Scene*, as it is painted by the profligate and profane Pen of *Alexander Pope* of *Twickenham*, Esq; in the following Letters, the Originals of which may be seen under his own Hand at one *Edmund Curll*'s, a Bookseller in the *Strand*. (p. vii)

Pope's letter to Cromwell, July 11, 1709 (*Corr.* I. 66–7), is then printed in part with the comment, 'Can anyone who reads this Letter, exempt Mr. *Pope* from the guilt either of *Lewdness* or *Profaneness*?' (pp. 3–4), and the *First Psalm* is printed with the suggestion that it was 'a Poetical Present made to some such Doxy as he here describes' (p. 4). Next is given part of Pope to Cromwell, April 25, 1708 (*Corr.* I. 47), and part of Pope to Cromwell, June 24, 1710 (*Corr.* I. 89–90), including the 'Rondeau'; this section ends, 'Thus endeth the first Chapter of *Records*, of the *Chastity* and *Sanctity* of *Alexander Pope*, of *Twickenham*, Esq; . . .' (p. 6). (See *Twick.* VI. 39–40, 61.)

Chapter II, after giving the account from Jacob's *Poetical Register* of Pope's early years, continues,

> I have already shewn the Exquisiteness of his Talents for *Immorality* and *Obscenity*, upon his arrival at the Years of Manhood, from 1688 to 1709, let us now see what *Improvements* he has made since, by his own *Industry*, in the polite Arts of *Rant* and *Bombast*, of which the following Letter is, I hope, a sufficient Specimen. It is likewise printed from the original Manuscript in his own Handwriting, *in haec verba* . . . (p. 7)

There follow the first part of Pope to Cromwell, December 21, 1711 (*Corr.* I. 137), and part of Pope to Cromwell, April 10, 1710 (*Corr.* I. 81), which, according to the pamphlet, was written during Passion Week. It was not, judging from the clear statement in the letter's opening paragraph; Easter fell on April 9 in 1710 (*Corr.* I. 81, n. 1). The *Court Ballad* and the *Worms* are then printed and the fourth (and usually omitted) stanza of the latter has the comment:

> Which is only saying in plain Prose, that, *it is doubtful if the Race of* Men *are the Off-spring of* Adam, *or of the* Devil. Now if he makes a Doubt of this, it is certain at least that his own Original is from *Satan*, otherwise he could never entertain such *Diabolical Imaginations*. However, in the *third* Volume of MISCELLANIES publish'd by him and his *Un-Theological* Fellow Labourer the Dean of St. *Patrick*'s, he has reprinted his WORMS, and omitted this last *Faecundifying*-Stanza. And I heartily wish his Repentance, upon many other Accounts, may be hastened, for his Life hitherto has been a sad one. (pp. 15–16)

'The New Metamorphosis' (pp. 42–8), the only other Pope item, is said, p. 16, to be by 'the ingenious Mr. *Foxton*'. On Foxton see *Twick.* v. 440. He is mentioned in the *Dunciad* A, iii. 151. The metamorphosis of the title is that of Pope into a libeller:

D

> A Poet renown'd for Politeness, and Fire,
> Has stain'd all his Laurels in Puddles and Mire,
> His Harp is unstrung, and his Trumpet so hoarse is,
> He ne'er will be able to rally his Forces.
> No Beauties of Wit can atone for ill Nature,
> And the World will but laugh at unmerited Satire.   (p. 43)

There are six pages of this, the point being that Pope should not have ruined his reputation by writing the *Dunciad*. There is a defence of Blackmore (p. 46), a hit at Pope's wealth from the Homer (p. 45), and indignation at Pope's attacks on the poverty of writers. This last occasions the charge,

2

> Mr. *Pope* has little Reason so to do, if he wou'd consider the former Distresses of his own Family. And that his Father was no Stranger to a *Statute* of *Bankrupt*. (p. 48, n.)

August 12, 1728 (*Monthly Chronicle*)

[Smedley, Jonathan.] Gulliveriana: Or, A Fourth Volume Of Miscellanies. Being A Sequel of the Three Volumes, published by Pope and Swift. To which is added, Alexanderiana; or, A Comparison between the Ecclesiastical and Poetical Pope. And many Things, in Verse and Prose, relating to the latter. With an ample Preface; and a Critique on the Third Volume of Miscellanies lately publish'd by those two facetious Writers. Sequitur pede, poena, claudo. Hor. London: Printed for J. Roberts, at the Oxford Arms in Warwick-Lane. M.DCC.XXVIII.

8vo.
Frontispiece, A⁸, b⁸, c⁴, d², B–Y⁸, Z⁴.
Frontispiece, [6 pp.], [vii]–xxi, [xxii], xxiii–xxxix, [xl], xli–xliv, [1]–282, [283], 284–344 pp. Page 215 misnumbered 521.
Case 351.
The frontispiece is Wimsatt 12.

This is No. 32 in Teerink who points out that it contains only two

genuine pieces by Swift, *Elegy on Demar*, and *The Journal*. He also points out that item 1975 in *Wagstaff's New Catalogue of Rare Old Books, For 1780*, mentions a copy dated 1727, with a portrait whole length. He has never met with such a copy, and I have not found any other mention of it.

On p. [283] is a drop-title: 'Alexanderiana: Or, A Comparison Between The Ecclesiastical and Poetical Pope; With Some Pieces, in Verse and Prose, relating to the Poet'. The 'Comparison' occupies only two pages, but the running-title on p. 284 is 'Alexanderiana' and continues to the end of the volume.

Pope attributed this to Jonathan Smedley (*Twick.* v. 208); the *Gulliveriana Secunda* he mentions, *Twick.* v. 212, seems never to have been published.

WORKS: A. *Iliad*; B. Atticus portrait; C. Pope–Swift *Miscellanies*; D. *Dunciad*.

CHARGES: 1. Pope a Roman Catholic; 2. Pope deformed; 3. Pope has contempt for anyone less wealthy; 4. Pope ungrateful to Addison; 5. Pope plagiarized from the dunces; 6. *Dunciad* an attack on poverty; 7. Pope has ridiculed the personal appearance of the dunces.

The badly organized Preface (pp. [vii]–xxi), devoted to the Pope–Swift *Miscellanies*, expresses surprise at Pope's and Swift's '*Consonancy of malevolent Thinking*, and *That uniform, scurrilous Cast of Mind*' (p. xi), since they differ in religion, physique, and politics.

1   *P—'s Religion*, indeed, allows him to demolish *Hereticks*, not only with his *Pen*, but with *Fire and Sword*; and such were all those unhappy *Wits* and *Poets*, who were sacrificed to his accursed *Popish Principles* ... (p. xi)

He is more eloquent on Pope's physique:

2   The *Frame and Make of P—'s Body* is thrown into the favourable Scale, and inclines People to excuse and forgive him; for it is generally remark'd, that crooked, minute, and deform'd People, are peevish, quarrelsome, waspish, and ill-natur'd; and the Reason is, the *Soul* has not Room enough to pervade and expand itself thro' all their nibbed, tiney Parts, and this makes it press sorely on the Brain, which is of a yielding Substance; and this *Pressure* again causes frequent Irritations and *Twinges on the Nerves*, which makes the crooked Person exert his Hands, his Feet, and his Tongue, in sudden *Starts* and *Fits*, which are very uneasy to himself, and which prove disagreeable and outragious, often, to others. (pp. xi–xii)

'A Critique On the Third Volume of Miscellanies' (pp. [xxii]–xxxix) is an attack on the *Peri Bathous* and Swift's verse. Pope is hardly mentioned, since Swift is credited with the *Peri Bathous*. At the end in 'a compleat View of the Captain's Body of Poetry' (p. xxxviii) the Atticus portrait is mentioned as well as *Sandys' Ghost, Umbra, Macer, Silvia, Artemisia, Phryne,* and the *First Psalm* (pp. xxxviii–xxxix).

In the book proper, pp. [1]–266 are devoted to Swift. But on p. 267, Smedley begins to reprint the attacks on the *Miscellanies* from the newspapers. See *A Compleat Collection Of all the Verses,* 1728, where I have indicated with a '†' the articles appearing there that are reprinted in *Gulliveriana.*

The following in *Gulliveriana* are new:

'The Comparison' (pp. [283]–4) has the usual play on Pope's name:

1   The two *Popes* profess the same Religion, but 'tis doubted whether either of them believe in Christ. The *Great Foreigner* pretends to forgive all manner of *Sins*; the *Little Briton* does not think there is such a Thing, as *Sin* in the World.

They both set up for *Infallibility,* but shew it in nothing except *Bulls* and *Blunders.* (p. 283)

From *Mist's Weekly Journal,* June 8, 1728, is reprinted (pp. 306–13) an important letter signed 'W.A.' (p. 313). Pope noted that the initials were meant for William Arnall and ascribed it to 'some or other of the Club of Theobald, Dennis, Moore, Concanen, Cooke' (*Twick.* v. 211, n.2); Hooker, II. ix, denies that Dennis had any hand in it. Largely on the *Dunciad,* the letter surveys Pope's career with insistence on his wealth.

3   Pope is distinguished 'by an uncommon Contempt of all Men less wealthy than himself ...' (p. 307).

A   Their version of the rival translations of the *Iliad* is, I think, the only one written by the dunces that implicates Addison:

It happen'd, a Translation[1] done by his Hand [Pope's], was not, in all Respects, conformable to the fine Taste, and exact Judgment of his Friend [Addison]; and, what was worse, the *tenacious* Gentleman would not be convinc'd a more perfect Piece was possible. *Maro* [Addison], to confute him, employ'd a younger Muse [Tickell] in an Undertaking of this Kind, which he supervis'd himself. When a Specimen of this was produc'd, the World allow'd it much more correct than our Author, closer translated, and yet retaining all the Beauties and Graces he could boast.

[1] *Homer's Iliad* (p. 308).

4   Addison had rescued Pope from obscurity and introduced him to
the great and powerful and it was still to Pope's advantage to preserve
his friendship with his benefactor. But as soon as Addison was dead,
Pope libelled him and made the scandal public (pp. 308–9). The mis-
reading of the Atticus portrait is extraordinary:

B   The Point of the Satire was not only wrong applied, but most
unnaturally and unjust [*sic*]; it reproach'd a Person for the
Exercise of his own private Judgment, and abus'd him for not
being severe, or ill-natur'd, to the Party he could not approve.
(p. 309)
There is an obscure charge of plagiarism from the dunces:

5   At this Time likewise, many Bickering [*sic*] and Skirmishes
happen'd; a barbarous unnatural Civil War being commenced
between *our Author*, and the *minor Poets*, some complain'd of
Characters abus'd, and others of Collections plunder'd; which
latter was unprecedented Cruelty; for the Gentleman might
have scorn'd to rob *those* Persons he had libell'd for their
Poverty . . . (p. 311)

6   There is no moral at all in the *Dunciad*; the whole is simply an attack
on poverty.

        It is, thro' the Whole, a merciless Satire on Poverty, the
Hunger, the Necessity and Distress of particular Men . . . He
reproaches his Enemies as poor and dull; and to prove them
poor, he asserts they are *dull*; and to prove them *dull*, he asserts
they are *poor*. (p. 312)
        . . . He thinks of nothing so much as his own Possessions, and
despises nothing so much as Poverty. In this View he compares
himself, and his Enemies; his own *Subscriptions* on one Side, and
their *Necessities* on the other. (p. 313)

7   Pope is charged with having 'libell'd a Person for his *rueful Length
of Face*' (p. 313; the reference is to the *Dunciad* A, ii. 134).

From *The Daily Journal*, May 28, 1728, a letter, p. 314, signed 'A.B.',
enclosing a poem, 'Alexander P—e's Nosegay: Or, The Dunciad
Epitomiz'd' (pp. 315–16). The eighteen-line poem collects the
more obvious obscene and scatological images of the *Dunciad* and
concludes,

        Thus *P—e* is dwindled to a Bog-house Wit,
        And writes as filthy Stuff, as others sh—.
        Who reads *P—e*'s *Verses*, or *Dean Gully*'s *Prose*,
        Must a strong *Stomach* have, or else no *Nose*. (pp. 315–16)
A Popp upon Pope is reprinted with a few minor changes (pp. 321–3).

'Part of Mr. Theobald's Letter to Mr. Mist, relating to Mr. Pope's Usage of him in his Dunciad. Dated June 22. 1728' (pp. 325–7). The justification of Popiana is interesting:

> My Notion is, that a *Poetical* War should confine itself to *Demerits* in the Science of Poetry ... But to draw into the Quarrel Parts of *private Character*, to fall on Persons independent even of the Fraternity of *Writers*, is intentionally to declare War against human Society. They, therefore, who oppose a Writer indulging himself in that *bad* Strain, employ their Pens in the common Cause of Mankind: And such a Writer should think it particular good Luck, if he is pursued as *Fair Game*, and not hunted down as one of a *Ferae Naturae*; a *Beast of Prey*, that ought to have a Price set on his Head. (p. 327)

The 'Postscript to the Whole; Containing Some Observations on the Preface, Advertisement and Postscript, of the Three Volumes publish'd by Pope and Swift' (pp. 333–6) denies that Pope can properly be said to have contributed to the *Miscellanies*:

> How Mr. *Pope* came to condescend to have his Name *tack'd* to this Volume, [the first volume] in which there is not one Line of his writing (except a Share, it may be, of the Preface) is a Riddle, that the Dean and He must unfold; ... it appears to me, that *Swift* impos'd on *Pope*'s Weakness in getting him to lend his Name, to help to blazon out Three Volumes, in which, truly, he has little or no share; for as to what *Pope* has writ in the Second and Third Volumes, it is very insignificant in *Matter*, and very small in *Quantity*. (pp. 333–4)

August 16, 1728 (*Monthly Chronicle*)

[Concanen, Matthew.] A Supplement To The Profund. Containing Several Examples, very proper to Illustrate the Rules laid down in a late Treatise, called The Art of Sinking in Poetry. Extracted from the Poetical Works of the ingenious Authors of that accurate Piece, and published for the Use of their Admirers. In Two Letters to a Friend. De Profundis Clamavi. Popish Psalm. London: Printed for J. Roberts, at the Oxford Arms in Warwick-lane. M.DCC.XXVIII. [Price 6d.]

8vo in half-sheets.

A in three leaves, B–E⁴, F in one leaf.

[2 pp.], [iii]–vi, [1]–34 pp.

Teerink 1287.

A MS. note on the fly-leaf of the copy in The Queen's College Library, Oxford, reads, 'Dr Warton tells me this 1st Feb. 1797 that he believed Concanen was assisted in this Pamplt by Bishp Warburton.'

WORKS: A. *Windsor Forest*; B. *Rape of the Lock*; C. *Eloisa to Abelard*; D. Homer; E. *Peri Bathous*; F. *Dunciad*.

In the Preface (pp. [iii]–vi) Concanen attacks the Homer, from which in the two following letters he draws most of his examples:

D
   ... Let it not be objected, that the Translator of *Homer* is not accountable for the Meannesses of his Work, which perhaps, says a Friend, are owing to the Original: It is demonstrable to all Readers of the *Greek*, that this Poet has stuck so little to the Original, as to give Occasion to have his Knowledge of it call'd in Question; and he and his Admirers seem to lay the whole Stress of his Merit upon the *fine Verses* of the Translation, not upon the Truth or Exactness of it. (p. v)

At the beginning of Letter 1 he explains:

E
   My Purpose, therefore, is in this and another Letter, to make a necessary Supplement to that stupendous Treatise [the *Peri Bathous*], by giving proper Examples of every kind of Style and Figure, which are the Ornaments of the *Profund*; and those I intend to draw, not like our Authors, from old, unknown, and damn'd Writers; but from Moderns of *their* Acquaintance, whose Works they have prais'd and approv'd ... (pp. [1]–2)

Letter 1 deals with the different styles which he lists as 'The *Vulgar*, the *Infantine*, the *Expletive*, the *Florid*, the *Pert*, the *A-la-mode*, the *Prurient*, and the *Cumbrous* or *Buskin* Styles' (p. 2). Since neither his definitions nor his examples are very clear, the letters are less interesting critically than they sound; most of his objections are to the heroic diction of the Homer translations.

The 'A-la-mode' 'is, when a Poet puts down for pretty Conceits, Things which have no Foundation in Truth or Nature' (p. 12), and he offers as an example,

Heav'n is feasting on the *World's green End*.

Iliad. 23 [l. 255] (p. 12)

Pope has noted in his own copy, 'Milton.'

C   For the 'Prurient', he offers 'the Description of Castration in
Eloisa's Epistle to *Abelard*'.

>   Cut from the Root, my perish'd Joys I see,
>   And Love's warm Tide for ever stop'd in thee.
>   [ll. 259–60] (p. 15)

Pope withdrew this couplet, perhaps because of Concanen's objection.

BF   His other examples are the usual ones in Popiana: *Rape of the Lock*,
iv. 54, and *Dunciad* A, ii. 154, *1728 a–f*.

The 'Cumbrous' or 'Buskin' style, 'A little Sense, moving, heavily,
under a Load of Metaphors, and trailing after it a Weight of Words'
(p. 16), he illustrates by,

D   So plain a Thing as (*they were destroyed*) is thus pompously express'd.

>   —The Gods these Objects of their Hate
>   *Drag'd* to Destruction by the *Links* of Fate.
>   3d Odyssey. [ll. 338–9] (p. 17)

Pope has noted in his own copy, 'Ignorance Greek.'

The 'Bathos' 'owing to *one choice Word that ends the Line*' (p. 19) he
illustrates by,

B   >   And dwells such Rage in softest Bosoms—*then*?
>   *Rape of the Lock* [i. 11, *1714–17*] (p. 20)

Letter II discusses the principal figures, which he lists as the varie-
gating, confusing, or reversing; the magnifying; and the diminish-
ing; each of these has numerous subdivisions.

He illustrates 'Jargon', 'Or, in plain Words, downright Nonsense,
which is no small Part of the *Profund*, and of which great Plenty is to
be found in their Writings' (p. 26) by,

D   >   *Prone* down the rocky Steep he rush'd *along*.
>   Iliad. 13. [l. 28]

Quere, if *along* does not always mean horizontally? If it does
how can a Man rush *down* and *along* at the same time? (p. 27)

Antithesis he illustrates by,

A   >   —Though all Things differ, all agree.
>   Windsor Forest. [l. 16] (p. 28)

August 29, 1728 (*Monthly Chronicle*)

Characters Of The Times; Or. An Impartial Account Of The Writings, Characters, Education, &c. of several Noblemen and Gentlemen, libell'd in a Preface to a late Miscellany Publish'd By P—pe and S—ft. Aw'd by no Shame, by no Respect controll'd: / In Scandal busy, in Reproaches bold: / With witty Malice, studious to defame; / Scorn all their Joy, and Laughter all their Aim. London: Printed, and Sold by A. Dodd without Temple-Bar; T. Read in White-Fryars; and by the Booksellers of London and Westminster. M.DCC.XXVIII. (Price One Shilling.)

8vo in half-sheets.
A–F⁴.
[2 pp.], iii–viii, 9–46 pp., [47–8] blank.
Teerink 1288.

Pope attributed this to Curll and Welsted but dropped the attribution from 1735 on. His ascription of it to Welsted is probably meant to be purely abusive, since the praise awarded Welsted in the pamphlet is extravagant. Curll in *The Curliad*, 1729, said he refused this 'very idle Pamphlet' because of its many errors (pp. 11–12).

WORKS: A. *Prologue to Cato*; B. *What D'Ye Call It*; C. *Iliad*; D. *Three Hours after Marriage*; E. Atticus portrait; F. *Umbra*.

CHARGES: 1. Pope a literary dictator; 2. Pope collaborated in *The Wife of Bath*; 3. Pope persecuted Dennis; 4. Pope ungrateful to Addison; 5. Pope a Jacobite and Roman Catholic; 6. Pope's career aided by his Roman Catholicism.

The author in the Preface explains the purpose of this hack work; he will make the seasonable attempt to vindicate the reputation of several distinguished men 'who have been lately very invidiously aspers'd, as well as in an absurd and foolish Manner, by a little Juncto of Authors, who have set themselves up to be Dictators to the World in what ever relates to *Polite Letters*' (pp. iii–iv).

He returns to this charge of dictatorship frequently, as, e.g.,

What they would be at, and wish in their Hearts, I believe, is to get it enacted by publick Authority, that no Man shall presume under the severest Penalties to write better than themselves:

> And that nothing good or bad, shall be publish'd without their
> Licence ... (pp. 11–12)

His list of 25 names which serves as a table of contents contains
many authors of Popiana, but his brief accounts are not biographies,
but senseless adulation. I give here only some of the major charges.
For the pamphlet's help in identifying the initials in *Peri Bathous*,
Chapter vi, see *The Art of Sinking*, ed. Edna Leake Steeves (New York,
1952), pp. 109–36.

A   The account of Eusden has a curious reference to Pope's *Prologue to
Cato*:

> ... *P—pe* had no Reason to be dull with him, since he cou'd not
> but be conscious to himself, that *Eusden's* Verses, prefix'd to *Cato*,
> were infinitely better than his own Prologue, in the Condition
> in which it was first shown to Mr. *Addison*. (p. 26)

BD2   The worst and meanest of Charles Johnson's plays 'is at least infinitely preferable to *The What d'ye Call it*, *The Wife of Bath*, *Three Hours
after Marriage*, or any other of the wretched Farces of *P—pe* and his
Coadjutors' (p. 20). The unusual suggestion that Pope had collaborated in *The Wife of Bath* had been made by Welsted in *Palaemon To
Celia*, 1717, q.v.

C   Tickell's translation of the first book of the *Iliad* was done 'in so
Masterly a Manner, as necessarily reduc'd *P—pe*'s Translation of it
into Contempt' (p. 31).

E   He repeats the classic charge of the Atticus portrait: 'the abomin-
able Ingratitude of the Wretch who has dar'd to insult him after his
Death in a low and stupid Satyr, to insult the Man, to whom he intirely owes his undeserv'd Success ... (pp. 29–30).

F   Pope's *Umbra* is said to be Walter Carey, an interesting claim. (On
this identification see James M. Osborn, 'Addison's Tavern Companion and Pope's "Umbra"', *PQ*, XLII (1963), 217–25.)

> This Gentleman is more flagrantly abus'd and affronted than
> any other Person mention'd by *P—pe*, who represents him in the
> Character of *Umbra*, that is, the most impertinent of all imperti-
> nent Fellows, and what is most extraordinary in the Matter, is,
> that *P—pe*, all the while, talks of himself as the most considerable
> of those great Wits whom *Umbra* is suppos'd to hang upon and
> tease ... (p. 36)

3   Pope has also persecuted Dennis whose 'too great warmth and vehe-
mence of Temper', one must admit, 'may have led him into some
Imprudences' (p. 39).

> 'Twas monstrously inhuman to persecute this unhappy

Gentleman in his decline of Life, and at a Time, when he had almost all Ills to struggle with, without any Support but the Friendship of a few worthy Men, who cou'd not persuade themselves, that a bare Contempt of *P—pe*'s Verses, and the prefering [*sic*] better Writers to him, was a Wickedness of the last Dye.

(p. 40)

The 'Cursory Account of S—ft and P—pe in the Conclusion' is interesting for its charge that Pope's Catholicism greatly aided his career:

Mr. *Alexander P—pe* was Educated a Roman Catholick under the Care of some Monk, or other puny Professor of that Religion: When he first set up for an Author, his Works lay for some Years the Refuse and Rubbish of the Booksellers Stalls, and had continued in the same Obscurity until this Day, had not Mr. *Addison*, out of his uncommon Generosity taken Notice of him. He was at that Time a little Flatterer of, and Hanger upon the late Mr. *Wicherley*, and had no Patrons that I cou'd hear of, excepting Mr. *Cheek* and Mr. *Cromwell*. No sooner had our great *Addison* given him a Figure in the Eye of Mankind, but he set himself to abuse and ridicule him, and all his Acquaintance in all Places and Companies, and by every poor Method he cou'd think of; then flew to *S—ft* and went *Pell-Mell* with him into the *Jacobite* Party, and to this laudable Conduct it is, that he chiefly owes the trifling Vogue he has since had in the World: Add to this, that his being a Papist, was a Circumstance vastly lucky for him, and contributed a great deal to that Zeal which a Set of Coxcombs had so remarkably exerted on all Occasions in his Favour. (pp. 45–6)

September 5, 1728 (*St. James's Evening Post*, September 5, 1728)

[Curll, Edmund, and Thomas, Elizabeth?] Codrus: Or, The Dunciad Dissected. Being The Finishing-Stroke. To which is added, Farmer Pope and his Son. A Tale. By Mr. Philips. Hic est Ille. Fellows, who ne'er were heard, or read of, / If Thou writ'st on, will write thy Head off. E. of Dorset, to Ned Howard. London: Printed for E. Curll in the Strand, 1728. Price 6d. Where may be had, The Progress of Dulness. The Popiad. And a Key to the Dunciad. Price 2s. 6d.

P

8vo.

A⁸, B⁴.

[2 pp.], [3]–10, [11]–24 pp.

Attributed by Pope to Curll and Mrs Elizabeth Thomas (*Twick.* v. 210). 'Mr. Philips', probably a pseudonym, is almost certainly not Ambrose Philips, but some Curll hack.

WORKS: A. *Iliad*; B. *Dunciad*.

CHARGES: 1. Pope's father a farmer; 2. Pope a Roman Catholic; 3. Pope ungrateful to Wycherley and his other friends; 4. Pope deformed.

Most of *Codrus* is given over to a fantastic biography of the poet. If Pope had been humbler, he would never have ridiculed poverty.

12   ... He would have remembered, that his Father was but a Husbandman on *Windsor-Forest*; and that the private Tutor which he seems to suggest his Father kept to teach him *Greek* and *Latin*, was a Secular Priest of the Church of *Rome*, whom his Parents, with other good Men of the same Way, in that Neighbourhood, sheltered by Turns, in order to make Proselytes.

   That by the Contribution of *Church* and *Friends*, he was enabled to make a Turn to the University of *Oxford*, was never deny'd, and a very short time it was, being but just enough to swear by: After which being of a Consumptive Constitution, and an only Son, he was by the Indulgence of his Parents, excus'd from the labouring Work of the Field ... (pp. [3]–4)

When he was about twenty, he was sent for a few weeks to a friend in London to see the world and seek a cure for his distemper which had increased. He met Wycherley who invited Pope to stay on with him. Pope's father refused to give his son more money, but Wycherley finally offered the young Pope board and lodging. Wycherley and Pope were called 'the Inseparable', Pope was introduced to all the great, and jokes about the difference in size of the two friends were popular. Once Pope found he was firmly established, he ridiculed Wycherley behind his back, and Wycherley never forgave him.

3   ... He had a peculiar Talent at private Slander, and his Absent Friends were always served up for a Dissért [*sic*] to the Present; which agreeable Faculty indear'd him to the several Parties which then reign'd in the Nation: He was a *Whig* with the *Whigs*, a *Tory* with the *Tories*; and some have carried their Par-

tiality so far, as to call him a *Popish-Whig*, an Epithet directly
inconsistent. (p. 7)

A With the large profit from his '*Nominal* Translation of *Homer*' (p. 9)
which he had taken so little pains to deserve he purchased an Estate
and dubbed himself a squire (pp. 9–10).

B   In the *Dunciad* Pope lampoons everything 'in Terms so Coarse and
Filthy, that few Readers can forbear Puking at his bare Ideas' (p. 10);
the essay ends with:

> To answer such as he with Words,
> Is like *Canary* washing *T—rds*;
> The *Wine* in Taste and Hue grows Meaner,
> But *T—rd* is ne'er a whit the Cleaner.   (p. 10)

'Farmer Pope and his Son: Or, The Toad and the Ox, A Fable',
pp. [11]–24, covers much the same ground as 'Codrus'. (There are
238 numbered lines, exclusive of the twenty-line 'Moral', but there
are errors in numbering which I have not corrected in my references.)
    An ancient toad and his wife who obey implicitly the church and
the priest have one son,

> A little scurvy, purblind-Elf;
> Scarce like a Toad, much less himself.
> Deform'd in Shape, of Pigmy Stature:
> A proud, conceited, peevish Creature.   (ll. 21–4)

He is taught Latin and Greek by the Parson, and when older goes to
the city against his father's wishes. On the way he meets 'a gentle,
amorous Swain' (identified in a note as Henry Cromwell), who is
amazed to hear a toad speak Greek. He introduces the toad to a bard,
Willy (identified in a note as Wycherley), who offers him bed and
board. The toad is made much of by city, court, and town, but he is
not content. His venom reveals itself in satire, directed chiefly against
his guardian:

> The stinking Venom; [*sic*] flows around,
> And nauseous Slaver hides the Ground.
> Yet not one Mortal, whom it hit,
> 'Twas just as harmless as his Wit.
> For take away the filthy Part,
> [1]Of T—rd, and Spew, and Mud, and Fart:
> (Words which no Gentleman could use,
> And e'en a Nightman would refuse.)
> There nought remain'd, save to the Elf
> A Disemboguement of himself.   (ll. 138–47)

[1] *Vide* First Book of the *Dunciad*.

Then one day the toad sees a lovely valley where sacred kine are feeding at the shrine of Apollo. He challenges a steer to fight, and when the steer replies that the toad is too small to be seen, bursts with his effort to swell his size.

September 17, 1728 (*Monthly Chronicle*)

The True ΠΕΡΙ ΒΑΘΟΥΣ: Or, The Art Of Sinking in Poetry, And Rising again. In Four Cantos. By Monsieur Boileau. The Third Edition, Revised and Compared with the Dunciad. London: Printed for E. Curll in the Strand. 1728. (Price One Shilling.)

12mo.
A⁴, B–C¹², D⁶, D² (second count). C1 missing.
[2 pp.] frontispiece, [2 pp.], v–[vi], [vii–viii] Curll book-list, 1–12, [13–14] blank, 15–47, [48] blank, 49–59 pp., [60] blank, [61–4] Curll book-list. Pp. 25–6 missing.

Rogers lists this as unlocated, giving what is apparently the first edition, with the imprint 'Printed for S. Chapman, E. Curl, and J. Brotherton.' I have been able to locate only the third edition above.

WORK: A. *Peri Bathous*.

'To the Reader' (A2v) is openly hostile to Pope:

A
>   To compare BOILEAU and POPE together, in all Respects, would be like drawing a Parallel between a Nobleman's *Valet de Chambre*, and a *Yorkshire* Boot-catcher on the Road.
>   Yet, in the Road of Writing, some Part of the Simile will hold; for as the *Twickenham-Imitator*, by his late Productions, has shewn us the New *Method* of *Sinking* in Poetry, so the *Gallic-Genius* demonstrates the *Old Art* of Rising again.

The 'Advertisement' (pp. v–[vi]) implies that the translation of Boileau's *L'Art Poétique* which follows and constitutes the rest of this misleadingly named pamphlet is by Sir William Soames, amended in versification and sense, and with the addition of several notes.

December 12, 1728 (*London Evening Post*, December 12, 1728)

[Ward, Edward.] Durgen. Or, A Plain Satyr Upon A Pompous
Satyrist.—in trutinâ ponetur eadem. Hor. Amicably Inscrib'd,
by the Author, to those Worthy and Ingenious Gentlemen mis-
represented in a late invective Poem, call'd, The Dunciad. London: Printed for T. Warner at the Black-Boy in Pater-noster-
Row. M DCC XXIX. Price 1s.

8vo in half-sheets.
A–H⁴.
[8 pp.], 1–56 pp.

For Ned Ward's authorship see his *Apollo's Maggot in his Cups*, 1729,
p. 36. *Durgen* is included in the bibliography of Ward's writings in
Howard William Troyer, *Ned Ward of Grubstreet* (Cambridge, U.S.A.,
1946), p. 237. Extracts from *Durgen* are given in *Notes and Queries*,
Ser. 2, IV, 340–2. 'Durgen' is defined in Bailey's Dictionary as 'a dwarf,
a little thick short person' (*ibid.* p. 509). *Durgen* was reissued in 1742
as *The Cudgel*, q.v.

WORKS: A. Homer; B. *Dunciad*.

CHARGES: 1. *Dunciad* a betrayal of Pope's friends; 2. Pope spent six
years writing half of the *Dunciad*; 3. Swift helped write the 1728 preface; 4. Pope forced to hire an Irish body-guard; 5. Untrue that in
the *Dunciad* Pope attacked only those who had published against him;
6. Pope bribed by the Duchess of Buckinghamshire to provoke the
rabble against John Ward in the pillory; 7. Pope plagiarized from his
friends.

2 'The Author to the Reader' (A2r–A4r) makes numerous charges. The
Dunciad is a betrayal of Pope's

> most serviceable Friends and Companions; upon whose trifling
> Foibles and unguarded Deportment in familiar Conversation,
> he has been many Years a Spy, in order to furnish out, with all
> imaginable improvements, the spightful Characters ... which,
> as the Publisher to the Reader very wisely confesses, cost the
> little celebrated Author above six Years retirement, from all the
> Pleasures of Life, to but half finish his most abusive undertaking;
> having as much more Matter in reserve as will require double
> the time to compleat his Satyr, with that Correction and Per-
> fection which the Design is worthy of ... tho' it is somewhat

difficult to conceive, from either the bulk or beauty of so ill-natur'd a Poem, that the unlucky Bird could be so long in hatch-ing, and at last come peeking into the World but by halves.

(A2r and v)

B3   Swift helped with the preface:

... the Prodigality and ill-Manners contain'd therein, are not entirely of *English* Extract, but savour of a little *Stall Pride* blended with *Hibernian Modesty*. (A3r)

Pope in his notes to the 1729 Preface incorporated both of the above (*Twick.* v. 201–4).

4   The enemies Pope has now made have put him

under the necessity of hiring an *Irish* Champion, when he walks abroad, to secure his Posteriors from the Feet of his Adversaries; which, by the way, is but a slender testimony of *the heroical dis-position and high Courage of the Writer* ... (A2v–A3r)

B5   He denies Pope's assertion that no one is attacked who had not published against him and solemnly protests

that he never, till now, ever wrote a line that could give to the little Gentleman the minutest Provocation; therefore thinks himself at liberty, with-out a breach of good Manners, to return him a scratch for his bite ... (A3v–A4r)

6   The poem is given over to similar charges, including the bizarre notion that Pope allowed himself to be bribed by the Duchess of Buckinghamshire to stir up the crowd against John Ward when he was pilloried. (Pope paraphrased this passage in his note to A, iii. 26.) Curll had first made this charge in the second edition of his *Compleat Key*, 1728, q.v.

Nor is the *T*[*wickenha*]*m* Bard intirely free
From mercenary throws of Obloquie;
The Lust of Mammon led him once astray,
And made him tag scurrility for pay;
If false, than [*sic*] let him clear up the mistake,
And to the following Queries answer make.

Who, for the lucre of a golden Fee,
Broke thro' the Bounds of Christian Charity,
To animate the Rabble, to abuse
A Worthy, far above so vile a Muse?
Tho', all in vain, for merit kept him free
From your intended base severity:
What envious Lady brib'd thee to express
Her Fury, in the Days of his distress? (p. 11)

7 Pope has palmed off as his own the writings (unspecified) of his
friends:

> Too long hast thou usurp'd the Throne of Wit,
> By fath'ring what your trusty Friends have writ;
> Their kind Assistance won you early Praise,
> And warm'd your Courage to attempt the Bays;
> Till your own rashness did untimely blast,
> The blooming Fame of all your Labours past,
> And forc'd your injur'd Friends to reassume
> Their own, and strip their Howlet of his Plume.   (p. 8)

B The heroic style used in the *Dunciad* is unsuitable to the subject:

> What Bard, but you, could think it worth his while,
> To dress Lampoon in such a lofty style?
> As if good language would your Malice drown,
> And make the gilded Pill go glibly down;
> Tho' the choice Words you lavishly bestow,
> Are too sonif'rous for a Theme so low,
> Like Kettle-drums and Trumpets to a Puppit-show.
>
> (p. 3)

A Pope's Homer translations are unsound:

> His Christian Muse, tho' Learn'd, disdain'd to seek
> For *Homer*'s sense, in *Homer*'s heathen *Greek*,
> But wisely took it, as before laid down,
> Disguis'd the antient Tale to gull the Town,
> And in a pompous Style, his Art to shew,
> Transform'd the old Translation to a new.   (pp. 50–1)

Ward fits into his verse a long list of offending expressions in Pope's
poems and translations taken from the *Daily Journal*, April 5, 1728
(see *A Collection Of Several Curious Pieces*, 1728), as he himself admitted
in *Apollo's Maggot in his Cups*, 1729, p. 36, though he denied that
Moore Smythe, to whom Pope had attributed the article, had any
hand in *Durgen*. Occasionally a comment emphasizes Ward's objection to epic diction:

> Next, a *Vermilian Prore* we must allow,
> Sounds better far, than a red painted Prow;
> Tho' such a Term as *Prore* was never heard
> On board of Ship, or in a Builder's Yard.
> What then, in Epick-Verse it may be good,
> And pass admir'd, because not understood.   (p. 26)

Rogers, pp. 27–8, prints part of this passage.

April 3, 1729 (*Monthly Chronicle*)

[Cooke, Thomas.] Tales, Epistles, Odes, Fables, &c. With Translations From Homer and other antient Authors. To which are added Proposals For perfecting the English Language. London: Printed for T. Green at Charing-Cross. M.DCCXXIX.

8vo.

Three unsigned leaves, A–N⁸, O⁴.

[2 pp.], [i]–iv, [1–3], 4–214 pp., [215] book-list, [216] blank.

This contains a greatly revised version of *The Battle of the Poets*, 1725, q.v.

Includes the following Popiana:

'To Mr. D.B.', pp. 50–3.
'The Battel Of The Poets. In two Cantos', pp. [105]–50.
'The Episode of Thersites, Translated From the second Book of the Iliad of Homer', pp. [169]–85.

Daniel A. Fineman, *Leonard Welsted, Gentleman Poet of the Augustan Age* (Philadelphia, 1950), p. 186, would apply to Pope 'The Ass', pp. 85–7, a retelling of the fable of the ass who disguises himself in a lion's skin. The 'Bard by Numbers rais'd, / By many read, and falsely prais'd' (p. 87) is probably meant for Pope, but the reference seems too vague to merit inclusion here.

WORKS: A. *Pastorals*; B. *Essay on Criticism*; C. *Windsor Forest*; D. *Ode on St. Cecilia's Day*; E. *Rape of the Lock*; F. *Temple of Fame*; G. Homer; H. *Eloisa to Abelard*; J. *Peri Bathous*; K. *Dunciad*.

CHARGES: 1. Pope a Bavius and a Labeo; 2. Pope venal about subscriptions; 3. Savage a spy for Pope.

I   The epistle 'To Mr. D.B.', dated, p. 53, 'June, 1728', contains a single hit, that in Pope we find 'a *Bavius* and a *Labeo* join'd' (p. 52).

'The Battel Of The Poets' is almost a new poem. The Preface (pp. [107]–11) dated, p. 111, January, 1729, claims that it contains less than 80 lines identical to the 1725 version. Cooke was induced to write the poem by reflecting on Pope's undeserved reputation.

K   . . . The Author of the *Dunciad* who, possessed of what Poets most pursue, and what his most lavish Hopes could indulge Him in, has at last convinced the thinking Part of his Admirers that he has no Title to the Praise which he has had. I am almost certain, had he not afforded this Opportunity to judge of him, his Date of

Fame would have ended soon after the Lives of those who were resolved, against Reason, to oppose him to superior Merit. (p. 108)
His criticism of the *Dunciad*, unfortunately not illustrated, includes
one of the rare objections in Popiana to its form:

> The *Dunciad* is not only gross and scurrilous, but so monstrous-
> ly foolish in the Conception and Execution of the whole, that we
> may immediately see it could not be the Work of a reasonable
> Man. Almost every Reader knows that Libertys are allowable
> in Poetry which are not in Prose; but when we find, in any Piece,
> a confusion of Figures, and evident Contradictions to Sense,
> with a Profusion of Words which mean Nothing, or what they
> ought not to mean, direct Calumnys, Lewdness, and Prophane-
> ness, and without Wit or Humour, we must conclude the Author
> not perfect in his Senses, and of an evil Disposition. (p. 109)

His objection that it is impossible from the poem to form an opinion
of the merit of the writers satirized is in itself ludicrous, but his example (p. 110) is shrewd – Bishop Hoadly's sermon – and is quoted,
Twick. v. 145, n.

The poem opens as in 1725, but the description of Pope is much
more severe:

First on the Plain a Haughty Gen'ral came,
Of *Rumour* born, the short liv'd Child of *Fame*,
In glaring Arms array'd, and *Pope* his Name.
Brittle the Helm he wore, no Artist's Care;
The Plume, *Belinda*, was thy ravish'd Hair.
See on his Shield's thin Boss the *Greecian* stand,
The lifeless Labour of the Painter's Hand;
Of *Greeks* the first, the deathless Son of Fame,
Not known for *Homer* but by *Homer*'s Name ...
Thy Lawns, O! *Windsor*, on the right were seen,
In Colours painted like autumnal Green.
Figures ill match'd of various Kinds were there,
The *Dunce's Bird* and *Eloisa* fair.   (p. 117)

Swift, now added to the poem, incites Pope to battle.

Call them, without Reserve, Dog, Monkey, Owl,
And splutter out at once Fish, Flesh, and Fowl.   (p. 120)

But Pope does not need his advice:

Who better knows than I his Dirt to throw?
To wound in Secret either Friend or Foe?
Go preach to *Gay*, and such as are inclin'd
Less to exert an enterprizing Mind, ...

> A Genius form'd like mine will soar at all,
> And boldly follow where Subscriptions call.   (p. 120)

The opposing army is commanded by Welsted, Theobald, Moore, and Tickell. (There is a neutral group, the witlings, but these are easily overcome by Welsted and Moore.) Theobald is now added and Tickell who in 1725 had been abused as a blind for Addison is treated quite differently:

> The Head of *Homer* painted on his Shield;
> The Lines so strong the master Pencil speak,
> All wish he'd draw'd at Length th'immortal *Greek*. (p. 125)

James Moore Smythe is paid the absurd tribute, 'Another *Dryden* shall arise in Thee' (p. 125)

Tickell fells Pope but Pope revives and attacks Welsted who is rescued by the god when Pope's men rush to their leader's defence. Pope then fights Theobald and is wounded by Moore. Darkness falls, leaving the contest undecided.

In Canto II Dennis's search for spoils is greatly expanded. He finds much less to burn in the enemy camp, but burns most of Pope:

> With the mar'd *Greecian* Storys feed the Flame
> Thy Praise *Cecilia*, and thy Temple *Fame*.

BDE

FG

> Light mounts, impartial Doom! the maukish Lay,
> Where Sylphs preside, and Belles at Ombre play;
> Where well bred Lords and softest Bosoms rage;
> And Clenches and Conundrums croud the Page.
> Not less severe the Fate of that dull Strain
> Where for the Critic's Wreath he strives in vain,
> Of Knowledge barren, much affects to know,
> While like the *Severn* rough his Numbers flow. (pp. 136–7)

A note points out that nothing is more false than the common view that Pope is a good versifier: his versification is as false as are his sentiments.

B   In the *Essay on Criticism* 'a nice ear can not distinguish fifty Lines which please' (p. 137, n.).

K   Another note objects to the *Dunciad* A, ii. 165, 'So Jove's bright bow displays its watry round', because the rainbow cannot be at the same time a bow and round (pp. 137–8, n.).

Dennis again meets Savage, but Savage is now 'one that seem'd, and was, a Spy' (p. 140). When Dennis promises to spare his life, Savage confesses that he is a spy for Pope in the enemy camp.

3

> I watch their Motions, and each Word they say,
> And all, and more than all, I know, betray:

In kind Return he cheers my Soul with Praise,
And mends, where such he finds, my feeble Lays.   (p. 143)

A   The battle begins again; Philips arrives and Swift deserts. Pope
fights Philips with his *Pastorals* which had been saved by Apollo from
Dennis for this end. There is a song contest between Pope and Philips.
The 'attendant Throng' finds Pope 'Like a Clown aukward in Sir
Fopling's Coat' (p. 146), but Philips 'A skilful, pure, and unaffected,
Swain' (p. 147). When Philips is judged the winner, Pope faints with
spleen and is rescued by Eliza, who lays him on a bed of nettles. Moore
Smythe nominates Philips the winner of the laurel.

'The Episode of Thersites' is a deliberate attempt to show up Pope
as translator. The Preface explains modestly that this version is a
'juster Copy of the Original than has yet been in *English*' (p. 172).
The translation reputed the best (clearly Pope's) 'has no more the
Likeness of *Homer* than the Person of *Thersites* had that of *Achilles*'
(p. 172). Considering the frequent use of Thersites as a name for Pope
in Popiana it is hard to believe that Cooke chose this passage from the
Iliad only, as he says, because it is one of the most difficult.

The translation is bad; the couplets are clumsily handled, the
rhythms uncertain. Numerous notes find fault with Pope for mis-
translation and for adding lines not in the original. For example,
Cooke says,

His Body such as might his Soul proclaim   [*Iliad*, II. 263]
is Pope's own. Homer's words are literally 'He was the vilest Man that
came to *Troy*' (pp. 174–5, n.). He sums up his basic criticism with
deftness unusual for him:

I may modestly assert that Mr. *Pope* might have used the whole
Speech of *Ulysses* to *Thersites*, as wrote by himself, in an original
Poem, without being accused of borrowing one Line from *Homer*,
(p. 180, n.)

The objections in the letter in *The Daily Journal*, April 23, 1728, printed in *A Complete Collection Of all the Verses*, 1728, are substantially incorporated into the notes on pp. 174–5. Edna Leake Steeves in her edition
of *The Art of Sinking* (New York, 1952), p. 151, states misleadingly that
the *Daily Journal* letter (which she dates incorrectly April 6, 1728) was
reissued in this volume.

Cooke reprinted 'The Episode of Thersites' and 'The Battel of the
Poets' in:

Mr. Cooke's Original Poems, With Imitations And Translations
of Several select Passages of the Antients, In four Parts: To

which are added Proposals For perfecting the English Language. London: Printed for T. Jackson in St. James's-Street, and C. Bathurst at the Cross-Keys in Fleet-Street. MDCCXLII.

12mo.

A⁶, B–O¹².

[2 pp.], [iii]–vi, [vii–xii], [2 pp.], 3–311 pp., [312] blank.

'The Episode of Thersites', unchanged, appears on pp. [241]–56.

'The Battel of the Poets' appears on pp. [175]–216. The Preface remains the same with the addition of a single note. The text of the poem is as in 1729; a few notes are changed, many are added. The only interesting feature of the reprinting is the Postscript, pp. 214–16, dated, p. 216, 'January, 1740–41.' Cooke would not now waste his time in writing 'a Poem of this Length on so ingrateful a Subject':

> ... and I must take this Occasion to say that I can not conceive very highly of Mr. *Pope*'s Philosophy, or Dignity of Mind, if he could be provoked by what a Boy writ concerning his Translation of *Homer*, and in Verses which gave no Promise of a long Duration. Poetical Contentions, unless attended with Fancy, Wit, and Humour, or with one of them at least, are unworthy the Attention of Men of Wisdom or Taste, and at best but little promote the public Good.
>
> I now dismiss this Poem from me with a Resolution never more to trouble myself about it, either to correct it, take from it, or add to it. To what Notes I have now added I have put the Date of the Year in which I made them, to distinguish them from those in the former Edition. (pp. 214–15)

But he says that he retains the same opinion of the merits of Philips and Welsted (p. 215).

April 30, 1729 (*Monthly Chronicle*)

[Curll, Edmund.] The Curliad. A Hypercritic Upon The Dunciad Variorum. With A farther Key to the New Characters. Pope, has less Reading than makes Felons 'scape, / Less human Genius than God gives an Ape. Dunciad. B.I. V. 235, 236. O may his Soul still Fret upon the Lee, / And nought attune his Lyre but Bastardy; / May un-hang'd Savage all Pope's Hours enjoy, /

And let his spurious Birth his Pen employ. Incerti Auth. London:
Printed for the Author. 1729. (Price One Shilling.)

8vo in half-sheets.
One unsigned leaf, B–E⁴, F in three leaves.
[2 pp.], [1]–38 pp.

Drop-title, p. [1]: The Curliad. A Critique Upon the New Edition
of the Dunciad Variorum. Soon will that Die which adds Thy Name
to Mine, / Let me then Live join'd to a Work of Thine. Steele.

The pamphlet is dated 'April 25. 1729' and signed 'E. Curll' (p. 38).

WORKS: A. *Worms*; B. *First Psalm*; C. Letters to Cromwell; D. *Dunciad*.

CHARGES: 1. Pope, under Wycherley's name, wrote verses in praise
of himself; 2. Pope wrote the flattering account of himself in *The
Poetical Register*; 3. Pope indecent and blasphemous.

I   Cleland's 'Letter to the Publisher' (*Twick*. v. 11–21)
        is undoubtedly wrote by Mr. *Pope*; as he formerly subscribed
        Mr. *Wycherley's* Name to a Copy of Verses before his *Pastorals*,
        wrote, in his own Praise, by himself. (p. [1])
    See Dennis's *Reflections Critical and Satyrical*, 1711, where this charge is
    first made.

2   The account of Pope given by Jacobs in his *Poetical Register*, 1720,
        was drawn up by Mr. *Pope* himself, and by him given to Mr.
        Jacob, with a Brace of *Guineas* to insert it. (p. 4)
    See *The Poetical Register*, 1719.

D   Of the Arguments to the Books of the *Dunciad*, he says,
        These are a direct Sneer, by way of Parody, upon *Milton's Argu-
        ments* to the *Books* of his *Paradise Lost*; and many of his Phrases
        are taken *Verbatim* ... (p. 9)
    But see *Twick*. v. 54, n., where so close a parallel is denied.
        He makes again his favourite charge:

C   In this Letter [A Letter to the Publisher], I observe *First*, the
3   mention of Mr. Pope's *Moral Character*, for which I only refer to
        his Satire called the *Worms*, his *Burlesque* of the first *Psalm*, and
        the *Stage-Coach-amour*, in his *Letters* to Mr. *Cromwell* [Pope to
        Cromwell, July 11, 1709; see *The Female Dunciad*, 1728] ...
        Parallels to which *Profane* Performances, I defy even Mr. *William
        Cleland* to produce. (pp. [1]–2)

Curll's valuable attributions of Popiana in his brief comments on
selected lines in the *Dunciad* have been noted here under the various
pamphlets mentioned.

The rest of the pamphlet is padded out with 'Lord Bacon's Essay on Deformity: Or, a Looking-Glass for Mr. Pope', pp. 32–4, and 'A farther Key: Or, New Characters; and, Additions to Old Ones, in the Dunciad Variorum' which comments on changes in the *Dunciad* and ends with ten lines of verse.

May 13, 1729 (*Monthly Chronicle*)

Pope Alexander's Supremacy and Infallibility examin'd; And the Errors of Scriblerus and his Man William Detected. With The Effigies Of His Holiness and his Prime Minister, Curiously engrav'd on Copper. Obscene with Filth the Miscreant lies bewray'd, / Fall'n in the Plash, his Wickedness had laid. Dunciad, Lib. II. ver. 71, and 72. London: Sold by J. Roberts in Warwick-Lane. M.DCC.XXIX. Price 1s. 6d.

4to. The format was planned so that it might be bound up with the 'last pompous Edition of the *Dunciad*' (p. 18).
Frontispiece, three leaves unsigned, B–E⁴, one unsigned leaf.
Frontispiece, [4 pp.], v–vi, 1–18, 1–6, 1–8 pp., [9] advertisement, [10] blank.
The frontispiece is Wimsatt 7. 11.

The authorship is vexed. Pope wrote to Lord Oxford, May 16, 1729,
> I see a Book with a Curious Cutt calld Pope Alexrs Supremacy &c. 4°. In it are 3 or 4 things so false & scandalous that I think I know the Authors, and they are of a Rank to merit Detection ... The book is writ by Burnet, & a Person who has great obligations to me, & the Cut is done by Ducket. I would fain come at the proof of this, for Reasons of a Very High Nature.
> (*Corr.* III. 33–4)

In 1735 Pope ascribed the book to Duckett and Dennis (*Twick.* v. 212); Dennis is, as Sherburn points out, 'strangely described as "a person who has great obligations to me"' (*Corr.* III. 33, n.3). Hooker does not think Dennis was involved in it (Hooker, II. ix–x) and David Nichol Smith thinks it unlikely Duckett had a part in it (*Letters of Thomas Burnet*, p. xix).

WORKS: A. *First Psalm*; B. Homer; C. *Court Ballad*; D. Pope's edition of Shakespeare; E. *Dunciad*.

Fronti Fides

MARTINI SCRIBLERI VERA EFFIGIES.

A Letter to the Publisher

The frontispiece to *Pope Alexander's Supremacy and Infallibility examin'd.*

CHARGES: 1. Pope deformed; 2. Pope ungrateful to Wycherley, Addison, and Steele; 3. Pope a spy for the Tories; 4. The dunces prepared a beating for Pope after the 1728 *Dunciad*, but Pope hid; 5. Philips hung up a rod for Pope in Button's, but Pope stayed away; 6. Pope never laughs.

The first item, pp. v–vi, in this miscellaneous compilation (I omit mention of several trivialities) is given under the drop-title, 'Inscriptions graven on the four Sides of the Pedestal, whereon is erected the Busto of Martinus Scriblerus, from which Original the Effigies prefix'd to this Work was taken' (p. v). There are inscriptions in Greek, Latin, Spanish, and English, the last being the most interesting:

> Chuse for this Work a Stump of crooked Thorn,
> Or Log of Poison Tree, from *India* born:
> There carve a *Pert*, but yet a *Rueful* Face,
> Half Man, half Monkey, own'd by neither Race.
> Be his Crown Picked, to One Side reclin'd,
> Be to his Neck his Buttocks closely join'd;
> With Breast protuberant, and Belly thin,
> Bones all distorted, and a shrivell'd Skin.
>   This his Misshapen Form: But say, what Art
> Can frame the monst'rous Image of his Heart.
> Compos'd of *Malice, Envy, Discontent,*
>   Like his Limbs crooked, like them impotent.   (p. vi)

See Wimsatt, p. 101.

The second item, pp. 1–8, has the drop-title, 'A Letter To The Writer of a Letter to my Lord—Occasion'd by a Letter to the Publisher of the present Edition of the Dunciad Variorum' and is signed, p. 8, 'Richard Smith'. The writer predicts hopefully that if the *Dunciad* survives, as the Publisher's Prefaces say it will, it will be only as

> a Monument of his Infamy; and those that come after us will and must believe, the Persons who stood the Marks of his petulant Malice, to be Worthy and Good Men; ... they will see a little invidious narrow Mind in every Line he has written; they will blush at his indecent Idaeas, and be shock'd at his Scurrility.
>   (pp. 2–3)

He is worried that posterity, should the *Dunciad* survive, may imagine its author to have been at least seven feet high; he therefore informs us,

> that this same Gyant, was but about four Foot and an Half high, of a Structure a little irregular, and his Genius Low and indecent as his Form. (p. 3)

The third item, pp. 9–18, under the drop-title, 'A Letter To A Noble Lord: Occasion'd by the late Publication of the Dunciad Variorum', is dated, p. 9, April 5, 1729, and signed, p. 18, 'Will. Flogg'. This constitutes the heart of the pamphlet.

The author explains that he has just been loaned the *Dunciad* by the nobleman to whom he is writing, a copy having been left at the peer's house, as copies were with so many peers. He has found out the true author and prefixed his effigy to the pamphlet; it is impossible Pope should have written it.

E   He admits that true and just satire may be beneficial; it may even be praiseworthy to expose the defects of a writer by ridicule or argument, if done with good manners, although never a writer's private reputation. Grubstreet had offended Pope; still, they had used either initials or feigned names. It was reserved for Pope 'to invent the *Ne plus ultra* of Scandal' by printing names at length, while suppressing his own (p. 13).

His version of Pope's friendship with Wycherley is the usual one:

2   I find, that upon his first coming to Town, out of pure Compassion for his exotick Figure, narrow Circumstances, and humble Appearance, the late Mr. *Wycherley* admitted him into his Society, and suffer'd him, notwithstanding his Make, to be his humble admirer at *Will*'s; and afterwards finding in him a glimmering of Genius, recommended him to some People of Rank, and introduc'd him to the most eminent Men of Letters; which Courtesy he soon after repaid with a satyrical Copy of Verses on his Benefactor ... (p. 13)

B 2   Addison and Steele set on foot a subscription for him for a work [the *Iliad*] they must have known he was unequal to. When the subscriptions were full, he wrote a satire on both, and later published an abusive libel on one of them [the 'Atticus portrait'] (pp. 13–14). What the earlier satire was, I do not know.

Pope was a Tory spy:

3   ... as many Things which has pass'd in private Conversation at *Button*'s Coffee-house, came to be known by the Lord *O*[*xford*], of which Infidelity *Scriblerus* was suspected, he was obliged to absent himself for some Years from thence. After this, he listed openly in the *Tory* Service, and every Week publish'd scandalous Invectives on those very *Whigs*, who had been his amplest *Subscribers*. (p. 14)

He was busy at this when the Queen died.

C   When after the Queen's death he had managed to be introduced

to some of the young ladies of the court, 'he abused in a Scurvy Ballad' [the *Court Ballad*] the four of them 'who were his best Friends and Patronesses' (p. 14). The ladies, however, felt only contempt for his malice.

> This did not hinder him from writing a second Lampoon, wherein he spared not the most exalted Characters, though under feigned Names; and adding Treachery to Ill-Nature, he threw the scandalous Imputation of having wrote this Libel, on a Lady of Quality, whose Wit is equal to her Beauty, and whose Character might have suffer'd by this impudent Forgery of his. (p. 14)

Does this refer to the *Court Poems* and Lady Mary?

A   Pope has also imitated the First Psalm 'in a most edifying Manner' (p. 16).

4   When Pope published the 1728 *Dunciad*, the gentlemen slandered in it did not think correction of the poet worth while, since they had been pointed at only by initials.

> Yet I have been credibly inform'd, that some of them resorted to no Place where *Scriblerus* might possibly be met with, without the Provision of a Rod, to whip this *Old Boy*, for his untoward Malice. (p. 15)

But Pope prudently absconded for over a month, and as only he himself had been hurt by the scandal, resentment cooled until the appearance in 1729 of the *Variorum*.

5   He also tells the story of Ambrose Philips and his rod; apparently this is the first mention of the incident (see Sherburn, pp. 120–1). Aretino, he says, had been reformed by a beating, but our poet

> must of Necessity expire under the very first Blow; and he can, by the Structure of his Person, only be liable to one Sort of Correction, that of the *Rod*; which some Years ago Mr. *Ambrose Philips*, being abused by him, bought for his Use, and stuck up at the Bar of *Button*'s Coffee-house; and which he avoided by his usual Practice after every Lampoon, of remaining a close Prisoner at Home. (p. 16)

6   No definition of man will include the author of the *Dunciad*. He is neither social, or rational, or risible. Pope has never

> been observ'd, since the Hour of his Birth, to have risen above a broad Grin, common to him with the Quadrupede, most resembling Human Nature. (p. 18)

The fifth item, pp. 1–7, third count, with the drop-title, 'A Curious Receipt, wherein is disclosed, the Art of writing Poetry with a small Genius, taken from Martinus Scriblerus's Writings', explains at length

Q

that the great secret of Scriblerus is alliteration, as e.g., in *Dunciad* A, i. 65–6,

> She sees a Mob of Metaphors advance
> Pleas'd with the Madness of the mazy dance.

Adjectives are selected only to fill up the measure and to alliterate. 'Thus must *Comfort* always be cold, the *Day* at Noon *Dawning* . . .' (p. 3).

The seventh item, p. 8, third count, with the drop-title, 'A Dialogue between Hurlothrumbo and Death. Inscrib'd to Martin and his Man William', consists of 24 lines of verse. Death, meeting Hurlothrumbo, tells him he is on his way to Twickenham to find a pigmy poet. Hurlothrumbo warns him,

BD
> *Homer* and *Shakespear* thou, in vain,
> Through many Ages would'st have slain;
> Our *Alexander*, at one Blow,
> Has laid th'Immortal Bards full low.   (p. 8)

May 14, 1729 (*Monthly Chronicle*)

[Henley, John?] Tom o' Bedlam's Dunciad: Or, Pope, Alexander the Pig. A Poem.—Popius cunctis è partibus Orbem / Aspicit accensum: nec tantos sustinet Aestus. Ovid Met. London: Printed for M. Turner at the Post-Office, Corner of Bow-Street, Covent-Garden; and Sold at the Booksellers in London and Westminster. 1729 (Price Six-Pence.)

Folio.
[A]–B².
[2 pp.], 3–8 pp.

Rogers, p. 138, observes that the style suggests 'Orator' Henley. The ascription seems probable. The same charge of Billingsgate made here was made in Henley's *Why How now, Gossip Pope*, 1743, q.v., and cf. the Oratory advertisement in the *Daily Post*, April 29, 1729, 'Tomorrow, at Seven o'Clock, will be held forth Tom o'Bedlam's Dunciad; or a Wager, who makes the best Hurlothrumbo, I, or Pope Alexander the Pig?' (*Twick.* v. 444).

WORK: A. *Dunciad.*

CHARGES: 1. Pope learns his language from watermen and Billings-gate; 2. Pope nearly illiterate.

The point, very clumsily made, is simply that Pope learns and re-news his invective from watermen and Billingsgate. The opening lines indicate the writer's confusion of satire with cursing:

> No Muse I seek, but summon to my Aid
> Each scolding Bard, and Bully of the Trade!
> Also my Pray'r, ye *Hackney* Drivers! hear:
> Ye Draymen! Link-boys! hearken to my Pray'r!
> Ye Tritons of the River help my Song;
> And Wives of *Billingsgate* about me throng!   (p. 3)

Pope learns his language from watermen:

> How oft, when settl'd in a studying mood,
> He walks along the Shore of *Isis*' Flood?
> And, when his own foul stock of Rage is spent,
> The neighb'ring Stairs for Knowledge do's frequent!
> Thus, what his own poor shallow Pate denies,
> Each cursing Hector of the Stream supplies.
>   O! wonder not, that he such Flights has shown,
> He shines in borrow'd Beauties; not his own.
> Well might his *Smithfield* Muse so sweetly sing,
> Since Watermen their due Assistance bring.   (p. 5)

There is an unpleasant picture of Pope's imagined distress:

> But see! he hears me, grins, and wildly stares,
> And deep in Wrath hangs down his *Midas'd* Ears.
> Too soon his Servant Wench, poor *Betty*! will,
> I fear, his raging-hot Displeasure feel.
> Up Stairs and down, in Anger he proceeds,
> And fumes and frets; scarce knowing where he treads.
> What wou'd I give to see his furious Tricks,
> Deep in his Heart when thorny Satyr sticks?   (p. 6)

Pope calls around him his doggerel scribblers and complains that their foes increase and are men of sense and wit who,

> Are better taught, and read than we! can tell
> The way to write; and we can hardly spell.   (p. 7)

He threatens suicide, but his friends suggest that he lacks the courage and attempt to comfort him by pointing out Billingsgate:

> 'There's *Billingsgate*! an unexhausted Spring,
> Whence we our Flights and Witticisms bring.'

                                                   (p. 8)

June 6, 1729 (*Monthly Chronicle*)

A Sequel To The Dunciad; Being The famous British Sh—rs. A Satire. Omne tulit punctum, qui miscuit utile dulci. London: Printed for A. Moore, near St. Paul's; and Sold at the Pamphlet-Shops. M.DCC.XXIX. [Price One Shilling and Six-pence.]

Folio.

[A]–F².

[2 pp.], 3–24 pp.

WORKS: A. Homer; B. Pope's edition of Shakespeare; C. *Dunciad*.

The nature of this poem forbids extensive quotation. English poets, including many of the dunces, are discussed and compared entirely in terms of their excrement, its amount, consistency, taste. The two references to Pope both concern his Homer.

A

But *P*— (with Vanity and Emptiness,
His Microcos'm grip'd to an Excess)
Like distant Thunder rumbles from behind,
Yet all he vents is little else but Wind;
The sovereign Lord of Poets he devours,
And makes him in a shitten manner, ours.   (p. 4)

A sh—g, Creature, of Repute of late
(Tho' more by Fortune sure, than Merit great)
With Excrement opprobrious, rough, and hard,
Fouly besmear'd th' illustrious *Grecian* Bard;
Oh! say (as *Homer* everlasting Fame)
Does he not merit everlasting Blame?   (p. 12–13)

As for Theobald:

BC

The *Dunciad's* Hero paid for Sh—g dear,
Yet still proclaims he does not sh—e for Fear.
He rakes, with searching Industry, among
The Hoard of *Shakespear's* antiquated Dung;
There Gold he finds, or what for Gold he'd pass,
And swears what *P*— collected there, was Brass:

              .   .   .

Pho! let the Sire's old Fundament alone,
And, if thou canst, void Treasure from thy own.   (p. 8)

July 7, 1729 (*Monthly Chronicle*)

Dennis, John. Remarks Upon Several Passages In The Preliminaries to the Dunciad, Both of the Quarto and the Duodecimo Edition. And Upon Several Passages in Pope's Preface to his Translation of Homer's Iliad. In both which is shewn, The Author's Want of Judgment. With Original Letters from Sir Richard Steele, from the late Mr. Gildon, from Mr. Jacob, and from Mr. Pope himself, Which shew the Falshood of the latter, his Envy, and his Malice. By Mr. Dennis. London: Printed for H. Whitridge, at the Corner of Castle Alley next the Royal Exchange in Cornhill. M.DCC. XXIX.

Half-title: Remarks Upon Mr. Pope's Dunciad.

8vo.

[A]^4, B–D^8, E^4.

[8 pp.], [1]–56 pp.

Reprinted in Hooker, II. 353–76.

WORKS: A. *Essay on Criticism*; B. *Windsor Forest*; C. *Narrative of Dr. Robert Norris*; D. *Temple of Fame*; E. *Iliad*; F. *Peri Bathous*; G. *Dunciad*.

CHARGES: 1. Pope teased Lintot to print Dennis's *Remarks upon Cato*; 2. Pope wrote the flattering account of himself in the *Poetical Register*; 3. Pope collaborated in *The Beggar's Opera*.

The *Remarks*, in the form of a letter to Theobald, discuss the 'preliminaries' before the duodecimo and quarto editions of the *Dunciad*, insisting, of course, that they are written by Pope himself. In an important passage, since it is one of the rare contemporary attempts to examine the structure of the *Dunciad*, Dennis attacks the statement in 'The Publisher to the Reader', 'The Dunciad is stiled Heroick . . .' and argues that the *Dunciad* is not an epic. Let us see, he says, what the proposition of an epic poem ought to be and then whether Pope's proposition conforms to the rules. He quotes Le Bossu as saying that the proposition must propose an action, and shows by quotation from Boileau and Butler that this rule holds for the comic epic. He then quotes the opening couplet of the *Dunciad* and comments:

> Thus *P*. sings Books, and not an Action; and the Author who pretends in an Epick Poem to sing Books instead of singing an Action, is only qualified to sing Ballads. (p. 17)

(The objection to 'Books' is odd, since Le Bossu in the passage Dennis himself has quoted says that we should not believe that Homer is proposing the wrath of Achilles as his subject – that would have been a passion, not an action. Homer is proposing the wrath that caused such suffering to the Greeks and the death of so many heroes, i.e. an action.)

> P. is so far from singing an Action, that there is no such Thing as Action in his whimsical Rhapsody, unless what proceeds from Dulness, that is, from Privation; a very pretty Principle of Action, and very worthy of P.'s Invention! The Thing is divided into Three Books. In the First, instead of Action there is Description and Declamation. In the Third, instead of Action we have nothing but a feverish Dream. The Second is made up of Nastiness, Obscenity, and Absurdity; and is so far from being Part of an Action, that it runs counter to the Design of the whole Thing, if there could be any Design in it; for Vigour of Action can never proceed from Dulness, though it may from Madness. The Hero of the Piece does nothing at all, and never speaks but once, unless it be half a Line in the Third Book. In the First Book, indeed, he offers to burn his Works, but is hinder'd by the Goddess: Now those Works are either Good or Bad; if they are Good, they render him incapable of being King of the Dunces; if they are Bad, the Offer to burn them shews his Judgment, and Judgment must be always contrary to Dulness, otherwise P. would be the brightest Creature that ever God made.
>
> (pp. 17–18)

An epic must also have 'Probability in all its Parts' (p. 18), as Dennis proves from Horace and Boileau.

> But what Probability is there in P.'s Rhapsody? What Probability in the Games which take up a third Part of the Piece? Is it not monstrous to imagine any Thing like that in the Master Street of a populous City; a Street eternally crowded with Carriages, Carts, Coaches, Chairs, and Men passing in the greatest Hurry about Private and Publick Affairs? (p. 19)

He then interrupts his discussion of the *Dunciad* to attack the Preface to Homer. When he returns to the *Dunciad* it is to discuss 'A Letter to the Publisher', signed 'W.C.', in the quarto. Dennis, of course, insists it is by Pope. The statement that most of the dunces had been the first aggressors provokes Dennis into giving a useful summary of his relations with Pope:

ABDE   At his first coming to Town, he was very importunate with the

late Mr. *Henry Cromwell* to introduce him to me: The Recommendation of Mr. *Cromwell* engaged me to be about thrice in Company with him; after which I went into the Country, and neither saw him nor thought of him, 'till I found myself most insolently attack'd by him, in his very superficial Essay upon Criticism, which was the Effect of his impotent Envy and Malice, by which he endeavour'd to destroy the Reputation of a Man who had publish'd Pieces of Criticism, and to set up his own. I was mov'd with Indignation to that Degree, at so much Baseness, that I immediately writ Remarks upon that Essay, in order to expose the Weakness and the Absurdity of it; which Remarks were publish'd, as soon as they could be printed. I afterwards writ and publish'd Remarks upon Part of his Translation of *Homer*, upon his *Windsor Forest*, and his infamous *Temple of Fame*. When I had done this, I thought I had Reason to be satisfied with the Revenge I had taken. As these several Remarks had made great Impressions upon the Minds of Persons of undoubted Sense, and so esteem'd by the Publick, *P.* began to repent of the Affront he had offer'd me, and the Injury he had attempted to do me ... (p. 39)

As proof of his repentance, Pope subscribed to the two volumes of Dennis's *Select Works* and to the two volumes of his *Original Letters*, from which Dennis had struck out the reflections on Pope. Dennis prints Pope's letter to him of May 3, 1721 (see *Corr.* II. 75–6). Dennis had ceased to be Pope's enemy, but he could not trust him entirely as long as he remembered the Cato incident, which he calls 'a Piece of monstrous Perfidy' (p. 41), and of which he gives the following account (he had first made the charge in *A True Character*, 1716, q.v.):

The great Success of Mr. *Addison*'s *Cato* fermented his Envy, and provok'd his Malice exceedingly. To discharge some Part of his Spleen, he goes to Mr. *Lintot* the Bookseller, and persuades him to engage me to write some Remarks upon Mr. *Addison*'s Play. He prevail'd upon the Bookseller, and the Bookseller upon me. I need not acquaint you that I wrote and publish'd such Remarks. But his Gratitude for my complying with his Request, may, perhaps, be a Piece of News, that will not a little surprize you: He writes a very scurrilous and impertinent Pamphlet, in which he acquaints his Reader, that I was in the Hands of Dr. *Norris*, a Curer of mad People, at his House in *Hatton-Garden*, tho' at the same Time I appear'd publickly every Day both in the

Park and in the Town. The Manuscript of this Pamphlet he offer'd to shew to Mr. *Addison* before it was printed, who had too much Honour, and too much good Sense to approve of so black a Proceeding. (p. 41)

And Dennis prints the letter he says Addison made Steele write Lintot, p. 42, and which Lintot sent on to Dennis who kept it (the letter is reprinted in *Corr.* I. 184; see *Prose*, I. xxv–xxviii). Dennis was thus unable to trust Pope, although he had ceased to be his enemy until Pope

FG gave him fresh provocation by 'his chimerical *Profund* and his filthy *Dunciad*, and so became a second Time the Aggressor ...' (p. 43).

Dennis is next concerned to disprove Pope's charge in his note to the *Dunciad* A, i. 104, that the character of Dennis in Jacob's *Lives* is written by Dennis himself. To do this he prints, pp. 44–9, a letter dated 'Thursday April 24, 1729' addressed to Dennis and signed 'Giles Jacob' which Dennis says he received unsolicited from Jacob. Jacob solemnly denies that Dennis knew anything at all of the praise of Dennis in the *Lives* until the book was printed and published. Pope's allegation is 'a malicious and scandalous Insinuation' (p. 45). He then quotes, very loosely, some of the praise of Pope in the *Lives* which, he says, Pope

2   particularly approv'd of, in a printed Proof of his Life and Character, which I transmitted to him for his Correction ... and by his Alterations and Additions therein, he entirely made the Compliment his own ... (p. 46)

(See *The Poetical Register*, 1719.)

Jacob laments his role in the *Dunciad*:

He has done all in the Compass of his Malice, to defame, injure, beat down every one he knew, except his Friend and Confederate the ingenious *John Gay*, on Pretence of my accusing of whom, for telling the Truth of that extraordinary Gentleman, I have the great and disproportion'd Share of his violent Invectives which run thro' his *Dunciad*. (p. 47)

Jacob's abuse of Gay refers apparently to *The Poetical Register*, 1719, q.v.

3   Jacob objects especially to being called a 'Blunderbuss of Law' (A, iii. 150); Pope is no judge of law (p. 47). He promises a just portrayal of Pope and Gay in a supplement to his account of them in the *Lives* and says Pope and Gay 'clubb'd their Wit' in *The Beggar's Opera* (p. 48).

Dennis concludes by listing ten differences between Pope and Boileau to show the wrongness of the comparison with Boileau with which

the 'Letter to the Publisher' closes. Pope, for example, never praises his contemporaries (p. 53).

E   To return to the middle section of the pamphlet devoted to the Preface to Homer, Dennis calls Pope's Preface

> neither a just Dissertation, nor a modest Encomium, but an extravagant hyperbolical Panegyrick on *Homer*; a Heap of dogmatical, elaborate, illiterate Pedantry ... (p. 21)

Pope has misused 'invention', taking it

> for a peculiar Faculty of the Mind, distinct from Memory, Imagination, and Judgment; whereas it is the Effect and Result of the confederate Powers and Operation of all the three. (p. 22)

(The sentences Dennis discusses are found in *Prose*, I. 224.) Pope was wrong in saying that it is to Homer's invention that we are to attribute his fire; on the contrary, it is to his fire that we are to attribute his invention.

> The more warm any one is by Nature, the more inventive is that Person, if the Organs be rightly dispos'd. (p. 28)

Nor should Pope have said that everything that Homer writes 'is of the most animated Nature imaginable' (p. 28).

> If everything that is said in Council is of the most animated Nature imaginable, the Characters of those who speak, either cannot be maintain'd, or cannot be diversify'd. (p. 29)

August 7, 1729 (*Monthly Chronicle*)

[Ward, Edward.] Apollo's Maggot in his Cups: Or, The Whimsical Creation Of A Little Satyrical Poet. A Lyrick Ode. Laudatur ab his, culpatur ab illis. Hor. Whilst Poets scribble for the Baies, / Some will condemn, what others praise: / Reader, do which will please thee best, / The Author only writes in jest, / And leaves the serious part o' th' Quarrel, / To Wits that scuffle for the Laurel. Merrily Dedicated to Dicky Dickison, the Witty, but deform'd Governour of Scarborough-Spaw. London: Printed and Sold by the Booksellers of London and Westminster. MDCCXXIX. Price 1s.

8vo in half-sheets.
A–G⁴, H in three leaves.
[14 pp.], 1–48 pp.

Texas has a copy, otherwise identical, with the imprint, 'Printed: and Sold by T. Warner at the Black-Boy in Pater-Noster-Row, and the Booksellers of London and Westminster'.

The authorship is made clear in the Postscript, and the pamphlet is included in the bibliography of Ward's writings in Howard William Troyer, *Ned Ward of Grubstreet* (Cambridge, U.S.A., 1946), p. 232.

WORKS: A. *Peri Bathous*; B. *Dunciad*.

CHARGE: 1. Pope deformed.

The verse Dedication (A2r–B1v) 'To the Worshipful Dicky Dickison, Esq; Distorted Governour of Scarborough-Spaw, and Jester in Ordinary to the Merry Northern Aquaepotes' is clearly directed to Pope.

1

> Nor do the Ladies that frequent
> The Wells, for Health and Merriment,
> Tho' to thy Merits over kind,
> Admire the Beauties of thy Mind,
> But like thee, as they do their Apes,
> Not for thy Wit, but Monkey-shapes.   (A3r)

> No charming Mortal can desire,
> To raise our admiration higher,
> Than you can do, when you're inclin'd
> To stir up Wonder in Mankind;
> Tis but appearing to Beholders,
> Without false Calfs and padded Shoulders;
> Then, with astonishment, they'll see
> A Chaos, few can show but thee,
> A frightful, indigested Lump,
> With here a Hollow, there a Hump;
> A true Epitome of *Wales*,
> Made up of ugly Hills and Dales.   (A3v)

AB1   'The Author To The Reader' (B2r–B3v) recounts the story from Pliny of the deformed Ephesian satirist Hipponax who so persecuted with 'terrible Heroick *Dunciads*, scurrilous *Profunds*' two painters who had secretly painted his picture, that they hanged themselves. Some ill-favoured Wits have made 'the present Age merry with their scare-crow Prints, as if they were proud of their Deformities' (B2v). Is a reference intended to the portrait of Pope in the 1717 *Works*?

The poem itself is too disgusting to quote. After a drunken feast of the gods, Apollo visits Parnassus and proposes to the Muses that they

form a satirist, a something between a monkey and a man. Having formed a body with muck, they urinate and defecate upon it. Apollo adds the brains and animates it with a bellows, 'plac'd to the backward Vent', and drops him down between Thames and Isis where he reigns 'as King of modern Wits'. It is clearly implied that Pope is impotent (pp. 18–20). I give a sample of a more quotable part:

> The Ladies that admire thy Strains,
>   When they behold the Poet
> Shall laugh in Scorn behind their Fans,
>   But thou, alas, not know it.
>
> Thy own Defects thou shalt not see,
>   Yet find out Faults in others,
> And shalt Flogmaster-Gen'ral be,
>   O'er all thy rhiming Brothers.   (p. 25)

The 'Postscript' or 'Falshoods by Alexander Pope against Edward Ward' (pp. 29–48) contains more railing at the *Dunciad* and replies to each of the passages mentioning Ward in the *Dunciad*. What rankled most with Ward was Pope's claim that Ward 'has of late Years kept a publick house in the City (but in a genteel way) and with his wit, humour, and good liquor (Ale) afforded his guests a pleasurable entertainment' (*Twick.* v. 87, n.). Ward, pp. 30–1, denies he ever kept a Public House in the City; he has kept a tavern in Moorfields for twelve years but has never 'sold a drop of Ale, or any other sort of Malt-Liquor since he has there resided' (p. 31). Pope had drunk wine at Ward's establishment and knew it was a tavern, yet turned it into an Ale-house to insinuate 'that *Ward* is possess'd of no other Qualifications than what are directly sutable [*sic*] to so humble a Station' (p. 38). Pope included part of Ward's correction in the note and in the *Errata* (*Twick.* v. 198), but made Ward protest that he sold port. On Ward's taverns see *Twick.* v. 474.

August 11, 1729 (*Monthly Chronicle*)

[Oldmixon, John?] Memoirs Of The Life, Writings, and Amours Of William Congreve Esq; Interspersed with Miscellaneous Essays, Letters, and Characters, Written by Him. Also Some very Curious Memoirs of Mr. Dryden and his Family, with a

Character of Him and his Writings, by Mr. Congreve. Compiled from their respective Originals, By Charles Wilson Esq; Poets have an unquestion'd Right to claim, / If not the Greatest, the most Lasting Name. Congreve. London: Printed in the Year M.DCC. XXX. (Price 5s.)

8vo.
Frontispiece, A–H⁸, A–K⁸, B–E⁴, F in one leaf.
Frontispiece, [2 pp.], [iii]–vii, [viii] blank, ix–xvi, [1]–112 [Part I]; 1–156 [Part II]; [4 pp.] index, 1–34 pp.; xiii misnumbered iix.

The *CBEL* ascribes this doubtfully to John Oldmixon, Straus without any question (Straus, p. 290). A second edition is listed in the *Monthly Chronicle*, January 13, 1730, but I have not located a copy.

WORK: A. *Dunciad*.

CHARGE: 1. Pope deformed.

Only the dedication ([iii]–vii) to George Duckett, signed and dated 'Cha. Wilson, Bath, July 14, 1729' (p. vii), attacks Pope.

A 1
He [Congreve] was likewise a *Brother-Commissioner*, which in these Days of *Dunciad-Scandal*, is, it seems a *notorious Sarcasm*; but the *Impotent Malice* of such Libellers (who love to *Laugh*, where they cannot *Ridicule*; and to *Rally*, where they cannot *Reason*) has no *Force*, and the *Effect* is fully summ'd up in this excellent Distich of my Lord *Rochester*'s Satire against Man.
　　So Magick Ointments make an old Witch fly,
　　And bear a cripled Carcass thro' the Sky.　　(pp. iv–vi)
There is some severe abuse of Dennis's pamphlets against Pope in Pt II, and on p. 141 a very mild reference to the Atticus portrait.

October 23, 1729 (*Monthly Chronicle*)

[Roberts, John.] An Answer To Mr. Pope's Preface To Shakespear. In a Letter to a Friend. Being A Vindication of the Old Actors who were the Publishers and Performers of that Author's Plays. Whereby The Errors of their Edition are further accounted for, and some Memoirs of Shakespear and Stage-History of His Time are inserted, which were never before collected and

publish'd. By a Stroling Player. Say from what Cause (by all condemn'd and curst!) / Still Bays the Second rails like Bays the First! Right Reading of the Dunciad Variorum from a Manuscript (revised and collated by this Author) which is interpolated by the last Editor. London: Printed in the Year MDCCXXIX.

8vo in half-sheets.
One unsigned leaf, A–E⁴, F in three leaves.
[2 pp.], [3]–48 pp.

Attributed in the *BM Cat.* to John Roberts, Comedian.

WORK: A. Pope's Preface to his edition of Shakespeare.

Roberts, with splendid confidence in his own knowledge of Shakespearean stage history and textual problems, attempts, in the part of the pamphlet which concerns us, a repetitious and badly reasoned refutation of some remarks by Pope in his 'Preface to Shakespeare'. Roberts objects especially to Pope's views on the social position of the Elizabethan player; he is sure that he was much more gifted intellectually and his social position much higher than Pope has made out. Pope

> speaks of them [the players] but very unskilfully, or *if his Knowledge were more, it is much darkned* [sic] *in his Malice*; and it may reasonably be said, that all his Calumny towards them proceeds from Envy, Folly, or Mistaking; Tho I am apt to assign it rather to his Ill-Nature than to his Ignorance ... (p. 41)

Theobald is said to have 'fully prov'd his Capacity superior to every *former Editor*' (p. 26), and there is a parody of Pope's unfortunate phrase:

> ... I have had a strict Regard to Truth, and very candidly observ'd *the dull Duty of an Author* (or in another Reading, *the Duty of a dull Author*) in delivering nothing but what is *ex fide codicum* ... (p. 43)

That it was the *Dunciad* that provoked this tardy reply to Pope's Shakespeare is suggested by the following typical remark:

> But this *universal Calumniator* scorns to confine himself to Sincerity and plain Matter of Fact in *this Preface* as much as in his *darling Poem* [the *Dunciad*?] ... (p. 44)

November 29, 1729 (*Monthly Chronicle*)

[Roome, Edward.] Dean Jonathan's Parody On The 4th Chap. of Genesis. London: Printed for Timothy Atkins, and Sold by the Booksellers of London and Westminster. 1729 [Price Sixpence.]

Folio.
Four leaves unsigned.
[2 pp.], [3]–7 pp., [8] blank.

Reprinted in *Tunbrigalia*, 1740, q.v., and, with the substitution of Cibber for Theobald, as *Blast upon Blast*, 1742, q.v. Pope attributed it to Edward Roome (*Twick.* v. 212).

WORK: A. Pope's edition of Shakespeare.

CHARGES: 1. Pope's father a hatter; 2. Pope deformed.

This is, as the title states, a fairly close parody of Genesis iv. It opens:

1   Verse 1. And it came to pass, that *Pope* the Hatter went in unto his Wife, and knew her; and she conceived, and bare a Son, and she called his Name *Alexander*, and said, I have gotten, as it were, a Man-child from the Lord.
        Verse 2. And behold the Child was exceeding fair, and comely to see to, and waxed tall, and in Favour with God and Man; and he became a Rhymer of Rhymes in those Days. But *Theobald* his Brother was a meek Man, and skilled in all the Learning of the Heathens. (p. [3])

A   Verse 3. And in Process of Time it came to pass, that *Pope* brought of the Fruits of his Leisure, an Edition of *Shakespear*, as an Offering to the Town.
        Verse 4. And *Theobald* he also brought of the Firstlings of his Study, even a Specimen of *Shakespeare*. And the Town had Respect unto *Theobald* and his *Shakespeare*. (p. 4)

But the town did not have respect unto Pope's. Finally Pope 'rose up privily against Theobald' in the field 'and cast stones and Filth at him, and evil entreated him' (p. 4). Pope, as a result, is cursed from the town. 'When thou beggest of the Town, she shall not henceforth yield her Subscriptions any more' (p. 5).

2   Pope is marked lest any man finding him beat him. He retires to Twickenham.
        Verse 18. And *Pope* knew his Nurse, and she conceiv'd and bare

a Child, and called his Name *Crambo*, and he builded a House and called it after his Son's Name; and it is called *Castle-Crambo* to this Day. (p. 6)

When the nurse dies she is buried 'in the Cave of *Twickenham*, called *Kneller's Cave* ... And then the Mourning of *Pope*, the Son of the Hatter, was ended' (pp. 6–7).

Mary Beach (*c*. 1647–1725) lived at Twickenham as a servant to Pope and his mother. She had no recorded children. The parish church at Twickenham had been rebuilt under the auspices of Sir Godfrey Kneller; her burial is recorded in the parish register under the date November 7, 1725 (*Horace Walpole's Correspondence with Sir Horace Mann*, ed. W. S. Lewis, Warren Hunting Smith, and George L. Lam (New Haven, 1954), II. 35, n.27 and n.28, 36, n.30).

'Crambo' is defined in the *OED* as '1. A game in which one player gives a word or line of verse to which each of the others has to find a rhyme; 2. *transf*. Rime, riming, said in contempt.'

1729 (?)

Durgen, A Satyr, To The Ceberbeted [*sic*] Mr. P—pe, On His Dunciad: By Namby Pamby.

Folio broadside. Since it has been pasted on to heavy paper, the verso is invisible. At the bottom is the imprint: 'Dublin: Printed by Rich. Dickson, in Silver-Court in Castle-Street; where Advertisements are taken in for the Dublin Intelligence, and other Printing-Work done Reasonably.'

CHARGES: 1. Pope's verse is smutty; 2. Pope deformed.

This poem in 24 couplets opens:

> Seraphic Brute! How else shall I address
> A Poet breathing Smut in shining Verse?
> Sweet and sublime thy lofty Numbers flow,
> And heav'nly Raptures in thy Periods glow,
> But the coarse Mixture of polluted Strains,
> Like some fell Blight the fair Creation stains.
> Beneath that gay Attire, those Robes of Light,
> A Fiend of Darkness opens to our Sight.

Mistake me not to ridicule thy Frame,
Which adds not to thy Glory, nor thy Shame,
Only 'tis something wond'rous to behold,
That Soul and Body both are of one Mould.

February 12, 1730 (*Monthly Chronicle*)

Claudian's Rufinus: Or, The Court-Favourite's Overthrow. Being A Curious and Correct Grub-street Edition of One of the best Satyrical Poems, of One of the best Poets, on One of the Worst Statesmen that ever liv'd. Ore legar populi. Ut pictura poesis erit, qua, si propiùs stes, / Te capiet magis; & quaedam, si longiùs abstes: / Haec amat obscurum, volet haec sub luce videri, / Judicis argutum quae non formidat acumen; / Haec placuit semel, haec decies repetita placebit. Hor. de Ar. Po. London: Printed for C. Guest, in the Strand. 1730 (Price Six Pence).

8vo in half-sheets.
One unsigned leaf, a⁴, b⁴, A–C⁴, one unsigned leaf.
[2 pp.], [iii]–xvi, [1]–26 pp., [27–8].

Yale has the second edition. The title-page omits 'Grub-street,' adds after 'Ar. Po.' 'The Second Edition', and has the imprint: 'London: Printed for E. Smith, at the Royal Exchange: Sold by the Book-Sellers, and Pamphlet-Sellers in London and Westminster. M.DCC. XXX. (Price Six Pence.)'

8vo in half-sheets.
One unsigned leaf, a–b⁴, A–C⁴, one unsigned leaf.
[2 pp.], [iii]–xvi, [1]–26 pp., [27–8].
My quotations are taken from the second edition.

WORK: A. *Dunciad.*

CHARGES: 1. Pope a literary dictator; 2. Pope a rich man; 3. Pope multiplies editions.

1   The Preface (pp. [iii]–xvi), which alone concerns us, has the drop-title: 'The Prefatory Introduction, Address'd to Alexander Pope, Esq;

requesting his Judgment of this extraordinary Piece', and is signed (p. xv) 'Nameless Name'. After running through, offhandedly, the life and reputation of Claudian and the characters of Rufinus and Stilicho, he begins a new section, headed, p. xi, 'A modest Appeal to Mr. POPE, about the real Value and Excellency of this Work, and requesting him to give an Impartial Judgment of the Performance'. This is apparently an attempt to sell the translation by using the notoriety of the *Dunciad*, although, if we can believe the writer, he is not mentioned in Pope's poem by name; it is certainly another fling at Pope, the would-be dictator, able to raise or crush a struggling author.

He asks Pope if he will not 'help a poor one of the Fraternity of *Grub-Street*' (p. xi) by recommending a subscription for the two books of his translation; he is too poor now to publish more than Book I. Perhaps he might be able to get £1,000. (Only Book I is translated here; an 'After-Thought', p. 27, repeats his hope for a subscription and the possibility of adding Book II of which he offers a summary.)

The author is, or claims to be, one of Pope's dunces. He has

> been ruin'd by having my *bare Name* put down among certain
> Nameless Names; ... and to say the Truth, *Claudian* was forc'd
> to appear by Pieces from *Grub-street* ... you may raise my
> Name, as the DUNCIAD depress'd it, it will be only saying
>> That I but slightly skim'd the sable Streams.
>> Then soar'd afar among the *Swans* of *Thames*.   (p. xiii)

This reference to the *Dunciad* A, ii. 285–6 is difficult. The original 'H—' in l. 283 referred to Aaron Hill, and was changed to asterisks, to be changed to 'P—' in *1735 a–b* and then back to asterisks again in *1736a*. None of these suggests our author. See *Twick.* v. 136–7.

He is sure he does not address Pope in vain since he is only trying

> to get something honestly in the way of your Profession, which
> has made you so rich ... (pp. xiv–xv)

He adds in a 'P.S.' that in his translation

> ... I politically left some Lines out, and pass'd by great Faults
> in the Manuscripts knowingly and on Purpose, because in the
> *next Edition* I intend to say, *With Additions and Corrections.*
> He! Monsieur Pope! Entendez vous bien? (p. xvi)

R

February, 1730 (*Monthly Chronicle*)

[Joseph Mitchell.] Poems on Several Occasions. The First Volume. London: Printed for the Author, And sold by L. Gilliver at Homer's Head against St. Dunstan's Church, Fleet-street. 1729.

8vo.
[A]–z⁸, Aa–Bb⁸. c3 incorrectly signed c4.
[16 pp.], [1]–384 pp.

This is the Bodleian copy. The second volume does not concern us; the first volume contains only one item of Popiana, 'An Anacreontique, To the Right Honourable John Earl of Stair: Occasion'd by a View of his Lordship's Wardrobe a Sunning before their Majesties Coronation, 1727. Caelum ipsum petimus stultitia. Hor.' The poem occupies pp. 350–8.

CHARGE: 1. Pope deformed.

This request in verse for clothes for the Coronation contains a single quite incidental but tactless reference to Pope's size. Mitchell would like to see an order with its own special decoration created for poets. He imagines the benefits this would confer:

I
> Lord! how *Young* and *Gay* wou'd strut?
> What a Figure *Hill* wou'd cut?
> Little *Pope* improve his Size
> Inches nearer to the Skies?   (p. 354)

Welsted, Philips, Savage, and Eusden are also mentioned (p. 355). It is possible that this poem explains Mitchell's presence in the *Dunciad* (*Twick.* v. 448).

April 4, 1730 (*Daily Journal*, Rogers)

[Hill, Aaron.] The Progress of Wit: A Caveat. For The Use of an Eminent Writer. By a Fellow of All-Souls. To which is prefix'd, An Explanatory Discourse to the Reader. By Gamaliel Gunson, Professor of Physick and Astrology. This Verse be thine, my Friend, nor Thou refuse / This, from no venal, or ungrateful, Muse. / Read these instructive Leaves. —Pope, to Mr. Jervas.

London: Printed for J. Wilford, at the Crown in Stationers-Court. M.DCC. XXX.

8vo in half-sheets.

A–D⁴. c² incorrectly signed c3.

Frontispiece, signed 'G. Van der Gucht', [2 pp.], v–xiii, [xiv] blank, 15–31 pp., [32] blank.

Reprinted in *The Works of The Late Aaron Hill In Four Volumes*. Vol. III. London: Printed for the Benefit of the Family. MDCCLIII, pp. 371–86, and in Anderson, R., *Works of the British Poets* (Edinburgh, 1794), viii. 701–3.

WORKS: A. *Peri Bathous*; B. *Dunciad*.

CHARGE: 1. Pope wastes his talent on obscenity and malice.

'To the Reader' (pp. v–xiii) is a mixture of strained humour and genteel prose. The writer explains that he found the following poem at the bottom of a Hackney-coach and, suspecting it might be an attack on the government, showed it to several friends. One found in it a description of a bawdy-house, another of a masquerade, or a slander on first ministers, but his son at the university replies in a letter (pp. xi–xiii) that it is 'no other, than *Satire*, written, by *One* Poet, on the Misapplication of *Another*'s Genius' (p. xi).

> What Pity, that the warmest of a certain Gentleman's Admirers are, lately, forc'd to confess, there are *Grossnesses*, in some of his Sallies, obscene enough to blot out any Wit, but their Author's! Insults, low enough to become the most vulgar-spirited among his Enemies: And Malice, animated enough to be beautiful, in any of his Friends, but Himself!
>
> It gives, however, a Kind of ill-natur'd Comfort to us, who are his distant *Contemporaries*, that among Virtues, which we must despair of equalling, we discover Errors, which we disdain to imitate. (pp. xii–xiii)

The inept poem tells of Alexis [Pope], who 'Poorly accepts a Fame, he ne'er repays' (p. 15), and who is at last deposed from the top of Pindus. He is taken by Fancy in her chariot to where he can see the stream of life rising from the sea of birth and falling into the sea of death. On one side of the stream is Oblivion's shore, with quicksands and rocks, where pebbles glisten like gems in the shoals and where bright insects play. On the other side is Fame's shore, green islands, with no port or landing place and guarded by swans who alone can give entrance.

As Alexis watches mankind sailing down the river, where some men drown in the whirlpools while a few reach Fame's shore, he notices a youth favoured by the Graces and Muses who reaches Fame's shore 'Ere yet one Third of the Stream's Length was try'd' (p. 27). The youth is welcomed by the swans, but, in disdain, leaves Fame's shore for the other tempted by the excitements of snatching at the pebbles, and catching the darting insects and wasps. He is so successful that he is hailed as 'Prince of Fly-Catchers', but his barque is all the while nearing destruction. Alexis cries out to warn the foolish youth when Fancy explains that the youth Alexis sees is Alexis himself.

AB

>Not surer *Fortune* is That dark Power's Name,
>That Left, *Oblivion*, and That Right Side, *Fame*,
>Than, that no Son of Wit dares, justly, hope,
>*Fame* dwells in *Folly's Paths*, but thou, O POPE!
> Alexis, starting, heard his own lov'd Name,
>Felt his Pride shrink, and blush'd with conscious Shame!
>Pitch'd from the Chariot, lost to *Fancy*'s Call;
>And, had not waiting *Judgment* broke his Fall,
>Contempt's cold Vale had caught him, wak'd and stunn'd,
>And deep intomb'd him, in his *own* Profund.   (p. 31)

April 28, 1730 (*Daily Journal*, April 28, 1730)

[Welsted, Leonard, and James Moore Smythe.] One Epistle To Mr. A. Pope, Occasion'd By Two Epistles Lately Published. Spiteful he is not, tho' he writ a Satire, / For still there goes some Thinking to Ill-Nature. Dryden. London: Printed for J. Roberts, in Warwick-Lane. [Price One Shilling.]

Half-title: One Epistle To Mr. A. Pope, Occasion'd By Two Lately Published. [To be Continued.]

Quarto.
A–C⁴.
[4 pp.], v–viii, [9]–24 pp.

Reprinted in *The Works in Verse and Prose of Leonard Welsted*, ed. John Nichols (London, 1787), and in my *Two Poems against Pope*, The Augustan Reprint Society, No. 114, 1965.

Pope's mention of this in Appendix II is confusing:

> Labeo, [A Paper of Verses written by *Leonard Welsted*.] which after came into *One Epistle*, and was publish'd by James Moore. *4to.* 1730. Another part of it came out in Welsted's own name in 1731, under the just Title of *Dulness and Scandal*, fol.
>
> (*Twick.* V. 211–12)

Savage in *An Author To Be Lett*, 1729, says, 'I have extracted curious Hints to assist *Welsted* in his new Satire against *Pope*, which was once (he told me) to have been christen'd *Labeo*. 'Tis yet an Embrio, and there are divers Opinions about the Birth of it' (pp. 5–6). Since no *Labeo* is known, it seems reasonable to conclude with Fineman that, though Welsted may have toyed with the idea of writing one, 'he either never did enough with it to warrant its publication, or discarded it entirely in favor of writing the collaborative *One Epistle to Mr. Pope* that appeared in 1730. Naturally, he would not broadcast his plans, and as a result the enemy camp continued to believe – or at any rate, to say – that Welsted would retaliate with a *Labeo*' (Daniel Fineman, *Leonard Welsted, Gentleman Poet of the Augustan Age* [Philadelphia, 1950], p. 190).

A letter from Welsted to Dodington shows that the poem was a collaborative effort, but it is clear that Welsted, though others may have made suggestions and additions, felt himself responsible for the poem (Fineman, p. 192). *The Grub-Street Journal* of May 14, 1730, attributed the poem to 'the son of an Alehouse keeper [Thomas Cooke?], the son of a Footman, and the Son of a —'. The same journal suggested on May 21, 1730, that Lady Mary had 'some hand in this piece'. But Lady Mary denied to Arbuthnot Pope's accusation that she had written it (*Corr.* III. 59–60, and n). *The Universal Spectator*, as early as February 1, 1729, had announced the pamphlet as 'the due Chastisement of Mr. Pope for his *Dunciad*, by James Moore Smythe, Esq; and Mr. Welsted' and it seems clear that the poem had been circulated before publication (*Corr.* III. 59, n.3). For a summary of the references to *One Epistle* in *The Grub-Street Journal* of May 14, May 21, May 28, and June 4, 1730, see James T. Hillhouse, *The Grub-Street Journal* (Durham, N.C., 1928), pp. 58–64. The Bodleian copy of *Of Fake Fame*, 1732, has a book-list (c4r) of books written by Welsted which gives *One Epistle*, 'this last by Mr. Welsted, and Mr. Moore Smythe'.

WORKS: A. *Pastorals*; B. Prologue to *Cato*; C. *Ode on St Cecilia's Day*; D. Epigram on 'Cato'; E. *Rape of the Lock*; F. Homer; G. *First Psalm*;

H. *Three Hours after Marriage*; J. *Elegy to the Memory of an Unfortunate Lady*; K. *Peri Bathous*; L. *Dunciad*.

CHARGES: 1. Pope's statement false that he attacked no one in the *Dunciad* who had not first attacked him; 2. Gildon dismissed by Buckingham for his dislike of Pope; 3. Pope libelled Lady Mary; 4. Pope libelled Addison after his death; 5. Gay forced to own Pope's worst work; 6. Pope quarrelled with Fenton and underpaid Broome; 7. Pope a plagiarist.

L I   The Preface denies Pope's statement that no one is attacked in the *Dunciad* 'who had not before, either in Print or private Conversation, endeavour'd something to his Disadvantage' (p. v; the reference is to *Twick.* v. 203, where conversation is not mentioned.) Even if Pope's assertion were true,

A F   sure no Man deserves a violent Injury to his Reputation, as a Gentleman, because perhaps at a Distance of several Years since he might have said, that Mr. *Pope* had nothing in him Original as a Writer, that Mr *Tickel* greatly excelled him in his Translation of *Homer*, and many of his Contemporaries in other Branches of Writing, and that he is infinitely inferior to Mr. *Philips* in Pastoral: And yet such Arguments or Apologies as these have been used by himself, or his Tea-Table Cabals, for calling Gentlemen Scoundrels, Blockheads, Gareteers, and Beggars,: If he can transmit them to Posterity under such Imputations, he is a bad Man; if he cannot, he is a bad Writer: I believe that he would rather suffer under the first Character, than the last ... (p. vi)

To prove Pope's statement wrong, he explains that

K L   Some Replies, which were made to the *Profund*, occasioned the Publication of the *Dunciad* which was first of all begun with a general Malice to all Mankind, and now appears under an Excuse of Provocations, which he had received, after he himself had struck the first Blow in the above-mentioned Miscellanies.
(p. vii)

The *Dunciad*, he says, 'contains only the Poetical Part of Dulness, extracted from a Libel, call'd, *The Progress of* it, and which included several other Branches of Science' (pp. vi–vii). Pope 'was teaz'd into a Publication of these Cantos, which regarded the Writers of the Age', by some attacks elicited by the *Peri Bathous*. Swift never saw the *Pari Bathous* until it was published. Arbuthnot wanted Pope to leave out the initials of the gentlemen abused and substi-

tute 'A or B, or Do or Ro', to make it a general satire on dull writers.
. . . This was refused by *Pope*, and he chose rather to treat a Set of
Gentlemen as Vermin, Reptiles, etc. at a Time when he had no
Provocation to do so, when he had closed his Labours, finish'd
his great Subscriptions, and was in a fashionable Degree of Reputation: Several Gentlemen, who are there ranked with the
dullest Men, or dullest Beasts, never did appear in Print against
him, or say any thing in Conversation which might affect his
Character . . . (p. vii)

His estimate of Popiana is surprisingly sound, however:

I cannot indeed say much in Praise of some Performances,
which appeared against him, and am sorry that Voluntiers
enter'd into the War, whom I could wish to have been only
Spectators: But the cause became so general, that some Gentlemen, who never aim'd at the Laurel, grew Poets merely upon
their being angry . . . (p. viii)

The poem and its notes is one of the most comprehensive attacks
on Pope's verse in Popiana.

Pope

> . . . *Cato*'s Muse with faithless Sneer belied,
> The Prologue father'd, and the Play decried.   (p. 12)

He also

> . . . from the Skies, propitious to the Fair,
> Brought down *Caecilia*, and sent [1]*Cloris* there.

[1] See Verses . . . to the Memory of an unfortunate young Lady (p. 11).

Welsted apparently means that Pope debased St Cecilia in his *Ode for
Musick on St Cecilia's Day* and glorified a suicide in his *Elegy to the
Memory of an Unfortunate Lady*. He is not saying, as did *The Life Of the
late Celebrated Mrs. Elizabeth Wisebourn*, 1721, that Pope caused the
lady's death. See *Of Dulness and Scandal*, 1732, where these lines are
discussed in connection with ll. 374–5 of the *Epistle to Arbuthnot*.

He was

> To lovely *F[ermo]r* impious and obscene,
> To mud-born *Naiads* faithfully unclean.   (p. 10)

The myth of Belinda's sunship is dismissed with,

> In the *Rape of the Lock*, *Belinda* and the Sun are very often said
> to be very much alike, which occasion'd two Lines in Praise of
> that Poem, written by a Friend of Mr. *Pope*;
> Here, like the Sun, *Belinda* strikes the Swain,
> In the same Page like the same Sun again.   (p. 23)

Pope has 'Strung to *Smithfield* Airs the *Hebrew* Lyre' (p. 10).

2   Charles Gildon was 'dismissed from the D[uke of Buckingham]'s
Pension and Favour, on Account of his Obstinacy in refusing to take
the Oaths to P—pe's Supremacy' (p. 22).

34   Pope has libelled Lady Mary and libelled Addison after his death –
these charges are obscurely made in the verse but clarified in the note,
p. 12.

H5   Gay is forced to yield his best pieces to Pope and own Pope's worst;
he was 'ordered to own *Three Hours after Marriage*' (p. 23).

F6   Pope

> By *F[ento]n* left, by Reverend Linguists hated,
> Now learns to read the *Greek* he once translated.   (p. 11)

At the end of the poem Pope is bid

F6
> Retire triumphant to thy *Twick'nam* Seat;
> That Seat! the Work of ¹half-paid drudging *Br[oo]me*,
> And call'd by joking *Tritons, Homer's* Tomb.   (p. 19)

> ¹ The Reverend Mr. *B[roo]me*, who translated a great Part of
> *Homer*, and construed the Rest: *N.B. A half-paid Poet* is oftentimes
> the Occasion of an *unpaid Taylor* (p. 24).

7   There is a sweeping charge of plagiarism:

> The Bard! that first, from *Dryden's* thrice-glean'd Page,
> Cull'd his low Efforts to Poetic Rage;
> Nor pillag'd only that unrival'd Strain,
> But rak'd for Couplets *Chapman* and *Duck-Lane*,
> Has sweat each Cent'ry's Rubbish to explore,
> And plunder'd every Dunce that writ before,
> Catching half Lines, till the tun'd verse went round,
> Complete, in smooth dull Unity of Sound.   (p. 10)

Pope is the

> Bane of the modern Laurel, like the past;
> While stupid Riot stands in Humour's Place,
> And bestial Filth, Humanity's Disgrace,
> Low Lewdness, unexcited by Desire,
> And all great *Wilmot's* Vice, without his Fire.   (pp. 18–19)

The *Grub-Street Journal*, No. 20, May 21, 1730, invited 'any Person of
Credit and Character to stand forth and attest any of the following
Facts . . .'

> That the late Duke of Buckingham paid any Pension to Charles
> Gildon, which he took from him since his acquaintance with
> Mr. P.

> That the present Archbishop of Canterbury hath past any
> Censure on Mr. P. . .

That Mr. F[ento]n and he ever were at distance or variance with each other. . .

That Mr. Addison or any other but Mr. P. writ, or alter'd, one line of the Prologue to Cato.

June, 1730 (*Monthly Chronicle*)

Maggot, Sir Butterfly [pseud.] The Gentleman's Miscellany, In Verse and Prose. Serious, Jocose, Satyrical, Humorous, and Diverting. Containing, [a list of 28 titles.] By Sir Butterfly Maggot, Kt. London, Printed, and Sold by J. Purser, in White-Fryars; and by the Booksellers of London and Westminster. 1730.

8vo in half-sheets.
[A]–G⁴, H².
[4 pp.], [5]–59 pp., [60] blank.
Case 358.

The Gentleman's Miscellany: In Verse and Prose. Serious, Jocose, Satyrical, Humorous, and Diverting. Containing, [a list of 35 titles.] Dedicated to the Most Fallibly Fallible Pope Alexander, or Alexander Pope. By Sir Butterfly Maggot, Kt. The Second Edition, with Additions. London, Printed and Sold by J. Purser, in White-Fryars; and by the Booksellers of London and Westminster. 1730.

8vo in half-sheets.
One unsigned leaf, A–G⁴. C2 incorrectly signed C3.
[4 pp.], [7]–60 pp.
Case 358 (b).

WORKS: A. *Peri Bathous*; B. *Dunciad*.

CHARGE: 1. Pope is a literary dictator.

The only Popiana in this trivial and salacious collection is the dedication, textually the same in both editions:

To the Most Fallibly Fallible *Pope* ALEXANDER, Or, *ALEXANDER POPE*, *Keeper of the* Profund, *Vicar of the* Dunciad, *Blunder-Master-General of* Dramatic *Poetry, Lord Paramount-wou'd-*

be of Mount Parnassus, *and Legate a latere from the* Dean *and the* Doctor, &c. &c. &c. The following *Miscellany* is most humbly Submitted and Address'd by his *Very Respectful Humble Servant*, Butterfly Maggot. ([A2r], 1st ed.; A1r in 2nd ed.)

August, 1730 (*Grub-Street Journal*)

[Concanen, Matthew.] The Speculatist. A Collection of Letters and Essays, Moral and Political, Serious and Humorous: Upon Various Subjects. London: Printed by J. Watts, for the Author. MDCCXXX.

8vo.

A⁴, B–S⁸, T⁴, U².

[8 pp.], [1]–283 pp., [284] blank.

The British Museum has the second edition with the imprint bearing the name of the bookseller 'J. Walthoe', 1732. The British Museum's copy is misplaced, and my repeated attempts to see it have yielded only a variety of nineteenth-century theological tracts.

WORKS: A. *Windsor Forest*; B. *Rape of the Lock*; C. *Epistle to Addison*; D. Pope's edition of Shakespeare; E. Pope–Swift *Miscellanies*; F. *Dunciad*.

CHARGE: 1. Pope venal.

Pope in his note on Concanen, *Dunciad* A, ii. 130, had said,

He was also author of several Scurrilities in the *British* and *London Journals* . . .

The 'Advertisement' to *The Speculatist* refers to this charge as the reason for publications of these essays from newspapers:

F   They were all published either in the *London* or *British Journal*, on the Days they bear date; and tho' many of them were favourably received, they are not now republished from any Opinion of their Excellence, but to refute the Calumny of a rancorous and foul-mouth'd Railer who has asserted in print that the Author of them wrote *several Scurrilities* in those Papers. (A3r)

The volume contains the following attacks: 'Of Motto's', pp. 12–15, dated and signed, p. 15, '*July*, 17. 1725. Will. Sharpsight', ridicules

the display of classical learning in the mottoes on title-pages, their inappropriateness and length. A Motto 'in its primitive Purity, should be Succinct, Apt, and Pointed,' he declares, 'as Mr. *Addison* observes in his Treatise of Medals' (p. 13). From this he launches an attack on Pope's 'To Mr. Addison, Occasioned by his Dialogues on Medals'.

> A certain great Poet has written a fine Copy of Verses in Praise of the Treatise above mentioned; which yet we will do him the Justice to believe he did not read, since he has so little observed the Rules laid down in it: He is contriving a Medal to be struck in honour of his Patron, and recommending a Motto proper to be inscribed in *lasting Notes* round the *Orb* of it, which he does in these Lines. [He quotes ll. 67–72, *Twick.* VI. 204.]
> Now, in the Name of God, is this an Inscription for the Orb of a Medal, or a Millstone? Sure I am, it's large enough for the latter: His Friends here are a little puzzled to excuse him; but I think it's easily done, by recollecting that the Medals were to be of *pure Gold*, and that he might reasonably expect one of them for his Pains. (pp. 13–14)

This constitutes, as far as I know, the only attack on this poem of Pope's.

In 'Of Modern Poetry', pp. 37–41, dated and signed, p. 41, '*Novem.* 13, 1725. W. Sharpsight', an attack on the use of pagan mythology in modern poetry, Concanen manages to praise and criticize Pope in one sentence:

> Mr. *Pope* has struck out a pretty discovery in the *Rosycrucian* Scheme, which he uses in the *Rape of the Lock*, but it's surprizing how the same Writer could stumble upon the School-boy Tale of *Pan* and *Lodona* in *Windsor Forrest* [*sic*]. (p. 40)

'Of Commentators', pp. 185–8, dated, p. 188, '*Sept.* 3, 1726', is a plea for good commentators on important English writers to preserve them from the change of language and customs. He concludes with the example of Shakespeare:

> To suppose that the greatest Poet in this Age is the only fit, or fittest Person, to revise the Sheets, and correct the Press, when the greatest Poet of the last is new published, is every whit as whimsical and absurd, as to imagine that no body but the best Sculptor living is proper to dig the Ground under which lie bury'd the Remains of the best antique Statues.
> I have been thrown into these Thoughts, by comparing a Book lately published call'd *Shakespear Restored*, with the late

Edition of that Poet set forth by Mr. *Pope*; in the former what Diligence and Accuracy is to be found, in the latter what Carelessness and Ignorance. Till I read *Pope*'s Work I hardly thought *Shakespear* wanted a Commentator; till I read *Theobald*'s, I scarcely believ'd he would ever find a good one. (p. 188)

E   The final attack and the only extensive one, 'On Pope's Miscellanies', pp. 260–5, dated, p. 265, '*Novem.* 25. 1727', reprints the letter from *The British Journal* of that date which had been already reprinted in *A Compleat Collection Of all the Verses*, 1728, pp. 1–6, q.v.

December 1–17, 1730 (*Grub-Street Journal*, December 17, 1730)

[Cooke, Thomas.] The Bays Miscellany, Or Colley Triumphant: Containing I. The Petty-Sessions of Poets. II. The Battle of the Poets, or the Contention for the Laurel; as it is now Acting at the New Theatre in the Hay-Market. III. The Battle of the Poets. An Heroic Poem. In Two Canto's [*sic*]. With the True Characters of the several Poets, therein mention'd; and just Reasons why not qualify'd for the Laurel. The Whole design'd as a Specimen of those Gentlemens Abilities, without Prejudice or Partiality. Written by Scriblerus Quartus. London: Printed for A. Moore; and Sold by the Booksellers and Pamphletsellers of London and Westminster. [Price Six-pence.]

8vo in half-sheets.
Two unsigned leaves, B–E⁴. c2 wrongly signed c3.
[2 pp.], [7]–8, [9–12], 13–38 pp., [39] advertisement, [40] blank.

WORKS: A. Homer; B. Pope's edition of Shakespeare.

CHARGES: 1. Pope deformed; 2. Pope a plagiarist.

The Battle of the Poets, or the Contention for the Laurel (pp. [9]–25) was first performed at the Little Theatre in the Haymarket, November 30, 1730 (Allardyce Nicoll, *A History of English Drama, 1660–1900*, 3rd ed. [Cambridge, 1952], II. 316). Both Nicoll and Wilbur L. Cross, *The History of Henry Fielding* (New Haven, 1918), I. 95–7, attribute the play to Thomas Cooke. See the Cross reference for a description of this brief farce which contains no attacks on Pope but satirizes Cibber,

Theobald, and Ralph. Cross, III. 350, describes a separate printing of it in 1730; I have seen the Bodleian copy.

The Battle of the Poets. An Heroic Poem (pp. 26–38) is the 1725 version of Thomas Cooke's *The Battle of the Poets*, q.v. It is surprising that the expanded 1729 version was not printed instead.

The only new Popiana in this miscellany is *The Petty-Sessions of Poets* (pp. [7]–8) which is a 53-line satire on the recent election of the laureate. The first candidate described is Pope:

> The first that appear'd, and who led up the *Van*,
> Was a peevish, mishapen'd, diminutive Man¹:
> A Bard, who by help of ²*Physician* and ³*Parson*,
> Went quickly to work, on his Chair set his A— on,
> And murder'd old *Homer*; but of his own head,
> *Flesh-dy'd* with Blood, murder'd, mangled poor *Shakespear*,
>   when dead.
> Like a *Butcher*, he knew how to *turn* an *old Coat*,
> But not *make* a *new one*; and just so he wrote.

¹ Mr. *P[op]e*.   ² Dr. *A[r]b[uthno]t*.   ³ Dr. *S[wif]t* (p. [7]).

Portraits of Swift, Hill, Henley, and others follow. One may tentatively ascribe this poem to Cooke.

December 1730 (*Monthly Chronicle*)

Johnson, Charles. The Tragedy Of Medaea. As it is Acted at the Theatre-Royal In Drury-Lane. With a Preface containing, Some Reflections on the new Way of Criticism. By Mr. Charles Johnson. London: Printed for R. Francklin in Russel-street, Covent-Garden. 1731. Price 1s. 6d.

8vo in half-sheets.
[A]⁴, a², B–I⁴, K².
[12 pp.], [1]–67 pp., [68] Epilogue.

Medaea was first performed at Drury Lane, December 11, 1730 (Allardyce Nicoll, *A History of English Drama, 1660–1900*, 3rd ed. [Cambridge, 1952], II. 339). Maurice M. Shudofsky, 'A Dunce Objects to Pope's Dictatorship', *Huntington Library Quarterly*, XIV (1951), 203–7, would take seriously Johnson's charge that Pope helped cause the

failure of the play, but presents no other evidence than this preface.

WORK: A. *Dunciad*.

CHARGES: 1. Pope has set himself up as dictator and helped cause the failure of *Medaea*; 2. Pope ridicules poverty.

The Preface, which is all that concerns us, is a long complaint against the damning treatment the play received on its first night, and, more especially, against the 'Set of noisy Criticks' ([A2r]) who, by creating a disturbance, condemn a piece without hearing it. In his wounded vanity, Johnson attacks Pope as a would-be dictator and manages to implicate him in the failure of the play:

A I 2   But perhaps we are not yet come to the Knowledge of the true Reason of this Treatment that has been given to some late Pieces as well as This. Many Years are not passed since a little Gentleman very well known and skill'd in Poetry, took it into his Head that he was really and truly the King of *Parnassus*, and that all People, who presumed to oppose this his Title to poetical Royalty or to make Verses without his Patent and Authority, were Rebels. Many of the Sons of the Muses did not like this Severity; ... upon which his versifying Majesty grew wrathful, and swore they should either stand in the Records of Fame as his Subjects, or as Dunces; and this Project we have seen him put in Execution ... Since that Time, whoever, it seems, stands attainted by Name in this Proclamation of his, is never to recover Fame or Bread; such is his poetical Will.

As visionary, as ridiculous, and as vain as this Scheme of his is, and must be thought to be by all sober People, he is certainly very solicitous to support it. I hope he is not concerned to support his Authority too in this tumultuary and unjust Way of suppressing the Labours of those, who have not the Honour of his Indulgence. Yet what may we not believe when we ... behold the calamitous Condition of Want, and Wretchedness, exposed and lashed, as if it were a decent or a proper Subject for Ridicule and Satire ... ([A2v]–a1r).

December ? 1730 (*Grub-street Journal*, December 3, 1730, 'Just published')

A New Miscellany. Containing, [a list of 31 titles.] London: Printed for A. Moore, 1730.

8vo in half-sheets.
Two unsigned leaves, B–G⁴.
[4 pp.], 1–48 pp.
Case 361.

WORK: A. Pope's edition of Shakespeare.

This contains a single twelve-line item of Popiana, 'On The Controversy Between Mr. Pope and Mr. Theobalds, 1729' (p. 47), Number XXX on the title-page which gives it as 'The Controversy between Mr. Pope and Mr. Theobalds, 1729'. Jones ascribes the epigram to William Duncombe (Jones, p. 119).

> In *Pope*'s melodious Verse the Graces smile;
> In *Theobalds* is display'd sagacious Toil;
> The Criticks' Ivy crowns his subtle Brow,
> While in *Pope*'s Numbers Wit and Musick flow.
> These Bards, so Fortune will'd, were mortal Foes,
> And all *Parnassus* in their Quarrel rose:
> This the dire Cause of their contending Rage,
> Who best could blanch dark *Shakespear*'s blotted Page.
> *Apollo* heard—and judg'd each Party's Plea,
> And thus pronounc'd th' irrevocable Decree;
> *Theobalds*, 'tis thine to share what *Shakespear* writ,
> But *Pope* shall reign supreme in Poesy and Wit.   (p. 47)

February 9, 1731 (*Grub-Street Journal*, February 11, 1731)

[Harte, Walter?] An Epistle To Mr. Pope, On Reading his Translations of the Iliad and Odyssy [*sic*] of Homer. To which are added, Some Examples of the Variety of Sound in Verse, consider'd with Mr. Pope's Accuracy in that Particular. A Short Character of Virgil and Homer. And, An Epistle to a Young Poet, concerning Mr. Pope: Also, The Condition of a Good Poet.

Parturiunt Montes—Hor. Aude aliquid brevibus Gyaris & Car-
cere dignum, / Si vis esse aliquis—Virtus laudatur & alget. Juv.
London: Printed for J. Wilford, behind the Chapter-House in
St. Paul's Church-Yard, 1731. (Price 6d.)

8vo in half-sheets.
A–B⁴, C².
[6 pp.], 7–20 pp.

This is ascribed to Harte in the *BM Cat.* and the *CBEL*, but it seems
an odd poem to have come from a professed admirer of Pope and is
not mentioned in the account of Harte in the *DNB*.

WORK: A. Homer.

CHARGE: 1. Pope undertook the Homer only for money and applause.

The verse dedication to Dennis (A2r) is more ambiguous than its
presence at the head of a Pope pamphlet would suggest. If Dennis is
only pursuing the Truth, then the author admires his firmness; if he
wants to tyrannize over human frailty, 'Thy Vanity and Folly I
despise.'

When everyone was praising Pope's Homer, Harte had taken the
liberty, he tells us in the Preface, to show how and why Pope was un-
qualified 'for such an accomplish'd Performance as his Translation
ought to have been'. But the world did not regard him and now he
would not 'be thought to take Advantage of his [Pope's] declining
State', but will only freely and impartially declare his own mind, now
as then. He is persuaded that the judgment of a future age on Pope's
productions will be his (A3r and v).

The 102 lines of the poem simply explain that Pope was unfit to
translate Homer and that he failed in his attempt; he undertook the
translations only to gain money and applause.

> How much are They deceiv'd—in Thee, *O Pope*,
> Who rashly place their Confidence or Hope?
> Thy Transmutations but provoke my Scorn,
> The Mountain labours,—and a Mouse is born!   (p. 8)

After conventional praise of Homer, he continues,

> And can'st thou, *Pope*! so choice a *Prize* acquire?
> Unqualify'd for thy immense Desire!
>
> .   .   .
>
> Beside thy Skill and Genius; thy Design

A I

Is mean, nor suits with an Attempt like thine:
Had'st thou directed well thy daring Aim,
And scorning Riches, sought the justest Fame;
Thou should'st have first examin'd well thy Mind,
And search'd thro' all the Ways of Human-kind.

(pp. 9–10)

He concludes his catalogue of what Pope ought to have done:

To know, thou should'st thy Faculties have strain'd,
If Fate had Thee for such a Task ordain'd!
Nor, unordain'd, and indiscreetly proud,
Been brib'd, or prompted by the shallow Crowd:
What hast thou thus (endeav'ring to display)
But satyriz'd Him, the severest Way!

.   .   .

Plunder'd, depriv'd of ev'ry noble Grace,
Thy mean Resemblance vilifies his Place:
In tawd'ry, Tinsel, fashionable Dress,
And with a trifling Air of Wantonness.   (p. 11)

Under the drop-title, 'A few Examples of the Variety of Sound in
Verse', he gives (pp. 12–13) seven examples from Pope, from two to
four lines each, with the concluding comment,

These few Examples may stand as an Epitome of all the soothing
Art, or Variety in Sound, with which Mr. *Pope* can be presum'd
to have embellish'd our *English* Poetry;—which it must be confess'd, after *Dryden*, he has done tolerably well, and perhaps
added something New;—tho', even here, he falls infinitely short
of *Virgil* ... (p. 13)

The examples seem to be chosen only for the echo of sound to sense:

Rude thrumming Harpers harshly rake their Strings;
Melodious Airs, lo *Philomela* sings!

See, see, the laughing Maids and jolly Swains,
Piping and dancing, frisking on the Plains!

The 'Epistle to a Young Poet' (pp. 15–18), after an obscure beginning,
repeats the criticism of the first poem.

February, 1731 (*Monthly Chronicle*)

[Cooke, Thomas.] The Letters Of Atticus, As printed in the London Journal, In The Years 1729 and 1730, On Various Subjects, With An Introduction, containing a short Survey of public Affairs from the Time of the Spaniards besieging Gibraltar to the Year 1731, and an Enquiry into the Reasons why some modern Writers assume to themselves the great Names of passed Ages. London: Printed by J. Chrichley, at the London Gazette, at Charing-Cross; and sold by J. Roberts in Warwick-Lane, 1731.

8vo in half-sheets.

A–I⁴.

[6 pp.], [7]–71 pp., [72] blank.

WORK: A. *Dunciad*.

CHARGE: 1. Pope gathers scandal from wretches for inclusion in the *Dunciad*.

About half of these ten letters are directly political. Only Letter v deals with Pope. It is headed 'Saturday, March 29. 1729. Letter V. An Examination into the Controversy betwixt the Poets and Mr. Pope. To the Author of the London Journal' (p. 33) and signed, p. 36, 'Atticus', as are the other letters. His main contention in this brief letter is that Pope has collected scandal for the *Dunciad* from wretches in order to hurt the reputations of the dunces. He points out that Theobald in *Shakespeare restored*, which 'seems to be the principal Cause of Mr. *Pope*'s writing the *Dunciad*' (p. 34), reflected on Pope only as an editor and left untouched his person and morals. Cooke admits that after the *Dunciad* many pieces 'unjustly and impertinently were directed at the Person and Morals of Mr. *Pope*' (p. 34). But Pope resorts to collecting scandal:

A1   Mr. *Pope*, apprised of some Preparations which have been making against him, has been industrious in collecting such particulars of the Lives of most Persons, who are mentioned in the *Dunciad*, as can possibly render them little in the Eyes of those who look farther than the real Merit of a Man to judge of him; nor has he wanted Wretches mean enough for the Collectors of Calumny and Scandal; Wretches who, rather than be thought unworthy their Employment, supplied their Master

with Materials from Invention where they failed in Facts ...
I hope such as are distinguished, by the Editor, with a Present
of this Work will know how to judge of the Merits and Abilitys
of a Writer who is forced at last to have Recourse to Scandal.

(pp. 34–5)

Cooke accused Savage of being a spy for Pope in the revised version
of 'The Battle of the Poets' published five days after this letter in his
Tales, Epistles, Odes, q.v.

March 13, 1731 (*Daily Journal*, Rogers)

Hill, Aaron. Advice to the Poets. A Poem. To which is Prefix'd,
An Epistle Dedicatory to the Few Great Spirits of Great Britain.
Written by Mr. Hill. Shame on your Jyngling, ye soft Sons of
Rhyme! / Tuneful Consumers of your Reader's Time! / Fancy's
light Dwarfs! whose Feather-footed Strains / Dance, in wild
Windings, thro' a Waste of Brains: / Yours is the Guilt of All,
who, judging wrong, / Mistake tun'd Nonsense for the Poet's
Song. London: Printed for T. Warner in Pater-Noster-Row.
M.DCC.XXXI.

4to.

A–E⁴.

[2 pp.], iii–xvi, 17–39 pp., [40] blank.

Reprinted in *The Works Of The Late Aaron Hill In Four Volumes*. Vol. III.
London: Printed for the Benefit of the Family. MDCCLIII, 209–24,
in Thomas Park, *Supplement to the British Poets* (London, 1809), VII.
146–55, and in Anderson, R., *Works of the British Poets* (Edinburgh,
1794), VIII. pp. 681–4.

WORK: A. *Dunciad*.

CHARGE: I. Pope envious and unwilling to forgive.

The poem is largely a plea for sublimity, for the recognition of the
poet as greater even than philosopher or saint. The good advice to
Pope occurs after the bombastic invocation to the Muse ('Thou *Flame*
of *Purpose*! and Thou *Flow* of *Mind*!' [p. 18]):

Let half-soul'd *Poets*, still, *on Poets* fall,

And teach the *willing* World to scorn them *All.*
But, let no Muse, pre-eminent as *Thine*,
Of Voice melodious, and of Force divine,
Stung by *Wit's Wasps*, all Rights of Rank forego,
And turn, and snarl, and bite, at, Every Foe.
No—like thy Thy own *Ulysees*, make no *Stay*:
Shun *Monsters*—and pursue thy streamy Way.

Shalt *Thou*—decreed, till Time's own Death, to *live*,
Yet *want* the noblest Courage—to *forgive*?
    Slander'd, in vain, *Enjoy* the Spleen of Foes:
Let These, from *Envy*, hate; from *Interest*, Those!
Guilt like the First your *Gratitude* requires;
Since none can *Envy*, till He, first, *admires*:
And *Nature* tells the Last, his Crime is *none*,
Who, to *your* Interest, but prefers His *own*.   (pp. 19–20)

January 3, 1732 (*Grub-Street Journal*, January 6, 1731)

Welsted, Leonard. Of Dulness and Scandal. Occasion'd by the Characters Of Lord Timon. In Mr. Pope's Epistle To The Earl of Burlington. Turno Tempus adest, magno cum optaverit emptum / Intactum Pallanta— / Pallas te hoc Vulnere donit. Virg. By Mr. Welsted. London: Printed for T. Cooper, the Corner of Ivy-Lane, next Pater-Noster Row. MDCCXXXII. [Price 6d.]

Folio.
[A]–B².
[2 pp.], 3–8 pp.

There was a 'second edition' in the same year, the old sheets, issued with 'The Second Edition.' inserted after 'Welsted' in the title-page as above.

Also a 'third edition' in the same year. Title-page as above with 'The Third Edition.' inserted after 'Welsted.' My quotations are taken from this third edition which introduces improvements in punctuation. The 'second' and 'third' editions were noticed in *The Grub-Street Journal* of January 13, 1731 (as was the false Latin of the title—*donit* for *donat*), and so must have appeared early in January.

Reprinted in *The Works in Verse and Prose of Leonard Welsted*, ed. John Nichols (London, 1787), pp. 196–9.

The Duke of Chandos wrote to his friend Anthony Hammond, January 1, 1732:

> I find by ye Advertisements M^r. Welsted is publishing some remarks upon it, I have reason to flatter my self, from ye friendship he has profest, he intends me no harm, but I should be very sorry, if he endeavour'd on my account to hurt M^r. Pope. I know not where to send to him my self, but as he is a particular acquainta[n]ce of Yours,—You may perhaps know where he lodges, & I desire You'l [*sic*] acquaint him I make it my request, that he will forbear printing any thing, on my behalf, that may tend to ye prejudice of a Person, who from what he has wrote, I ought to beleive [*sic*] neither hath nor had any ill will towards me. (George Sherburn, ' "Timon's Villa" and Cannons', *The Huntington Library Bulletin*, VIII [1935], p. 140.)

WORKS: A. *Rape of the Lock*; B. *Iliad*; C. *First Psalm*; D. *Epistle to Burlington*.

CHARGES: 1. Victoria died from reading Pope's *Iliad*; 2. Pope ungrateful to Chandos; 3. Pope wrote verse in his own praise and palmed it off on Walsh and Wycherley.

1 Victoria, who here makes her only appearance in Popiana, died from reading Pope's Homer:

> BEHOLD the Charmer, wasting to Decay;
> Like Autumn faded in her Virgin *May*!
> To pore o'er curs'd Translation Rest she flies,
> And dims, by Midnight Lamps her beamless Eyes;
> With *Iliads* travestied, to Age she stoops,
> In Fustian withers, and o'er Crambo droops.
>   No Conquest now, VICTORIA, shalt thou boast;
>   The second Victim to ACHILLES' Ghost!   (p. 4)

Victoria has died, then, from reading Pope's *Iliad*. Daniel A. Fineman, 'The Case of the Lady "Killed" by Alexander Pope', *MLQ*, XII (1951), 137–49, on the basis of a remark of Theobald's in a letter to Warburton, would identify Victoria as Lady Frances Vandeput. Pope, Fineman argues, is thinking of these lines in his note to l. 375 of the *Epistle to Arbuthnot* when he accuses Welsted of having 'had the Impudence to tell in print, that Mr. *P*. had occasion'd a *Lady's death*, and to *name* a person he never heard of' (*Twick*. IV. 123). Sutherland,

in his continuation of Pope's note, confuses this charge with the earlier one about Cloris in *One Epistle*, 1730. The difficult line later in *Of Dulness and Scandal*, 'We've lost a ST. LEGER, and gain'd a POPE', Fineman points out, does not give us the name of the heroine of the *Elegy to the Memory of an Unfortunate Lady*, as Courthope thought. He would explain it as a reference to St Leger, martyred at Ebroin in 678 after being horribly mutilated, to be taken with the usual pun on 'Pope'; this seems strained, but I have no other suggestion to offer.

There is, however, a recompense for Victoria:

> Thy Fame, thy Wrong shall go to future Times;
> While POPE damns SHEFFIELD with his Bellman's Rhimes.
>
> (p. 4)

(This last line must be a hit at Pope's edition of Buckingham's poetical works in 1723.)

D2 Welsted's main charge is Pope's ingratitude to Chandos (on this charge see *An Epistle To The Little Satyrist Of Twickenham*, 1733):

> See! POLLIO falls a Victim to the Rage,
> Which Goodness could not charm, nor Friendship swage;
>
> . . .
>
> INGLORIOUS Rhimer! low licentious Slave!
> Who blasts the Beauteous, and belies the Brave:
> In scurril Verse who robs, and dull Essays,
> Nymphs of their Charms, and Heroes of their Praise:
> All laws, for Pique or Caprice, will forego;
> The Friend of CATILINE, and TULLY's Foe!

Welsted's abuse has a certain vigour:

> A softling Head! that spleeny Whims devour;
> With Will to Satyr, while deny'd the Power!
> A Soul corrupt, that hireling Praise suborns!
> That hates for Genius, and for Virtue scorns!
> A Coxcomb's Talents, with a Pedant's Art!
> A Bigot's Fury, in an Atheist's Heart!
> Lewd without Lust, and without Wit profane!
> Outragious, and afraid! contemn'd, and vain!
>
> IMMUR'D, whilst young, in Convents hadst thou been;
> VICTORIA, still, with Rapture we had seen:
> But now our Wishes by the Fates are crost;
> We've gain'd a THERSITE, and an HELEN lost:
> The envious Planet has deceiv'd our Hope;
> We've lost a ST. LEGER, and gain'd a POPE.
>
> A LITTLE Monk thou wert, by Nature, made!

Wert fashion'd for the *Jesuit*'s Gossip—Trade!
A lean Church-Pandar, to procure, or lie!
A Pimp at Altars, or in Courts a Spy!   (pp. 6–7)

That Pope wrote verses in his own praise and palmed them off on Wycherley was by 1732 an old charge, but Welsted here makes Pope play the same trick on Walsh:

Forgot the self-applauding Strain shall be;
Tho' own'd by WALSH, or palm'd on WYCHERLEY:
While Time, nor Fate, this faithful *Sketch* erase,
Which shews thy Mind, as REISBANK's Bust thy Face. (p. 7)

He introduces the *Rape of the Lock* and the *First Psalm*:

Debase, in low Burlesque, the Song divine;
And level DAVID's deathless Muse to thine:
Be Bawdry, still, thy ribald Canto's Theme:
Traduce for Satyr, and for Wit blaspheme:
Each chaste Idea of thy Mind review;
Make CUPIDS squirt, and gaping TRITONS ¹spew.   (p. 8)

¹ *Pope's Epistle* [*to Burlington*] ... [l. 111; l. 154].

January 15, 1732 (*Grub-Street Journal*, January 20, 1731)

[Concanen, Matthew.] A Miscellany On Taste. By Mr. Pope, &c. Viz. I. Of Taste in Architecture. An Epistle to the Earl of Burlington. With Notes Variorum, and a Compleat Key. II. Of Mr. Pope's Taste in Divinity, viz. The Fall of Man, and the First Psalm. Translated for the Use of a Young Lady. III. Of Mr. Pope's Taste of Shakespeare. IV.—His Satire on Mrs. P[ultene]y. V. Mr. Congreve's fine Epistle on Retirement and Taste. Address'd to Lord Cobham. No Author ever spar'd a Brother, / Wits are Game-Cocks to one another. Gay's Fab. the 8th. London: Printed; and sold by G. Lawton, in Fleet-street; T. Osborn, below Bridge; and J. Hughes in High-Holborn. 1732. Price 1s.

8vo in half-sheets.

Frontispiece, one unsigned leaf [G4 folded back], B–F⁴, G in three leaves.

Frontispiece, [2 pp.], 1–24, [25], 26–41, [42–3], 44–5 pp., [46].

Griffith 266. But there are two errors in both the Yale copies, which

are identical, not mentioned by Griffith: D2 is signed D3; G is signed F. The British Museum copy has the same errors and lacks the frontispiece.

The frontispiece (Wimsatt 13.2) is a reduced copy of the engraving 'Taste' (Wimsatt 13.1) reproduced as the frontispiece to *Twick*. III. ii.

This volume is said in the *CBEL* to be 'edited by Concanen'. *Twick*. III. ii. 128 quotes Warton, *Works*, III. 289, as saying that the notes were written 'by Concanen and Welsted, as was supposed'. Straus, p. 294, suspects that this is a Curll publication and notes that several items appear also in *The Female Dunciad*, 1728. The *Mr. Pope's poem on Taste; with a Compleat Key and Notis Variorum* advertised in *The Grub-Street Journal*, January 20, 1731, and listed as unlocated in Rogers is almost certainly this Concanen *Miscellany*.

WORKS: A. *Worms*; B. *First Psalm*; C. Pope's edition of Shakespeare; D. *Epistle to Burlington*.

CHARGES: 1. Pope ungrateful to Chandos; 2. Pope deformed; 3. Untrue that Theobald was asking favours of Pope at the same time that he was concealing from Pope his plans to edit Shakespeare.

A B C   The chief interest of the volume is its notes to the *Epistle to Burlington*, but it contains as well one other attack on Pope, Theobald's letter on Shakespeare from *The Daily Journal*, April 17, 1729 (reprinted in Nichols, *Illustrations of the Literary History of the Eighteenth Century*, II. 214–22), as well as two poems by Pope, 'Of Mr. Pope's Taste of Religion. Being a Translation of the First Psalm. For the Use of a Young Lady', p. [42], and 'Of Mr. Pope's Taste of Original Sin. To the Ingenious Mr. Moore, Author of the Celebrated Worm-Powder', pp. [43]–45; also, 'Mr. Pope's Satire on Mrs. P— The Looking-Glass', p. [46]. (See *Twick*. VI. 419–20 for the reasons for refusing to attribute this last poem to Pope.) Their inclusion and titles were obviously designed to annoy Pope.

D I   The 'Clavis' [G4r] provides identifications that have been used in *Twick*. III. ii; Timon is, of course, identified as the 'Duke of C[handos]'.

The text of the *Epistle to Burlington* printed here which I have used in my quotations is an early unauthorized edition with several differences in punctuation and spelling from Griffith 259 and 265 (e.g., ll. 124, 139).

The notes are largely composed of quibbles and irrelevancies. Two

of the notes are important because they were probably responsible for changes Pope made in the poem. He objects, e.g., to l. 25,

> Just as they are, yet shall your noble Rules
> Fill half the Land with *Imitating Fools*;

This, as it stands, is down-right Nonsense, . . . that is, your noble Rules, such as they are, good or bad, rough as they run, shall fill . . . Your Aim was to have said, Yet shall your noble Rules, as just as they are, fill, *&c.* This would have been Sense, and something to your Purpose, but then it would have stretch'd your Verse out a Syllable too long, and you rather chose to transgress against Sense, than Sound. However, for once, I will help you to an Expression which shall suite you exactly. *Just tho' they be, yet shall—* (p. 21)

Pope altered the line to,

> Yet shall (my Lord) your just, your noble rules.

The discrepancy between l. 127,

> Behold! my Lord advances o'er the Green,

and l. 132,

> Just at his Study-door he'll bless your Eyes,

was shrewdly noted:

Here we find my Lord, first of all, advancing o'er the Green on purpose to expose his Person to view;—And now we are told that our Eyes must not be blest with the Sight, till he appears at this Study-door.—*Quere*, Whereabouts, upon the Green, my Lord's Study-door stands? (p. 16)

Pope altered l. 127 to read,

> My Lord advances with majestic mien.

These criticisms, however, are exceptional. Much more typical is the objection to 'Who but must laugh the Master when he sees?' (l. 107),

Who but must laugh at our Poet for writing such barbarous English? I am really surpriz'd to think how he suffered such an Impropriety to excape him. The Truth is, *laugh at the Master* would have stretch'd the Verse a Syllable beyond its ordinary Length, for which Reason He, having more Regard to Sound than Sense, chose to omit the Particles.   (p. 13)

He is annoyed by 'The Wood supports the Plain' in l. 81:

I have heard of a Plain supporting a Wood a thousand Times, because the Plain was below, and the Wood above.—But how Mr. *Pope's* Wood comes to support his Plain, I own myself unable to determine . . .' (p. 9)

To 'What Sums are thrown away!' in l. 100 he objects that since the money is being paid to English workmen and almost all the building material is English, this private expense does not constitute a public loss (pp. 12–13).

There is little directly personal abuse, but l. 108, 'A puny Insect shiv'ring at a Breeze!' was too tempting to pass over:

2
> Every one who has the Honour to be acquainted with Mr. *Pope*, owns him to be a fine, tall, proper, well-shap'd, agreeable, jolly Gentleman, with a Constitution strong enough to enable him to defy Winds and Weather ... (p. 13)

c   Theobald's letter, pp. 31–41, is simply headed 'To the Author', and dated and signed 'April 16, 1729. Lew. Theobald' (p. 41). In Nichols, *Illustrations*, II. 214, it is headed 'To Mr. Matthew Concanen, Fleet-street', and a note adds that it appeared in *The Daily Journal*, April 17, 1729. Jones includes it in his bibliography of Theobald (Jones, p. 351).

Theobald will, he says,
> attempt to show with what Fidelity he [Pope] has perform'd the *dull* Office of an *Editor*, hardly without aiming to understand his Author himself, or having any Ambition that his Readers ever should: Or, where he does aim, to shew he has such a happy Fatality at Mistaking, that we wish he would not explain the Author into *Nonsense*. (p. 32)

He then gives nine errors in Pope's edition and their corrections (pp. 32–9).

c3   Theobald goes on to protest against Pope's statement in the note to the *Dunciad* A, i. 106, that at the same time that he was soliciting favours from Pope he concealed from him his design to edit Shakespeare. Theobald protests that he had no such design until he saw how incorrect Pope's own edition was; he only asked Pope for two favours: to buy a few tickets for a benefit performance of his play and to recommend his Aeschylus subscription. To the first request Theobald received a letter saying Pope had been away and had received the letter too late to do anything about it. To the second request Pope wrote that he would ask some of his friends, but Theobald never received one subscriber from Pope's recommendations, nor did Pope himself subscribe. Theobald cannot, then, be accused of ingratitude towards Pope (pp. 39–41).

January 22, 1732 (*Grub-Street Journal*, January 27, 1731)

Of Good Nature. An Epistle Humbly Inscrib'd to His G[ra]ce the D[u]ke of C[hando]s. Homo sum; humani nihil a me alienum pato [*sic*]. Ter. London: Printed by J. Hughs in High-Holborn, For T. Dormer at the Star and Garter, over-against the Castle Tavern in Fleetstreet. 1732.

Half-title: Of Good Nature. An Epistle Humbly Inscrib'd to His G—ce the D—ke of C—s. Price Six-pence.

8vo in half-sheets.
[A]–B⁴.
[4 pp.], [5]–15 pp., [16] blank.

Listed as unlocated in Rogers.

This is attributed to the Rev. John Cowper by John Butt, 'A Master Key to Popery', *Pope and his Contemporaries* (Oxford, 1949), p. 43, n.2.
    Some 30 lines from *Of Good Nature* are quoted in *Ingratitude*, 1733, including the first quotation below.

WORKS: A. Atticus portrait; B. *Epistle to Burlington*.

CHARGES: 1. Pope ungrateful to Chandos; 2. Pope libelled Addison; 3. Pope deformed; 4. Pope's library consists mostly of his own works.

Another in the series of attacks on Pope for his supposed ingratitude to Chandos. After praise of Chandos's liberality and kindness, the author reveals his purpose:

> AND yet there lives (oh! Shame to human Race!)
> A Wretch who boasts within Your Heart a Place:
> Who like an Adder, swoln with cherishing,
> Darts at his Patron his relentless Sting:
> Well-treated, yet not pleas'd, caress'd, yet rude,
> And proud of the base Crime—INGRATITUDE.
>   (pp. 6–7)

There follows a long portrait of Maevius (Pope) who lures the good and great with his 'soothing Harmony', only to tear and devour their spotless fame.

> AH! hapless they on whom unknown you [Pope] smile,
> Whose yielding Hearts thy Flatteries beguile:
> Soon shall they see themselves with wild Surprise
> Adorn'd, as Victims, for the Sacrifice:

So ADDISON—Peace to his gentle Shade—
Was to thy seeming Merit once betray'd:
So C[HANDO]s, GEN'ROUS LORD, is taught to know
That to oblige, is to exasp'rate You:
So the same Change shall many others see,
And B[UR]L[INGTO]N Himself be stab'd by Thee. (pp. 7–8)

3 Pope's size is, of course, relevant:

MAGNIFICENCE and GRANDEUR hurt thy Eyes,
Objects too mighty for thy Pigmy Size:

.   .   .

As well thy Stature might the Standard be,
And Six Foot high be rank Deformity.   (p. 9)

4 This leads to ridicule of the Lilliputian size of his house and grotto,
and a curious charge against his library:

His Library, of Books no ample Store,
His own Works neatly bound, and little more.   (p. 10)

The metaphor of a wasp deserves notice:

To Vice indulgent, Vertue he pollutes,
And preys, like Wasps upon the fairest Fruits:
He singles out, his little Rage to spend,
The Good, the Kind, the Generous, and the Friend. (p. 14)

He indulges in the pleasing fantasy, so common in the attacks, of a
Pope at last exposed and humiliated, in an image that makes one
think of Cowper:

I see Thee stript of Honours thou has worn,
Expos'd to private Jest, and publick Scorn,
Driv'n from the Herd all pale with wild Despair,
Panting, and breathless, like the tainted Deer.   (p. 13)

February 1, 1732 (*Grub-Street Journal*, February 10, 1732)

Malice Defeated. A Pastoral Essay. Occasioned By Mr. Pope's
Character of Lord Timon, In his Epistle to the Earl of Burling-
ton, and Mr. Welsted's Answer. As long as Moco's happy Tree
shall grow, / While Berries crackle, or while Mills shall go; /
While smoaking Streams from silver Spouts shall glide, / Or
China's Earth receive the sable Tide; / While Coffee shall to
British Nymphs be dear; / While fragrant Steams the bended

Head shall chear; / Or grateful Bitters shall delight the Taste, /
So long, O Pope! This Image Of Thy Mind Shall Last. See Pope's
20th Letter to H. Cromwell, Esq; —To break thy Faith, / And
turn a Rebel to so good a Master, / Is an Ingratitude unmatch'd
on Earth. Rowe's Tam.

A folio broadside, unsigned, unnumbered, the verses being printed in
double columns on both sides. The imprint is on the verso, about
three-quarters down the page: London: Printed for J. Millan, near
the Horse-Guards. M.DCC.XXXII. [Price Two Pence.]

Listed as unlocated in Rogers.

WORK: A. *Epistle to Burlington.*

CHARGE: 1. Pope ungrateful to Chandos.

The form, a dialogue between Daphnis, Thyrsis, and Strephon, shows
an originality surprising in Popiana. The hint for pastoral may have
been taken from Welsted's use of 'Pollio' for Chandos in *Of Dulness
and Scandal*, 1732.

Thyrsis explains to Daphnis the cause of his grief; Rancor has
blasted great Pollio's fame. Daphnis is horrified but knows that the
attacker can only bring disgrace on himself. Thyrsis replies,

I
> 'Tis true, indeed, and that is RANCOR's Fate;
> More Foes by this one Action he'll create,
> Than ever Friends he gain'd. But he deserves
> No Friends, who from the Laws of Honour swerves.
> There was a Time (I know not by what Art)
> When ev'ry Swain, nay, POLLIO took his Part;
> But now the Rebel can't expect to find,
> Virtue will be to its Defamer kind.   (v.)

Although Daphnis is sure that 'good POLLIO don't regard / The base
Design of the Inglorious Bard' (v.), Thyrsis feels he deserves punish-
ment, and both are relieved when Strephon arrives with the news that
Satyrus [Welsted] has come to Pollio's defence:

> In mighty Numbers, foreign to these Times,
> He has display'd the proud Imposter's Crimes;
> Made RANCOR be by ev'ry Swain abhorr'd,
> *And injur'd* POLLIO *to Himself restor'd.*   (v.)

Daphnis concludes with praise of Welsted:

> Expiring Numbers shall thro' him revive,
> *And whate'er* HORACE *was, shall in* SATYRUS *live.*   (v.)

February 3, 1732 (*Daily Journal*, Rogers)

Welsted, Leonard. Of False Fame. An Epistle. To the Right Honourable the Earl of Pembroke. Judice, quem nosti, populo, qui stultus honores / Saepe dat indignis, & famae servit ineptus; / Qui stupet in titulis & imaginibus. Quid oportet / Nos facere, à vulgo longè latéque remotos? Hor. By Mr. Welsted. London: Printed for T. Cooper, the Corner of Ivy-Lane, next Pater-Noster Row. M.DCC.XXXII.

Half-title: Of False Fame. An Epistle To the Right Honourable the Earl of Pembroke. Price 6d.

8vo in half-sheets.

[A]–C⁴.

[4 pp.], 5–21 pp., [22] blank, [23] book-list, [24] blank.

Reprinted in *The Works in Verse and Prose of Leonard Welsted*, ed. John Nichols (London, 1787), pp. 200–6.

WORKS: A. *Windsor Forest*; B. *Rape of the Lock*; C. Pope's edition of Shakespeare; D. *Dunciad*; E. *Epistle to Burlington*.

CHARGES: 1. Pope's reputation undeserved; 2. Pope's wealth gained by fraud; 3. Pope malicious and fond of libel.

1   The point is simple and conventional. The poet must scorn false fame which is awarded by the vulgar to the undeserving, while in every age the true genius goes unrewarded. True fame consists in the applause of the wise. Pope throughout is Welsted's chief example of false fame. 'The Rabble's Cry'

A B   Nor adds to PLUME, nor takes from CHANDOS Taste; ...
                The Marsh becomes not, hence, a limpid Rill;
                Nor WINDSOR FOREST shines a COOPER's HILL.   (p. 7)
False fame is 'What POPE once had, and DRYDEN could not gain!' (p. 9).

C   Pembroke may see Shakespeare
                Defac'd ¹so late, who was so early scorn'd!
                ¹ The Quarto Edition of *Shakespear*, by *Pope* (p. 10).

He illustrates the fate of poets by a parable. Celia, robbed of her virtue by Lord Jasper, is brought by him to the city where he soon abandons her. She is taken from the streets, a 'fleering, faithless, fluttering, flimsy Whore!' (p. 15) by Lord Lovemore and transformed

into a fashionable lady. Lavinia, on the other hand, lives out her innocent life in the country, unknown. The application of the whore to
Pope is made clear:

> BAVIUS, the while, till Fate decreed his Fall,
> A Dunce triumphant reign'd, and captiv'd all:
> Dull, on the golden Harvest, did he gaze;
> Grew envious with Success, and pale with Praise:
> Still brew'd, in Gall, his teizing, trifling Song;
> And spar'd no Malice, tho' he knew no Wrong:
> Writ, rail'd, and DUNCIFY'D, from Year to Year:
> The JESUIT's Hate inflam'd the EUNUCH's Fear.
>
> UNMARK'D at first! necessitous and scorn'd!
> No Patron own'd him, and no Bays adorn'd:
> One [1]Critic's Pupil, with one [2]Bard he vy'd;
> And knew not to be 'sick with civil Pride'[3].
> A hungry Scribbler, and without a Name;
> Till Fraud procur'd him Wealth, and Falshood Fame!
> That Wealth obtain'd, Faith, Friendship he disclaims;
> Sneers, where he fawn'd, and where he prais'd, defames;
> No Virtue leaves unwrong'd, or Vice untry'd;
> No Fame not scarr'd, no Genius not decry'd.

[1] Cromwell.   [2] Gildon.
[3] *See* Pope's *Epistle to the Earl of Burlington.* [l. 166] (pp. 19–20).

February 8, 1732 (*Grub-Street Journal,* February 10, 1732)

On P[op]e and W[elste]d. Occasion'd by their late Writings.
O Cives! Cives! querena [*sic*] Paecunia primum est, / Virtus post
Nummos—Hor. With Advice To A Modern Poet. —Cui lumen
adeptum. Virg. London: Printed for R. P. and Sold by E. Nutt
under the Royal-Exchange; A. Dodd without Temple-Bar; and
J. Jollysse in St. James's-Street. 1732. (Price 6d.)

Folio.

A–B².

[2 pp.], 3–8 pp.

This pamphlet seems to have been elicited by Pope's *Epistle to Burlington* and Welsted's *Of Dulness and Scandal.*

WORK: A. *Epistle to Burlington* (?).

CHARGE: 1. Pope fails to attack the rich.

The not very intelligible title poem in its 50-odd lines calmly joins Pope and Welsted. The criticism of Welsted is clear: in order to make money, he asserts that the rich can do no wrong. The criticism of Pope is obscure, but the writer seems to be saying that the same charge applies to Pope. It is clear that the writer feels that contemporary satirists lack the courage to attack the rich. He begins,

I
> How greatly, by our modern Poets Rage,
> Charm'd and instructed is our modern Age?
> While, in their smooth and varnish'd Lines, is seen
> Nothing—but Partiality and Spleen!
> Such are the Motives of thy mighty Mind,
> Oh, mighty P[op]e! with Arrogance combin'd;
> And W[elste]d, with the Zeal of Gain inspir'd,
> (But Zeal of Justice in Pretension fir'd)
>
> .   .   .
>
> They strive the World, but more themselves to please;
> They court Applause, adoring Wealth and Ease.   (pp. 3–4)

Pope is clearly meant in the following:

A?
> What Miracles are now, by Fortune wrought!
> The Poor have no Desert!—the Rich, no Fault!
> Our Poets first, thro' spleenful Discontent,
> Not Love of Truth, satirick Meanings vent;
> And afterward (observe the glorious End)
> Recant those Meanings—least [*sic*] they shou'd offend:
> Yet Truth it self is call'd Abuse—and Satire,
> For rightly representing Things—Ill-Nature.   (p. 5)

He seems to be suggesting that after Pope had attacked Chandos as Timon, he tried to pretend that he hadn't meant him at all. His criticism of Pope's verse is more specific:

> What e'er the Theme, the Manner is the same;
> They Energy, like Truth, avoid—profound
> In specious Show, and undulating Sound;
> As Lovers 'Plaints, their Satires softly move,
> Melodiously they fill the vocal Grove;
> Their Wrath, howe'er invet'rate, never seems
> Like Torrents Rage—but glides like purling Streams:
> Well Suits indeed their Principles, their Strain;
> So false! affected! impotent! And vain!

P[*op*]*e* does (exorbitantly fond of Fame)
    Pour out the Vengeance of aspersing Blame.   (pp. 4–5)
The title poem is followed by the brief ironic 'Advice To A Modern Poet', pp. 6–7, which mentions Pope once, and by a contemptuous six-line epigram, p. 8, 'On Welsted's Motto, To His Dulness and Scandal'.

April 5, 1732 (*Grub-Street Journal*, April 13, 1732)

Mr. Taste, The Poetical Fop: Or, The Modes Of The Court. A Comedy. By the Author of the Opera of Vanelia; or the Amours of the Great. That I the Humour of this Age may hit, / Where Blockheads often sneer for want of Wit: / Fools of each various Cast I hither call, / With Sawny Taste, who in one Fool is All. London: Printed for E. Rayner, and sold by the Booksellers in Town and Country. (Price One Shilling and Six Pence.)

8vo in half-sheets.
Two leaves unsigned, B–I⁴, K in one leaf.
[4 pp.], [5]–74 pp.
Several errors in pagination: there are no pp. 61, 62, 68, or 69.
    'The End of the Second Act' (p. 57) should read 'The End of the Fourth Act'.
    Mlle Flipant, Jenny Wheedle, and several other minor characters are omitted from the Dramatis Personae.

Re-issued with a new title-page on April 17, 1733, as:

The Man of Taste. A Comedy. As it is Acted By a Summer Company near Twickenham. No more, O Pope! what Chandois [*sic*] builds deride, / Because he takes not Nature for his Guide; / Since, wond'rous Critick! in thy Form we see / That Nature may mistake as well as he. London: Printed for L. Gulliver, and sold by the Booksellers in Town and Country. M DCC XXXIII. (Price 1s.6d.)

8vo in half-sheets.
Two leaves unsigned, B–I⁴, K in one leaf. B1 incorrectly signed A2.
[4 pp.], [5]–74 pp. Errors in pagination as above.

The drop-title, p. [5], 'The Poetical Fop: Or, The Modes of the Court', is used for the running-title throughout. The title-page and incorrect signing of B1 constitute the only differences between the editions. Since the second unsigned leaf, recto, is still 'Books lately published by E. Rayner', E. Rayner was probably still the proprietor; 'L. Gulliver' was an invention. See James T. Hillhouse, 'The Man of Taste', *MLN*, XLIII (1928), 174–6.

'The author may have been Mrs. Eliza Heywood, as hinted in the dedication (May 27, 1733) to Lady Mary of *The Neuter: or, A Modest Satire on the Poets of the Age*' (Halsband, p. 139, n.4). As Hillhouse pointed out, the *DNB*'s ascription of *The Man of Taste. A Comedy* to James Miller rests on a confusion with Miller's play *The Man of Taste: or the Guardians* (1735). Hillhouse identifies the *Vanelia* of the title-page as one of a number which made scandalous gossip out of the amour of the Prince of Wales and the Hon. Anne Vane.

WORK: A. Homer.

CHARGES: 1. Pope's offer of marriage rejected by Lady Mary; 2. Pope's father a farmer; 3. Pope ungrateful; 4. Pope deformed.

1   In the Dramatis Personae (verso of second unnumbered leaf) appears 'Mr. *Alexander Taste*, A Poet who, in spite of deformity, imagines every Woman he sees in love with him, and imprudently makes Addresses to *Lady Airy*'. Both Hillhouse and Halsband identify Lady Airy with Lady Mary and the latter calls this the 'first mention in print of Pope's rejection by Lady Mary' (Halsband, p. 140).

The play is a confused and silly affair. Lady Airy is courted by Sir William Heartfree and Taste. To get rid of Taste, Heartfree has a servant, Jenny Wheedle, disguise herself as an heiress. Lady Airy, offended by a song Taste has composed in her honour, accepts Heartfree. Taste is deceived into thinking Jenny an heiress and is led into a mock marriage with her which is interrupted at the end of the last act when the plot is revealed. Taste, conceited and foolish, is a figure of fun to all. He is clearly meant for Pope (and is so identified in Genest's copy of the play, now at Yale).

The Homer is the chief butt of the jokes. In Act I when Sir William Addle is asked if he knows the name of Taste's current mistress for whom he is writing a song, he replies,

A   I am as ignorant of his Affairs as he is of the *Greek* tongue; I take them from common Report, and he understands that by the *Latin* on t'other Side. (p. 10)

And in Act IV:

> Mr. *Taste*. How do you like *Pope*'s *Homer*? 'tis an admirable *English* Poem.
>
> Mr. *Brit*[on]. There you are right, Mr. *Taste*; 'tis indeed an *English* Poem.
>
> Mr. *Taste*. What do you mean, Sir? I aver it is absolutely the most finish'd Work in the World.
>
> Mr. *Brit*[on]. And I aver, Sir, that it is no more a Translation of *Homer*, than the good old Ballad call'd the Siege of *Troy* is one ... (pp. 46–7)

Then Harry Oldcastle intervenes:

> The very best Lines in that Work are stole from *Dryden*, and in several Places copied *verbatim*: not to mention the innumerable Thefts committed upon several other celebrated Authors. 'Tis like a Piece of Patch-Work, Madam, made up with Scraps of various Colours; nay, what's worse, it is an inhuman Murder committed upon the Prince of Poets, and the *Greek* Tongue.
>
> (pp. 47–8)

Taste is shown as ridiculously vain. In a brief discussion of the latest works in Act III he says to Lady Airy,

> Our present Sett of Authors are despicable Creatures, they have neither Genius nor Learning; and yet are too proud to be instructed: I have given them the true Standard of Poetry in all my Performances, but to no purpose; for, instead of endeavouring to imitate me, they rail at my Works, because they are above their Understanding. (p. 36)

And in Act IV, he announces that there are more faults in Waller and Prior 'than can be explain'd in one Conversation, I'll give you in writing the necessary Rules to judge by' (p. 46).

There is in Act v the by now familiar account of his early life.

> His Father ... was a Farmer; however, he made a shift to keep this Son at a Grammar-School: the Lad had always a great Inclination to Poetry, and some Gentlemen of Worth happening to see his juvenile Performances, took a Fancy to him; and from that time provided for him in a handsome manner, sparing no Charge in his Education. He behaved with great Modesty, and wrote several Things which met with universal Applause.
>
> (p. 64)

That, of course, was a very long time ago. He has forgotten his modesty as quickly as he did the obligations he owed his benefactors. As soon as he had gained a reputation, he

3   treated those Gentlemen who had rais'd him from nothing with
the utmost Contempt, taking all the vile methods he could
think of to do them Injuries; nay, he was so much lost to Shame,
that he wrote a Work on purpose to abuse them. (p. 64)

4   Taste's career 'verifies the common Saying, *as crooked in Mind as in
Body*' (p. 64). The familiar ape metaphor appears both when Lady
Airy explains that she allowed Taste 'the Liberty of hopping about
my Rooms sometimes, because the Folly and Vanity of the Creature
diverted me' (p. 51), and when Jenny, now that the plot has been
discovered, says that she would rather take a soldier than Taste for a
husband 'for fear our Children should have resembled Baboons, Ha,
ha, ha!' (p. 73).

May, 1732

[Cooke, Thomas.] The Comedian, Or Philosophical Enquirer.
Numb. II. May. 1732. [two lines of Greek.] Epictet. Cap. 10.
London: Printed for J. Roberts, at the Oxford-Arms, in War-
wick-Lane, 1732. (Price Six Pence.)

8vo in half-sheets.

A–E⁴.

[4 pp.], [5]–40 pp.

Bound together with the other eight numbers of *The Comedian*, No. 1,
April, 1732–No. 9, [April] 1733, with a general preface and under the
general title:

A Demonstration Of The Will of God by the Light of Nature,
In Eight Discourses., Containing [a list of eight titles] ... London: Printed for F. Cogan, at the Middle-Temple-Gate. 1733.

WORKS: A. Homer; B. *Epistle to Burlington*.

The second item in this issue is 'A Letter in Prose to Mr. Alexander
Pope, occasioned by his Epistle in Verse to the Earl of Burlington',
pp. 13–24, dated, p. 23, 'April. 1732'.

He will, he says, try to correct a few of the inaccuracies and absurdities in Pope's *Epistle to Burlington*; there are too many to correct them
all.

B   Most of Cooke's criticisms are tedious quibbles over wording. He
does not mention Chandos at all. His most important objection is to

'Rarities for Sloan' in l. 10. He suggests the reading 'Butterflies' and corrects the spelling of 'Sloane' (pp. 15–16). Pope altered both words accordingly. See *Twick.* III. ii. 136 for Cooke's comments. They were noticed in *Notes and Queries*, Ser. 1, VII, 541.

B   Since Aldus's editions of the classics are valuable only for their correctness and not at all for their typographical beauty, he suggests altering ll. 135–6,

> To all their dated Backs he turns you round,
> These *Aldus* printed, those *Du Sueïl* has bound,

to

> To all their *gilded Backs* he turns you round;
> These *Lintot* printed, and those *Brindley* bound.   (p. 22)

This gives him a chance to work in a reference to Pope's Homer. As Lintot, he continues, has published some bad books,

A
> ... my Lord may be supposed to have a few of them: and, tho thou sayest that he has no modern Authors in his Study, he may have *Homer* in *English,* with a View that his Visitants may believe that he bought the Volumes for the Sake of the Notes; and some Editions of them thou knowest to be very well printed: thus the Satire would be compleat; for having those Volumes, he would have Books well printed, and yet worth little. (p. 22)

The level at which Cooke works here may be seen in his comment on l. 5, 'Not for himself he sees, or hears, or eats.'

> To say he neither sees, nor hears, for himself are Expressions allowable in Poetry or Prose; but that he should not eat for himself is very odd. Dost thou really mean that he does not eat for himself? Indeed thou can'st not mean so; for if thou dost, thou meanest that he chews the Victuals for his Company as Nurses do for Children: thou surely had'st not so filthy a Meaning; therefore what thou must mean is, that his expensive Dishes are not provided for himself, but, thro Vanity, for those who dine with him ... (p. 14)

The letter ends with a 'Postscript to Posterity' which opens,

> *Alexander Pope* was a Man who lived in the 18th Century of the Christian Aera, Cotemporary with the Author of this Letter, but was near twenty Years older: he continued *making Verses,* and *Lys,* almost from the Day in which he could first speak to the Day of his Death; and yet he always expressed a tender Concern for his *moral* Character. (pp. 23–4)

March 2, 1733 (*Daily Post*, March 2, 1733)

[Burnet, Atex.] Achilles Dissected: Being a Compleat Key Of the Political Characters In that New Ballad Opera, Written by the late Mr. Gay. An Account of the Plan upon which it is founded. With Remarks upon the Whole. By Mr. Burnet. To which is added, The First Satire of the Second Book of Horace, Imitated in a Dialogue between Mr. Pope and the Ordinary of Newgate. What's good for the Goose, is good for the Gander. Ray's Prov. London: Printed for W. Mears, at the Lamb, on Ludgate-Hill, 1733. (Price Six Pence.)

8vo in half-sheets.
One unsigned leaf, B–D⁴, E in three leaves.
[2 pp.], [1]–30 pp.

In 1734 the old sheets were reissued with a new title-page:

The Case Of Alexander Pope, of Twickenham, Esq; And His Counsel learned in the Law. Transver'd To a Friendly Dialogue Between Him and the Ordinary of Newgate. By Way of Allusion To the First Satire of the Second Book of Horace. To which is prefix'd, A Dissection, and Compleat Key to Mr. Gay's Post-humous Opera of Achilles. By Alexander Burnet Esq; The Second Edition. London: Printed for W. Mears, at the Lamb on Ludgate-Hill. M.DCC.XXXIV. Price 6d. [Texas.]

'Achilles Dissected, &c. In a Letter to Lady P****' (pp. [1]–20) is signed, p. 20, 'Atex. Burnet'. 'Atex.' may or may not be a misprint. Swift twice refers to him as 'Alexander Burnet' (Ault, p. 215), and the 'second edition' spells it as 'Alexander'. Whatever his first name, he is almost certainly not Thomas Burnet who is not known to have published against Pope after 1716 and never seems to have signed himself either 'Atex.' or 'Alexander'; the references to Duckett and the *Homerides* may be deliberately misleading. Ault, pp. 215–21, would accept the attribution of the Prologue to *Achilles* to Pope, but it is rejected in *Twick.* VI. See the review of *New Light on Pope* by Maynard Mack, *PQ*, XXIX (1950), p. 291.

The 'Imitation' (pp. 21–30) is signed 'Guthry' (p. 30), the ordinary of the prison.

'Achilles Dissected' is dated, p. [1], 'Feb. 12, 1733'. *Achilles* had been produced on February 10, 1733, at the Theatre Royal (Ault,

p. 218). The 'Imitation' is dated, p. 30, 'Feb. 26, 1732/3'; *Sat.* II. i had appeared on February 15, 1733. *Achilles* was not published until March 3, 1733 (*Universal Spectator*, March 3, 1733) and is therefore in the pamphlet referred to as not yet published.

WORKS: A. Homer; B. *First Psalm*; C. *Sat.* II. i.

CHARGES: 1. Pope wrote prologue and songs for *Achilles*; 2. Pope a spy for Pulteney and a contributor to *The Craftsman*.

Despite the title-page, *Achilles Dissected* contains very little political satire, indeed, very little original writing. A letter to *The Daily Courant*, February 16, 1733, and several lines from *The Auditor* of the same date are included, pp. 5–11; pp. 14–19 contain quotations from *Homerides: Or, Homer's First Book Moderniz'd*, 1716, q.v.

The writer in *The Daily Courant* charges Pope and his friends with having got together after Gay's death (he had died on December 4, 1732) to finish the play. '. . . the *little Satyrist* tags the Verse, and *points* the Song' (p. 10). Pope is thus clearly implicated in the writer's ridicule of the play and of the songs. Gay's friends 'have gone farther in wounding his Reputation, by *writing for him*, than his most inveterate Enemies (if he had any) could by writing against him . . .' (p. 10). The obscenity of the poetry equals the dullness of the prose (p. 11).

Burnet agrees both on authorship and on obscenity:

> Some Songs were likewise wanting, and his Friends Mr. *Pope*, Dr. *Arbuthnot*, &c. who have undertaken to supply that Defect, have really overloaded it . . . Some of them are very *low*, and others very *luscious*. (pp. 4–5)

According to *The Daily Courant* writer, the presence of Pope and his friends at the opening night made the people suspect 'a worn-out Artifice of bad Authors to support a bad Play' (p. 6).

Burnet, in an ironic attempt to justify Gay's modernization of Achilles against *The Daily Courant* writer, shows by quotations from *Homerides: Or, Homer's First Book*, 1716, that Gay was not the first to modernize Homer and charges in his conclusion that Pope had first had the idea:

> Mr. POPE burlesqued the Story of our Hero ACHILLES, from the *Greek* Original, by his Translation. (p. 19)

Burnet, at the end of his letter, introduces the 'Imitation' as a parody upon Pope's '*vain* Imitation of this *Satire*' (p. 20). The 'Imitation' involves little more than an obvious inversion of the poet's self-portrait.

B
> *I love to pour out all myself*, PROFANE,
> And *mock* the SCRIPTURES in *Heroick Strain*.

> .   .   .

> In a false Partial Light my Muse intends,
> *Fair* to set forth *myself*, and foul *my Friends*.   (p. 28)

2   Pope is accused of being a spy:
> Envy'd I've always liv'd *among the Great*,
> Tho' I've been Pimp, and often *Spy of State*.[1]

> [1] For Mr. P[ultene]y; and wrote the Character of a *Norfolk-Steward* in the *Craftsman* (p. 28).

There is a single aesthetic objection:

C
> *You could not do a worse Thing for your Life*,   [*Sat.* II. i. 15]
is footnoted, 'How ten low Words here creep in one dull line!' (p. 22).

March 9, 1733 (*Grub-Street Journal*, March 29, 1733)

[Montagu, Lady Mary Wortley and John Lord Hervey.] Verses Address'd to the Imitator Of The First Satire Of The Second Book of Horace. By a Lady. London: Printed for A. Dodd, and sold at all the Pamphlet-Shops in Town. (Price Six-pence.)

Folio.
[A]–B².
[2 pp.], 3–8 pp.

Drop-title: To The Imitator Of The First Satire of the Second Book of Horace.

The Bodleian copy, Dom c.23 (7), is another issue of this. The Bodleian copy, Godwyn Pamphlets 1661 (18), is another edition: title-page as above but adding after 'Lady' 'Si Natura negat, facit Indignatio versus. Juvenal.' Collation and pagination are the same.

Advertised on the same day in *The Daily Post* was a piracy of this:

To The Imitator Of The Satire Of The Second Book of Horace. London: Printed for J. Roberts, near the Oxford-Arms in Warwick-Lane. M.DCC.XXXIII.

Half-title: To The Imitator Of The Satire Of The Second Book of Horace.

Folio.
[A]–C².
[4 pp.], [1]–7 pp., [8] blank.

Drop-title: To The Imitator Of The Second Book of Horace.

There are numerous differences in accidentals between this and the Dodd. Yale has a 'Fifth Edition Corrected', 1733, 'a tribute not to its own popularity but to that of Pope's *Epistle to Arbuthnot*, which had encouraged the bookseller' (Halsband, p. 150): title-page as in the Dodd first edition, adding after 'Lady' 'Si Natura negat, facit Indignatio versus. Juvenal. The Fifth Edition Corrected.'

Folio.
[A]–B².
[2 pp.], 3–8 pp.

There is in the British Museum a duodecimo:

Verses Address'd to the Imitator Of The First Satire Of The Second Book of Horace. By a Lady. Si Natura negat facit Indignatio versus. Juvenal. London: Printed for A. Dodd; Dublin: Reprinted by Christopher Dickson in the Post-Office-Yard, 1733.

12mo.
A⁴.
[2 pp.], 3–8 pp.

WORKS: A. Homer; B. *Epistle to Burlington*; C. *Sat.* II. i.

CHARGES: 1. Pope ignorant of Greek; 2. Pope ungrateful to Chandos; 3. Pope incapable of loving; 4. Pope deformed.

The most famous of attacks on Pope and perhaps the only one where Pope has found a worthy adversary. To summarize the charges made is to falsify the total impact of the poem. There is Pope's inability to understand Horace:

C   Whilst on one side we see how *Horace* thought;
       And on the other, how he never wrote.   (p. 3)
his ignorance of Greek – who can believe,
1   That the dull Copist better understood

> That *Spirit*, he pretends to imitate,
> Than heretofore that *Greek* he did translate?   (p. 3)

his ingratitude to Chandos (made clear in a footnote: 'See *Taste*, an Epistle', p. 5)

B 2
> But even Benefits can't rein thy Hand:
> To this or that alike in vain we trust,
> Nor find Thee less Ungrateful than Unjust.   (p. 5)

But it is the brilliant thrusts one remembers, as at his verse:

> Weeds, as they are, they seem produc'd by Toil.   (p. 4)

Or the sickeningly insistent personal abuse:

3
> Whilst none thy crabbed Numbers can endure;
> Hard as thy Heart, and as thy Birth obscure.   (p. 4)

She cannot insist enough on the absurdity of his claims to be a man:

4
> If Limbs unbroken, Skin without a Stain,   ⎫
> Unwhipt, unblanketed, unkick'd, unslain;   ⎬
> That wretched little Carcass you retain:
> The Reason is, not that the World wants Eyes;
> But thou'rt so mean, they see, and they despise.   (p. 6)

His other enemies, though there is no evidence that they lacked the will, lacked the imagination and the experience of years of friendship, possibly of love, that made it possible for Lady Mary to wound deepest of all:

34
> But how should'st thou by Beauty's Force be mov'd,
> No more for loving made, than to be loved?
> It was the Equity of righteous Heav'n,
> That such a Soul to such a Form was giv'n;
> And shews the Uniformity of Fate,
> That one so odious, shou'd be born to hate.   (p. 5)

In the appalling final lines she rises to a full command of the rhetoric of hate:

34
> Like the first bold Assassin's be thy Lot,
> Ne'er be thy Guilt forgiven, or forgot;
> But as thou hate'st, be hated by Mankind,
> And with the Emblem of thy crooked Mind,
> Mark'd on thy Back, like *Cain*, by God's own Hand,
> Wander like him, accursed through the Land.   (p. 8)

March 30, 1733 (*Grub-Street Journal*, April 5, 1733)

An Epistle To The Little Satyrist Of Twickenham. Peras imposuit Jupiter nobis duas: / Propriis repletam vitiis post tergam dedit, / Alienis ante pectus suspendit gravem. / Hac re videre nostra mala non possumus: / Alii simul delinquunt, Censores sumus. Phaed. London: Printed for J. Wilford, at the Three Golden Flower de Luces behind the Chapter-House in St. Paul's Church Yard. 1733. (Price, Six-Pence.)

Folio.
[A]–B², c in one leaf.
[2 pp.], [3]–10 pp.

WORKS: A. Homer; B. *Dunciad*; c. *Epistle to Burlington*; D. *Sat.* II. i.

CHARGES: 1. Pope ungrateful to Chandos; 2. Pope venal; 3. Pope proudly boasts of his virtue.

The central indictment is Pope's ingratitude to Chandos:

> A kind Compassion prompts me to conclude,
> That *Timon*'s Study you had never view'd;
> Not LOCK, nor MILTON, nor *a modern Book*,
> Has Truth your Tongue, or Sight your Eyes forsook?
> An English'd *Homer* there you might have found, }
> Not b'*Aldus* printed, nor *du Suëil* bound, }
> Which cost, a [*sic*] I have heard, *Five Hundred Pound*.   (p. 6)

This passage may be the source for the figure of 'five hundred pounds' which Pope named in *Epistle to Arbuthnot*, p. 375, n., as the present Welsted accused Pope of taking from Chandos. Welsted, though he clearly means by 'Pollio' Chandos in *Of Dulness and Scandal*, 1732, q.v., and in that poem clearly accuses Pope of ingratitude to him, does not specify a present of money from Chandos to Pope and names no figure. The sentence in Butt's note, 'No mention is made in Welsted's poems of the Duke of Chandos or of his supposed present . . .' (*Twick.* IV. 124, n.), is, therefore, misleading, and *Twick.* III. ii. 172, n.3, which states, '£500 was the figure mentioned by Welsted . . .', needs correction. For the same charge repeated, see *Ingratitude*, 1733.

The *Dunciad* is 'A Mixture of Ill-Nature, Spleen, and Scorn' (p. 9).

He goes a step further and suggests that Pope's satire is marked not only by malice but by avarice:

> And 't has been urg'd, you write for odious Gain,

And know that nothing but the rankest Satire
Will sell, the Town's so poison'd with ill Nature.
From this sad Crime, pray Heav'n you may be free,
For what's so vile as Scandal for a Fee?   (pp. 8–9)

It is Pope's pride, his ambition to be thought virtuous, that the writer
finds especially offensive:

D 3

To Virtue only, and her Friends, a Friend;
But him so bless'd, to hear, it wou'd offend.
For when that Virtue is indeed possess'd,
It is in Silence, and the Owner's bless'd.   (p. 8)

You say, *impartially your Muse intends*
Fair to expose yourself, your Foes, and Friends.
And Leaf by Leaf your Writings I have turn'd
To find the Page wherein your Faults are mourn'd;
Still self-blown Praise presents itself to View.   (p. 10)

March 24–31, 1733 (*Weekly Miscellany*, March 31, 1733)

[Morrice, Bezaleel.] On The English Translations Of Homer:
A Satire. Parturiunt Montes. Hor. With the Characters of
Homer, Virgil and Horace. And the Character of a truly accomplished Poet. This Satire was printed in the Year 1721. (With
the Character of Homer) but is here improved and enlarged.
London: Printed for John Oswald, at the Rose and Crown in
the Poultry, near Stocks-Market. 1733.

8vo in half-sheets.
[A]–c⁴.
[4 pp.], 5–24 pp.

WORK: A. Homer.

As the title-page indicates, this contains an enlargement of 'On the
British Translations of Homer' which appeared in *An Epistle To Mr.*
Welsted; And A Satyre on the English Translations of Homer . . ., 1721, a
volume which had also contained 'A [*sic*] Essay on the Character of
Homer'. See also the first version in *Three Satires*, 1719.

The present volume contains 'On The English Translations Of

Homer' (pp. 5–13), 'The Character Of Homer' (pp. 14–16), 'An Encomium on Virgil' (pp. 17–18), 'An Encomium on Horace' (pp. 19–21), and 'The Character Of a Truly Accomplish'd Poet' (pp. 22–4).

The volume is dedicated, in what must be a deliberate affront to Pope, to Lady Mary Wortley Montagu.

Only 'On The English Translators of Homer' concerns us here.
A   The 1721 version had had 100 lines; the present version contains 142 lines. The changes affecting the Pope references are minor: changes in punctuation, a slight verbal difference. A triplet is added to the passage I have quoted from the 1721 version beginning 'all things rightly', while a number of lines are added to the passage I have quoted from pp. 20–1.

The poem now concludes with an apostrophe to 'Advent'rous Britons!'

> Ye shou'd not have presumptuously inclin'd
> To view the most approv'd of Human Kind,
> Despoil'd of native Glory! uninspir'd!
> But—at—just Distance—awfully admir'd!   (p. 13)

May 10, 1733 (*Grub-Street Journal*, May 17, 1733)

[Jacob, Giles.] The Mirrour: Or, Letters Satyrical, Panegyrical, Serious and Humorous, On The Present Times. Shewing The great Improvement of Wit, Poetry and Learning, of Art and Sciences, natural Phylosophy, the Law, Physick, Religion, Morality, modern Greatness, Dress, Fashions, &c. To which is added A legal Conviction of Mr. Alexander Pope of Dulness and Scandal, in the high Court of Parnassus. This, Reader, is a faithful Glass to thee; Here All their Beauties and their Faults may see. London: Printed for J. Roberts in Warwick-Lane, and Sold at all the Pamphlet-Shops in London and Westminster, 1733. (Price One Shilling.)

8vo in half-sheets.
A², b–k⁴, l².
[2 pp.], 3–80 pp.

WORK: A. *Dunciad.*

CHARGES: 1. Pope wrote his own praise in *The Poetical Register*; 2. Pope's statement untrue that in the *Dunciad* he mentioned only those who had first written against him; 3. Pope deformed; 4. *Dunciad* hurt James Ralph financially.

'Miscellaneous Letters, Satyrical, Panegyrical, &c' (pp. 5–75) consists of twenty letters arranged chronologically from December 18, 1729, to October 12, 1730. The 'Preface' (pp. 3–4), having explained that publication has been delayed for two or three years, tells us that,

> *THESE Letters* are intended, not only as a *Mirrour* to Mr. *Alexander Pope* and his Creatures, the Admirers of the famous *Dunciad* and more famous *Tom Thumb*, but to many others ...
>
> (p. 3)

Only the first three letters refer to Pope.

The first and most important letter, 'To Mr. J[oh]n D[enni]s, on Mr. Pope, and his Poetry' (pp. 5–9), is dated December 18, 1729

1   (p. 5). The opening mentions in passing the familiar Jacob charge (see *The Poetical Register*, 1719) that Pope wrote his own praise for *The Poetical Register*. In an earlier letter to Dennis (April 24, 1729; see Dennis, *Remarks Upon ... the Dunciad*, 1729), Jacob says, he gave some reasons why about ten years ago he commended Pope when

> he was generally thought to be a rising Genius; and therefore, I was willing to compliment him with an exalted Character, of his own drawing up and approving. (p. 5)

But now that Pope has 'exerted his noble *Billingsgate* Talents in the most shameless and unprecedented Abuse of all his Contemporaries' he must retract his good opinion and draw his pen against him (p. 6). What were Pope's motives in 'entering the Lists against almost half Mankind'? His pretence in the *Dunciad* is 'that the great Number of Persons he hath so flagrantly abused, were first guilty of writing against him ...' (p. 6).

A2   This, however, is false. Jacob was one among many

> who never writ, or said the least Thing against him, 'till he first became the most notorious Agressor by writing against us ...
>
> (p. 6)

Pope's real reason for the attack is vanity. And what has he to be vain of?

3   As to his Person, there can be nothing seen there in the most flattering Mirror to highten [*sic*] his Self-Opinion, but, on the contrary, to humble and mortify him: So that it is from his Mind

alone, whence this Source of Vanity essentially springs; and as his Body is so very unpromising a Figure, his Mind should be rare and excellent to lift him to that Pitch of Pride which he hath lately so eminently display'd. (p. 7)

His mind, of which he is so vain, is shown in his verse. Is there in his poems any appearance of Horace's '*Mens divinior*'?

Or is there any Thing appears in the Poetry of Mr. *Pope*, but either the most trifling Imitation of celebrated Poets; or smooth flowing Words and jingling Rhime, adapted to the Ear only?
(p. 7)

If he has not the sublimity of a great poet, he has nothing to boast of but Impudence (p. 8). There is only one instance Jacob can find of a *Mens Divinior*:

> Renew'd by ordure's sympathetic force,
> As oil'd with magick juices for the course,
> Vig'rous he rises, from th'effluvia strong
> Imbibes new life, and scours and stinks along.
>
> [*Dunciad* A, ii. 95–8]

This is 'a sufficient Example and Testimony of the Sublimity of this Poet's Genius, his Fire and his Judgment' (p. 8).

The second letter, 'To R—t J—m, Esq; on Wit, Learning and Judgment' (pp. 10–12), dated January 20, 1729, has one interesting remark on Pope and judgment, putting him in odd company:

Mr. *Alexander Pope*, Mr. *Richard Savage* and Mr. *Stephen Duck*, fancy they possess it, and a Multitude of others: Tho' Mr. *John Dennis*, and three, or four more, are the only Persons who have any just Pretensions to this Heavenly Gift ... (p. 12)

The third letter, 'To B—m G—d, Esq; on the Judgment of the Town' (pp. 13–15), dated February 16, 1729, finds Pope a useful example.

Wit has been long since Languishing, and is now Dead: With *Prior* and *Congreve* it made its Exit; and Folly is triumphant, by *Pope* supported. (p. 14)

His '*Dunciad* Infamy' is an example of what ignorant patrons commend to the town (p. 15), and the poem is listed along with *Tom Thumb* and *Hurlothrumbo* as some of the wretched things the town cries up (p. 13).

'Addenda. The legal Tryal and Conviction of Mr. Alexander Pope of Dulness and Scandal, before Mr. John Dennis, Mr. Lewis Theobald and Mr. Aaron Hill, Apollo's Deputy Judges of the High-Court of Parnassus, held in the Great Room of the Devil-Tavern near

Temple-Bar, on the first Day of February, in the Year 1729' (pp. 76–80), a rather mild lawyer's joke, is important for its charge that Pope hurt the reputations and earning powers of the dunces.

The bill of John Ralphe (James Ralph is apparently meant; see *Twick.* v. xxiii) against Pope is first given. In the 1728 *Dunciad*,

A4   the said *Alexander* has abused, vilified and scandalized, not only
the said *John Ralphe* ... but hath also endeavoured to make
Asses, Owls, Fools, Blockheads, Blunderers, Coxcombs, Rogues,
Rascals and Scoundrels of many Gentlemen of superior Rank
and Figure ... in Expectation that his own Character would
stand and remain the Brighter by such a Procedure; and having
frequently defamed his Adversaries for no other Reason but
because they had better Faces and handsomer Bodies than himself, being thoroughly sensible of his own Defects of Body and
Mind; and particularly having called the said *John* a stupid Ass
and Owl, whereas he the said *John* has neither the long Ears of
that foolish Animal, nor the least Resemblance of any Species of
Owls, but being credited by many ignorant Persons, the Fame
and Reputation of the said *John* hath greatly suffer'd with his
Booksellers, Printers and Hawkers, by the false and malicious
Aspersion aforesaid; whereupon he the said *John* says he is the
worse, and hath Damage to the Value of 500 *l.* and therefore he
brings his Suit. (pp. 77–8)

Pope is defended by his Proctor, Richard Savage, who claims Pope
is not guilty because all of the persons satirized

deserve his just and extraordinary Names and Characters, because they have more Sense, Learning, Judgment, Sincerity,
Modesty and Virtue than the said *Alexander*; and therefore he
the said *Alexander* was for beating down these Men, especially
the said *John Ralphe* ... (p. 78)

The jury declares Pope 'guilty of the greatest Dulness and Scandal,
throughout his nonsensical and filthy *Dunciad*' (p. 79). John is to recover damages of £500 and Pope is to be cast headlong from Parnassus, which is accomplished with cries of 'down with this *Pope* and
Pretender to Poetry' (p. 80).

Years later, Jonathan Richardson, in his notes on Pope's works in
the 'Later Anecdotes Collected by Jonathan Richardson and tran-
scribed for Bishop Percy by Mr. Gregson, Richardson's Grandson',
published by George Sherburn in *Notes and Queries*, ccIII (1958),
348, noted on *Dunciad* A, III. 159–60, 'Ralph complained that he had
near being famished by this Line. None of the Booksellers would em-

ploy him.' Sherburn adds, 'Ralph found employment – perhaps not so much as he wished – and did not go hungry.'

May 29, 1733 (*Daily Journal*, Rogers)

Ingratitude: To Mr. Pope. Occasion'd by a Manuscript handed about, under the Title of, Mr. Taste's Tour from the Land of Politeness, to that of Dulness and Scandal, &c &c. Ingratitude's the Growth of ev'ry Clime. Addison's Cato. London: Printed and Sold by J. Dormer, next Ludgate. (Price One Shilling.) 1733.

Folio.
[A]–c².
[2 pp.], [3]–10 pp., [11] advertisement, [12] blank.

The frontispiece is missing in the Yale copy; it is No. 1935 in the *Catalogue of Prints and Drawings in the British Museum, Political and Personal Satires*, II, where it is described. In the full print Pope is shown with three noblemen, one of whom is probably Chandos. One of them is urinating on Pope.

WORKS: A. Homer; B. *First Psalm*; C. Atticus portrait; D. *Dunciad*; E. *Epistle to Burlington*.

CHARGES: 1. Pope wrote the as yet unpublished *Mr. Taste's Tour*; 2. Savage a spy for Pope; 3. Pope ungrateful to Chandos who had given him £500; 4. Pope libelled Addison after Addison's death.

His first charge is Pope's authorship of an unpublished satire:
> I am inform'd, that there is in the Press, and in a few Days will be publish'd, a satirical Poem, or rather a Libel, on several Noblemen, of which (as it is said) you are the Author: The great Personages whom you therein most falsely calumniate, if you are really the Author, have a Design, as I am inform'd, to truss you by turns under one of their Arms, and then, by lowering your Worship, to *piss* upon you as an Insect beneath their Resentment any other way: Nor can you deny that you deserve such Treatment. (p. 3)

He has read some part of the libel now in the press and implicates Savage in it:

U

2   The Diction is good, the Verse smooth and even, but the charges
against the Noblemen at whom it is level'd, are full of *Falsehood*
and *Defamation*. This gives me Cause to suspect the Libel was
pen'd by the same Hand, who writ the others; and I think I have
good Grounds for my Suspicion, for therein I perceive some
Strokes of Scandal which the Gleaner of it, I mean *unhang'd*
S[ava]ge, vented not long since in certain Coffee-houses within
a Mile of *Charing-Cross* and *Fleet-Street*. (p. 8)

He has, in other words, read some verses in manuscript which contain, he thinks, libels against certain noblemen. Pope, therefore, must
have written it. See the following pamphlet, *Mr. Taste's Tour*.

He preaches an impressively moral sermon on Ingratitude, filled
with classical references, and as an example of one of the blackest
pieces of Ingratitude he gives an unusually vivid account of the Pope–
Chandos story, his second major charge:

ACE   A Certain *Animal* of a diminitive [*sic*] Size, who had translated
3   a Book into English-Metre, (or at least had it translated for him)
addressed himself to a Nobleman of the first Rank, and in the
Style of a *Gentleman-Beggar*, requested him to Subscribe a *Guinea*
for one of his Books; the Nobleman entertain'd him at Dinner
in a sumptuous Manner, (and continued so to do) as often as the
insignificant Mortal came to his House. After Dinner this Generous Man of Quality, taking him aside, put a Bank Note for Five
Hundred Pounds into his Hands, and desired he might have but
one Book. But what was the Consequence of this? Why truly,
the Wretch, who is a Composition of *Peevishness*, *Spleen*, and *Envy*,
having no Regard to the Benefits he had receiv'd, in a few Years
after, and without any manner of Provocation, or the least
Foundation for Truth, publishes a Satire, as he terms it, but in
Reality it is an Infamous and Scandalous Libel, calculated, with
all the Malice and Virulency imaginable to Defame and render
Odious the Character of his best Benefactor. (pp. 7–8)

His third charge is the usual one about Addison. Addison's merits
drew upon him 'the Malice, Envy and Hatred of *Maevius*' who pretended to be his friend until after 'that good, that moral, and Christian
Man's death'; then,

CD4   knowing that he could not answer for himself, he writ a most
virulent Satire against him, which was very smoothly reply'd to
by a young Gentleman, who (if I mistake not) was for his Wit
and Ingenuity honour'd with a Place in the *Dunciad*. [Neither
Tickell nor Markland appears in the *Dunciad*.] (p. 8)

There is also an interesting Congreve–Pope anecdote:

> That Satire writ by *Maevius* brings to my Remembrance [*sic*] what
> Mr. *Congreve* said *inter alia*, viz. *That he was in great Hopes of work-*
> *ing a perfect Cure upon* Maevius; *for the* Violence *of his* pevish [*sic*]
> *and* sowre Temper *began to abate, nor were his* Malice *and* Ill-nature
> *so* predominant *as they had been*: But when a Gentleman shew'd
> him the Satire on the deceased Mr. *Addison*, Mr. *Congreve* sighing
> said, *From this Day forward I number him among the* Incurables.
>
> (pp. 8–9)

He concludes by asking Pope to admonish his 'Friend and old Acquaintance Mr. *Maevius*' who, he pretends, is not Pope, lest in time
he be guilty of as 'infamous a Crime, as his, who *prophanely* burlesqued
the First Psalm' (p. 10).

May 31, 1733 (*Grub-Street Journal*, June 7, 1733)

The Neuter: Or, A Modest Satire On The Poets Of The Age.
By a Lady. Dedicated to the Right Honourable Mary Wortley
Montague. As the soft Plume gives swiftness to the Dart, / Good
breeding sends the Satire to the Heart. Young. London: Printed
for T. Osborne, in Gray's-Inn, near the Walks; and sold by A.
Dodd at Temple-Barr. [Price Six Pence.]

Folio.
[A]–B².
[4 pp.], [5]–8 pp.

WORK: A. *Dunciad*.

CHARGE: 1. Pope's verse scandalous and abusive.

The pamphlet, dedicated in flattering terms to Lady Mary Wortley
Montagu ([A2]r and v), attacks the dunces, but also censures Pope
for having stooped to their level. The authoress says to Lady Mary,

> I presume Madam, the following Lines will discover a greater
> Veneration for Mr. *Pope*, than Contempt for his Adversaries:
> But I can never be so much blinded by partiality, as to think the
> *Dunciad* without Faults [*sic*]: He has certainly made his Enemies
> more sigrificant [*sic*] than they cou'd possibly make themselves;

and since he was so much above the reach of their *Malice*, I heartily wish he had been above committing their *Crime*! ([A2r])

The only passage in the poem which attacks Pope is the following:

A 1

> See *Pope*! the Monarch of the tuneful Train;
> *Pope*! who alone can touch the charming Strain!
> He whose sweet Songs have gain'd immortal Praise!
> Even *Pope* with Scandal, has defil'd his Lays:
> What can excuse his Breach of ancient Rules?
> To make deformity the Jest of Fools;
> Why shou'd a sad, unpleasing Form, degrade,
> A Man whom Nature has unkindly made?
> Can *Moor* his large, unhandsome Shape reduce?
> That can't be Satire,—but low, mean abuse.   (pp. [5]–6)

Her reference is apparently to *Dunciad* A, ii. 35–40.

May 31, 1733 (*Daily Journal*, Rogers)

Mr. Taste's Tour From The Island of Politeness, To That of Dulness and Scandal.

> —Last, those who boast of mighty Mischiefs done,
> Enslave their Country, or usurp a Throne;
> Or who their Glory's dire Foundation laid,
> On Sov'reigns ruin'd, or on Friends betray'd;
> Calm thinking Villains, whom no Faith can fix,
> Of crooked Counsels, and dark Politicks:
> Of these a gloomy Tribe surround the Throne,
> And beg to make th' immortal Treasons known.
> The Trumpet roars, long flaky Flames aspire,
> With Sparks that seem'd to set the World on fire,
> At the dread Sound pale Mortals stood aghast,
> And startled Nature trembled with the Blast.

London: Printed for S. Sloe, and sold at the Pamphlet-shops of London and Westminster. 1733.

Half-title: Mr. Taste's Tour From The Island of Politeness, To That Of Dulness and Scandal, &c. (Price One Shilling.)

Folio.

[A]², B* in one leaf, B–D², one unsigned leaf.

[6 pp.], 5–17 pp., [18] blank.

Advertised in *The Post Boy*, May 31, 1733, as 'Being the Poem for which Mr. Pope was so unhandsomely attacked in an impudent Pamphlet, called Ingratitude, to which a scandalous Picture was prepared'.

See a letter by A. N. L. Munby, *TLS*, January 10, 1935, and Howard P. Vincent, 'A Pope Problem', *TLS*, February 14, 1935. This is the pamphlet mentioned in *Ingratitude*, published two days earlier. Rejecting as most improbable Vincent's suggestion that *Mr. Taste's Tour* was, as it purports to be, written by Pope himself in answer to *Ingratitude*, the most probable explanation is that both pamphlets were written by hacks, perhaps both by one author, in order to capitalize over the Chandos scandal. *Ingratitude*, then, would have been contrived to help pass off as Pope's the insipid verse of *Mr. Taste's Tour*. Or perhaps no one was really meant to be deceived and *Mr. Taste's Tour* is quite simply another Pope attack.

WORKS: A. Atticus portrait; B. *Epistle to Burlington*.

CHARGES: 1. Pope libelled Addison after his death; 2. Pope ungrateful to Chandos.

The 'Introduction' (B*r and v, an insertion, and not part of the unsigned leaf) pretends to be by Pope himself:

> To mention every particular Pamphlet, wherein I am misrepresented, and vilely traduced, would take up more Time than I can spare; and to refute 'em would be the Labour of an Age. I shall therefore, at present, only vindicate myself, in relation to what is charged upon me in a Pamphlet, call'd INGRATITUDE; to which is prefix'd an impudent Picture. (B*r)

He then refutes the charges in such a way that his refutation becomes in itself an attack.

> The heavy Allegation against me is, that I am guilty of *Ingratitude*; a Crime, I must confess, in its Nature vile and detestable. To maintain this, two Instances are produced; the first is concerning a Disgust that I took at the late Mr. *Addison*; I own it; but then give me leave to put the Question, were we not reconciled after *this*? *This* is allow'd; but then I am charged again, *with publishing a Satire on the aforesaid Gentleman, after his Death, though our Reconciliation had continued to the End of his Life*. This,

truly, I cannot deny; but in Alleviation thereof, I must say, *That I did inadvertently deliver one Satire to be printed instead of another.*

The *Second* is, concerning a *noble Peer*, to whom I went to *beg a Subscription, who was very liberal to me*; this I freely own: But who can say, *I am guilty of Ingratitude?* Can they prove that *I have mention'd his Name, or that the Character of Lord Timon was design'd for him?* If People will draw wrong Conclusions from false Premisses, who can help it? The Fault is theirs, and not mine. (B*v)

Congreve's assertion he will neither own nor deny:

> ... the Person is *defunct*, and if they can *subpoena* him from the Shades below, let 'em do it; I will then answer for myself ...
>
> (B*v)

The poem, which has no connection with the Introduction, is a rambling satire on the abuse of riches, lacking both plan and wit, and probably a bad imitation of Pope's *Epistle to Bathurst*. Though corruption is attacked in juries, court life, military life, etc., the poem does not at all fulfil the expectations aroused by the description in *Ingratitude*. The following may indicate the quality of the verse supposed to be Pope's:

> GOLD, tho' so pow'rful, yet thou'rt oft misus'd,
> By those that love the [*sic*] most, thou'rt most abus'd. (p. 7)

> MONEY first tempted *Judas* to betray,
> 'Tis the *false Guide* that *leads Mankind astray*;
> It makes Men warmly labour to deceive
> Others with what themselves do not believe.   (p. 16)

November 3, 1733 (*Grub-Street Journal*, November 15, 1733)

The Muse in Distress: A Poem. Occasion'd by the Present State of Poetry; Humbly Address'd to the Right Honourable Sir William Yonge Bart. and Knight of the Bath, &c. Qui nescit Versus, tamen audet fingere. Quidni? / —fungar vice cotis, acutum / Reddete quae ferrum valet, exors ipsa secandi. Hor. Art. Poet. Curam impende brevem, si munus Appoline dignum / Vis complere libris, & vatibus addere calcar. Ibid. Epis. Lib. 2. London: Printed for T. Cooper, at the Globe in Ivy-Lane, near Pater-Noster-Row. MDCCXXXIII. (Price One Shilling.)

Folio.
[A]–D².
[2 pp.], [3]–16 pp.

WORK: A. *Sat.* II. i.

CHARGES: 1. Pope a friend of Bolingbroke; 2. Pope libels women.

The title is misleading; this is almost entirely a plea for patronage addressed to Yonge and such other prominent patrons as Dodington. There is a Whig bias in his attack on Pope:

> The *Twitt'nham* 'SQUIRE, grown petulant and bold,
> Forgets the Notes with which he charm'd of old;
> To *Spleen* he prostitutes his noble Art,
> Alike a Bigot in his *Verse* and *Heart*:
> With Him the Best of *Patriots* are but *Tools*,
> *All*, but his Party, if not worse, are *Fools*.
> *St. John* with Him ne'er knew the Guilt of Treason,
> *He is the Flow of Soul the Feast of Reason*:
> *Judges* are Hangmen, *H*— cannot write,
> And who but *M*—, now alive, can fight?
> Would He with Harmony awake the *Nine*,
> *And sweetly flow thro' all the Royal Line*;
> Still virtuous might we think his *Satire*'s Ends,
> Still might we think Mankind and He were *Friends*.
>
> (pp. 12–13)

There is a further attack, this time on his abuse of women, with a reference to *Sat.* II. i. 81–4.

> In *vain* the snowy Breast, the blooming Cheek,
> Their due Applauses from the Gazers seek;
> The Old the Young, th' Imprudent and Discreet,
> *Sappho* and *Delia* in one Libel meet.
>
> (p. 14)

November 10, 1733 (*Grub-Street Journal*, November 15, 1733)

[Hervey, John Lord.] An Epistle From A Nobleman To A Doctor of Divinity: In Answer to a Latin Letter in Verse. Written from H—n C—t, Aug. 28. 1733. London: Printed for J. Roberts, near the Oxford-Arms in Warwick-Lane. M DCC XXXIII. (Price Sixpence.)

Folio.

[A]–B².

[2 pp.], 3–8 pp.

Reprinted twice, in 1733 and 1734, in *Tit for Tat*, q.v., in Appendix B.

'This characteristic example of Hervey's unfortunate facility for writing letters in rhyme had been published without his consent or ap-
proval by Dr. Sherwin, the clergyman to whom it was addressed.
However, when approached by Arbuthnot on behalf of Pope, he
owned himself the author of the Epistle . . .' (Hervey, John Lord,
Some Materials Towards Memoirs of the Reign of King George II, ed.
Romney Sedgwick (London, 1931), I. xliv). See *Twick.* IV. xix–xx.

WORKS: A. *Essay on Criticism*; B. *Rape of the Lock*; C. Homer; D. *Epistle
to Burlington*; E. *Epistle to Bathurst*; F. *Sat.* II. i.

CHARGES: 1. Pope only a translator and plagiarizer; 2. Broome translated the Homer.

These rather foolish verses which seem to have provoked far more
satire on Hervey than on Pope (see Appendix B) end with a section
devoted to Pope. He first endeavours to turn against Pope, *Sat.* II. i. 6:

F
>Guiltless of Thought, each Blockhead may compose
>This nothing-meaning Verse, as fast as Prose.
>And *P—e* with Justice of such Lines may say,
>*His Lordship spins a thousand in a Day.*
>Such *P—e* himself might write, who ne'er could think.

(pp. 6–7)

He then makes his major charge – that Pope lacks all invention and
is only a translator and plagiarizer:

C 1
>[Pope] is call'd Poet, 'cause in Rhyme he wrote
>What *Dacier* construed, and what *Homer* thought;
>But in Reality this Jingler's Claim,
>Or to an Author's, or a Poet's Name,
>A Judge of writing would no more admit,
>Than each dull *Dictionary*'s Claim to Wit;
>That nothing gives you at its own Expence,
>But a few modern Words for ancient Sense.

(p. 7)

He then surveys Pope's poetical career for its originality:

A B C
D E
1 2
>But had he not, to his eternal Shame,
>By trying to deserve a Sat'rist's Name,
>Prov'd he can ne'er invent but to defame:

Had not his *Taste* and *Riches* lately shown,
When he would talk of Genius to the Town,
How ill he chuses, if he trusts his own.
Had he, in modern Language, only wrote
Those Rules which *Horace*, and which *Vida* taught;
On *Garth* or *Boileau*'s Model built his Fame,
Or sold *Broome*'s Labours printed with *P—pe*'s Name:
Had he ne'er aim'd at any Work beside,
In Glory then he might have liv'd and dy'd;
And ever been, tho' not with Genius fir'd,
By *School-boys* quoted, and by *Girls* admir'd.
So much for *P—pe* . . .   (pp. 7–8)

The Olympian dismissal of Pope in these last four words is particularly admirable.

1733

Verney, Richard. Dunces Out Of State. A Poem. Address'd to Mr. Pope. By the Right Honourable the Lord Willoughby De Broke. Ex nihilo nil fit. London: Printed in the Year M.DCC. XXXIII.

Half-title: Dunces Out Of State. A Poem. Addressed to Mr. Pope.

Folio.
One unsigned leaf, [A]², B in one leaf.
[4 pp.], 3–6 pp.

Richard Verney, Baron Willoughby de Broke, is mentioned in the *Dunciad* A, i. 250, n.

The verse, of which the following is a very fair sample,

Hasten we, Wings, from such a Theme to fly away;
I wish I could, but want of Words won't let me stay,   (p. 4)

is so badly written, the syntax so careless, that much is simply unintelligible. It seems that in intention at least this is a satire against dunces, Pope figuring twice. After praise of Walpole's Houghton the writer says,

Then, Bard, if these rich Motives don't excite
You're worse than *Ogilby*, who cou'd not fairly write;
Even *Pope* is worse than him, that all must say

These eligible Gifts from him claim no Array;
Pope breathes his Satyr without Wit,
And plainly in his Face dull Fool is writ.   (p. 5)

After mentioning other dunces he returns with new energy to Pope:

Tho' these are very dull, yet *Pope* exceeds them all;
Merits a worse Fate than *Praetion* [*sic*], a worse Fall.

.   .   .

His Poetry is fowler than the Common-Shore,
And hurts more than Perfumes of rotten Core;
Shun his vile Poetry, like Tanners Hide,
Unless when vapour'd, you would laugh, and much deride;
But if in Spirits you once take his Verse in Hand,
Throw it, like stinking Fish, upon the Land.   (p. 6)

1733 or later.

The Satirists: A Satire. Humbly Inscrib'd To his Grace the Duke
of Marlborough. The Spirit of Satir [*sic*], rises with Ill-Mood;
and the Chief Passion of Men thus diseas'd, and thrown out of
Good-Humour, is to find fault, censure, unravel, confound and
leave nothing without Exception. Shaftsbury's Characteristicks.
London: Printed for C. Corbett, at Addison's Head over-against
St. Dunstan's-Church, Fleetstreet, and Sold by the Pamphlet-
sellers of Loudon [*sic*] and Westminster. (Price One Shilling.)

Folio.
[A]–D².
[2 pp.], [3]–16 pp.

Dated in the *BM Cat.* and in the catalogue of the Sterling Library
[1710?] but the quotation of *Sat.* II. i. 84 fixes February 1733 as a
terminus a quo.

WORK: A. *Sat.* II. i.

CHARGE: I. Pope venal.

An attack on contemporary satirists named only by initial letters and
for the most part difficult to identify. Much of the bias is clearly political and pro-Walpole. Pope is his first victim:

I

> And first the Bard, most favour'd of each Muse,
> Shou'd I *P*—'s self here venture to accuse;
> Shou'd I this gross, this shocking Line repeat,
> 'Pox'd by her Love and Libel'd by her hate';
> Or yet presume to call it Common Place
> All that is said of Bribery, Courts, his Grace,
> Wou'd he refrain from calling Whore and Knave?
> This a great Fool? and that a pension'd Slave?
> Wou'd he for this his darling Slander quit?
> Or pay regard to Beauty, Birth or Wit?—
> Or shou'd I tax him with the Venal Stain;
> Praise He, or Censure, say 'tis all for Gain,
> Wou'd he one Copy gen'rous give away?
> Nor keep his various Gillivers in Play,
> T'enhance the Price of every Satire sold,
> And wring from each Competitor more gold?
> Wou'd he if less imperfect in his make
> The lucrative Employ refuse to take?   (pp. 4–5)

And so on for ten more lines. The next satirist mentioned, '*W*—',
'*P*—'s servile Son' (p. 5), is probably Whitehead.

January, 1734 (*Gentleman's Magazine*)

Theobald, Lewis, ed. The Works Of Shakespeare: In Seven
Volumes. Collated with the Oldest Copies, and Corrected; With
Notes, Explanatory, and Critical: By Mr. Theobald. I, Decus,
i, nostrum: melioribus utere Fatis. Virg. London: Printed for
A. Bettesworth and C. Hitch, J. Tonson, F. Clay, W. Feales, and
R. Wellington. MDCCXXXIII.

8vo.
Frontispiece, two unsigned leaves, A⁸, a–e⁸, B–Z⁸, Aa–Hh⁸, Ii⁴.
Frontispiece, [14 pp.], [i]–lxviii, [lxix–lxxxvi], [1–2], [3]–487 pp.,
[488] blank.

A portrait of Shakespeare facing title-page, 'B. Artaud del.' Also a
separate title-page for volume, giving a list of six plays, following the
general title-page.

Reprinted in 1740:

The Works Of Shakespeare: In Eight Volumes. Collated with the Oldest Copies, and Corrected: With Notes, Explanatory, and Critical: By Mr. Theobald. The Second Edition. I, Decus, i, nostrum: melioribus utere Fatis. Virg. London: Printed for H. Lintott, C. Hitch, J. and R. Tonson, C. Corbet, R. and B. Wellington, J. Brindley, and E. New. MDCCXL.

12mo.
Frontispiece, A^{12}, a^{12}, B–R^{12}.
Frontispiece, [48 pp.], [1–2], [3]–382 pp., [383–4] blank.
Portrait of Shakespeare facing title-page, 'G. Van der Gucht sculp.'
Five plates inserted, one before each play, 'H. Gravelot in. & del.'

For other editions see Jones, pp. 353–4.

The eight emendations of the classics are omitted at the end of the preface, as well as the poems on Shakespeare and list of subscribers that had appeared in the first edition. The notes are also abridged and some omitted.

WORKS: A. Pope's edition of Shakespeare; B. *Dunciad.*

A The Preface, [i]–lxviii, contains animadversions on Pope and his edition.

> The same mangled Condition [of Shakespeare, acknowledged by Rowe] has been acknowleg'd too by Mr. *Pope,* who publish'd him likewise, pretended to have collated the old Copies, and yet seldom has corrected the Text but to its Injury. (p. xxxv)

He claims that Pope in his last edition has used far more of Theobald's own emendations than the 25 words he admitted to (p. lii). He says as well:

AB > It is not with any secret Pleasure, that I so frequently animadvert on Mr. *Pope* as a Critick; but there are Provocations, which a Man can never quite forget. His Libels have been thrown out with so much Inveteracy, that, not to dispute whether they *should* come from a *Christian,* they leave it a Question whether they *could* come from a Man ... It is certain, I am indebted to Him for some *flagrant Civilities*; and I shall willingly devote a part of my Life to the honest Endeavour of quitting Scores: with this Exception however, that I will not return those Civilities in his *peculiar* Strain, but confine myself, at least, to the Limits of *common Decency.* (pp. xxxvi–xxxvii)

The notes throughout, as one would expect, criticize and ridicule Pope's editing.

At the end of Vol. VII, under the rubric 'Editions of no Authority', he lists the editions of Rowe and Pope (pp. [502–3]).

February 12–14, 1734 (*London Evening Post*, February 14, 1734)

Gerard, —. An Epistle To the Egregious Mr. Pope, In Which The Beauties of his Mind and Body are amply display'd. By Mr. Gerard. [One line of Greek.] Plato. London, Printed for the Author; And sold by M. Harris, at the Bee-Hive, opposite St. Clement's-Church, in the Strand. MDCCXXXIV. (Price One Shilling.)

Folio.
[A]–D², one leaf unsigned.
[2 pp.], 3–17 pp., [18] blank.

A second edition with additions, which I have not been able to locate, was, according to Rogers, advertised in *The Daily Post Boy*, April 11, 1734.

WORKS: A. *Essay on Criticism*; B. *Guardian No. 40*; C. *Three Hours after Marriage*; D. Atticus portrait; E. *Odyssey*; F. *Epistle to Burlington*; G. *Sat.* II. i.

CHARGES: 1. Pope ungrateful; 2. Pope plagiarized the *Essay on Criticism* from Wycherley; 3. Pope cheated the public with his *Odyssey*; 4. Pope's father a hatter; 5. Pope threatened by Philips; 6. Pope refused to pay Rysbrack for the unflattering bust he made of Pope.

After an ironic invocation to Pope there is the usual charge of ingratitude, although this time with Lady Mary as one of the examples:
> Thy Venom's Taint our [1]*Addison* would damn,
> And stain with Virulence the fairest Fame:
> Coward! insult thy Patron when deceas'd!
> Whom living both thy Hopes and Fears caress'd!

> How rank that Mind, how keen his inborn Hate,
> Whom God-like Benefits exasperate!
> Great *Chandois* [*sic*] Stream of *Bounty* flow'd too high,

And [2]*Sappho's* Crime was *Generosity*:
Chandois, high Soul, forgets as he bestows;
In *Sappho Wit* with Beauties Radiance glows.

[1] *Pope*'s satire on Mr. *Addison*.
[2] This Lady assisted *Pope* in his Subscription (p. 4).

A 2   The *Essay on Criticism* Gerard calmly attributes to Wycherley:

[1]The first gay Colours which thy Muse assum'd,
Were false—the Jay in Peacock's Beauties plum'd:
This Work, 'tis true, was nervous, learn'd, polite,
The Sound an artful Comment to the Wit;
With *Sheffield* and *Roscommon* claim'd the Prize,
And justly too—the Piece was WITCHERLEYS.

[1] Art of Criticism – *Mr. Witcherley* sent it to *Pope* to revise, upon which *Pope* published it as his own: This Fact is well known, and mentioned by the Gentlemen of *Shropshire* with great Indignation (p. 7).

The other charges of plagiarism are the usual ones, that Pope has stolen from Denham, Garth, and Dryden. Gerard questions Pope's share in the Homer:

E 3   *Homer* appears the Lyon in Disgrace;
His Royal Grandeur mimick'd by an Ass:
If to this Work thy Nerves unequal found,
Bend with the Massive Solid to the Ground,
Broome like an *Atlas* can Assistance lend,
While thou maintain'st thy Ground by Wit-ensuring Friend.
Thou *undertak'st*, th'*Odyssy*, dost not *write*,
Pope Jobs *imaginary* Stock—a *Bite*.   (pp. 8–9)

These plagiarism charges end with an attack on Pope's father

4   Mechanick Wretch! assume thy Father's Trade,
Thy Sire could make a *Hat*[1], but not a Head.
Hereditary Craft! how apt t'express
Thy Genius, turn'd to *furbish* up and *dress*!

[1] *Pope*'s Father was a Haberdasher of Hats (pp. 10–11).

Three Hours after Marriage is introduced:

C   Thou once club'st Nonsense for [1]dramatick Stuff,
And there thy Folly met a just Rebuff;
Th'indignant Town cou'd easily divine
The Grain of *Wit* was *Gay*'s, the Mass of *Scandal* thine.

[1] A Comedy called *Three Hours after Marriage*, wrote by *Gay* and *Pope*, and damned the first Night (p. 12).

The story of Ambrose Philips and his rod at Button's, first told apparently in *Pope Alexander's Supremacy*, 1729, q.v., is here repeated:

> Mr. *Phillips* Author of the *Distress'd Mother*, having been abused by *Pope*, hung a *Rod* over the Chimney at *Button's Coffee-House*, and declared he would take down our little Poet's breeches and whip him in Publick, the next Time he caught him there;—which obliged *Pope* to leave the House. (p. 17, n.)

See *Corr.* I. 229, n.2.

There is an interesting reference to Rysbrack's bust of Pope, who

> Shews his[1] own Picture, in Burlesque a *Lord*,
> And stands a matchless Monster on Record.

> [1] *Pope* ordered several Pictures and Busts of himself, in which he would have been represented as a comely Person: But Mr. *Rysbrack* scorning to prostitute his Art, made a Bust so like him, that *Pope* returned it without paying for it (p. 13).

See Wimsatt, p. 104.

Pope is called a '*Human Devil*' (p. 15) and we overhear his 'curst Soliloquy' (p. 16):

> Since Heav'n has form'd my *Body* thus, in Spite
> Let Hell make crook'd my *Soul* to answer it:
> Were I but absolute one precious Hour,
> Detested *Man* should groan beneath my Power.

March, 1734 (*Gentleman's Magazine*)

The False Patriot. An Epistle To Mr. Pope.—Intabescitq; videndo / Successus hominum; carpitq; & carpitur unà. Ovid. London: Printed for James Roberts, near the Oxford-Arms in Warwick-Lane. MDCCXXXIV. (Price Sixpence.)

Folio.
[A]–c².
[2 pp.], [3]–12 pp.

WORK: A. *Essay on Man.*

CHARGE: I. Pope seriously misguided in his praise of Bolingbroke.

This pamphlet has a double aim, to reprove Pope for disfiguring his

verse with a dangerously false picture of Bolingbroke, and to attack and expose Bolingbroke.

A 1   What is Pope's own ruling passion? Love of Truth? Love of Satire?
>Nor this, we hope, supreme; nor that, we fear;
>The one too light, the other too severe.   (p. 4)

Nor is Pope's ruling passion ambition, pleasure, or avarice; it is 'Devotion to a *Friend*':

1   For him what Lengths you run! what Projects try!
>How bend your noblest Faculties awry!
>For him you speculate, and speak, and write;
>And fiercely plunge into the Party-Fight:
>For him you shut your Eyes, and steel your Heart,
>Shedding, without Remorse, vindictive Smart:
>For him, alas! too rich a Sacrifice!
>Humanity expires, and Honour dies.   (p. 5)

Friendship is good or bad only as its object deserves praise or blame; Bolingbroke deserves no praise. After severe condemnation of the false patriot, Bolingbroke, the writer concludes by commanding Pope to renounce his misguided political engagement:

>Recall your Muse, lur'd into Factions Cause,
>And sing, great Bard, of Heav'ns and Natures Laws:
>But sing unsquinting; keep a guiltless Eye;
>Nor dart Contagion at the Standers-by.
>Beware how prostitute your noble Theme
>To Party-Views, and Politicians Dream:
>Nor taint immortal Lines with mortal Rage;
>Posterity will mourn the spotted Page.   (p. 11)

1734

A Satirical Essay On Modern Poets. —facilis descensus Averni, / (Noctes atque dies patet atri janua Ditis) / Sed revocare gradum, superasque evadere ad auras, / Hic labor! hoc opus est!—Virgil. Into the writing Vein (seduc'd by Pride) / 'Tis ever open—easily we slide; / But, all its real Graces to comprize, / Here, here, the Task, or Difficulty, lies! / Almost as well, from everlasting Night, / May Souls returning, view th'oetherial Light. London: Printed and Sold by J. Wilford, behind the Chapter-House, in St. Paul's Church-Yard, 1734. (Price Six-Pence.)

Folio.

[A]–c².

[4 pp.], 1–[10] pp.

Conventional praise of the Ancients, with this denigration of the Moderns:

> Who bears the Prize of instant Fame away,
> *Pope*—is the Joy and Wonder of a Day!
>
> .   .   .
>
> *Cowley* redundant, trifling, incorrect;
> *Milton* is tedious, *Dryden* has Neglect;
> *Waller* is dark! and often sweeps the Ground;
> And *Pope* is far more splendid, than profound.   (p. 2)

February 4, 1735 (*Daily Journal*, Rogers)

An Epistle To Alexander Pope, Esq; Occasion'd by some of his Late Writings. Integer vitae, Scelerisque purus / Non eget Mauris jaculis, neque arcu, / Nec venenatis gravidâ sagittis, / Fusce, Pharetrâ. Horat. London: Printed for J. Wilford behind the Chapter-house in St. Paul's Church-yard. MDCCXXXV. (Price Sixpence.)

Folio.

One unsigned leaf, b², c in one leaf.

[2 pp.], [1]–6 pp.

WORKS: A. *Sat.* II. i(?); B. *Sober Advice* (?); c. *Epistle to Arbuthnot* (?).

CHARGES: 1. Pope steals jests from an impoverished poet; 2. Pope plots treason; 3. Pope a Jacobite; 4. Pope misled by Bolingbroke.

There is at Yale another copy of the above, identical except that '(Price Sixpence.)' does not appear on the title-page, on which in the autograph of Lady Mary Wortley Montagu is written, 'not by me except a Correction or two' and, beneath this, the letter 'M.' This copy has an 'x' in ink in the margin at ll. 1–2, a small mark beside ll. 6–7, and an 'x' at ll. 39–40. Halsband describes this as Lady Mary's own copy (Halsband, p. 150, n.2).

v

1   A poem of only 140 lines, with a strong political bias. Pope, in the
most interesting section, boasts of his wealth and is accused of stealing
half his jests from a needy bard whom he has entertained at his table
only to laugh at him when he leaves:

C I 2   As he departs, thou rattlest in the Throat
                    To see his uncurl'd Wig, and thread-bare Coat;
                    His Poverty, his Debts, are Pastime, good
                    Things if unfelt, but lightly understood.
                    In future Time, oh! may some Poet rise,
                    And strip *Thee*, Tyrant Wit, from all Disguise;
                    Discover to the World thy inborn Hate
                    To Wits of Worth, to all the loyal Great;
                    Unfold the Secrets of thy boasted Grot,
                    The addled Treason, and the groundless Plot.   (p. 3)

Pope himself is made to say,

B?   ... my Friendship is a Gem,
                    But then my Libels, there's no standing them;
                    See this old Cloak, 'twas *Horace's* of Old,
                    Patch'd thus by *Bentley*, worth its Weight in Gold;
                    In this I domineer, repeat old Saws,
                    And sell 'em to the Crowd, *Apollo's* Laws:
                    Sweet Cadence cheats their Ear, the Soul suspends,
                    The Reason's dazled, and its Kingdom Ends.   (p. 2)

A series of political portraits is ironically proposed:

3   Paint Liberty (but deaden every Charm)
                    Forc'd from her Seat, by *William's glorious Arm*.
                    On either Hand a learned *Jesuit* Place,
                    Let *them* hand down the Crown to *Brunswick's Race*. (p. 3)

Lady Mary and Hervey are introduced:

A?   Draw M[o]nt[a]g[u]e in a gay Idiot's Dress,
                    But not her Beauty, nor her Air express,
                    From the known East, turn her experienc'd Eye,
                    And homebred stile her to the Stander by.
                    Dress S[u]ff[o]lk up like Truth, and let her Face
                    Glow with the Sunshine of the royal Grace;
                    Sit there for H[e]rv[e]y, and the Piece will be
                    As like, as that we in thy Verses see.   (p. 4)

Bolingbroke is seen as Pope's evil genius, largely responsible for the
faults into which Pope has fallen:

4   St. J[oh]n thou know'st, when with wild Faction prest
                    He takes a Part from off thy frantick Breast,

Sooths thee with Prophecies, his Grandame told,
And makes thee in thy conscious Treason bold.   (p. 5)
Pope must fly from such friends, quit faction's train, and 'Reign
secure, the Monarch of sweet Lays' (p. 6).

March 1–4, 1735 (*London Evening Post*, March 4, 1735)

[Bentley, Thomas.] A Letter To Mr. Pope, Occasioned By Sober
Advice from Horace, &c. Quia lacessisti prior. Terent. London:
Printed for T. Cooper at the Globe in Pater-noster-row. [Price
Six Pence.] M.DCC.XXXV.

4to.

A–B⁴, C².

[2 pp.], 3–19 pp., [20] blank.

On p. 11 the catchword reads, incorrectly, 'Truths' for 'You'.

WORKS: A. Homer; B. *Sat.* II. i; C. *Essay on Man*; D. *Sober Advice*;
E. *Epistle to Arbuthnot*; F. *Of the Characters of Women*.

CHARGES: 1. Pope abuses Richard Bentley in *Sober Advice* because
Bentley had spoken against the Homer; 2. Pope sells the same poem
several times; 3. Pope deformed.

Bentley, who is sure that Pope is the author of *Sober Advice*, ridicules
its device of the admirer's dedication:

> Here has he published a most obscene thing, worse than any
> *Bacchanalian Song* made for a Bawdy-house, and gravely told the
> World, that 'tis *in the Manner of Mr. Pope*. (p. 4)

It is soon clear that Bentley is writing to protect his uncle's reputation:

> An admirable Expedient, and worthy of your Sagacity, *to get
> upon the Back of Horace*, that you may abuse every body you don't
> like, with Impunity! But this Imitator did not know himself, nor
> you. You are a *Rasor*, he a *Wedge*. You please and ravish every
> where without Affectation; he blasphemes and talks Bawdy.
> You make a man's Blood crawl upon his Back, even whilst you
> are describing and tearing to pieces one of the finest Gentlemen
> and politest Scholars in the Kingdom. Your Imitator thinks
> there's *Wit* in Calling Horace's *Sermones*, Sermons[1]; in naming

Reverend Doctor, and *Doctor in Divinity*; in putting *Bentley* to Notes that wou'd be pointless and stupid, but that they are swoln with *rigid C—i*, & *caudae turgent*. To see a Man of Dr. *Bentley's* Age and Dignity and incomparable Learning, writing *Bougre* and *Foutre* Remarks, how delicious it must needs be!

¹ As *delivered* in his second *Sermon. Delivered* too very smart! *Vid. Title Page* (p. 4).

A 1   He attacks the Homer and gives us a Pope–Bentley anecdote:

You are grown very angry, it seems, at Dr. Bentley of late. Is it because he said (*to your Face*, I have been told) that your Homer was *miserable Stuff*? That it might be called, Homer *moderniz'd*, or something *to that effect*; but that there were very little or no *Vestiges* at all of the *old Grecian*. Dr. Bentley said right. Hundreds have said the same *behind your Back*. For Homer *translated, first* in English, *secondly* in Rhyme, *thirdly*, not from the Original, but, *fourthly*, from a *French Translation*, and that in *Prose*, by a *Woman* too, how the Devil should it be *Homer*? (p. 14)

He offers another version a little later:

I have been told, that the great Critic himself, who did not read the *Sermon*, till he heard something about his Son and you, said after, *'Tis an impudent Dog; but I talked against his* Homer, *and the portentous Cub never forgives*. (p. 15)

His objections to *Sober Advice*, its ridicule of his uncle aside, are, not surprisingly, largely to its indecency, which he underlines. While reproaching Pope for blasphemous use of Scripture, he alludes to the Gospels himself:

D   Now Fufidia, because she hungers and thirsts only at one End, [*Sober Advice*, l. 24] she shall be filled; as you'll find it written in another Sermon besides Flaccus's.

After all, it may be useful to have some Women complaisant with the *lower Labia*, and some with the *upper*; for as our Imitator tells us,

Different Taste in diff'rent Men prevails,
And one is fir'd by *Heads*, and one by *Tails*.

[*ibid*. ll. 35–6.]

The very next Lines to a Verse of yours; a delicate one indeed, and worthy to be had in everlasting Remembrance,

Spread her Fore-buttocks to the Navel bare. [*ibid*. l. 34]

a verse too you seem to be fond of; for I had read it in the *Miscell*. and *Dunciad* before it came here.

I can't help remarking how dextrous our *sober Adviser* is at *engrafting Bawdy* upon the Word of God. (pp. 5–6)

He has as well a long passage on the notes to the Latin text, ll. 45 and 70. He objects to giving Avidienus a wife and to making Fufidius a woman. He has been told that Fufidia [Lady Mary]

> has a great deal of Wit and Learning, that she is Mr. Pope's very own Sister in Poetry, and writes almost as well as himself; not *inferior* to the *Grecian* Sappho for Spirit and Delicacy ...
>
> (p. 7)

Bentley has a good deal to say about the *Essay on Man*, as well, and Bolingbroke, whom he detests. His objections to the poem are the traditional ones:

> c   There are Starts and Flights of Poetry very fine, but you *prove* nothing. You are often obscure, twice or thrice unintelligible. You make false Judgments of Things, and reason wrong from *Premisses*. When we fancy we are going to learn some valuable thing, you fly off, and leave us in a Smoak. (p. 9)

He finds that the sentiment in the *Essay on Man*, ii. 31–4, is not just. Since apes are ugly and ridiculous because they are like a man in shape and manners, if the gods show Newton as we would show an ape, they must think Newton absurd, ugly, and ridiculous (p. 10). He is unable, he says, to understand *Essay on Man*, iv. 267–8.

'To Virtue Only and Her Friends, A Friend' [*Sat.* ii. i. 121] annoyed Bentley as it did so many others:

> You make a great ado with your *Virtue only*, and your *Uni aequus virtuti atque ejus amicis*. VIRTUE ONLY in Capitals is one of the Marks to know you by. Is Bolingbroke one of your Virtutis Amici? Pray, let us know then what you mean by *Virtue*. Is it *Graian* or *Roman*? Or do you mean *Evangelical Graces*? Is it *Charity*, that *suffereth long, and is kind*, that *vaunteth not itself, nor is puffed up*? Is it *Humility, Love of Enemies, &c*? He has nothing of them: You have but little your self. I have sometimes thought, that you put *Virtue* for *Self*, and that *Virtue only* is *Self only*; and that *Uni aequus virtuti atque ejus amicis*, means only, *Uni mihi aequus, & mihi amicis*;
>
> To my self only and my Friends a Friend. (p. 12)

It is too bad that this passage degenerates into personal abuse. The attempt to fit Pope's 'virtue' into Pauline categories points up one of the central problems of the poem.

Bentley also objects at some length to Pope's habit of publishing the same thing several times – obviously out of greed. He observes that in the *Epistle to Arbuthnot*:

E 2   From Verse 146 to Verse 209 [see the note on the line numbering in *Twick.* IV. 92–3], above Threescore Lines, of this Epistle was printed before, twice or thrice, I think, in the Volumes of the *Miscellanies*. 'Tis called there, *the Fragment of a Satire*; and instead of *From slashing B—ley*, 'tis *From sanguine Sew—*. Who this Sew— is, I don't know; but why must Bentley come *slashing*, and take his Place? (pp. 13–14)

The business methods behind the publication of the *Imitations* and the second Moral Essay he finds equally suspect:

F 2   You sold those Imitations already published for 40 or 50 Pounds each. Fifty Pounds for 150, or 200 lines! ... Is the *Epistle* to a Lady, *Of the Characters of Women*, all we are to expect? I wonder you would set your Name to such a Piece of poor unmeaning *Galimatias*, patch'd up out of the Third Volume of *Miscellanies*? *Silvia, a Fragment*, and *Verses to Mrs. M.B. &c.* makes a great part of it. How dare you impose upon the Public at this rate?

(pp. 15–16)

The motto to the *Epistle to Arbuthnot* affords him an opportunity to introduce Pope's deformity:

3   'Tis very amazing, to see a little Creature, scarce four Foot high, whose very Sight makes one laugh, strutting and swelling like the Frog in Horace, and demanding the Adoration of all Mankind, because *it* can make fine Verses ... Enough for you, sure, to be called as Horace was by Augustus, *Putissimum penem, the purest Wag-prick* ... (pp. 17–18)

B C   In his able defence of verbal criticism (in the course of which he points out the superiority of Theobald's edition of Shakespeare to Pope's) he observes that several errors have already crept into Pope's own work. His examples, pp. 8–9, 'Bear the mean Heart' for 'Bare the mean Heart' (*Sat.* II. i. 108) and 'this faithful Dog' for 'his faithful Dog' (*Essay on Man*, i. 112), are, however, nowhere recorded in the textual notes in the Twickenham Edition.

June 24–6, 1735 (*General Evening Post*, June 26, 1735)

The Poet finish'd in Prose. Being A Dialogue Concerning Mr. Pope And His Writings. —Nunquamne reponam / Vexatus toties rauci Dunciade Codri? Juv. London: Printed for E. Curll, in Rose-Street, Covent-Garden, 1735. [Price 1s. 6d.]

Drop-title: A Dialogue Concerning Mr. Pope And His Writings.
[p. 3]

8vo.

A–E⁸.

[2 pp.], [3]–80 pp.

Apparently written for Curll. Rogers lists the British Museum copy of
Post-Office Intelligence, 1735, which reprints this. It has been misplaced,
and all my efforts to see it have failed.

WORKS: A. Homer; B. *Epistle to Burlington*; C. *Epistle to Bathurst*;
D. *Sat.* II. i; E. *Essay on Man*; F. *Epistle to Dr. Arbuthnot*; G. *Of the Characters of Women*.

CHARGES: 1. Pope's poems obscure and incorrect; 2. Pope subject to
delirious fevers as the result of a fall; 3. Pope afraid of being raped
by Lady Mary; 4. Pope prefers self-abuse to women; 5. Pope has
plagiarized from his servant John; 6. Pope refuses to hire tall servants;
7. Pope boasts of his money and possessions; 8. Pope has injured the
sale of Theobald's Shakespeare; 9. Philips threatened to whip Pope;
10. Pope sells the same poem several times; 11. Pope has mistranslated Homer; 12. Pope's father a mechanic; 13. Pope sensitive to
criticism and hires spies.

A dialogue between A., a stranger to the town who dislikes Pope's
recent work, and B., who endeavours to justify Pope.

A. complains in general of,

> that affected Obscurity which runs thro' most of his late Works.
> The Essays on *Man*, otherwise most excellent Performances, are
> not free from it. That on *False Taste*, and that on *The Use of Riches*
> are full of it. And, in general, you meet with a great deal of it in
> all these Poems which are call'd his *Aethick Epistles*. (p. 11)

Pope is also guilty of incorrectness. Now that he thinks his reputation secure, he has become careless.

> Can Mr. *Pope* therefore be said to be consistent, when he conveys to us the filthy Ideas of a Lady's *dirty Smock* [*Of the Characters
> of Women*, l. 24]; *Plaisters* on a Man's Tail [*Epistle to Bathurst*,
> l. 90]; the *Pox* in plain Terms, and that too in a *Woman* [*Sat.* II.
> i. 84]; with many other Things of the like Kind. (p. 12)

B. excuses these defects by explaining that when, several years ago,
Pope was routing 'a whole Army of Scriblers' who had attacked him,

> his Horse *Pegasus* made a false Step, and tumbled him down

upon a Dunghill, which broke his Fall, enough to save his Neck; but the Violence of the Concussion threw him into a Fever attended with a Delirium, into which he has frequent Relapses. 'Tis no Wonder therefore that he is sometimes a little obscure and incorrect. Much less should we be surprized that his Imaginations [*sic*] is, during these Paroxysms, a little dirty, if we reflect that the Dunghill which sav'd him, happened unluckily to be a Place where the neighbouring Chambermaids every Morning us'd to disembogue the Ordure of half the Parish. (p. 13)

The inhumanity, lies, scandal, and immorality in Pope's recent work is not his fault but his doctor's who has allowed him to write during his paroxysms (pp. 14–15).

DF   They then decide to examine the *Epistle to Dr. Arbuthnot*. The fear Pope shows in the opening lines of the Epistle, A. says, is caused by Sappho,

> for I remember he was once before afraid least that Lady should do him an Injury, which he seems to dread more than Poison or a Halter. (p. 16)

He blames Pope for *Sat.* II. i. 84. B. replies with an unparalleled charge on Pope's sexual habits:

34   Sir, our Author took an extravagant Aversion to this Lady, upon a Suspicion he had that she intended to ravish him. I make no doubt but there were some Grounds for these Apprehensions of a Rape, otherwise a Man of strict Virtue, which Mr. *Pope* assures us over and over again, he is, could never have been guilty of so vile an Insinuation. Taking this for granted, I say, she could not be us'd too ill; for nothing can be imagin'd more terrible than a Rape, to a Gentleman who has not the least Passion for the Sex. Whether this want of Inclination proceeds from Constitution or Habit, it is not worth our while to examine at present. Be that as it will, I say, every Man has a Right to pursue his Pleasure by such Ways as his Taste inclines him too; and no Body disputes the Elegance of Mr. *Pope*'s ... 'Tis possible his Fondness for Retirement may have given him this Disrelish for the Sex; but no doubt he has found out some other Amusement, equally entertaining to him in his Solitude, and which makes him less sollicitous about losing the Favour of the Ladies. (pp. 17–18)

F5   B. explains that Pope's servant John has written 'several *admirable Jokes*' which Pope has versified and passed off as his own (p. 20). Pope has also overheard John's quarrels with his mistress, Margery Termagant, a dairy maid, and was so entertained with them

that he was at the Trouble of taking down some of them in Short-hand, and has given us Extracts from those valuable Manu-scripts in *this Poem* and other of his *late Works*. (p. 22)

6   John is as little as his master, since 'Mr. *Pope* would not keep a *Footman* five Foot tall for the *Indies*' (p. 70).

*7   Why has Pope chosen to talk almost entirely in the first person, to tell us he has a footman, a grotto, a chariot, and a barge? This is pride, to introduce by Head and Shoulders such Particulars, which relate to no Man in the World by *himself* . . . (p. 24)

He has mentioned the poverty of poets derisively eight times in the poem and boasted that he could relieve a fellow tradesman by a dinner (pp. 30, 27).

*8   He has ridiculed Bentley, and hurt Theobald by prejudicing people against the subscription for his edition of Shakespeare and spoiling its sale (pp. 53–5).

Pope abuses Philips because Addison had decided in his favour over Pope, since which time Pope cannot endure either of them. Philips
9   had threatened to whip Pope, but Pope was too prudent to stir abroad until Philips had left for Ireland (pp. 48–50).

F   Several verses are criticized. L. 131 is made up of 'ten low words' (p. 51), and there is 'little or no Meaning' in l. 326:

Did ever Smock-face act so vile a Part?

He simply needed a rhyme for 'Heart' says B. (p. 71). (The line was altered in 1735 in the *Works*, vol. II, which had appeared in April.) In the Paris (Sporus) portrait the sentiment is low and dirty, the phraseology vulgar and ill-bred (p. 63); B. explains that it is the sub-stance of the first conversation Pope overheard between John and Margery (p. 64).

G   Pope manages to sell the same poem several times over. Almost a
o   hundred lines in the *Epistle to Dr. Arbuthnot* Pope sold to Lintot many years ago. (This would seem to refer to ll. 151–214, but these were first published by Pope in Motte's *Miscellany*, 1727; see *Twick.* VI. 283–5.) The only good things in *Of the Characters of Women* had been printed long since in Pope's own Miscellany and later in his and Dr Swift's. (See *Twick.* VI for the complicated incorporations Pope made in this poem.) He has also published in the same poem the very lines (ll. 243–8) he and Moore Smythe had such a long dispute about (pp. 35–6).

The Homer, too, is abused:

Instead of keeping up that noble and majestick Grandeur of the best of Poets, *Pope* plays the *Buffoon*, and tickles your Ears with a *Witticism* or a *Conceit*. (p. 37)

He has mistranslated some thousand passages out of ignorance or malice (p. 38).

F 12   As to Pope's father, Pope in the *Epistle to Dr. Arbuthnot*,

> says he was descended of a *noble Family*: So he might, and yet 'twas possible for him to be a Hatter, a Pedlar, or any other Kind of Mechanick. (p. 73)

13   An interesting general comment on poet-baiting suggests that the pamphlet was written for Curll:

> ... Poet-baiting is a modern Entertainment; and *Pope* has had the Honour of shewing the World, for the first Time, how this *excellent Diversion* should be managed in Order to provoke sufficiently the *poor Devil* at the Stake. Talk of a *Monkey* and he kicks; mention *Tonson, Shakespear*, or Subscriptions, and he roars: But name *Curl*, or the *House of Lords*, and he runs full butt at you as far as his Rope will give him Leave. (p. 39)

After A. has compared Pope to Lady Betty Modish's monkey, B. warns A. that Pope has a great many spies about; B. is one himself:

> As simple as I stand here, Mr. *Pope* has some Opinion of my Abilities, and has employ'd me to discover his impertinent *Calumniators*. I have already some Reason to hope I may do him Service; for tho' I have not been much at leisure to attend to this Business, I have, however, got already a *Catalogue* of more than *five Millions*, who accuse Mr. *Pope* of *Vanity, Insolence, Arrogance, Impiety, Knavery, Ingratitude*, and many other Crimes of the like Kind. (p. 75)

July 14, 1735 (Griffith 386)

Mr. Pope's Literary Correspondence. Volume the Second. With Letters To, and From, [a list of ten names in two columns] London: Printed for E. Curll, in Rose-Street, Covent-Garden. M.DCC. XXXV.

For collation and complete description of contents see Griffith 386. He states that there are twelve names on the title-page but in listing them gives only ten. In his pagination, after [i]–xvi, add another [i]–xvi. Griffith includes these pages, however, in his description of the contents. In one of the two copies at Yale, the frontispiece is not the Kneller portrait of Pope.

There was a duodecimo edition, Griffith 403. I have examined the Bodleian copy.

WORKS: A. *First Psalm*; B. *Worms*; C. *Three Hours after Marriage*; D. *Dunciad*; E. *Essay on Man*; F. *Sober Advice*; G. *Epistle to Arbuthnot*; H. *Letters*.

CHARGES: 1. Pope equivocated over the *First Psalm* and publication of his letters; 2. Pope as a schoolboy wrote a satire on his master.

Much of the introductory material deals with the publication of the correspondence. I omit this here, except where it turns to direct attack on Pope.

In 'To Mr. Pope' (pp. [v]–xvi, first count) the most interesting accusation is the following (for the advertisement on the *First Psalm* see Ault, p. 158; Curll had made this charge years earlier in his *Compleat Key To The Dunciad*, 1728, q.v.):

D
I   *To believe nothing is yours, but what you own,* would be merely ridiculous. Did you not deny the *Dunciad* for seven Years? Did you not offer a Reward of three Guineas, by an Advertisement in the *Post-Man*, to know the Publisher of your Version of the *First-Psalm*? And when you were inform'd, did you ever pay the Premium? Did you not publish the *Worms* yourself, and leave out the Foecundifying Stanza? And do you *own* any of these in the Preface to the second Volume of your works. (p. xii)

He presents Pope with the bill:

I   *Mr.* Alexander Pope, *Debtor to Mr.* Edmund Curll.

To an *Advertisement* in the *Post-Man*, 1717, promising Three Guineas to discover the Publisher of his Version of the *First* Psalm,	3	3	0
To a Promise of Ten Pounds, on producing one of Bishop *Atterbury's* Letters,	10	0	0
To discover the *Publishers* of Mr. *Pope's Letters*,	42	0	0
Total	55	3	0

All these Articles I have made good, and therefore think myself justly intitled to the promissory Rewards above-mention'd.
    A fitter Couple, sure, were never hatch'd,
    Some marry'd are, indeed, but we are match'd.
                      E. CURLL. (p. xvi)

'The Initial Correspondence: Or, Anecdotes Of The Life and Family of Mr. Pope' (pp. [1]–32) prints a letter (pp. 6–7) addressed to Curll by 'E.P.' who claims to have been Pope's school-fellow and who is writing, he says, in reply to Curll's advertisement for accounts of Pope. The letter contains an account of Pope's early schooling which, as Sherburn observes, 'while very specific, has never been accepted' (Sherburn, p. 40, n.).

2   The last School he was put to, before the twelfth Year of his Age, was in *Devonshire-Street* near *Bloomsbury*, there I also was, and the late Duke of *Norfolk*, at the same time. It was kept by one *Bromley*, a *Popish Renegado*, who had been a Parson, and was one of *King James's* Converts in *Oxford*, some Years after that Prince's Abdication; he kept *a little Senary* [*sic*], till upon an advantagious offer made him, he went a *Travelling-Tutor* to the present Lord *Gage*.

Mr. *Alexander Pope* before he had been four Months at this School (or was able to construe *Tully's Offices*) employed his Muse in satirizing his Master. It was a Libel of at least one hundred Verses, which a Fellow-Student having given information of, was found in his pocket, and the young Satirist was soundly whipp'd, and kept a Prisoner to his Room seven days; whereupon his Father fetch'd him away, and I have been told, he never went to School more. (pp. 6–7)

The rest of the 'Initial Correspondence', except for a brief biographical sketch, deals with the correspondence.

DG   It is followed by 'The 17th Epode of Horace Imitated. A Palinody to Mr Pope, by one of the Heroes of the Dunciad, occasion'd by his Epistle to Dr Arbuthnot' (pp. 37–47). This has a dedication to Curll (p. [33]) and a letter to him (p. [35]) explaining that the writer is here making his submission to Pope. It is signed only 'The Author'.

The poem is an ironic plea for forgiveness:

CF   By the dear Manes of your [1]joint-writ Play,

.   .   .

By those fore-Buttocks, which You sucking kiss'd,
I here conjure You wou'd some Pity take.   (pp. 38–9)

[1] Three *Hours* after *Marriage*. (p. 38)

(For the second line here, see *Sober Advice*, l. 34.)
He attacks as well the dedication to Bolingbroke of the *Essay on Man*, and *Sober Advice*:

EF   I'll mark how You your Morals dedicate

To pious *St John's* Name immaculate.
From thence I'll shew your natural Transition
To *Sober Advice* for casual *Fruition*[1].

[1] See, *Sober Advice from Horace, to the young Gentlemen about Town*. This Profane and Lewd Satire is the Production of Mr. *P.* and was by sold [*sic*] to four Booksellers for sixty Guineas, as can be proved. E.C. (p. 45)

September 20 (?), 1735 (Griffith 402)

Mr. Pope's Literary Correspondence. Volume the Third. With Letters To, and, From [a list of eight names in two columns] London: Printed for E. Curll, at Pope's-Head, in Rose-Street, Covent-Garden. M.DCC.XXXV.

For collation and complete description of contents see Griffith 402.

There was a duodecimo second edition, Griffith 404, which I have not seen.

WORK: A. *Dunciad*.

'To the Subscribers', pp. [iii]–x, a dialogue between Curll and Squire Brocade on the contents of volumes II and III of the *Literary Correspondence*, contains many references to Pope, but nothing of any importance. 'E. Curll and A. Pope', pp. [xiii]–xvi, concerns the quarrel over the publication of Pope's letters.

'A Letter To Mr. P***', pp. 29–39, and signed 'Philo-A—s' (p. 39) is probably addressed to Pope. It is a silly essay on the dignity of asses. It contains (pp. 33–4) a long quotation from the *Dunciad* A, ii. 225–6, 237–54, with the comment,

> Scarce do I know whether the Ass is more indebted to the Poet for this excellent description of him, or the Poet to the Ass, for those Qualifications of his, which were the Occasion of it . . .
>
> (p. 35)

December 9, 1735 (*St James's Evening Post*, December 9, 1735)

Post-Office Intelligence: Or, Universal Gallantry. Being, A Collection Of Love-Letters, Written By Persons, in all Stations, from most Parts of the Kingdom. Faithfully published from their Originals, returned into the General-Post-Office in Lombard-Street, the Parties to whom they were directed being either Dead, or removed from their usual Places of Abode. The Am'rous Quaker here, is set to View; / The Cook-Maid, Courtezan, and Liv'ry-Crew; / Th'intriguing Priest, the Soldier, All Degrees / Encamp'd with Mars, or Venus, which you please, / In ev'ry Class th'Advent'rers take their Turn, / In Love they Languish; and for Love they Burn. With Rational Remarks upon Mr. Pope's Letters, and some of his former and late Productions. London: Printed for E. Curll, at Pope's Head, in Rose-Street, Covent-Garden. 1736. Price 3s.

8vo.
A⁶, B–F⁸, A⁸. F² unsigned.
[12 pp.], [1]–80 pp., [1]–16 pp.; p. 80 misnumbered '88'.

The above is the copy at the University of Texas. Professor Edward Ruhe has kindly sent me a description of the copy at the University of Kansas, which lacks A8 entirely and thus does not contain the 'Rational Remarks On Mr. Pope's Letters'. Rogers lists only the copy in the British Museum which includes both the 'Rational Remarks' and *The Poet finish'd in Prose*, 1735, q.v.

WORKS: A. *Eloisa to Abelard*; B. *Dunciad*; C. Pope's letters.

CHARGES: 1. Pope unforgiving and a libeller; 2. Pope blasphemous and indecent.

A   'To the Reader' (A2r–A3v) ends with 'Of Love. By Mr. Pope', which is *Eloisa to Abelard*, ll. 91–6; and 'Of the Use of Letters', which is ll. 51–8 of the same poem.
     The only Popiana in the copy I have examined is 'Rational Remarks On Mr. Pope's Letters' (pp. [1]–16, second count).
     These remarks, in the form of a letter dated (p. [1]) 'York, Oct. 1. 1735', are much more rational than the Curll imprint would lead one to expect; they constitute a kind of advertisement for Curll's *Literary Correspondence*. There is praise of *The Rape of the Lock* (pp. 2–3), and

sensible comment on the correspondence with Wycherley (pp. 8–9).

Pope is, however, seen as an unforgiving libeller; he

> has libelled fifty Times as many People as poor *Dryden* ever did,
> who was forced to write a Court-Satire (his *Absalom* and *Achito-*
> *phel*) for Bread. This Taste in *Pope* made me desirous to see how
> he would stand upon a Correspondence of thirty Years; and he
> appears to be the very inconsistent Creature, which his Poetical
> Works had before denominated him. He puts his Bible and
> *Homer* in Equipage together; He professes he should not have
> resented *Dennis*'s Criticism, had he known of his Poverty, and
> yet as well in these Letters, as in the *Dunciad* and elsewhere, he
> has carried this Resentment to the Extent of his Power. (pp. 4–5)

One regrets that Pope did not follow Arbuthnot's wise advice to him
to *study* more to *reform than chastise*: But such is the unhappy Condition of human Nature, that the Mind partakes of the Faults
of the Body, of its Crookedness, of its Craziness, and the Per-
verseness of old Age, which happens in some Constitutions thirty
Years earlier than in others; of miserable old Age, which generally renders Men querulous and malevolent. (pp. 12–13)

The only charge developed at any length, however, is the charge
that Pope in his letters indulges in blasphemy and indecency.

> Tho' he quotes the *Rhemish* Bible to *Papists*, yet it is plain he has
> read our English Translation often; for he has it at his Finger's
> Ends to Profane it, by applying the Phrases of it on trivial and
> ludicrous Occasions. (p. 5)

One of the examples given is from the letter of Pope to Teresa and
Martha Blount, September 13, 1717, 'In short, I heard of no Ball,
Assembly, Basset-Table, or any place where two or three were gatherd
together, except Mad. Kilmanzech's, to which I had the honour to be
invited, & the grace to stay away' (*Corr.* I. 427). If this is witty, it 'is
only so by being horribly profane' (p. 6).

He quotes the two sentences Pope omitted from his letter to Cromwell, December 21, 1711, calls them painting himself 'in a very ram-
pant Goatish Altitude' [*sic*] (p. 13), and approves of their omission.
(See *Corr.* I. 137, n.1 and n.3.) He also notes with satisfaction (p. 14)
the omission of two letters 'in the smutty Vein'; he quotes as examples
of these ll. 29–31 of Pope to Cromwell, July 12 or 13, [1707] (*Twick.* VI.
25), and ll. 24–5 of Pope to Cromwell, April 25, 1708 (*Twick.* VI. 39).
The implication is that Pope's letters are full of indecencies.

March 25, 1736 (Griffith 415)

Mr. Pope's Literary Correspondence. Volume the Fourth. With Letters, &c. To, and From, [a list of seven names in two columns] To which are added, Muscovian Letters. London: Printed for E. Curll, at Pope's-Head, in Rose-Street, Covent-Garden, M.DCC. XXXVI.

For collation and full description of contents see Griffith 415. In the Yale copy I have used, the frontispiece is a portrait of Pope; there is no other plate. The quarter-sheet book-list has been inserted following the bastard title to *Muscovian Letters*.

WORKS: A. *Essay on Criticism*; B. *Court Poems*; C. *Dunciad*; D. *Sober Advice*.

CHARGE: 1. Pope challenged Bentley's son to a duel.

'To The Sifters', pp. [iii]–vii, surveys the contents of the book, with Curll's usual small hits at Pope.

'A Character Of Mr. Edmund Curll, Bookseller. By Mr. Pope', pp. 148–52, with the epigraph (a parody of *Dunciad* A, ii. 53–4),

C
> *Before the Lords*, Alone, untaught to fear,
> Stood dauntless Curll (*and spoke to ev'ry Peer.*)
> He triumph'd, Victor of the high wrought Day!

reprints Pope's note on Curll, *Dunciad* A, II. 54, n. Curll changes 'printed it twelve years' (*Twick.* V. 104, second line from bottom) to 'printed it above *Eighteen* Years'. The following epigram is added at the end:

B
> *Court Poems* to this Work are join'd,
> That All the World may see;
> *Pope*'s Falshood manifested here,
> *Hinc illae Lacrymae.*   (p. 152)

To Pope's note Curll has added footnotes attacking Pope and the truth of his assertions, particularly about the *Court Poems*.

Following the printing of letters to and from Henry VIII and Anne Boleyn is a letter from Curll to Pope, pp. 25–8, on these letters and containing what must be a thrust at Pope's alleged fondness for obscenity.

> There appears not the least Pretension to the *Last-Favour*, nor Aim towards it, till the *Holy Legate* and *Mother Church*, had paved the Way to Consummation, (and then, *He! Monsieur* Pope! *Entendez vous bien.*) (p. 27)

He says, as well,

> The *New-Year*'s Gift I sent you was from *Paris*; and this im-
> maculate Intercourse of *Royal* Affection, comes from *Rome*,
> (p. 28)

and adds a note to this (I am unable to explain the '*New-Year*'s Gift')
which notices a change in the *Essay on Criticism*:

> The *New Year*'s *Gift*, I sent by a Special Messenger, to Mr. *Pope*
> at *Twickenham*, was a little Book (neaty [*sic*] Bound in *Red Turky*
> Leather, Ruled, and the Capital Letters illuminated with Gold,
> and various Colours) intitled, 'Heures des Prierres: Dedie à
> Madame la Duchesse de Chartres. Avec les Sept Pseaumes Peni-
> tentieux. à Paris, 1696.' ... One good Effect I find they have
> produced, for you have recanted, and razed out, this *Distich*
> against the *Dutch*.
>
> > Then *first* the *Belgian* Morals were extoll'd;
> > We their *Religion* had, and they our Gold.
> >   *Ess. on Crit.* (ll. [546–7])
>
> You now say, as these Lines *contain a National Reflection, in your*
> *stricter Judgment*, it is what you *cannot but disapprove, on any People*
> *whatever*. Were you not as sensible, that this was a *National Re-*
> *flection*, when you wrote it, as it is now? (p. 28)

Sober Advice from Horace is reprinted, pp. [49]–62, with some notes
by Curll added. He footnotes 'To Alexander Pope, Esq;' which heads
the dedication, 'i.e. Alexander Pope, Esq; to *Himself*.' (E2r) and footnotes the first sentence,

> This Assertion proves most True. *There farther runs a Rumour, that*
> Mr. *Pope challenged* Dr. Bentley's *Son, to a Pistol Combat on this*
> *Occasion*, but how true this is I know not. E.C. (E2r)

Richard Bentley, Jr, threatened to horsewhip Pope if he was the
author of *Sober Advice*, but later apologized (*Corr.* III. 446, n.3; 451).
Thomas Bentley, Dr Richard Bentley's nephew, is said to have sent
Pope a challenge (*Twick.* v. 429). See Isaac Disraeli, *The Quarrels of*
Authors (London, 1814), I. 155, n.

I give Curll's notes to the poem with the line numbers:

l. 10   This is a Piece of Travelling Scandal, related of the late
        Duchess of *C[levelan]d* and the late Duke of *M[arlboroug]h*.
        E.C. [See *Twick.* IV.] (p. 52)

l. 34   [Adds to Pope's note:] Of which, Mr. *Pope* is so fond, that he
        has made use of it, no less than *three* Times. E.C. (p. 53)

l. 44   [Adds to Pope's note:] *Cork* would have stopt this Hole. E.C.
        (p. 54) [*Twick.* IV suggests 'York'.]

l. 60   [Adds to Pope's note:] This *Opinion* I agree to as *True*, but that this Note was *Mine*, is *False*. E.C. (p. 55)

l. 129   There is a famous *Staye-Maker* of this Name, which stiffens the *Double Entendre* here meant. E.C. [Quoted in *Twick*. IV where the date 1757 is apparently an error for 1736.] (p. 59)

l. 133   A *Quondam* Bawd of high Renown,
                In whose Apartments P— has oft been seen,
                Patting Fore-Buttocks, to divert the Spleen. (p. 59)

l. 150   A noted Tavern for Eating, Drinking and Gaming, in *Southampton-Street, Covent-Garden.* (p. 60)

l. 86   A famous Rope-Dancer. (p. 57) [Not signed E.C., or obviously his, but not in *Twick*. IV.]

The Curll book advertisements are, as Griffith pointed out (Griffith 415), part of the Curll warfare against Pope.

1736

[Hanmer, Sir Thomas?] Some Remarks On The Tragedy Of Hamlet Prince of Denmark, Written by Mr. William Shakepeare. London: Printed for W. Wilkins, in Lombard-Street, M,DCC, XXXVI. Price 1s.

8vo in half-sheets.
A–I⁴.
[2 pp.], [iii]–viii, [1]–63 pp., [64] blank.

Reprinted in: Reprints Of Scarce Pieces Of Shakespeare Criticism. No. 1. Remarks On Hamlet, 1736. London: John Russel Smith, 1864.
    Also reprinted in: *Some Remarks on the Tragedy of Hamlet, Prince of Denmark, Written by Mr. William Shakespeare (1736)*, ed. Clarence D. Thorpe, The Augustan Reprint Society, 3rd Ser., No. 3 (September 1947). A selection appears in Scott Elledge, ed., *Eighteenth-Century Critical Essays* (Ithaca, 1961), I. 448–55, which contains a useful note on the authorship, I. 564.

Twick. V. 442 suggests that Hanmer may have been the author. The principal reason for Hanmer's inclusion in the *Dunciad* (B, iv. 105) was, however, his quarrel with Warburton over his edition of Shakespeare. See *Corr*. IV. 438, n.2. Thorpe rejects Hanmer's authorship emphatically and points out that the attribution rests only on a state-

ment by Sir Henry Bunbury, one hundred years after the essay, in his *Correspondence of Sir Thomas Hanmer, with a Memoir of his Life* (London, 1838) (Thorpe, p. [1]).

WORK: A. Pope's edition of Shakespeare.

The Preface contains a handsome tribute to the *Essay on Criticism* (pp. vi–vii), but the following passage with its decided preference for Theobald's edition over Pope's may have annoyed Pope, although it is hardly an 'attack':

> In the Course of these Remarks, I shall make use of the Edition of this Poet, given us by Mr. *Theobalds*, because he is generally thought to have understood our Author best, and certainly deserves the Applause of all his Countrymen for the great Pains he has been at to give us the best Edition of this Poet, which has yet appear'd. I would not have Mr. *Pope* offended at what I say, for I look upon him as the greatest Genius in Poetry that has ever appear'd in *England*: But the Province of an Editor and a Commentator is quite foreign to that of a Poet. The former endeavours to give us an Author as he is; the latter, by the Correctness and Excellency of his own Genius, is often tempted to give us an Author as he thinks he ought to be. (pp. 3–4)

Theobald's notes are referred to frequently throughout.

June, 1737 (Griffith 462)

Mr. Pope's Literary Correspondence. Volume the Fifth. With Letters of [six names in two columns] London: Printed for E. Curll, at Pope's Head, in Rose-Street Covent-Garden. M.DCC.XXXVII.

This is the Bodleian copy, which has, preceding the above title-page, the title-page of *New Letters*, 1736. For collation see Griffith 462. It has as well an additional leaf after p. 250 and before the Curll advertisement. The Yale copy has the title-page and preface of *Dean Swift's Literary Correspondence*, London, E. Curll, 1741, Griffith 534. Except for this, the Yale copy agrees with Griffith 462 (part one); the frontispiece is the same as in Griffith 534 and may be the correct one for this edition also; the portrait of Bolingbroke is wanting; sig. R (pp.

241–50, one leaf?) has no R3, but the text is complete. Following p. 250 is Curll's advertisement [2 pp.]. It is not clear whether this is part of sig. R or is inserted; p. 237 is misnumbered 273; 238 is misnumbered 240; 240 misnumbered 140.

WORKS: A. *Iliad*; B. *Sober Advice*.

CHARGES: 1. Pope disavowed *Sober Advice*; 2. Pope translated Homer only for money.

The additional leaf in the Bodleian copy contains a two-page 'Parodie on the Imitation of the Second Epistle of the Second Book of Horace', pp. [242]–3, signed, p. 243, 'E. Curll.'

B 1   *Sober Advice* from Horace you have giv'n,
              Yet disavow it in the face of Heav'n.   (p. [242])

A 2   It was for *Lintot*'s Gold that you begun
              To rime from *Greek* the wrath of *Peleus*' Son.   (p. 243)
       The only other Popiana here is the reprinting, pp. 136–46, of *Madame*
A *Dacier's Remarks*, 1724, q.v.

1737

Crousaz, J. P. de. Examen De L'Essay De Monsieur Pope Sur L'Homme. Par Monsieur De Crousaz, Membre des Académies Royales des Sciences de Paris & de Bourdeaux. A Lausanne, Chez Marc-Mich. Bousquet & Comp. M.DCCXXXVII.

12mo.
†⁸, A–H¹², I⁴, K⁸.
[2 pp.], [iii]–iv, [v]–xvi, [1]–214 pp., [215] Fautes principales à corriger, [216] blank.

The 'Avis Du Libraire', †2r and v, is omitted in the Elizabeth Carter translation, November 21–3, 1738, q.v.

For a discussion of this and the other Crousaz items see *Twick.* III. i. xix–xxi.

August, 1738 (*London Magazine*)

A Dialogue On One Thousand Seven Hundred and Thirty-eight: Together With A Prophetic Postscript As To One Thousand Seven Hundred and Thirty-nine. London: Printed for T. Cooper, at the Globe in Pater-noster-Row. M.DCC.XXXVIII. (Price One-Shilling.)

Folio.

[A]–D².

[2 pp.], [3]–15 pp., [16] blank.

WORKS: A. *Dunciad*; B. Pope's letters; C. *Epilogue to the Satires, Dial. I* (and *II*?).

CHARGES: 1. Pope a false patriot; 2. Pope equivocated over the publication of his letters; 3. Pope venal.

A dialogue between A. and B. A. complains throughout that B. no longer writes poetry and encourages him to do so. B. answers that it is not that he lacks subjects,

> ... but that I dread my Fate,
> When I appear the Friend of Church and State;
> Sneer at no Bishop, at no Member strike.   (p. 4)

He would lose his good reputation at the hands of his brother wits who spread scandal and lies about the living and the dead. A. answers that it is 'a Shame / That Love of Truth shou'd yield to Love of Fame'.

        (p. 5)

> B. You reason right, I nothing can reply,
> And yet if H[e]rv[e]y 'scapes not, how shall I?
> H[e]rv[e]y! whose Sense the wisest Men approve,
> And whose just Conduct all who know him love;
>
>   .   .   .
>
> Him, if such Virtues screen not from their Spite,
> Tho' Reasons [*sic*] bids me, yet I dare not write;
> Lest these sour Critics shou'd upon me fall,
> From P[o]pe to Whit[hea]d, furious One and All.   (p. 6)

B. argues against A.'s pessimism that the English cannot be long deceived by their corrupt statesmen and false patriots:

> P[ope] in his *Dunciad* might hurt You, or I;
> The Verse might strike, and the Prose-note might lye:
> But at the Constitution shou'd he rail,

E'en all the Pow'r of pompous Verse wou'd fail;
As little Weight in such a Case his Words
Wou'd with the Public have as with the L[or]ds;
When after much Debate the Truth came out,
Himself against Himself had form'd a Plot;
In which at last to do Himself but Right,
He prints his *Letters*, and gets Money by't:
The Public laugh'd, but still the Public read,
When in his Verse fresh Reputations bleed:
This well he knows, and this he will pursue,
While profit tells him All he writes is true:
But shou'd the Public bilk a Satire's Sale,
This virtuous Poet soon wou'd change his Tale;
Try a new Way his Customers to fit,
And write with Rapture who correctly writ.
A. Is this the Case then! *P[ope]* alone You fear,
    For only he well heard in Verse can sneer.   (pp. 12–13)

Pope, then, is clearly the chief reason why B. remains silent. When A. says he will print their present conversation, B. allows him to, but indulges in his fiercest attack on Pope when he assures A. that the lines will be

c   Good in themselves, but writ in a bad Taste;
            Without that Salt, that Spirit, Force and Fire,
            Which *P[ope]*'s malicious Dialogue inspire;

            Yet let him mark this Prophecy of mine,
            His *Thirty-eight* shall, before *Thirty-nine*,
            Be own'd ev'n by his Friends a partial Song,
            Writ for a Day, unfit to prosper long.   (pp. 14–15)

October 24, 1738 (*General Evening Post*, October 24, 1738)

A Supplement To One Thousand Seven Hundred Thirty-eight. Not written by Mr. Pope.—Hoc te / Crede modo insanum, nihilo ut sapientior ille / Qui te deridet caudam trahit—Hor. Lib. ii. Sat. 3—Uni aequus virtuti, atq; ejus amicis—Idem. Dublin: Reprinted for the Booksellers, M,DCC,XXX,VIII.

8vo in half-sheets.

A–D⁴.

[2 pp.], [3]–32 pp.

My quotations are taken from the above edition which spells out more proper names than the London edition (at Harvard):

Title page as above but 'thousand' and 'hundred' are not capitalized, and with the imprint: 'London: Printed for J. Roberts, near the Oxford-Arms, in Warwick-Lane. MDCCXXXVIII.'

Half title: A Supplement To One thousand Seven hundred Thirtyeight. [Price One Shilling].

8vo in half-sheets.

A–D⁴, E². A3 incorrectly signed A2.

[4 pp.], 5–35 pp., [36] blank.

Since *One Thousand Seven Hundred and Thirty Eight. A Dialogue Something like Horace* appeared in May 1738 and *One Thousand Seven Hundred and Thirty Eight. Dialogue II* in July 1738, this pamphlet, apparently by a Walpole hack, was probably intended as an 'answer' to both.

WORKS: A. *Epistle to Cobham*; B. *Ep.* II. ii; C. *Epilogue to the Satires. Dial. I*; D. *Epilogue to the Satires. Dial. II.*

CHARGES: 1. Pope a Catholic; 2. Pope a Jacobite; 3. Pope praises anyone in the Opposition; 4. Pope writes satire to make money; 5. Pope's satire ill-natured.

In the form of a dialogue between B., the poet, who is clearly meant for Pope, and A., who attacks B.'s satire and exposes his weaknesses, the poem is an attack on Pope's political involvement with the Opposition and on his anti-government satire. It closes with A.'s prayer for Walpole, King, and Country.

Pope's religion is insincere:

> I fear what may, and may not come to pass,
> Which keeps me oft from church—sometimes from mass.
>
> (p. 4)

> *Luther* and *Loyola*, whene'er I see
> Room for a sneer, are saints alike with me!   (p. 13)

Pope is also a Jacobite:

> Two things, you know, I ever gave right names,
> Call'd B[oli]ngb[ro]ke my friend, my sovereign J[a]mes.
>
> (p. 13)

CD   B.'s disaffection from the reigning monarchs is obvious:

      A. Plant royal virtues in your sovereign's breast—
      B. Father and Son, by turns, have been my jest!
      A. Write somewhat moving of *Britannia*'s Queen
         If *Clark*, and *Harvey* have not rais'd your spleen.
      B. With libels on her reign, on ev'ry shelf,
         Her praise wou'd be a satire on myself.   (pp. 19–20)

ABCD   The political key to Pope's praise or blame is simple:

3
      A. Why heap'd on *Cobham* such rare gifts, and grace?
      B. —What? ask a reason? when he lost a place!
         Whoever quits his golden key or staff,
         I reverence, I adore—while others laugh!   (pp. 7–8)

B. explains that he pours over the new-made Tory 'the patriot chrism'
which purges him of every vice (p. 8), and A. asks,

      Does *Stow*'s pure air, or *Dawl*[e]*y*'s, in an hour,
      Cleanse just like soap; like purgatory scour?   (p. 8)

      Blest *Twikenham*! scourge and cure of every vice!
      What reformation's finish'd in a trice?
      Here, to refine your sense, and mend your tail, [*sic*]
      Sages of *Bedlam*, nuns of *Drury* sail!
      At *Temple-stairs* you may each virtue lack,
      Yet swim a *Cato*, or a *Barnard* back:

          .   .   .

      Rome's deities a change as nimbly make;
      See there a God—last moment 'twas a cake!   (p. 10)

4   B. writes satire, A. implies, because it makes money. He can get
£50 for a satire – more in half a year than Horace in a lifetime (p. 6).
To A.'s suggestion that B. write panegyric, B. replies,

      Most people love to buy their neighbours crimes;
      Who send to *Dodd*, and for the scandal press,
      For publick vices make our own seem less!   (pp. 26–7)

A. sums this up:

      Tho' virtue's praise each page of your's, begins,
      You seem to make much more of people's sins;
      Guilt is your gain, 'tis honesty you fear!
      A court of saints undoes you in a year.   (pp. 27–8)

5   B.'s satire is severe; Horace's muse was free from spleen. B. admits,

      Applause runs heavy in my muse's strain,
      I lash with rapture, but commend with pain!   (p. 23)

When A. urges him to show the virtues as well as the vices of his victims, B. replies,

> I've rail'd so long, I scarce know how to praise.

.   .   .

> Think as I please, direct it as I will,
> Nothing but satire follows from my quill!   (p. 19)

November 21–3, 1738 (*General Evening Post*, November 23, 1738)

Crousaz, J. P. de. An Examination Of Mr Pope's Essay On Man. Translated from the French of M. Crousaz, Member of the Royal Academies of Sciences at Paris and Bourdeaux; and Professor of Philosophy and Mathematics at Lausanne. London: Printed for A. Dodd, at the Peacock, without Temple-Bar. M.DCC.XXXIX.

12mo in half-sheets.
A–U⁶ (A1 [blank?] wanting).
[2 pp.], [i]–viii, [1]–227 pp., [228] advertisement for Crousaz' *A Commentary on Mr. Pope's Principles*.

B1, B5, C1, D3, and G6 are cancels in the Yale copy. This copy is signed on the fly-leaf in the translator's hand 'E Libris Eliza Carter', and under this is the autograph of her nephew and literary executor, Montagu Pennington.

This translation was formerly thought to be by Samuel Johnson. Elizabeth Carter's notes frequently come to Pope's defence against Crousaz. See *Boswell's Life of Johnson*, ed. George Birkbeck Hill, revised and enlarged by L. F. Powell (Oxford, 1934), IV. 494–5.

November, 1738 (*London Magazine*)

[Forman, Charles, trans.] A Commentary Upon Mr. Pope's Four Ethic Epistles, Intituled, An Essay on Man. Wherein His System is fully Examin'd. By Monsieur De Crousaz, Counsellor

of the Embassies from his Majesty the King of Sweden, and Land-grave of Hesse-Cassel; formerly Governour to his most Serene Highness Frederick Prince of Hesse; and Member of the Royal Academy of Sciences of Paris and Bourdeaux. Translated from the French Original, printed at Geneva, with Remarks. London, Printed for E. Curll, at Pope's-Head in Rose-Street, Covent-Garden. 1738.

12mo in half-sheets.
Two unsigned leaves, a⁶, A–F⁶, G⁴.
[4 pp.], v–xvi, 1–79 pp., [80] blank.

The advertisement in *The London Magazine*, November 1738, gives 'Translated by Ch. Forman, Esq;'.

Emile Audra, *L'Influence Française dans l'œuvre de Pope* (Paris, 1931), p. 93, says that the preface, pp. v–x, is by Curll; if this is so, the tone seems surprisingly mild. On Forman, see Georges Bonnard, 'Notes on the English Translations of Crousaz' Two Books on Pope's *Essay on Man*', *Receuil de travaux publiés à l'occasion du quatrième centenaire de la fondation de l'université* [de Lausanne] (Lausanne, 1937), pp. 178–80. The Forman translation gives only an abridged version of Crousaz's commentary on Epistle 1. See also Samuel Johnson's translation, 1739. The preface ends with 'The COMMENTARY of Monsieur DE CROUSAZ upon Mr. POPE's *Second* EPISTLE is in the Press' (p. x), but no more seems to have been published.

The Bodleian has a copy of:

Commentaire Sur La Traduction En Vers De Mr. L'Abbé Du Resnel, De L'Essai De M. Pope. Sur L'Homme, Par M. De Crousaz, Conseiller des Ambassades de S.M. le Roi de Suede & Landgrave de Hesse, ci-devant Gouverneur de S.A.S. le prince Frederic de Hesse, & Membre des Académies Royales des Sciences de Paris & de Bourdeaux. A Geneve, Chez Pellissari & Gopp. MDCCXXXVIII

12mo.
* in 3 leaves, A–P¹², Q⁸.
[6 pp.], [1]–375 pp., [376] blank.

The unsold sheets of the *Commentary* with the title-page and original preface suppressed were issued again, pp. 1–79 second count, by Curll in his:

December 6, 1740 (Straus, p. 308)

Miscellanies In Prose and Verse, By the Honourable Lady Margaret Pennyman. Containing I. Her late Journey to Paris, giving an Account of the present State of the Court of France, and of all that is curious and remarkable in that famous City. II. Poems on several Occasions, with Familiar Letters to a Friend. Published from her Original Manuscripts. To which are annexed, Some other curious Pieces. London: Printed for E. Curll, at Pope's Head, in Rose-Street, Covent-Garden. 1740. Price 3s.

12mo in half-sheets.
A⁴, A–I⁶, K², A–F⁶, G⁴, A–E⁶, [A2–A7], B–E⁶.
Frontispiece, [2 pp.], [iii]–viii, [1]–112, 1–79, [80] blank, [3]–59, [60] blank, [3]–52 pp., [1]–8 Curll book-list.

WORK: A. *Essay on Man.*

The preface is not so much hostile to Pope as to Crousaz. The author ridicules Crousaz's use of Du Resnel's translation, his ignorance of English, and the errors he falls into through trusting Du Resnel. Crousaz chose Du Resnel not because, as he said, he loved verse better than prose, but because it afforded him 'more Opportunities to display his own self-boasted Talents in criticizing Mr. *Pope*' (p. x). The only important reference to Pope is:

> But still there is enough of the Commentary which may much more properly be called a Critical Satire on the *Essay on Man*, to set Mr. *Pope* to work; and had we not been persuaded, that he will think his Honour engaged to make some Reply or other, to the heavy Charge brought against him by a Frenchman, we would have enlarged the Remarks we made in translating *Crousaz* ...   (pp. viii–ix)

The 'Remarks' of the title-page are footnotes added throughout, pointing out mistranslations and defending Pope. The following is typical:

> All this is the pert Babble of a Frenchman; the Original no way authorizes it ... (p. 19, n.)

March 13, 1739 (*Daily Advertiser*, March 13, 1739)

Characters: An Epistle To Alexander Pope Esq; And Mr. White-head. [one line of Greek] Iliad. Lib. ix. Cernenda autem sunt diligenter, ne fallant ea nos vitia, quae virtutem videntur imitari. Tully. London: Printed for T. Cooper, at the Globe in Pater-Noster-Row; and sold by the Booksellers of London and Westminster. MDCCXXXIX.

Folio.

One unsigned leaf, B–D².

[2 pp.], [5]–15 pp., [16] blank.

WORKS: A. *Sober Advice*; B. *Of the Characters of Women*; C. *Epilogue to the Satires, Dial. I*; *Dial. II*.

CHARGES: 1. Pope treasonous; 2. Pope influenced by the traitor Bolingbroke.

An attempt written probably by a Walpole hack to discredit the anti-government satires of Pope and Whitehead. The notes display the writer's classical learning. The poem is offensive not only on Pope's politics but in its ranking of Pope with Whitehead. It opens,

> Shall *Pope* and *Whitehead*, with the rankest Hate,
> Disgorge a Stew of Satire on the State,
> As if a *Verres* or a *Nero* reign'd,
> Who all the Laws of God and Man profan'd;
>
> .   .   .
>
> And I in its Defence not draw my Pen,
> To strip the Varnish from invidious Men?   (p. 5)

He sees Pope as almost Satan-like:

C I

> Good Actions are the Test of virtuous Men;
> And not the Dashes of a *Madman*'s Pen.
> These only dignify the godlike Man,
> And make him greater than a Monarch can.
> Till these appear,—*Pope*'s but a specious Knave;
> A Tool to Envy, and Ambition's Slave;
> Link'd with Division, Prejudice and Hate,
> In Anarchy would fain involve the State:
> Of Soul too covetous to sit at Ease;
> And too ill-natur'd any more to please:
> His talent is to cast a Slur on all
> That grace the Court, the Senate, or the Hall.   (p. 7)

He makes one of the few attacks on *Sober Advice*:

> Go!—after *Ethicks* write a bawdy Piece;
> To put it off, relenting *Rufus* fleece;
> Then with a spurious Title force it down:
> Yet, as it ought, 'tis damn'd by all the Town.
>
>   .   .   .
>
> Now drop with *St. John* to the deepest Hell,
> And unto Traitors there your Poems sell:
> There let your Hawkers cry 'em on a String,
> And spread Sedition to dethrone your King.
> Yet blot out all Encomiums ere you vend,
> With which you dawb and flatter ev'ry Friend;
> Or you'll be scourged severely for a Fool,
> And double damn'd for an *Apostate*'s Tool.
> There *Sapho* [*sic*] too must wear a cleaner Smock;
> Nor must the Lover fear to catch the Pock:
> Or by a Legion of the stoutest Whores
> *You*'ll suffer Vengeance for your bawdy Scores.   (pp. 8–9)

For the reference to Sappho see *Of the Characters of Women*, l. 24.

March 13, 1739 (*Daily Advertiser*, March 13, 1739)

Ayre, William. Truth. A Counterpart to Mr. Pope's Essay on Man. Epistle The First, Opposing his opinions of Man with respect to the Universe. By Mr. Ayre. London: Printed in the Year M.DCC.XXXIX.

4to in half-sheets.
[A]–D².
[4 pp.], 1–11 pp., [12] blank.

'*Truth* . . . *Epistle the Second*, opposing his [Pope's] Opinions of Man as an Individual' was announced in *The Daily Advertiser* of June 13, 1739. I have not located a copy. The *BM Cat.* lists the first epistle as appearing in *Four Ethic Epistles, opposing some of Mr Pope's Opinions of Man, as set forth in his Essay*. London, 1753. I have not seen a copy.

WORK: A. *Essay on Man*.

'The Contents' give a fairly clear idea of this attack on Pope's hetero-
doxy in the *Essay on Man*:

> Subjects of this Nature must be consider'd without any regard
> to Poetry—There is positive Evil—All things can have but one
> original Author—The Impossibility of the Whole being perfect,
> and not the Parts— . . . A Gradation from Infinite to nothing
> denied . . . (A2r)

Ayre's attitude toward Pope in this very weak poem may be indicated by,

A
> Far be from me to do such Numbers wrong;
> I love the Musick but condemn the Song:
> That tells me *Reason* must from *Knowledge* flow,
> Yet sings of Things which Man can never know:
> That proudly tells me, in my Reason's spight,
> Without a Proof; *Whatever is, is Right.*
>
>   Then Right are all the Paths which Men have trod,
> This makes a *Demon* Right as well as *God*;
> Break down the Pale, Confusion enter in,
> If Holiness is Right, why so is Sin.　　　　　　　(p. 2)

November 17, 1739 (*Daily Advertiser*, November 17, 1739)

One Thousand Seven Hundred Thirty Nine. A Rhapsody. By
Way of Sequel to Seventeen Hundred Thirty Eight: By Mr.
Pope. Semper ego Auditor tantum? Juven. Excursusque Leves
tentat. Virg. Veritas pluribus Modis infracta: Primùm Inscitia
Reipublicae, ut alienae; Mox Libidine assentandi, aut rursus
Odio adversus Dominantes. Obtrectatio & Livor pronis Auribus
accipiuntur: Quippe Adulationi faedum Crimen Servitutis, Ma-
lignitati falsa Species Libertatis inest. Tacit. London: Printed
for J. Cooper, in Fleet-Street. MDCCXL. Price Sixpence. Where
may be had All Mr. Pope's Works.

Folio.

[A]–B².

[4 pp.], [5]–8 pp.

Rogers, who lists this as unlocated, gives the imprint as: 'Printed for

J. Cooper, Mess. Jackson and Jolliffe, H. Chappelle, and E. Curll.'
Yale also has a 'second edition'; title-page as above, adding after
'Tacit.' 'The Second Edition'; collation and pagination the same as
above.

WORK: A. *Epilogue to the Satires, Dial. I*; *Dial. II.*

CHARGE: I. Pope malicious and venal.

This 70-line pro-Walpole poem consists of a long series of 'when'
clauses and a brief main clause at the end. The Pope passage occurs
at the very beginning:

POPE wrote a *Satire*,—took it in his Pate
To call it *Seventeen hundred thirty-eight*;
In Imitation therefore tack to mine,
One Thousand seven hundred thirty-nine.

When Nonsense from the Tongue of *Hervey* flows,
And *P—pe* no Malice or no Envy shows;
Whose peevish Pride, without Distinction, flings
His Dirt, on Players, Poets, Peers, and Kings:
Or if he praises, modestly replies,
'Praise undeserv'd, is Satire in Disguise.'
With Names at length behold his Poems swell;
Scandal and Slander make a Poem sell:
Italics, CAPITALS, each Page supply,
Like *C—bb—r*'s Play-Bills, set to catch the Eye,
And raise Curiosity in Passers-by:
This Peerless Poet we as justly name,
A Bookseller for Bread, as Bard for Fame.
When *St. J—n* to his Country dare be just,
Or watchful *Walpole* shall betray his Trust . . .   (pp. 5–6)

The conclusion, however, 'Then will I cease to wish that Charmer
mine' (p. 8), turns the poem unexpectedly into a tribute to 'Mira' and
makes it difficult to take the attack on Pope too seriously.

1739

[Benson, William.] Letters Concerning Poetical Translations, And Virgil's and Milton's Arts of Verse, &c. London: Printed for J. Roberts, near the Oxford-Arms in Warwick-Lane. MDCCXXXIX.

Half-title: Letters Concerning Poetical Translations, &c. (Price One Shilling.)

8vo.
Two unsigned leaves, B–F⁸, G².
[4 pp.], [1]–83 pp., [84] blank.

On William Benson see *Twick.* v. 428–9.

WORKS: A. *Essay on Criticism*; B. Homer.

Not at all a personal attack on Pope. The criticism of Pope's verse and theories of versification is incidental to his examination in ten letters of such things as rhyme and caesura in Virgil and Milton.

In Letter 1 Benson quarrels with Pope's view of expletives and monosyllables.

A   It is commonly apprehended from a Passage in Mr. *Pope*'s *Essay on Criticism* [ll. 346–7], that all auxiliary Verbs are mere *Expletives*.

> While Expletives their feeble Aid *do* join,
> And ten low Words oft creep in one dull Line.

But this I believe Mr. *Pope* never intended to advance. (p. 8)

He gives several examples where he feels the expletive is poetically used, though neither these nor his argument is very clear. He does say that the auxiliary verb

... occasions suspence, which raises the attention; or in other Words, the auxiliary Verb gives notice of something coming, before the principal thing itself appears, which is another Property of Majesty. (p. 9)

He gives as an example of their improper use,

> His Heart, his Mistress and his Friends *did* share. *Pope*, on *Voiture*.
> (p. 10, n. ['Epistle To Miss Blount, With the Works of Voiture', *Twick.* vi. 62, l. 9, where 'Friend' is the reading given]).

He goes on to criticize Pope's translations of the opening lines of the *Iliad*:

B   As to Mr. *Pope*'s two Translations, I don't understand why the

latter ought to be preferr'd to the former. Mr. *Pope*'s first Translation stood thus.

> The Wrath of *Peleus*' Son, the direful Spring
> Of all the *Grecian* Woes, *O* Goddess sing.

Mr. *Pope* had reason to be dissatisfy'd with the *O* in the second Line, and to reject it; for *Homer* has nothing of it. But now let us see how the Vacancy is supplied in Mr. *Pope*'s new Translation.

> *Achilles*' Wrath, to *Greece* the direful Spring,
> Of Woes un-number'd, *Heav'nly* Goddess, sing.

Is not *Heav'nly* as much an Expletive as *O*, and can either of these Couplets deserve to be plac'd in the Front of the Iliad? I could wish Mr. *Pope* would return these two Lines once more to the Anvil, and dismiss all Expletives here at least. (p. 11)

Monosyllables, he says, 'seem to be absolutely condemn'd in the second line [*Essay on Criticism*, l. 347] ...' (p. 11). Pope's line may be indeed applied to Cowley 'whom Mr. *Pope* has formerly celebrated with no mean Encomiums' (p. 12), but there are hundreds of beautiful monosyllabic lines, and he gives some examples from Milton. (He has failed to consider Pope's specifying 'ten *low* words'.)

He disagrees as well, in Letter x, with

> And such as *Chaucer* is, shall *Dryden* be.   (l. 483)

It did not occur to that ingenious Writer, that the State of the *English* Language is very different at this time from what it was in *Chaucer*'s Days: It was then in its Infancy: And even *the publick Worship of God was in a foreign Tongue*, a thing as fatal to the *Language* of any Country, as to *Religion* itself. (p. 82) But we now have the Bible in English, and as long as it continues to be publicly used, there can be no great alteration in our language (p. 82). There is commendation of Pope, pp. 52, 76, 80.

1739

Crousaz, J. P. de. A Commentary On Mr. Pope's Principles of Morality, Or Essay on Man. By Mons. Crousaz, Member of the Royal Academies of Sciences at Paris and Bourdeaux, and Professor of Philosophy and Mathematics at Lausanne; In Answer to a Letter of Remarks on his Examen, &c. Containing Also I. The Letter of Remarks to Mons. Crousaz. II. The Abbe Du

x

Resnel's Translation of the Essay into French Verse. III. An Interlineary English Version of the same. IV. A Preliminary Discourse, by Du Resnel, on French and English Poetry: and V. Some cursory Annotations by the Translator. London: Printed for A. Dodd without Temple-Bar. M. DCC. XXXIX.

12mo.

A^{12} [4 leaves marked 'Contents' inserted between [A2] and A3], B–L^{12}, M–O^6, P^3, A^3, Q–S^6, T^2.

[12 pp.], [i]–xx, 1–84, [85]–157, [158]–207, [208]–82, [283]–99, [300], 301–26 pp., [327], [328] blank.

Samuel Johnson was the translator. The unused sheets were reissued in:

November, 1741 (*Gentleman's Magazine,*)

Crousaz, J. P. de. A Commentary On Mr Pope's Principles of Morality, Or Essay on Man. By Mons. Crousaz, Member of the Royal Academies of Sciences at Paris and Bourdeaux, and Professor of Philosophy and Mathematics at Lausanne; In Answer to a Letter of Remarks on his Examen, &c. Containing Also I. The Letter of Remarks to Mons. Crousaz. II. The Abbe Du Resnel's Translation of the Essay into French Verse. III. An Interlineary English Version of the same. IV. M. Du Resnel's Preface, with his Observations on the French, Italian, and English Poetry. V. Some Annotations by the Translator. London: Printed for E. Cave, at St John's Gate M,DCC, XLII.

An errata sheet giving four corrections has been inserted immediately after the title-page. Immediately following the errata sheet are the four leaves of contents.

At the end is an eight-page list of Cave publications. See A. T. Hazen, 'Crousaz on Pope', *TLS*, November 2, 1935, p. 704; A. T. Hazen and E. L. McAdam, Jr, 'First Editions of Samuel Johnson', *The Yale University Library Gazette*, x (1936), 45–51. A convenient summary of the Pope–Crousaz argument may be found in Jacqueline E. De La Harpe, *Jean-Pierre de Crousaz (1663–1750) et le conflit des idées au siècle des lumières* (Berkeley and Los Angeles, 1955), p. 231, n.

1739

Candour: Or, An Occasional Essay On The Abuse Of Wit and Eloquence. —Homo ingeniosissimè nequàm, / Et facundus malo publico. Vel. Paterculus. Non obtusa adeo gestamus pectora— Virgil. London: Printed by M. Watson, in Chancery Lane. MDCCXXXIX.

Folio.

Two unsigned leaves, A–E².

[8 pp.], [5]–19 pp., [20] blank.

After praise of Pope's 'divine' poetry, the author reproves him:

> To pry, to rail, to menace, and accuse,
> Seem not the Marks of a celestial Muse,
> Vengeance to wake, and Coals of Wrath to blow,
> The Province is of Man's infernal Foe.   (p. 8)

He urges Pope 'in healing ways' to employ his powerful pen (pp. 8–9).

July, 1740 (*London Magazine*)

[Johnson, T.] The Tryal Of Colley Cibber, Comedian, &c. For writing a Book intitled An Apology for his Life, &c. Being A thorough Examination thereof; wherein he is proved guilty of High Crimes and Misdemeanors against the English Language, and in characterising many Persons of Distinction. Lo! He hath written a Book! Together With An Indictment exhibited against Alexander Pope of Twickenham, Esq; For Not exerting his Talents at this Juncture: And The arraignment of George Cheyne, Physician at Bath, for the Philosophical, Physical, and Theological Heresies, uttered in his last Book on Regimen. London: Printed for the Author; and sold by W. Lewis in Russel-Street; and E. Curll in Rose-Street, Covent-Garden; Mess. Dodsley, Jackson, Jolliffe, and Brindley, in St. James's and Bond-Street, and at all Booksellers in London and Westminster. 1740. Price One Shilling.

8vo in half-sheets.

A–F⁴.

[2 pp.], [iii]–viii (misnumbered 'vii'), [1]–40 pp.

CHARGES: I. Pope fears reprisals for his political satire. The satires in question were probably *Epilogue to the Satires, Dial. I* and *II*. See *Twick.* IV. xl.

The dedication 'To Mr. Ralph of Redriff', pp. [iii]–viii, is signed, p. viii (misnumbered 'vii'), 'T. Johnson'.

Concerned almost entirely with Cibber and his *Apology*, the pamphlet reprints several attacks on the *Apology*, as much apparently to ridicule 'Captain Hercules Vinegar', who is credited with them, as to ridicule Cibber.

Pope appears only as brought to trial together with Dr Cheyne and Cibber 'at a Court of Censorial Enquiry held before Capt. Hercules Vinegar' (p. 27). This section of the pamphlet, pp. 28–37, is misleadingly given the drop-title, p. 28, 'The Indictment of Alexander Pope Esq;' since Pope is mentioned only on pp. 28–30.

Pope is indicted because 'He, being a Person to whom Nature had bequeathed many Talents, in Order and with Design that he might well and duly give People their own' had '*too much* Fear before his Eyes' to do anything to deter 'one *Forage*, alias *Guts*, alias *Brass*, and many other sad Fellows to the Jurors unknown' from committing 'all Sorts of Roguery' (p. 28). But his counsel pleads that Pope's holding his tongue was no crime, although speaking or writing against Guts is, and the court dismisses the case. The only sting at all, other than being dragged into this foolishness, is a footnote:

1   The Satire call'd *Manners*, written by Mr. *Whitehead*, two Years ago, and for which his Publisher was taken into Custody by the *House* of *Lords*, struck Mr. *Pope* with such a Pannic, [*sic*] and trembling in his Nerves, that he has not since been able to hold a Pen. (p. 30, n.)

1740

Tunbrigalia. Or, The Tunbridge Miscellany, For the Years, 1737, 1738, 1739. Being A Curious Collection of Miscellany Poems, &c. Exhibited upon the Walks at Tunbridge Wells, in the three last Years. By a Society of Gentlemen and Ladies. London: Printed for T. Webb near St. Paul's, and sold by the Booksellers of London and Westminster. M.DCC. XL. (Price 6d.)

8vo in half-sheets.

A–C⁴, D in one leaf.

[2 pp.], 3–26 pp.

Case 429.

WORK: A. Pope's edition of Shakespeare.

A This reprints, pp. 17–19, under the title 'A Parody on the 4th Chapter of Genesis' (there is no table of contents), *Dean Jonathan's Parody On The 4th Chap. of Genesis*, 1729, q.v. There are only nineteen verses, verses 11 and 12 being run together. There are many differences in punctuation and the use of italics, and several verbal differences from the 1729 text. Proper names are not spelled out, but dashes are substituted for several letters. The Theobald–Pope quarrel was out of date in 1740, and it seems odd that this piece should have been reprinted.

There are two other poems dealing with Pope, 'Verses found in a Lady's Pocket Book, With the Picture of Mr. Pope inclosed' (p. 11) and 'On Mr. Pope. By Mrs. W—ll—tt' (p. 12). The first is only twelve lines long, the second eighteen. 'Mrs. W—ll—tt' also contributed two other equally brief poems to the volume, 'Verses on Mr. Nash' and 'Verses on Dr. Young' (p. 16). In each of the poems on Pope the authoress expresses her love of Pope's mind, but in each there is more emphasis on the disparity between the beauty of his mind and his physique than seems complimentary. Or perhaps they are only tactless, not intentionally wounding.

'Verses found in a Lady's Pocket Book' opens,

> Oft on the Lillyputian GOD I look,
> Which is confin'd within my Pocket Book.   (p. 11)

She would like to see the original, but is confined 'Alone to gaze on his illustrious mind' (p. 11).

In the second, the authoress confesses,

> I form Ideas of him with Delight:
> Whose Person I have ne'er so much as seen,
>
>   .   .   .
>
> Admitting all that vulgar Scandal say,
> His Soul lives there: Its Mansion I'd approve,
> And tell him, I was his *Platonic* Love.   (p. 12)

May, 1741 (*Gentleman's Magazine*)

The Bath Miscellany. For the Year 1740. Wrote By The Gentle-
men and Ladies at that Place. Containing All the Lampoons,
Satyrs, Panegyrics, &c. For that Year. Bath: Printed for W.
Jones, and sold by W. Lobb there; and by Jacob Robinson,
Bookseller, in Ludgate-street; and the Pamphlet Shops of Lon-
don and Westminster. 1741 [Price One Shilling.]

8vo in half-sheets.
Two unsigned leaves, B–F⁴, G².
[4 pp.], [1]–43 pp., [44] blank.
Case 431.

CHARGE: 1. Pope and Swift think themselves the only living poets.

This collection of light verse contains a single hit at Pope, in 'The
Publisher's Apology To The Reader', signed 'W.J.' (second unsigned
leaf, r):

1   The Publisher of these Amusements of the Gentlemen and
        Lady's [*sic*] leisure Hours, hopes to stand excused, since his In-
        tentions [*sic*] was to oblige the Publick, by shewing these Speci-
        mens of concealed Genius's [*sic*], and to convince *Pope* and *Swift*
        that there are more Poets in *England* than themselves.

See the *Dunciad* B, iii. 156, n.

April 3–6, 1742 (*London Evening Post*, Rogers)

[Morrice, Bezaleel.] To The Falsely Celebrated British Homer.
An Epistle. Sense, Language, Measure, living Tongues, and
dead, / Let all give way, and M[orri]ce may be read. D[uncia]d.
London: Printed for the Author: And sold by the Booksellers of
London and Westminster; and the Pamphlet Shops at the Royal-
Exchange. 1742. [Price One Shilling.]

Folio.
[A]–E².
[4 pp.], [5]–20 pp.

Listed as unlocated in Rogers.
The poem is signed 'Bazaleel [*sic*] Morrice' (p. 20).

WORKS: A. *Windsor Forest*; B. *Ode on St Cecilia's Day*; C. *Rape of the Lock*; D. Homer; E. Pope's edition of Shakespeare; F. *Dunciad*; G. *Essay on Man*.

CHARGES: 1. Pope a literary dictator; 2. Pope a plagiarist.

The opening makes clear that the pamphlet is a reply (an oddly belated one) to the *Dunciad* A, ii. 118, n.:

> Both by the world and thee contemptuous made,
> And bury'd long, in dull oblivion's shade;
> Rouz'd from the dreary regions of the dead,
> By arrogance like thine, I raise my head;
> I now to haunt thy guilty conscience, rise;
> The guilty mind a ¹phantom terrifies;
> Nor thee for this disdainful title blame,
> For, what art boastful thou! beside a name?
> Oh, thou! demanding all men to submit
> To thee, and own the wonders of thy wit.
>
> ¹ Called phantom in the *D[uncia]d*. (p. [5])

Morrice's chief target is the Homer. Pope's is intent

> All others worth, with jealous rage to wound,
> And lessen by presumption, things profound;
> *Homer* to rob of all heroic rage,
> And dress like modern mimic of the stage;
> This was thy first, or principal offence.   (p. 6)

> HOMER (whom thou prompted by evil fate
> Wou'd'st, strangely metamorphosing, translate)
> Was, like th'expanded aether, unconfin'd;
>
> .   .   .
>
> Such was the force of his informing lays;
> Ennobling to the height, the lowest theme,
> His frogs and mice, as gods and hero's seem;
> Thro' thee, and thy heroical device,
> His gods and hero's, seem as frogs and mice!
>
> .   .   .
>
> His great ACHILLES to deprive of might,
> Thou seem'st to reclaim as thy peculiar right;
> But, F[ENT]ON, in conspiracy with B[ROO]M,
> And thee, pronounce his wand'ring hero's doom:
> Of HOMER see the lamentable state!

> The cruelty of this triumvirate!
> The soul, or genius of the poet flies,
> He by proscription, or subscription dies.   (pp. 10–14)

ABC2   *Alexander's Feast* is preferred to Pope's St Cecilia ode (p. 8), Garth's *Dispensary* to the *Rape of the Lock* (p. 9), Denham's *Cooper's Hill* to *Windsor Forest* (p. 7).

G2

> If thy *Essay on Man* some value shows,
> 'Tis what the bounteous *Shaft'sbury* bestows;
> His only, all that's solid and sublime;
> Thine are the measure, and melodious chime.   (p. 8)

E

> SHAKESPEAR, whom thou rais'd by an impious spell,
> (As once the witch of *Endor—Samuel*;
> Tho' thou, with feebler skill, or worse inclin'd,
> The body rais'd, and left the soul behind) ...   (p. 17)

And he attacks, of course, the *Dunciad*:

F

> Where arrogance erects its tow'ring head,
> And reigns alone—thy *D—d* may be read;
> Be read, where men benevolence disown,
> Where modesty, as yet, was never known ...   (p. 6)

July 24–30, 1742 (*London Evening Post*, Rogers)

[Cibber, Colley.] A Letter From Mr. Cibber, To Mr. Pope, Inquiring into the Motives that might induce him in his Satyrical Works, to be so frequently fond of Mr. Cibber's Name. Out of thy own mouth will I judge thee. Pref. to the Dunciad. London, Printed: And Sold by W. Lewis in Russel-Street, Covent-Garden. M DCC XLII. Price 1s.

Half-title: A Letter From Mr. Cibber, To Mr. Pope. Price One Shilling.

8vo in half-sheets.
Four leaves [the first leaf, the half-title, is signed A2; the other three leaves are unsigned], B–H⁴, I².
[4 pp.], [5]–66 pp., [2 pp.] blank.

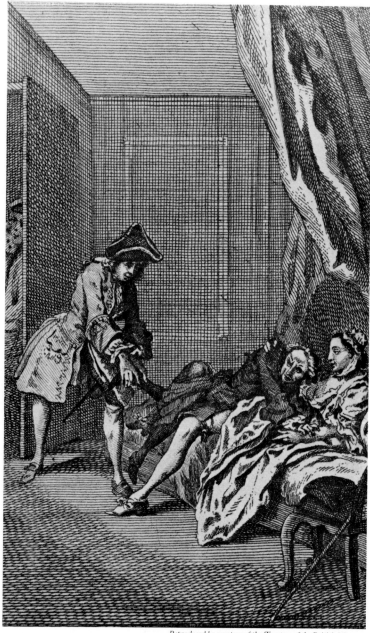

The frontispiece to the third edition of *A Letter From Mr Cibber, To Mr Pope.*

The catchword, p. 39, reads, correctly: —*Si*.

Laid into this copy is a folded plate illustrating the quotation on p. 44, entitled at bottom 'And has not Sawney too his Lord and Whore? Vide Cibber's Letter. Publish'd according to Act of Parliament by P. Uriel in Temple Lane, over against Chancery Lane, August 9th 1742.'

A variant of the above, also at Yale, has the catchword on p. 39: —*S*.

There was a Dublin edition, printed for A. Reilly, 1742, which I have not seen.

The second edition, with title-page as above, inserting 'The Second Edition.' after 'Dunciad.'

Three unsigned leaves, B–H⁴, I in one leaf.
[2 pp.], [5]–66 pp.

The ornamental initial on p. [5] differs from the first edition, as does the position of the tail-piece on p. 66.

The third edition, with title-page as in the first edition, omitting comma after 'Works' and adding after 'Dunciad':

The Third Edition. Glasgow: Printed for W. Macpharson. [Price One Shilling.]

Half-title: A Letter From Mr. Cibber, To Mr. Pope. [Price One Shilling.]

Gathered as an octavo in half-sheets, but the chain lines are horizontal.
Two unsigned leaves, B–K⁴.
[4 pp.], [1]–72 pp.

Another edition: Title-page as in the first edition, but reading 'thine own' for 'thy own', and with the imprint: London: Printed in the Year M.DCC. LXXVII.

Half-title: A Letter From Cibber to Pope. [Price One Shilling.]

8vo in half-sheets.
Two unsigned leaves, B–F⁴, FI signed E.
[4 pp.], [1]–40 pp.
In the two Bodleian copies FI is correctly signed.

Cibber's famous *Letter* either provoked Pope into making Cibber the new hero of the *Dunciad* or gave him an excuse for continuing the revisions he had already contemplated. See *Twick.* v. xxxii–xxxv.

WORKS: A. *What D'Ye Call It*; B. *Key to the Lock*; C. Homer; D. *Three Hours after Marriage*; E. *A Clue to the Comedy of the Non-Juror*; F. *Dunciad*; G. *Epistle to Arbuthnot*; H. *New Dunciad*.

CHARGES: 1. Pope insulted Cibber after a performance of *The Rehearsal*; 2. Pope has forgotten Cibber's recommendation of Dodsley's *The Miller of Mansfield*; 3. Cibber rescued Pope from a bawdy house; 4. Ambrose Philips once threatened to whip Pope.

Cibber explains at the beginning that he has been 'really driven' to write this '*At the Desire of several Persons of Quality*' (p. [5]); he has formed a resolution (often mentioned during the Pope–Cibber quarrel): 'I will now, Sir, have the last Word with you . . .' (p. 8).

Why, Cibber wishes to know, has Pope so often fallen foul upon him? Cibber has always been a warm admirer of Pope's writings and has never printed anything against him. Pope must think of him as one of those ' "two, or three Persons only, whose Dulness or Scurrility all Mankind agreed, to have justly intitled them to a Place in the *Dunciad*" ' (p. 14; Cibber is quoting 'The Publisher to the Reader', *Twick.* v. 203–4, n.). Cibber's objection to this shows his utter inability to grasp what the *Dunciad* is all about:

F   Now let us enquire into the Justness of this Pretence, and whether Dulness in one Author gives another any right to abuse him for it? No sure! Dulness can be no Vice or Crime, or is at worst a Misfortune, and you ought no more to censure or revile him for it, than for his being blind or lame; the Cruelty or Injustice will be evidently equal either way. (pp. 14–15)

What follows has a touching naïveté. Supposing Dulness to be actually criminal, he will leave it to Pope's own conscience

to declare, whether you really think I am generally so guilty of it, as to deserve the Name of the Dull Fellow you make of me. Now if the Reader will call upon My Conscience to speak to the Question, I do from my Heart solemnly declare, that I don't believe you *do* think so of me. (p. 15)

He promises to offer nothing against Pope that he cannot prove by known facts and gives us his famous explanation of how he once offended Pope. *The Rehearsal* was revived shortly after *Three Hours after Marriage* 'had been acted without success' (p. 17). Cibber in the

role of Bays, a character whom tradition allowed to *ad lib.* on current theatrical matters, introduced a reference to the unfortunate mummy and crocodile:

› I   . . . I, Mr. *Bays*, when the two Kings of *Brentford* came from the Clouds into the Throne again, instead of what my Part directed me to say, made use of these Words, viz. 'Now, Sir, this Revolution, I had some Thoughts of introducing, by a quite different Contrivance; but my Design taking air, some of your sharp Wits, I found, had made use of it before me; otherwise I intended to have stolen one of them in, in the Shape of a *Mummy*, and t'other, in that of a *Crocodile*'. Upon which, I doubt, the Audience by the Roar of their Applause shew'd their proportionable Contempt of the Play they belong'd to . . . But this, it seems, was so heinously taken by Mr. *Pope*, that, in the swelling of his Heart, after the Play was over, he came behind the Scenes, with his Lips pale and his Voice trembling, to call me to account for the Insult: And accordingly fell upon me with all the foul Language, that a Wit out of his Senses could be capable of—How durst I have the Impudence to treat any Gentleman in that manner? &c, &c. &c. Now let the Reader judge by this Concern, who was the true Mother of the Child! When he was almost choked with the foam of his Passion, I was enough recover'd from my Amazement to make him (as near as I can remember) this Reply, *viz.* 'Mr. *Pope*—You are so particular a Man, that I must be asham'd to return your Language as I ought to do; but since you have attacked me in so monstrous a Manner; This you may depend upon, that as long as the Play continues to be acted, I will never fail to repeat the same Words over and over again.' (pp. 18–19)

On this incident see Ault, p. 300; it is not at all certain that we can accept Cibber's account here.

E   Cibber then begins his charges against Pope. The first concerns *The Non-Juror*. He quotes (p. 21) Pope's references to the play in his letter to Jervas, July 9, 1716, and (pp. 28–9) in his letter to Digby, March 31, 1718 (*Corr.* I. 347; 473 and n.), and insists that Pope's real objection to the play was to its attack on Jacobitism. He claims that Pope sent him four guineas for four tickets to the author's night obviously to discharge his indebtedness to Cibber for the latter's subscription to the Homer (pp. 24–5). (See Pope's mention of this, *Twick.* V. B, i. 133, n.)

He accuses Pope as well of being the author, under the name of Barnevelt, of a pamphlet, the title of which Cibber has forgotten,

which claimed that *The Non-Juror* was 'a closely couched Jacobite Libel against the Government' (p. 26). Ault, who reprints Cibber's charge, identifies the pamphlet as *The Plot Discover'd; or, a Clue to the Comedy of the Non-Juror*, 1718, and argues for Pope's authorship (*Prose* I, cxvii–cxxiv). Pope's having published the same kind of charge against his own *Rape of the Lock* convinced Cibber that Pope must have written the pamphlet, and he gives his view of the motives behind *A Key to the Lock*:

B   . . . he might hope, that such a ludicrous Self-accusation might soften, or wipe off any severe Imputation that had lain upon other parts of his Writings, which had not been thought equally Innocent of a real Disaffection. This way of owning Guilt in a wrong Place is a common Artifice to hide it in a right one. (p. 27)

(The anonymous author of *A Blast upon Bays*, 1742, finds Cibber's reasoning faulty: 'The honest, stupid Vulgar are to take one Piece of Drollery literally, because it makes against Mr. *Cibber*, and the other, which is just in the same Taste, as Banter only, because it makes for Mr. *Pope* . . .' [p. 15].)

Cibber next examines the most offensive passages in the *Dunciad*. He finds inept the statement in the note to A, i. 240, that he is 'particularly admirable in Tragedy'; if he has

D   made so many crowded Theatres laugh, and in the right Place too, for above forty Years together, am I to make up the Number of your Dunces, because I have not the equal Talent of making them cry too? Make it your own Case: Is what you have excell'd in at all the worse, for your having so dismally dabbled (as I before observ'd) in the Farce of *Three Hours after Marriage*?
                                                                              (p. 36)

AD   Earlier Cibber had referred derisively to 'those polite Pieces, *The What d'ye call it*, and *The Three Hours after Marriage* (both which he [Pope] had a hand in)' (pp. 21–2).

He attributes to Pope the epigram on Cibber as laureate, A, iii. 319, n. ('The probabilities point to Pope's authorship' [*Twick.* VI. 305]), but says, typically, that he can hardly help laughing at it himself (p. 39).

He next takes up the *Epistle to Arbuthnot*.

G2   There (thank my Stars) my whole Commission ends,
                    Cibber and I are, luckily, no friends   (ll. 59–60)

insinuates that Cibber had a 'certain Prejudice to any thing, that had your Recommendation to the Stage' (p. 42). But his treatment of Dodsley's *The Miller of Mansfield* should have convinced Pope that

Cibber did not allow his judgement to be influenced by Pope's treatment of him. He had met Pope in a visit to the late General Dormer and when both gentlemen asked Cibber's advice and assistance for the play, he gave it, and is sure his recommendation helped it to be performed (pp. 42–3). Malcolm Goldstein, *Pope and the Augustan Stage* (Stanford, 1958), p. 56, thinks this Cibber anecdote probably true. Pope has, Cibber notices, altered the offensive line to

The Play'rs and I are, luckily, no friends.

By far the most galling passage to Cibber is l. 97 which he quotes as

And has not *Colley* too his Lord, and Whore?   (p. 44)

This elicits his celebrated account of the 'Tom-tit episode', the best-known and most important part of his letter and one of the cruellest charges ever made against Pope.

He may remember, then (or if he won't I will) when *Button's* Coffee-house was in vogue, and so long ago, as when he had not translated above two or three Books of *Homer*; there was a late young Nobleman (as much his *Lord* as mine) who had a good deal of wicked Humour, and who, though he was fond of having Wits in his Company, was not so restrained by his Conscience, but that he lov'd to laugh at any merry Mischief he could do them: This noble Wag, I say, in his usual *Gayetè* [*sic*] *de Coeur*, with another Gentleman still in Being, one Evening slily seduced the celebrated Mr. *Pope* as a Wit, and myself as a Laugher, to a certain House of Carnal Recreation, near the *Hay-Market*; where his Lordship's Frolick propos'd was to slip his little *Homer*, as he call'd him, at a Girl of the Game, that he might see what sort of Figure a Man of his Size, Sobriety, and Vigour (in Verse) would make, when the frail Fit of Love had got into him; in which he so far succeeded, that the smirking Damsel, who serv'd us with Tea, happen'd to have Charms sufficient to tempt the little-tiny Manhood of Mr. *Pope* into the next Room with her: at which you may imagine, his Lordship was in as much Joy, at which might happen within, as our small Friend could probably be in Possession of it: But I (forgive me all ye mortified Mortals whom his fell Satyr has since fallen upon) observing he had staid as long as without hazard of his Health he might, I,

Prick'd to it by foolish Honesty and Love,

As *Shakespear* says, without Ceremony, threw open the Door upon him, where I found this little hasty Hero, like a terrible *Tom Tit*, pertly perching upon the Mount of Love! But such was my Surprize that I fairly laid hold of his Heels, and actual-

ly drew him down safe and sound from his Danger. My Lord, who staid tittering without, in hopes the sweet Mischief he came for would have been compleated, upon my giving an Account of the Action within, began to curse, and call me an hundred silly Puppies, for my impertinently spoiling the Sport; to which with great Gravity, I reply'd; pray, my Lord, consider what I have done was, in regard to the Honour of our Nation! For would you have had so glorious a Work as that of making *Homer* speak elegant *English*, cut short by laying up our little Gentleman of a Malady, which his thin Body might never have been cured of?   (pp. 47–9)

On this charge see Ault, pp. 301–7. The least that may be said in Pope's favour is that Cibber's story is to be accepted with extreme caution. If Cibber really had such a weapon as this story in his possession, why had Pope dared to attack Cibber repeatedly?

Proceeding to the *New Dunciad* he objects to l. 20:

H   Soft on her lap her Laureat son reclines.

Pert and *Dull* at least you might have allow'd me; but as seldom asleep as any Fool. (p. 53)

He objects with rather more force to Pope's exceedingly disingenuous quotations from Cibber's *Apology*. *Dunciad* B, iv. 20, n., supplies, as Cibber does here, the omitted phrases (pp. 54–6).

He concludes with one last charge – that Ambrose Philips threatened to whip Pope:

4   When you used to pass your Hours at *Button*'s, you were even there remarkable for your satyrical Itch of Provocation; scarce was there a Gentleman of any Pretension to Wit, whom your unguarded Temper had not fallen upon, in some biting Epigram; among which you once caught a Pastoral Tartar, whose Resentment, that your Punishment might be proportion'd to the Smart of your Poetry, had stuck up a Birchen Rod in the Room, to be ready, whenever you might come within reach of it; and at this rate you writ and rallied, and writ on, till you rhym'd yourself quite out of the Coffee-house. (p. 65)

On this well-known gesture of Philips see Sherburn, pp. 120–1.

July 26, 1742 (*Daily Post*, July 26, 1742)

[Ward, Edward.] The Cudgel, Or, A Crab-tree Lecture. To the
Author of The Dunciad. By Hercules Vinegar, Esq; Tough
Answers, we confess, but sometimes fit / To tame the Wildness
of ill-natur'd Wit, / Which often, unprovok'd gives mortal
Wounds, / And would without Correction, know no Bounds: /
But if the injur'd Person cannot draw / A Pen, or seek due
Remedy at Law; / When with Resentment warm'd, he need not
want, / A Crab-tree Cudgel or an oaken Plant. London: Printed
for the Author, and sold at his House, the Crab-Tree, in Vinegar-
yard, near Drury-Lane. [Price 1s.] MDCCXLII.

8vo in half-sheets.
One unsigned leaf, B–H⁴.
[2 pp.], 3–4, 3–56 pp.

The use of Henry Fielding's pseudonym in *The Champion* is deliberately misleading. This is a reissue of the left-over sheets of *Durgen*,
1728, q.v., with a new title-page. 'The Author to the Reader' has been
omitted and B1 has been reset because of the new drop-title on B1r:
'The Cudgel, Or, A Crab-Tree Lecture, &c.'; B1 is incorrectly numbered 3–4. The lines on the title-page above are from the poem, p. 9,
where they appear in a different order. See Knox Chandler, 'Two
"Fielding" Pamphlets', *PQ*, XVI (1937), 410–11, and *Blast upon Blast*,
1742. Ward had died in 1731. The mention of *The Cudgel* in *Dunciad*
A, iii. 26, n., does not make clear that it is a reissue of *Durgen*.

August 19–21, 1742 (*London Evening Post*, Rogers)

[Hervey, John Lord.] A Letter To Mr. C[ib]b[e]r, On his Letter
to Mr. P[ope]. Tu ne cede malis sed contra audentior ito. Virg.
London: Printed for J. Roberts, near the Oxford-Arms in Warwick-Lane. MDCCXLII.

8vo in half-sheets.
One unsigned leaf, B–D⁴, E in one leaf.
[2 pp.], 1–26 pp.

The *BM Cat.* and the *DNB* ascribe this to Hervey, as did Horace Walpole in *A Catalogue Of The Royal and Noble Authors of England* (Strawberry-Hill, 1787), p. 452.

WORKS: A. Homer; B. *Dunciad*; C. *Imitations of Horace*; D. *Essay on Man.*

CHARGES: 1. Pope venal and sells same work several times; 2. Pope's conversation laboured and motivated only by vanity.

A Letter From Mr. Cibber, 1742, serves as a pretext for Hervey's general abuse of Pope. Pope has no right to the tribute Cibber has paid to him as a poet, since he lacks Perspicuity and Invention (p. 6). Hervey finds the Satires and Epistles lacking in Perspicuity (p. 7), but he does not particularize the charge. Nor is his comment on the *Dunciad*'s lack of Perspicuity very enlightening:

AB   ... there is no one Article you can name, in which it is not so obscure, that, according to *Milton*'s Phrase, it is *a Darkness to be felt* in ev'ry *Line* by ev'ry *Reader*. The *Plan* is *obscure*, the *Grammar* is obscure, the *Sense* is obscure, the *Stories* are obscure, the *Allusions* are obscure, and the *Characters* are so obscure, that the Persons of the *Satirized* are as obscure as the Stile of the *Satirist*. Which made me admire extremely a little Epigram I saw in a Visit written on the Title-Page of this Poem when it first came out, that at once did Justice to Mr. *Pope* as a Translator, and as an Author. The Epigram was this:

> Whilst in thy Verse we hear old *Homer* speak,
> And in thy *Dunciad* thy own Meaning seek,
> His *Greek* grows *English*, and thy *English Greek*. (pp. 8–9)

On Pope's lack of Invention he is rather more satisfactory. As to Pope's Invention in his satires:

BC   ...Tho' I grant there is as much as is necessary to make *a great Liar*, yet I protest I do not see the least Glympse of that sort which is necessary to make *a Great Poet* ... (pp. 9–10)

What Pope calls his 'Strokes of Satire' are not poetry:

BC   ... I can no more admit that Mr. *Pope* has any Merit in this Sort of Writing, or deserves the Title of a Satirist; than if I heard a drunken Scold of an Apple-woman quarrelling with a foul-mouth'd Hackney-Coachman, I shou'd think in my next Visit of describing what had pass'd, by saying, I had seen at the Corner of the Street coming thither, two of the *keenest Satirists* I had ever met with in my Life. (p. 11)

He is able, however, to praise Pope's metrics and his translations:

> Mr. *Pope* was certainly once so good a Versificator, that his
> Predecessor Mr. *Dryden*, and his Cotemporary Mr. *Prior* ex-
> cepted, I think the Harmony of his Numbers equal to any
> body's; and when other People thought for him (that is, when
> he was a Translator) he had all the Merit that a Man can
> have in the Execution of a Task where Genius is not neces-
> sary, and to which no Man of true Genius can, or will submit.
> (pp. 11–12)

After this back-handed compliment, he points out that 'flowing numbers' cannot of themselves make a poem good (p. 12), and goes on to
object to the verse of the satires:

> But even this Merit of Versification ... Mr. *Pope* in his late
> Epistles, and what he calls Satires, has either from Age and Rust
> entirely lost, or from an Affectation of the *sermo pedestris* chosen
> to abdicate. (p. 13)

He allots to the *Essay on Man* a more extended treatment, but does
little more than repeat the usual objections:

> ... He has jumbled together my Ld *Shaftsbury*, *Montagne*, Lord
> *Herbert*, *Mandeville*, and fifty *&* caeteras; till from these fine
> uniform Originals drawing only some incongruous Scraps, his
> whole Work is nothing but a Heap of poetical Contradictions,
> and a jarring Series of Doctrines, Principles, Opinions and Sen-
> timents, diametrically opposite to each other ... (p. 15)

Hervey draws a parallel of five or six pages between Cibber and
Pope. Cibber may have squandered his money, but Pope

> constantly robs, cheats, and plunders the Publick within the
> Limits of the Law, by selling the same Work over and over again
> under the Pretence of correcting, altering, and adding here and
> there a Word, in *Folios*, *Quarto's*, *Octavos's*, *Duodecimo's*, *Loose-
> Sheets*, *collected Volumes*, and all the *Proteus-Shapes* which the *Press*
> can furnish. (pp. 18–19)

His comments on Pope as a conversationalist are at least original:

> Your Conversation [Cibber's] is always flowing and easy; his
> affected and constrain'd. You always talking in the Character
> for which *Nature* designed you; he in That, which in Spite of
> *Nature*, he designed himself for, and is constantly labouring to
> obtain, and keep up by *Art*; till his poor tortur'd Imagination,
> perpetually on the Stretch to act the Wit, the Refiner, and the
> Humorist, yields Maxims, Sentences, Observations and Senti-
> ments, just as poor Wretches upon the Rack make Confessions,

Y

and extorts every Word from himself, as every Word of theirs is extorted by other People. (pp. 19–20)

Cibber tries to entertain and amuse the people he is with; Pope only tries 'to tax their Admiration, and excite their Flattery' (p. 20). While Cibber is welcomed into society, Pope is excluded. He is 'only read and fear'd' (p. 21). Pope, Hervey predicts with relish, will drag out the close of his life in 'continued unpitied Solitude' (p. 22). In short, Hervey finds Pope,

> at best *a second-rate Poet*, a *bad Companion*, a *dangerous Acquaintance*, an *inveterate, implacable Enemy, no body's Friend*, a *noxious Member of Society*, and *a thorough bad Man*. (p. 25)

August 21, 1742 (*Daily Post*, August 21, 1742)

Vinegar, Capt. Hercules [pseud.] Blast upon Blast, And Lick for Lick; Or A New Lesson For P—PE. A Parody on the Fourth Chapter of Genesis. By Capt. H[ercule]S Vinegar. London: Printed for W. Webb, near St. Paul's; and sold by the Booksellers and Pamphlet-Shops, of London and Westminster, 1742.

Folio.
One unsigned leaf, B², one unsigned leaf.
[2 pp.], 3–8 pp.

Reprinted in Horace Walpole's letter to Mann, August 28, 1742, Old Style, *Horace Walpole's Correspondence with Sir Horace Mann*, ed. W. S. Lewis, Warren Hunting Smith, and George L. Lam (New Haven, 1954), II. 31–6, in *The Yale Edition of Horace Walpole's Correspondence*, ed. W. S. Lewis, vol. 18.

And, from a manuscript copy in the British Museum, in *Sawney and Colley* (*1742*) *and other Pope Pamphlets*, ed. W. Powell Jones, The Augustan Reprint Society, No. 83 (Los Angeles, 1960).

WORK: A. *Three Hours after Marriage*.

This is a revision of *Dean Jonathan's Parody*, 1729, with the substitution of Cibber for Theobald, *Three Hours after Marriage* for Pope's Shakespeare, and *The Careless Husband* for Theobald's *Shakespeare Restored*. Since the parody had been reprinted in 1740 in *Tunbrigalia*, it is not clear whether this was used as the basis for the text or whether *Dean*

Jonathan's Parody was used. Since, however, in at least three instances the *Tunbrigalia* text differs verbally from *Dean Jonathan's Parody* and in each of these instances *Blast upon Blast* returns to the original reading, it may be inferred that the 1729 text was the source. The use on the title-page of Fielding's pseudonym in *The Champion*, 'Hercules Vinegar', was deliberately misleading. See the denial of Fielding's authorship in Wilbur L. Cross, *The History of Henry Fielding* (New Haven, 1918), I. 367–8, and Knox Chandler, 'Two "Fielding" Pamphlets', *PQ*, XVI (1937), 410–11.

The following may illustrate the revision:

III. And in Process of time it came to pass, That *P[o]pe* brought of the Fruits of his Leisure, a Farce for the Stage, as an Offering to the Town, and lo! it was called, *Th[r]ee H[ou]rs Af[te]r M[a]rr[ia]ge.*

IV. And *C[i]bb[e]r* he also brought of the Firstlings of his Study, even a Play for the Stage; and he called it the *C[are]l[e]ss H[u]sb[an]d*, and the Town had respect unto *C[i]bb[e]r* and his Play. (p. 4)

The rest, with the Cibber substitutions, continues as in 1729.

August 21–4, 1742 (*London Evening Post*, Rogers)

[Hervey, John Lord, and Cibber, Colley.] The Difference Between Verbal and Practical Virtue. Dicendi Virtus, nisi ei, qui dicit, ea, de quibus dicit, percepta sint, extare non potest. Cic. With A Prefatory Epistle from Mr. C[i]b[be]r to Mr. P. Sic ulciscar genera singula, quemadmodum à quibus sum provocatus. Cic. post Redit. ad Quir. London: Printed for J. Roberts, near the Oxford-Arms in Warwick-Lane. M DCC XLII.

Drop-title: The Difference Between Verbal and Practical Virtue Exemplify'd, In some Eminent Instances both Ancient and Modern. (p. [1]).

Folio.

[A]–C².

[4 pp.], [1]–7 pp., [8] blank.

Horace Walpole in *A Catalogue of the Royal and Noble Authors of England* (Strawberry-Hill, 1787), p. 452, attributes this pamphlet to

Hervey. The introductory letter, [A2r and v] under the drop-title, 'Mr. C[i]b[be]r to Mr. P.', is apparently genuinely by Cibber and is so accepted by Ault, p. 304. The letter, however, implies that the poem which follows is by Cibber, aided by others, and this is much less certain. Reprinted in *The Scribleriad and The Difference Between Verbal And Practical Virtue*, ed. A. J. Sambrook, The Augustan Reprint Society, No. 125 (Los Angeles, 1967).

WORK: A. *Epilogue to the Satires, Dial. I; Dial. II.*

CHARGES: 1. Cibber rescued Pope from a bawdy house; 2. Pope a usurer; 3. Pope deformed; 4. Pope libels and defames for money.

There is, of course, a reference to the 'Tom-tit' episode:

1   ...With what reasonable and equitable Pleasure may I not pursue my Blow till I make you repent, by laying you on your Back, the ungrateful Returns you have made me for saving you from Destruction when you laid yourself on your Belly. ([A2v])

The poem states its theme in ll. 5–8:

> Few Authors tread the Paths they recommend,
> Or when they shew the Road, pursue the End:
> Few give Examples, whilst they give Advice,
> Or tho' they scourge the vicious, shun the Vice.   (p. [1])

This is then illustrated by the lives and writings of Horace, Seneca, and Sallust. When the author arrives at Pope, he charges him, oddly enough, with usury:

A2   How many Authors of this Contrast kind
> In ev'ry Age, and ev'ry Clime we find.
> Thus scribbling *P—* who *Peter* never spares,
> Feeds on extortious Interest from young Heirs:
> And whilst he made Old *S[e]lkerk*'s Bows his Sport,
> Dawb'd minor Courtiers, of a minor Court.   (pp. 4–5)

I am unable to explain the reference to 'Selkerk's Bows'.

The long passage on Pope's malice and deformity is remarkably vicious:

34   He rails at Lies, and yet for half a Crown,
> Coins and disperses Lies thro' all the Town:
> Of his own Crimes the Innocent accuses,
> And those who clubb'd to make him eat, abuses.
> But whilst such Features in his Works we trace,
> And Gifts like these his happy Genius grace;
> Let none his haggard Face, or Mountain Back,

The Object of mistaken Satire make;
Faults which the best of Men, by Nature curs'd,
May chance to share in common with the worst.
In Vengeance for his Insults on Mankind,
Let those who blame, some truer Blemish find,
And lash that worse Deformity, his Mind.

      .   .   .

That Mind so suited to its vile Abode,
The Temple so adapted to the God,
It seems the Counterpart by Heav'n design'd
A Symbol and a Warning to Mankind:
As at some Door we find hung out a Sign,
Type of the Monster to be found within.

      .   .   .

Then let him boast that honourable Crime,
Of making those who fear not God, fear him;
When the great Honour of that Boast is such
That Hornets and Mad Dogs may boast as much.
Such is th' Injustice of his daily Theme,
And such the Lust that breaks his nightly Dream;
That vestal Fire of undecaying Hate,
Which Time's cold Tide itself can ne'er abate,
But like *Domitian*, with a murd'rous Will,
Rather than nothing, Flies he likes to kill.
And in his Closet stabs some obscure Name.   (pp. 5–7)

August 31, 1742 (*Daily Post*, August 31, 1742)

Sawney and Colley, A Poetical Dialogue: Occasioned by A Late
Letter From The Laureat of St. James's, To The Homer of
Twickenham. Something in the Manner of Dr. Swift.—Par No-
bile Fratrum. / Strange! that such dire Contest should be, /
'Twixt Tweedledum and Tweedledee! London: Printed for
J. H. in Sword and Buckler Court, on Ludgate-Hill. (Price One
Shilling.)

Quarto in half-sheets.
One unsigned leaf, A–E², one unsigned leaf.
[2 pp.], [1]–21 pp., [22] blank.

The British Museum copy I have used for my text is conveniently reproduced in *Sawney and Colley (1742), and other Pope Pamphlets*, ed. W. Powell Jones, The Augustan Reprint Society, No. 83 (Los Angeles, 1960).

This pamphlet on the Pope–Cibber quarrel was prompted by Cibber's *A Letter From Mr. Cibber, To Mr. Pope*, 1742. Cibber is attacked here as well as Pope, but Pope comes in for much the greater share of abuse.

works: A. Homer; B. *First Psalm*; C. *Three Hours after Marriage*; D. Pope's edition of Shakespeare; E. *Dunciad*; F. *Epistle to Burlington*; G. *Sat.* II. i; H. *Essay on Man*; J. *Sober Advice*; K. *Of the Characters of Women*; L. Pope's letters.

charges: 1. Savage is Pope's spy; 2. Pope's Homer translated from Dacier; 3. Pope ungrateful to Chandos; 4. Pope a friend of Bolingbroke; 5. Pope sexually inadequate and deformed; 6. Pope's mother a whore at heart, and Pope illegitimate; 7. Martha Blount is Pope's mistress; 8. Pope sells same poem several times.

1   Pope is brought Cibber's letter by Setter, identified in a note as 'A notorious poetical Pander, or Jack-call, to Sawney, which provides *Savage* Provender for that *roaring Lyon*' (p. 2); Richard Savage is clearly meant.

'Cold Horrors' thrill Pope's veins when he comes on the Tom-tit episode:

> Nay, he be-paw'd himself – and then,
> Wiping, in fierce tho' sh—ten Mien,
> With Colley's Sheets, his *Bumkin* clean,   (p. 2)

he rushes off to Cibber.

AE   Cibber is sorry now he rescued Pope:

> I meant it well for Homer's Sake,
> But oft lament my dire Mistake.
> Could Homer from Elysium steal
> O! how he'd curse both Hands and Heel.
>   *Much Thanks* to *France*, but *none* to *Greece*,
>   A *patch'd, vamp'd, old, reviv'd, new Piece*,
>   [cf. *Dunciad* A, i. 237–8]

2   *Translation* from Dacier's *Translation*,
         A Homer of his *own* Creation

         .   .   .

         A purling Riv'let void of Oar;
         Not the strong Stream the *Grecian* flows,

       Whose Depth with Golden Bullion glows:
       In short, poor HOMER, in thy Wit,
       Is dwindled to a mere TOM-TIT.   (pp. 13–14)

Pope 'clubb'd in that damn'd *Farce* Obscene', *Three Hours after Marriage* (p. 20).

       Twas you made [1]DAVID talk low *Smut*,
       And [2]sober HORACE sent to *rut*.

       [1] Alluding to an infamous, obscene Parody on the *first Psalm*, affirmed to be written by the *pious* SAWNEY.
       [2] To another Performance of the same delicate and virtuous Bard ... (p. 20)

Pope has cheated the town with his Shakespeare:

       SAWNEY took in an immense Subscription, for a new and, as he set, [*sic*] forth, more correct Edition of *Shakespear*; but it appear'd, upon its Publication, that the Chief he had done in it was giving the *Publisher* Liberty to prefix his Name in the Title-page ... (p. 17, n.)

Pope was ungrateful to Chandos:

       He, at whose Table thou wer't fed,
       Lampoon'd for *filling Thee with Bread*.   (p. 14)

Sat. II. i. 121 is here turned against Bolingbroke:

       Saw. *Fair Virtue, and her Friend are mine*,
       Col. Yes!—virtuous B[o]L[ING]B[RO]KE is thine.   (p. 15)

The *Essay on Man* and Bolingbroke are criticized together:

       You, and your *God-A'mighty*, club
       Your uncreating Pates, and dub
       Poor mortal MAN *a Thing of Nought*,
       Just what the *pamper'd Gander* thought,
       And bravely prove, in *Reason's Spite*,
       That Right is *wrong*, and Wrong is *right*.   (p. 10)

Of the Characters of Women, l. 216, provokes a passage of unusual abusiveness:

       Then *Women* felt your righteous Fury,
       Hung all at once without a Jury;

       .   .   .

       For, *ev'ry Woman*, you are sure,
       Is, in her *Heart*, a *very Whore*.
       'Troth, TIT-TE, I'll allow this much,
       You never knew *Woman* but was *such*.
       For who, except a venal *Punkey*,
       That car'd not whether Man or *Monkey*,

> But set to Sale her *Titillation*,
> For Bread, not carnal Recreation,
> Would suffer Thee, *small* Friend, to come
> Within ten Foot of her *Fore-bum*? (pp. 10–11)

The innuendo is clear from earlier references:

> At length he [Pope] light at COLLEY's Door,
> And rapp'd for Entrance—but, before,
> Lugg'd out, and shook his *pigmy Oar*. (p. 3)

> Saw. 'Tis well, you'll see me draw my *Quill*.
> Col. Oh! Sir, I've seen your *Quill* before,
> So did your *Lord*, and eke your *Whore*;
> But 'twas so *very, very small*,
> I trust, it holds but little *Gall*. (p. 6)

K6   For the only time, I think, in the pamphlet attacks, Pope's mother is abused:

> But, SAWNEY, if thy Maxim's true!
> Let's see how well 'twill fit on you:
> What think'st thou, then, of thy own *Mammy*,
> ¹'Bout whom thou talk'st, and talk'st so?—Damn ye?
> She had the *like at Heart*, no doubt;
> If so, *'Gad, split me*! it would out;
> No Woman ever wish'd *that same*,
> But got, by Hook or Crook, her Aim:
> So, SAWNEY, Thou'rt, perhaps, the Spawn,
> Not of thy good Old *Name-sake* gone,
> But of some *Serpent*-JESUIT,
> Or other petulant TOM-TIT. (pp. 11–12)

¹ *Vide* his *Letters, &c.* where he is perpetually TRUMPETTING forth his *filial Piety* to his *Mamma*, and the many Virtues and Excellencies of that good old Lady, whilst at the same Time he runs riot on all the rest of her Sex ... (p. 11, n.)

To refute Cibber's charge that Pope's carcase and '*Wezel* Face',

> Could only cold Contempt procure,
> And 'gainst thee barr'd the *fringed* Door:
> Hence all thy Libels on the *Fair*,
> Born not of *Hatred*, but *Despair*, (p. 12)

7   Pope appeals to *B*—. The note on this referring to Pope's letters to 'Mrs. B—t' makes clear that Martha Blount is intended (p. 13).

L8   Pope's intrigues over the publication of his letters is mentioned (pp. 17–19), and Pope's business methods are compared to Curll's:

SAWNEY and C[URL]L are said to be *Akin* by Trade, on Account of the former's having lately turned *Bookseller* to himself, selling all his own Pieces by Means of a *Publisher*, without giving his Bookseller any Share in them; and likewise practising, in all respects, the lowest Craft of the Trade, such as different Editions in various Forms, with perpetual Additions and improvements, so as to render all but the *last* worth nothing; and, by that Means, fooling many People into buying them several times over. (p. 19, n.)

December, 1742 (*London Magazine*)

The Blatant-Beast. A Poem. What is that Blatant-Beast? Then he reply'd. / It is a Monster bred of hellish Race, / Then answered he, which often hath annoy'd / Good Knights and Ladies true, and many else destroy'd. Spencer's Fairy Queen, Book VI. Canto I. No Might, no Greatness in Mortality / Can Censure 'scape: Back-wounding Calumny / The whitest Virtue strikes. What King so strong, / Can tye the Gall up in a sland'rous Tongue? Shakespear. London: Printed for J. Robinson, at the Golden Lyon in Ludgate-Street. MDCCXLII.

Folio.

[A]–C².

[2 pp.], [3]–12 pp.

Reprinted in my *Two Poems Against Pope*, The Augustan Reprint Society, No. 114 (Los Angeles, 1965).

WORKS: A. Homer; B. *First Psalm*; C. *Three Hours after Marriage*; D. Pope's edition of Shakespeare; E. Epitaphs on Shakespeare and Gay; F. *New Dunciad*.

CHARGES: 1. Pope deformed; 2. Pope venal; 3. Pope wrote his Homer on the backs of personal letters; 4. Pope rescued from a bawdy house by Cibber; 5. Pope's verse partly by Swift and Arbuthnot.

Almost an omnium gatherum of the charges against Pope. There is a certain fittingness in its appearance towards the end of our study. The first page leaves us in no doubt, with its forthright handling of the theme of personal deformity, of what is in store:

1

    If Beauty be the Subject of our Praise,
A rude, mishapen Lump Contempt must raise.
    When *Lucifer* with Angels held first Place,
Seraphic Beauty sparkled in his Face.
By Pride and Malice tempted to rebel,
Vengeance pursu'd him to the lowest Hell:
Not sulph'rous Lakes suffic'd, nor dreary Plains;
Deformity was join'd t'improve his Pains.
    Paint then the Person, and expose the Mind,
Who rails at others, to his own Faults blind.
Sly *Sancho*'s Paunch, meagre *Don Quixot*'s Love,
The Satyr and the Ridicule improve.   (pp. [3]–4)

The blatant beast is Pope, of course, not his libellers; the almost
insane shower of abuse recalls Dennis:

DEF

12

    The Blatant-Beast once more has broke his Chains,
Disperses Falshoods, and remorseless reigns.

.   .   .

    Distorted Elf! to Nature a Disgrace,
Thy Mind envenom'd pictur'd in thy Face;
Malice with Envy in thy Breast combines,
And in thy Visage grav'd those ghastly Lines.
Like Plagues, like Death thy ranc'rous Arrows fly,
At Good and Bad, at Friend and Enemy.
To thy own Breast recoils the erring Dart,
Corrupts thy Blood, and rankles in thy Heart.
There swell the Poisons which thy Breast distend,
And with the Load thy Mountain Shoulders bend.
Horrid to view! retire from human Sight,
Nor with thy Figure pregnant Dames affright.
Crawl thro' thy childish Grot, growl round thy Grove,
A Foe to Man, an Antidote to Love.
In Curses waste thy Time instead of Pray'r,
[1]And with thy Breath pollute the fragrant Air.
There doze o'er *Shakespear*; then thy Blunders sell
[2]At mighty Price; this Truth let *Tonson* tell.
Then frontless intimate, (oh perjur'd Bard!)
Thy Labours were bestow'd without Reward.
On that immortal Author wreak thy Spite,
[3]And on his Monument thy Nonsense write.   (pp. 4–5)

[1] It is surely allowable to treat a Man after this manner who abuses
all others and to make this just Reflexion, since in his new *Dunciad*

he not only calls *Mummius* a Fool, but uses this filthy Expression—
who stinks above the Ground. [*Dunciad* B, iv. 372]

² See this farther explained in the ingenious Dialogues of *Sawney*
and *Colley*.

³ Tho' he was informed that Wreck was improper, yet he was resolv'd it should be inscrib'd, because the Nonsense was in his Edition of *Shakespear*. (p. 5, n.)

Pope was, with several others, responsible for the Latin inscription on
the Shakespeare monument in Westminster Abbey; it does not seem
that he had anything to do with the lines from *The Tempest*, IV. i.
152–6, which were added several months later. These lines are given
in *Twick.* v. 268 and, in slightly different form, in *The Gentleman's
Magazine*, XI. 276. The last line reads, 'Leave not a wreck behind'.
Pope's version of the lines in both his 1725 and 1728 editions of Shakespeare (Griffith 149 and 210) does not commit the errors of the inscription and reads, 'Leave not a rack behind!' For the debate over
the Latin inscription see *Twick.* VI. 395–6 and *The Gentleman's Magazine*, XI. 105. The bantering note about the monument which begins
the *Dunciad in Four Books* may have been prompted by this passage in
The Blatant-Beast as well as by the comment of Theobald which
Sutherland refers to.

C   The old *Three Hours after Marriage* charge is repeated:
          Cibber shall foremost in thy Satyrs stand;
          His Plays succeed, and thine was justly damn'd.   (p. 6)
There is a curious objection to Pope's habit of using the backs of
letters for his poems:

3   Beware all ye, whom he as Friends carest,
          How ye entrust your Secrets to his Breast.
          ¹On Backs of Letters was his *Homer* wrote,
          All your Affairs disclos'd to save a Groat.
          He valu'd not to whom he gave Offence;
          He sav'd his Paper, tho' at your Expence.   (p. 6)

¹ When he sent his *Homer* to his Acquaintance for their Emendations, it was written on the Back of the Letters of his Correspon-
dents, whether of Business, Complement or Secrecy. A shameful
Instance of Avarice and Treachery! (p. 6, n.)

Pope ridicules the fathers of the Church, and the English universities.
F   Thy Muse, by *Virgil's* Harpies taught to write,
          Scatters her Ordure in her screaming Flight;
          Sacred Religion and her Priests defames,
          And against Monarchs saucily exclames.

¹The Fathers, of our Church the surest Guides,
As a poor Pack of Punsters she derides.
But chief O *Cam*! and *Isis*! dread her Frown,
Chain'd to the Footstool of the Goddess' Throne.

(pp. 6–7)

¹ *Vide* Notes on the new *Dunciad*. [B, iv. 247, n.] (p. 7, n.).

He attacks the *New Dunciad*, ll. 110–12, as well as Pope's epitaph on Gay.

BEF

B[e]ns[o]n abuse for raising *Milton*'s Bust,
And impiously molest learn'd *Johnston*'s Dust.
Religious, he the Psalms in *Latin* sung,
From hence the Malice of the Deist sprung.
While with a just Derision we survey,
The wretched Epitaph on poor *John Gay*.   (p. 8)

The Gay reference may be to 'Epitaph. On G—' (*Twick*. VI. 295–7) or to 'Epitaph on Mr. Gay' (*Twick*. VI. 349–52).

He includes a most unkind reference to Cibber's famous charge:

4

With Malice swoll'n, Pride, Envy, Avarice,
Ingratitude attends this Train to Vice.
Yet one remains untold; with Lust endu'd,
Behold the Fribler lab'ring to be lewd.
Kind *Cibber* interpos'd, forbad the Banns,
He'd peopled else this Isle with *Calibans*.   (p. 9)

Pope is avaricious:

2

Had *Peter*, *Charters* thee with Gold supply'd,
Peter and *Charters* had been deify'd.
But ev'ry Lord, each gen'rous Friend implore,
And by Subscriptions meanly swell thy Store.
When to the Town by sordid Int'rest led,
Mump for a Dinner, flatter for a Bed.
Then to thy Grot retire, indulge thy Spite,
And rail at those who for Subsistence write.   (pp. 8–9)

Arbuthnot and Swift are awarded a large share in Pope's work:

5

Thy Notes pedantic shall no more engage;
Arbuthnot's Wit enlivens not the Page.
Thy Muse, that Prostitute abandon'd Jade,
Now flounders in the Mire without *Swift*'s Aid.   (p. 7)

January 11, 1743 (*London Daily Post and General Advertiser*, Rogers)

[Cibber, Colley?] The Egotist: Or, Colley upon Cibber. Being His own Picture retouch'd, to so plain a Likeness, that no One, now, would have the Face to own it, But Himself. But one Stroke more, and That shall be my Last. Dryden. London, Printed: And Sold by W. Lewis in Russel-Street, Covent-Garden. M DCC XLIII. [Price One Shilling. [bracket not closed.]

8vo in half-sheets.

A–K⁴.

[4 pp.], [5]–78 pp., [2 pp.] blank.

On the authorship see De Witt C. Croissant, 'A Note on *The Egotist: Or, Colley upon Cibber*', *PQ*, III (1924), 76–7.

WORKS: A. Pope's *Letters*; B. *Dunciad in Four Books* (?).

Pope is probably glanced at in the Preface:

> *Self* is too sacred a Subject to be prophan'd; ... as well we might expect a Pope to jest upon his Infallibility, as a Satyrist to be the Subject of his own Ridicule! (A2r)

Almost all of this long bantering pamphlet in dialogue form between the Author (Cibber) and Frankly is devoted to an argument over Cibber's contention that satyrical libels ought never to be answered and to discussion of Cibber's conduct and vanity, but there are several clear references to the Pope–Cibber quarrel.

Cibber argues at some length against Frankly that the wise man will ignore all attacks on his character and reputation. Frankly objects that Cibber's practice has belied his doctrine, and Cibber grants that his letter to Pope, 'as far as doing an unnecessary thing is so', is 'an idle thing' (p. 21). Frankly doubts that Cibber will be able to persuade many people that in his desire to please his friends, his letter did not also intend to hurt his aggressor:

> *Auth.* Unless my keeping my Temper could make him lose his, I won't suppose I *have* hurt him: If I did him wrong I hurt myself, if Justice he has nothing to complain of; let Truth answer for herself then—what I did was by her Direction: In a word, I had no other way of turning the Jest upon my Ralliers [*sic*], than by getting the Publick to head it against them; in which I have so far succeeded that they are now, it seems, forced to be fond of a new Joke that is not come out yet.

> *Fran.* What do yo [*sic*] mean?
>
> *Auth.* Terrible Rods in Poetical Pickle for me, that are to give them a tickling Triumph!

The 'new Joke' is probably the *Dunciad in Four Books.* See *Twick.* v. xxxiv on the spurious proof sheet sent to Cibber.

A   There is probably a reference early in the pamphlet to Pope's famous intrigues with Curll over the publication of his letters. Cibber has some papers which he does not think worth printing. Frankly says his conscience is too nice. He should get them printed without his consent by having a third person sell them to '*Buckle* the Bookseller' without Cibber's consent. When the surreptitious edition comes out, he will then have an excuse for publishing a genuine edition, and be paid twice for the same copy (pp. 7–8).

February 15, 1743 (*Daily Post*, February 15, 1743)

Cibber, Colley. A Second Letter From Mr. Cibber To Mr. Pope. In Reply to some additional Verses in his Dunciad, which he has not yet publish'd. My old Friend wishes me well at the last I find. Vanbrugh's Aesop. London, Printed for A. Dodd, without Temple-Bar. 1743. [Price Three Pence]

Folio.
One unsigned leaf, B².
[2 pp.], 3–5 pp., [6] blank.

WORK: A. *Dunciad in Four Books.*

CHARGE: 1. Pope deformed.

Cibber, in this brief letter dated and signed, p. 5, '*From my easy Chair,* Feb. 13, 1742. COLLEY CIBBER.', says (see *Twick.* v. xxxiv) that he has lately received

A   an undoubted Copy of some new Lines, which in the next Edition of your *Dunciad,* now in the Press, you intend to honour my Name with. I take it for granted they were sent me by your own Direction, because I cannot imagine any other Person could be equally impatient to doe me that Sort of Favour. (p. 3)

The lines, which he quotes, are *Dunciad* B, i. 29–32:

> Close to those walls where Folly holds her throne,

And laughs to think Monroe would take her down,
Where o'er the gates, by his fam'd father's hand
Great Cibber's brazen, brainless brothers stand.

Cibber, reminding Pope that he had promised to have the last word (p. 3), points out that the statues were of stone, not brass, and gives what he says is Scriblerus's ingenious note on these lines:

The Criticks have disputed, whether these Images were of Brass, or two Blocks; let this be decided according as the Person related to them is judg'd to have the greater Share of Assurance or Stupidity. (p. 4)

Cibber objects to Pope's continual use of *brazen* and *brainless* for himself, says again that calling a man stupid does not make him so, and includes a little personal abuse:

... these Figures, upon the Gates of *Bedlam*, do not *stand* but *lye*. Do you observe, *Sir*? I say they are no more *upright* than you are when you *stand*, or write ... (p. 4)

He concludes with eight lines of verse. These end,

On me, thy Wit's so worn, so void of Smart;
I read, I yawn, and (by your leave too) *F—t*.   (p. 5)

February 21, 1743 (*Daily Post*, February 21, 1743)

Mr. P[O]PE's Picture in Miniature, But As Like as it can stare; A Poem: With Notes. Hic Niger est. Hor. London: Printed for G. Lion, near Ludgate-street. 1743. (Price Six-pence.)

Folio.
[A]–B².
[2 pp.], 3–7 pp., [8] blank.

WORKS: A. Atticus portrait; B. Pope's edition of Shakespeare; C. *Odyssey*; D. *Dunciad*; E. *Epistle to Burlington*; F. *Sat.* II. i; G. *Essay on Man*; H. *Epistle to Arbuthnot*.

CHARGES: 1. Pope attacked Bishop Hoadly gratuitously; 2. Pope ungrateful to Addison; 3. Pope traitorous and a friend of Bolingbroke; 4. Pope ungrateful to Chandos; 5. Pope encouraged Walter Harte to write a poem in Pope's praise; 6. Pope revised Spence's *Essay on Pope's Odyssey* to remove unfavourable criticism.

A poem of only 53 numbered lines, but a very comprehensive attack.

The first charge is the familiar one of malicious attacks on those who had never hurt him:

D I

> Whose venom'd Arrows still at random fly,
> The same let *Cibber*, or let *Hoadly* die.[1]
> The Bard perhaps provok'd his envious Quill;
> But when did *Hoadly* stoop to use him ill?[2]

> [1] It has by some been argued, that Mr. *P.* was led into his Censure on a Right Reverend Prelate, from not rightly understanding those Pieces, at which his Satire is pointed; while others of his Friends, more tender of his Reputation as a Man of Learning, have taken it for granted, that he never read them.
>
> [Pope's 'Censure' seems to be *Dunciad* A, ii. 368]

> [2] It has often been the Boast of Mr. *P.* that he was indeed resolv'd to keep close to the Menace of his Brother Poet, *Nemo me impune lacessit*, but that he never became an Enemy till he was provok'd. (p. 4)

A 2

There is the usual reproach of ingratitude to Addison who 'rais'd from Dust th' ungrateful Miscreant's Head' (p. 5), and an attack on the *Essay on Man* and *Sat.* II. i:

FG 3

> Unequal to the Task, who needs must aim
> To raise by *wild Philosophy* his Name;[1]
> Fond of new Paths, where Nature never trod,
> He blindly blunders thro' the Works of God.
> See o'er each Page a sacred Mist arise,
> Which Reason rarify'd to Smoak supplies:
> Yet that were little were his greatest Crime
> His vain Attempt to reason well in Rhyme.
> But if, unaw'd, He speaks his *Rebel Heart*,
> Spurns at the Throne, and takes *Sedition*'s Part,
> If his dear Self He as a Friend commends,
> To Virtue only, and to Virtue's Friends,
> Yet (what the Muse must blush but to rehearse)
> To treach'rous *S[t John]* dedicates his Verse.

> [1] Read the Essay on Man quite thro'. (p. 5)

B

Pope loaned 'his Name, without any other Labour than that of writing a Preface, to an incorrect and ill-judg'd Edition of *Shakespear*'s Works' ... (p. 6, n.).

The old Chandos story is revived:

EH 4

> If, *C[hando]s*, when thy Aid no more he needs,[1]
> His Satire thanks thee for thy past good Deeds.

> [1] ... The Satirist, asham'd of what he had done, (a very special

Instance of his Modesty) has been pleased flatly to deny that he intended the noble Peer as the Object of his Raillery. It is worth remarking, however, that he could not do this, without at the same time indulging his Spirit of Ingratitude, by endeavouring to persuade his Readers, that the utmost Obligation he was under to that noble Lord was a bare Subscription to his Translation of *Homer* [see *Epistle to Arbuthnot*, l. 375, n.]. He thinks, I suppose, that nothing can be an Obligation, but what is paid down in *Specie*. (p. 6)

The concluding lines of the poem attack Pope's relations with both Walter Harte and Joseph Spence in a parody of the Atticus lines:

If, as his Soul, or *Pride*, or Meanness sways,
Peers he insults, or flatters *Hart* for Praise;[1]
With saucy Censure other's Faults has shewn,
Yet poorly begg'd of *Spence* to spare his own;[2]
Who would not grieve if such a Man there be?
Weep then, O *Twick'nam*, for thy Bard is He. (pp. 6–7)

[1] This Gentleman, who in his younger Days shew'd an inkling for Poetry, was soon listed as a kind of Under-Trumpeter to Mr. *P.* Among other Poems he wrote one in Praise of his Master, which that Poet, having first modell'd it to his own liking, enduc'd the Youngster to make public, and then himself quoted it in his Preface to the Dunciad, among the *Testimonia* of his own good Character [*Twick.* v. 36]. (p. 6)

Pope, according to Harte, had corrected 'with his own hand' every page of his *Poems on Several Occasions*, 1727; it contains complimentary verse to Pope (*Corr.* II. 429–30, n.4).

[2] This learned and ingenious Critick wrote an Essay on Mr. *P*'s Translation of the *Odyssey*; the first Volume of which answered exactly to the Design specified in the Title-Page, of remarking the Beauties and Blemishes of that Work. When this Volume was made publick, Mr. *P.* alarm'd at the many enormous Blunders pointed out by this Author, sent immediately an Invitation to him, expressing an earnest Desire of waiting on him at *Twick'nam*; where, after having used all the Art he was Master of to ingratiate himself, ... he prevail'd upon his Guest to leave the Manuscript Copy of the second Volume in his Hands; which having obtain'd, he made such Remarks upon it as he thought might best answer his own Purposes, and then remitting it to the Author, entreated him in almost every Page, to omit such Strokes of Criticism as he look'd upon to be the most *just*, and of consequence the most offensive to himself ... The Author, in short, complied with his Request, and by that Means, he publishing the second Volume quite alter'd from what it was, when first deliver'd into Mr. *P*'s Hands, the Work itself sunk greatly

in its Reputation, and the learned World lost the Completion of a most ingenious Undertaking. (p. 7)

Pope 'revised the MS. of the last two dialogues [of the *Essay on Pope's Odyssey*], but without excessive pruning of adverse comment' (*Corr.* II. 379, n.1).

March 3, 1743 (*London Daily Post*, Rogers)

[Henley, John.] Why How now, Gossip Pope? Or The Sweet Singing-Bird of Parnassus taken out of its pretty Cage to be roasted: In one short Epistle (Preparatory to a Criticism on his Writings) to that Darling of the Demy-wits, and Minion of the Minor Criticks. Exposing the Malice Wickedness and Vanity of his Aspersions on J.H. in That Monument of His Own Misery and Spleen, the Dunciad: An siquis atro Dente me petiverit / Inultus ut flebo Puer? Hor. The Second Edition. London: Printed in 1736. Reprinted in 1743, for J. Roberts in Warwick Lane [Price Four-pence.]

8vo in half-sheets.
One unsigned leaf, A–B⁴.
[2 pp.], [1]–16 pp.

I have been unable to locate a copy of the 1736 'edition' mentioned on the title-page.

WORKS: A. Homer; B. *First Psalm*; C. *Dunciad*; D. *Essay on Man*

CHARGES: 1. Pope deformed; 2. Pope a Catholic; 3. Savage a spy for Pope; 4. Pope made wealthy by the Homer subscription; 5. Pope's language is Billingsgate.

Henley is replying in vituperative and heavy-handed prose to Pope's inclusion of him in the *Dunciad* (A, iii. 195–208 and n.).

CD   ... It would be *ridiculous* to be *serious* to *you* about *Injury* and *Satisfaction*, who are exalted by your Genius and Fame above all *right Sense*, and *moral Virtue*, those Regards are only fit for the *Gentlemen of the Dunciad, not the Author*: Let *the Dull* keep their Understanding and Integrity to themselves, Mr. POPE is *above both*; in *him, whatever is, is right*: as his *Catholick Epistles* on MAN divinely *sing* ... (p. 2)

Most of his attention is given to refuting Pope's account of him (see *Twick.* v. 173–4, n.); he denies that he attacked Pope first and abuses at once Pope's deformity and his religion:

2   You shrewdly call *the Orator this Person,* and *this extraordinary Person*: any *Spectator* may judge, whose PERSON is more EXTRAORDINARY, Mr. HENLEY's or Mr. POPE's … If there be such another *grinning Lover of Mischief in the World,* in whom *Nature has mimicked and mocked* the *Species*: the MONKEY's *Paw* of a low Faction, one that can only use *the Old Woman's Weapon of malicious Gossiping, venomous Scandal,* and *lying Chit-chat,* like a TRUE SON of an impudent WHORE of BABYLON, famous these 1700 Years for *bespattering, stripping,* and *murdering* … (p. 4)

Savage, he claims,

3   was entertain'd by you to give you Tittle-tattle for Bread, of my self and others; fit Company, for you and your Associates are *all half-hanged,* and only want a *Burlesque-Psalm,* like that *written by yourself,* for a *Peroration.* (p. 6)

See the passage on Savage in *The Hyp Doctor* (*Twick.* v. xxvi).

He includes a hit at the Homer:

4   In the Fling, that I wrote for Booksellers, is imply'd an Imputation on my Fortune, as to which, my Education was better than your's, and not on Charity … nor on *Subscription,* which is the *Basis* of your *Toy-Shop* at *Twickenham* … (p. 7)

He is most eloquent on Pope's Catholicism:

2   A *Gilt Tub* [A, ii. 2] is a sparkling Metaphor: you call the Pulpit of *a Dissenter, a Tub,* if so, *your Priest,* to whom you ought to *confess your Dunciad* as a *mortal Sin,* is entitled to your *Tale of a Tub,* for *Papists* are *all Dissenters in England,* and was the Government as sharp as you, the Priests would *be hang'd by the Statute* …

It is odd, that one, who has used Men so cavalierly, and has dar'd to appear in the House of L— and in other Courts, to *claim Rights* in a Country, where, by Law, and Reason he *ought to have no Right at all,* has not rouz'd *the Execution of the Penal Laws,* as an Answer to *the Persecution of his Dunciad* … (p. 3)

The *Dunciad* is simply Billingsgate:

5   Your *whole Piece* is only refining on the low Jests of *Porters* and *Fish-Women, as you live by the Water-side*; or dressing the *insolent Scurrility* of *Link-Boys* and *Hackney-Coachmen* in something (not much) genteeler Language … (p. 16)

January 19, 1744 (*London Daily Post and General Advertiser*, Rogers)

Cibber, Colley. Another Occasional Letter From Mr. Cibber To Mr. Pope. Wherein The New Hero's Preferment to his Throne, in the Dunciad, seems not to be Accepted. And the Author of that Poem His more rightful Claim to it, is Asserted. With An Expostulatory Address to the Reverend Mr. W. W[arburto]n, Author of the new Preface, and Adviser in the curious Improvements of that Satire. By Mr. Colley Cibber.—Remember Sauney's Fate! / Bang'd by the Blockhead, whom he strove to beat. Parodie on Lord Roscommon. London, Printed: And Sold by W. Lewis in Russel-Street, Covent-Garden. M DCC XLIV. [Price One Shilling. [bracket not closed.]

8vo in half-sheets.
Three unsigned leaves, B–G⁴.
[2 pp.], [5]–56 pp.

Another edition, dated [1744] in the *CBEL*, title-page as above, but with the imprint: 'Glasgow: Printed for W. Macpharson'.

Half-title: A Letter From Cibber to Pope. [Price One Shilling.]

8vo in half-sheets.
Four unsigned leaves, C–H⁴, C2 signed B2.
[4 pp.], [5]–56 pp.

There was also, according to the *CBEL*, an edition in 1777 which I have not located.

WORKS: A. *What D'Ye Call It*; B. *Three Hours after Marriage*; C. Pope's edition of Shakespeare; D. *Dunciad in Four Books*.

CHARGES: 1. Cibber rescued Pope from a bawdy house; 2. Pope has a venereal disease.

The last of the Cibber attacks, written in the same bantering and occasionally amusing vein. The title suggests one of his main points – Pope is himself the King of the Dunces.

He speculates on the cause of the new *Dunciad*:

D   To say, then, that you did it, with an eye to your getting off another Edition of your Book, by making more ample mention of Me in it, (whatever small Probability it may carry) that, I doubt, you will not care to own, and will, again, call it Vanity,

in me, to suppose had the least Temptation in it ... (p. 14)
He sees the new edition, of course, as an answer to his first letter,

> ... for I cannot but say, that thy low Invention of making the
> Laureat the new Hero of thy *Dunciad*, without producing the
> least Evidence of his Pretence to the Title, is but a wretched
> Reply to his Letter, and leaves him but the same Laughing-
> Fellow he was before thy Weakness was angry with him ...
>
> (pp. 42–3)

He criticizes, as many have done since, the way Pope has substituted
Cibber without sufficiently altering some details of the poem:

> The bare Change of one Name for another is his whole Expence
> of Thought about it! The Materials, and Furniture of the
> Character, even to the same Books, in his Study (which he
> knew would never be looked into) stand just in their old Places!
>
> (p. 29)

D   His most detailed charges concern 'Ricardus Aristarchus Of The
Hero of the Poem' and its attempt to establish Cibber's vanity, impudence, and debauchery. He first shows that Pope in the paragraph
on Cibber's vanity (*Twick.* v. 257) has deliberately misquoted from
his *Apology*, and as to his 'glorying in those *Vices*', 'To call the Confes-
sion of his *Follies* a Glorying in his *Vices*, is the insolent Logick of a
Jesuit' (p. 47).

The charge of impudence he finds equally ill-founded in '*His daring
Figure in Speech, which is taken from the Name of God!*' [*Twick.* v. 258]
(p. 48).

> All the Meaning, then, we can pick out of this Abortive Para-
> graph is—That he is a Swearer— ... But thou shouldst con-
> sider that his Title to the Throne thou hast given him, is not
> founded on his *Wickedness*, but his *Stupidity*! And farther, that
> Swearing is a Sin, which Men of quick Spirits are more apt to
> be guilty of than *Blockheads*! (p. 48)

The proof of gentle love [*Twick.* v. 258], Cibber says, is in 'That
the Man is, sure enough Hero, who has his Lady at fourscore' (p. 50).

> Even thou thy self, my little *Tom Tit*, I suspect wouldst be glad
> of the same Reproof, with the Power of deserving it ... Is a hale,
> or wanton Constitution (even at Four-score, if thou wilt [)]
> —Any Proof of the Mud in his Brain? Or are Vice, and Dullness
> synonimous Terms? (p. 50)

This leads Cibber to bring up again the 'Tom-tit episode', which

> has hurt thee more, and lain deeper in thy Mind, than all the
> severer Attacks he has made upon thy Character. Now, there,

I must own, thou seemest to me, to have been quite uneasy, in the wrong Place! For, sure, to have been exposed, as a *bad Man*, ought to have given thee thrice the Concern, of being shewn a *ridiculous Lover*! ... Thy taking it, then, so bitterly to heart, to have been compared to so pretty a little Creature, as a TOM-TIT, is a Weakness, I am ashamed to think thou wert capable of! Yet this, I am told is the unpardonable Provocation, which has once more, and so particularly, inflamed thee! ... What now restrains him, from once more reminding thee of the former friendly Office he did thee, when in thy dangerous Deed of Darkness, crawling on the Bosom of thy dear Damsel, he gently, with a Finger and a Thumb, picked off thy small round Body, by thy long Legs, like a Spider, making Love in a Cobweb; why, I say, might not such a human Insect, such a dismal Devil of a *Dunce* in Love, make as proper a Figure on the Throne of Stupidity, as the more wholesome Sinner with *his Lady at Fourscore?*

(pp. 51–2)

He then makes a very unpleasant charge indeed. Cibber has no complaints to make of his former abuse of love,

2   a Happiness I do not hear thou hast yet arrived at; for by the inadvertent Commiseration of thy Health which lately escap'd from a Person of Honour in my Hearing we are afraid, that if the earthen Receiver on thy Night-table could speak, it might tell us, by how slow a Distilment of Drop by Drop (passing through the *Strainers* of a Stricture [a reference to the *certain strainers* of the *Essay on Man*, ii. 189, mentioned by Aristarchus, *Twick.* v. 258]) thy Tears of Penitence, to this Hour fall from thee! (pp. 52–3)

A B   Cibber includes a glance at Pope's plays. Why, he asks, does Pope insist as regarding as a rival, every man

that meets with Success, though but in a single Play! a Work, which by thy having so dirtily and often dabbled in, it is plain thou never hadst an equal Courage, alone, and unassisted, to undertake. (p. 44)

D   The middle section of the pamphlet is addressed 'To The Supposed Author of the Preface to Mr. Pope's last Edition of his Dunciad, in Quarto, published October the 29th, 1743', pp. 20–40, dated, p. 40, 'December *the 20th*, 1743', and signed 'C. Cibber'. Most of this deals with Theobald, but there are inevitably attacks on Pope. He quotes *Dunciad* B, ii. 352 and 355–8, and discourses at length (pp. 34–9) on what he considers the licence of this attack on the Church. He ridi-

cules Warburton's note which insists that the passage must be understood in a 'confined sense', pointing out that an Army can hardly
be called 'confined' (p. 34). Apropos of Warburton's mention of those
clergy who have aspired to interfere in the government, he does not
miss the opportunity to allude clearly to Pope's friendship with Atterbury (pp. 35–6).

He has a spirited summary of the Pope–Warburton friendship:

c   No one sure that knows how a Clergyman ought to employ his
        Time, will wonder I should be a little surprised, though not
        totally displeased, to hear, that the very Person, who had
        so judiciously assisted Mr. *Tibbald* in his Edition of *Shakespear*
        (wherein the idle Guesses and Errors of Mr. *Pope*, in the same
        Undertaking, are so justly exposed and refuted) should now,
        almost in the same Breath, blow Hot and Cold, and enter into
        so unexpectedly an Alliance with Mr. *Pope*, whose Labours he
        had so unluckily disgraced! ... No Comedy ever concluded
        with so intire Satisfaction on all Sides! *Pope* pardons you! You
        forgive *Pope*! *Tibbald* is released! and *Colley* the Coxcomb is the
        only ridiculous Person to the End of the Piece! (pp. 27–8)

APPENDIXES

APPENDIX A

Pamphlets which I have been unable to locate

The Pope-ish Controversy compleat. Prose, i. cix, reprints the advertisement for this in *The Daily Post,* April 12, 1720, but dismisses it as a 'phantom publication'. Straus, p. 264, also questions its existence. It was advertised again in *The St James's Evening Post,* July 22, 1729 (Straus, p. 290), and in *The Monthly Chronicle* for the same date, but no copy has been located. It was advertised again by Curll in his book-list at the end of *Miscellanies In Prose and Verse, By the Honourable Lady Margaret Pennyman* ... *1740,* where the contents are listed as *The Progress of Dulness, The Popiad, The Curliad, The Twickenham Hotch-Potch, The Female Dunciad,* and Curll's *Complete Key To The Dunciad.* Again, no copy is known.

1726

Jo. Hervey. *A Collection of Miscellany Poems* ... Edinburgh, 1726. Accuses Pope of incompetence, p. 8 (Sherburn, p. 265, n.1).

1731

The Monthly Chronicle lists for December 1731 *A Petition to Pope, from several Noblemen and Gentlemen of great Estates, in behalf of themselves and many Thousands of Gardeners, Builders, Bricklayers, Masons, Carpenters,* &c *humbly requesting that (during his Stay in* England*) he will be pleas'd to lay aside his Supremacy and Infallibility. Sold by the Booksellers of* London *and* Westminster. *pr. 1* s. Was it ever published?

1732

A Letter to a Noble Lord, on the Conduct of Mr. Pope, in first defaming a Great Man, and next in abusing the Town for their Resentment of the Libel. John Butt, ' "A Master Key to Popery" ', *Pope and his Contemporaries* (Oxford, 1949), p. 43, notes this as advertised for publication in the last week of January, 1732.

1733

March, 1733 (*London Magazine*). *Sappho to Adonis, after the manner of Ovid.* Popiana?

1736

London Evening Post, May 20, 1736. *The Law of Liberty and Property; or a New Year's Gift for Mr. Pope. Wherein those between Men and Women are*

particularly recited, relating to double Marriages, Stealing Heiresses, Rapes, Sodomy, &c., by Giles Jacob, Gent. 2s. (Straus, p. 302). Straus is unable to identify the volume. It was advertised at least four or five more times in succeeding months and appears again in the Curll book-list at the end of *Miscellanies In Prose and Verse, By the Honourable Lady Margaret Pennyman* ... 1740.

1739

Daily Advertiser, June 13, 1739. Ayre, William. *Truth* ... *Epistle the Second.* Was it ever published?

APPENDIX B

Lists of Popiana hitherto available (chiefly those in Rogers and in the *CBEL*) give not only attacks on Pope but defences of Pope and his satire, imitations of his style, parodies, etc. In order to help the reader use these lists more easily I give here titles and brief descriptions of pamphlets in those lists which are not, but which from their titles alone might well seem to be, attacks on Pope. I have excluded all works by the friends and epigoni of Pope: Bramston, Dodsley, Harte, Lyttelton, Mallet, Miller, Savage, Warburton, Whitehead, and Young, as well as the pamphlets and articles of Fielding and Samuel Johnson.

April 13, 1733 (*Grub-Street Journal*, April 19, 1733)

Advice To Sappho. Occasioned by her Verses on the Imitator Of The First Satire Of The Second Book of Horace. By a Gentlewoman. London: Printed for the Authoress, near White's Chocolate-House; and sold by J. Roberts, in Warwick-Lane. M.DCC.XXXIII. [Price Six-Pence.]

Attacks Lady Mary for her abuse of Pope, urges her to do Pope justice, and then pleads with Lady Mary to reform her character.

1737

[Beach, Thomas.] Eugenio: Or, Virtuous and Happy Life. A Poem. Inscrib'd to Mr. Pope. [One line Latin.] London: Printed for R. Dodsley, in Pall-mall. M.DCC.XXXVII. [Price One Shilling.]

A flattering invocation to Pope at the beginning and some obvious indebtedness to the *Essay on Man*.

1738

Bickerstaff the Younger [pseud.] August The Second, One Thousand Seven Hundred and Thirty Eight. A Prediction; In the Manner of Many. By Bickerstaff The Younger. [Eight lines from *Hudibras*.] London: Printed for T. Cooper, at the Globe in Pater-Noster-Row. MDCCXXXVIII. Price Sixpence.

A dull political satire which opens with several neutral references, pp. 3–4, to Pope's *One Thousand Seven Hundred and Thirty Eight*.

August 3, 1742 (*Daily Post*, August 3, 1742)

A Blast upon Bays; Or, A New Lick at The Laureat. Containing, Remarks upon a Late Tatling Performance, entitled, A Letter from Mr. Cibber to Mr. Pope, &c. And lo there appeared an Old Woman! Vide the Letter throughout. London: Printed for T. Robbins in Fleet-street, and sold at all the Booksellers and Pamphlet-Shops in Town and Country. 1742 [Price Sixpence.]

The second edition, which Rogers was unable to locate, has the same

title-page with 'The Second Edition' inserted before the imprint. The third edition was included in *Lick upon Lick* . . . 1744.

A defence of Pope against Cibber. Ault in *Prose*, i. cxxiii, attributed this to Pope, promising to give his evidence in the second volume.

1714

Burnet, Thomas. A Second Tale of a Tub.

See *Letters of Thomas Burnet*, pp. 306–7, for a full description. I have been unable to discover in it any references to Pope at all, and do not understand its inclusion in Griffith's list of Popiana in the *CBEL*.

1737

The Contrast To The Man of Honour. Read, Judge, Try. Quacks Bill. London: Printed for J. Morgan in the Strand. 1737.

A defence of Walpole. Listed as Popiana in the catalogue of the Dyce Collection, but the only Pope reference is the quotation of *Sat.* ii. i. 121, which is footnoted, 'This line I think I have read in Mr. *Pope*'s Works' (p. 10, n.).

June, 1733 (*Gentleman's Magazine*)

The Court Dunciad. Inscrib'd to the Honourable Mrs Fitz—ms. [Two lines of verse.] London: Printed for J. Irons, and sold at the Pamphlet-Shops of London and Westminster. 1733. [Price 1 s.]

Listed in Rogers as unlocated. Nothing in the volume is Popiana; the title-piece, typical of the rest of the book, is a brief story about Alexis and his seven mistresses, full of indecencies.

1734

The Court Monkies. Inscrib'd to Mr. Pope. [Two lines of verse.] [Price (with the Copper-Plate) One Shilling. London: Printed and sold by J. Dormer, at the Printing-Office, the Green Door, in Black and White Court in the Old Bailey. M.DCC.XXXIV.

Listed in the *BM Cat. sub* Popiana, but the only Pope reference is on the title-page. A political satire on the court and politicians, closing with praise of Pulteney. Illinois.

August, 1737 (*Gentleman's Magazine*)

[Dale, Thomas?] An Epistle To Alexander Pope, Esq; From South Carolina. [Three lines Latin.] London: Printed for J. Brindley, Bookseller to his Royal Highness the Prince of Wales, at the King's-Arms in New Bond-street; and C. Corbett, at Addison's-Head, over-against St. Dunstan's-Church, Fleetstreet. MDCCXXXVII.

Tentatively attributed to Thomas Dale in the *CBEL*. Praise of Pope and defence of his satire. See Austin Warren, 'To Mr. Pope: Epistles from America', *PMLA*, XLVIII (1933), 61–73, where, however, no proof is offered that the poem was genuinely written from South Carolina. Texas.

March 31, 1736 (*London Daily Post and General Advertiser*, Rogers)

Divine Wisdom And Providence; An Essay. Occasion'd by the Essay on Man. London: Printed by J. Huggonson, and sold by J. Roberts, at the Oxford Arms in Warwick-lane. MDCCXXXVI. (Price One Shilling.)

A second edition, corrected, was announced in *The London Evening Post*, April 19, 1737, and a third edition in *The Weekly Miscellany*, September 22, 1739 (Rogers, p. 147). I have not seen either of these. The title-page of the second edition states that the poem was written by 'Mr. Bridges'. See Rogers, p. 95, n.7.

The Preface makes clear that this is not in any sense a personal attack on Pope but an attempt to refute certain ideas or implications in the *Essay on Man*. The poem itself, with its long, learned notes, is not despicable; it is an attack on the idea of fitness, arguing that Good, not Variety, is Heaven's great end (see p. 14). Rogers, p. 95, would attribute to the influence of the poem *Ep*. II. ii. 280–3, where Pope affirms his belief in free will.

March 27, 1739 (*London Daily Post*, Rogers)

[Dudgeon, William.] A View Of The Necessitarian or Best Scheme: Freed From The Objections of M. Crousaz, in his Examination of Mr. Pope's Essay on Man. [Seven lines of prose.] London: Printed for T. Cooper, at the Globe in Paternoster-Row. 1739.

An answer to Crousaz's *Examen*; the *Essay on Man* is quoted twice, p. 19, pp. 21–2, but Pope is not mentioned by name.

March, 1739 (*Gentleman's Magazine*)

Epidemical Madness: A Poem In Imitation of Horace. [One line Greek.] London: Printed for J. Brindley, Bookseller to his Royal Highness the Prince of Wales, in New-Bond-Street; and sold by Mrs. Dodd, at the Peacock without Temple-Bar, and the Booksellers of London and Westminster, 1739. [Price One Shilling.]

An imitation of the *Epilogue to the Satires*.

March 14, 1734 (*Grub-Street Journal*, March 14, 1734)

An Epistle From A Gentleman at Twickenham, To A Nobleman at St. James's. Occasion'd by an Epistle From A Nobleman, To A Doctor of Divinity. [Four lines of verse.] London: Printed for William Guess, near Temple-Bar, and Sold at the Pamphlet-Shops. [Price Six-Pence.]

An attack on Hervey, pretending to be by Pope.

January 29, 1732 (*Daily Post*, January 29, 1732)

An Epistle To Mr. Pope. London: Printed for H. Whittridge, under the Royal Exchange. MDCCXXXII. Price 6d.

Mr. Pope's Literary Correspondence, II. 39–40, prints a brief poem 'To the Author of an Epistle to Mr Pope; Occasion'd by his Epistle to the Earl of Burlington'; a note tells us the *Epistle* was printed in folio in 1732 and gives the author's name as 'Mr. *Jos. Turner*' (II. 39, n.). The present pamphlet is probably the one in question. It is a defence of Pope and an attack on Welsted. But see Rogers, p. 153, who lists the Turner poem as unlocated.

1735

An Epistle To the Author of the Essay On Reason. [One line Latin.] London: Printed for T. Cooper, in Pater-Noster-Row. M.DCC.XXXV.

An attack only on Walter Harte's *Essay on Reason*. Illinois.

1717

An Essay On The Poets. [One line Latin.] London: Printed for
Tho. Harbin, and Sold by J. Morphew near Stationers-Hall, and
N. Dodd without Temple-Bar. 1717.

Listed by Sherburn in 'The Fortunes and Misfortunes of *Three Hours
After Marriage*', *MP*, xxiv (1926–7), 91–109, as unlocated and possibly containing references to that play. It contains, however, no Pope
references. Chicago.

1714

Fiddes, Richard. A Prefatory Epistle Concerning Some Remarks
to be published on Homer's Iliad. Occasioned by The Proposals
of Mr. Pope towards a new English Version of that Poem. To the
Reverend Dr. Swift, Dean of St. Patrick's. By Richard Fiddes,
B.D. Chaplain to the Right Honourable the Earl of Oxford.
[One line Greek.] London: Printed for John Wyat, at the Rose,
and Henry Clements, at the Half-Moon in St. Paul's Church-
yard. 1714.

It contains, pp. 9–10, in a passage too long to quote here, a flattering
reference to the *Essay on Criticism* and Pope's expected translation of
Homer. British Museum.

November–December, 1733 (Rogers)

Flavia To Fanny, An Eipstle [*sic*]. From a Peerless Poetess, to a
Peerless P— in immortal Dogrill. Occasioned by a late Epistle
from Fanny to her Governess. [Sixteen lines of verse.] London:
Printed for T. Reynolds, in the Strand, and Sold by the Booksellers of London and Westminster. (Price 6d,) [*sic*.]

A foolish poem attacking Hervey for his *An Epistle From A Nobleman*,
1733.

1726

[Gordon, Thomas.] A Learned Dissertation On Dumpling; Its
Dignity, Antiquity, and Excellence. With a Word upon Pudding.
And Many other Useful Discoveries, of great Benefit to the Pub-
lick. [Five lines Latin — Maeb. de Fartophagis.] The Second

Edition. London, Printed for J. Roberts in the Oxford-Arms-
Passage, Warwick-lane; and Sold by the Booksellers of London
and Westminster. 1726. [Price 6 d.]

In no sense an attack on Pope. Listed under Popiana in the *BM Cat.*
because it contains, pp. 26–9, 'Namby Pamby: Or, A Panegyric on
the New Versification address'd to A— P— Esq;', a coarse attack on
Ambrose Philips.

The *BM Cat.* records a fifth edition, 1726, and a seventh, 1727 (Yale
also has the seventh).

April 17, 1742 (*Daily Post*, April 17, 1742)

The History Of Martin. Being A Proper Sequel to The Tale of a
Tub. With A Digression concerning the Nature, Usefulness, and
Necessity of Wars and Quarrels. By the Rev. D—n S—t. [Two
lines of verse.] To which is added, A Dialogue between A— P—e,
Esq; and Mr. C[harle]s C[o]ffe[y], Poets, in St. James's Park.
London: Printed for T. Taylor, at the Rose, in Exeter-Exchange.
MDCCXLII.

Teerink 783. The *BM Cat.* lists a copy with a different title-page,
dated '1735?', Teerink 784. The dialogue between Pope and Coffey
may have been meant to annoy Pope, but it is too innocuous (and
unclear in detail) to be considered an attack. Coffey accuses Pope of
having impolitely refused his request for a subscription. Pope explains
his conduct and at the end gives him five guineas. Most of their conversation concerns the hostility between the English and the Irish.

1740

The Laureat: Or, The Right Side of Colley Cibber, Esq; Con-
taining, Explanations, Amendments and Observations, On a
Book intituled, An Apology for the Life, and Writings of Mr.
Colley Cibber. Not Written By Himself. With some Anecdotes
of the Laureat, which he (thro' an Excess of Modesty) omitted.
To which is added, The History of the Life, Manners and Writ-
ings of Aesopus the Tragedian, from a Fragment of a Greek
Manuscript found in the Library of the Vatican; interspers'd
with Observations of the Translator. [Two lines of verse.]
London, Printed for J. Roberts in Warwick-Lane, and Sold at

the Pamphlet-Shops of London and Westminster. 1740. (Price 1s. 6d.)

An attack on Cibber and his *Apology*. The several Pope references are either neutral or favourable.

February 16, 1744 (*London Daily Post*, Rogers)

Lick upon Lick; Occasion'd by Another Occasional Letter From Mr. Cibber to Mr. Pope. To which is added, [The Third Edition.] A Blast upon Bays; Or, A New Lick at the Laureat: Containing Remarks upon that Tattling Performance, Mr. Cibber's first Letter to Mr. Pope, &c. And lo there appeared an Old Woman! Vide both the Letters throughout. London: Printed for T. Robbins in Fleet-street, and sold at all the Booksellers and Pamphlet-shops in Town and Country. 1744. [Price Sixpence.]

An attack on Cibber and a defence of Pope. See *A Blast upon Bays*, 1742. Library of Congress.

April 14, 1740 (*Daily Post*, Rogers)

[Lorleach, —.] A Satirical Epistle To Mr. Pope. [Six lines Latin.] London: Printed for the Author; and Sold at the Pamphlet-Shops. MDCCXL. (Price Six Pence.)

For authorship see *Notes and Queries*, Ser. 1, xi, 378. Praises Pope highly but counsels him to abandon satire as useless, since the times are grown too desperate to remedy. Texas.

March 8–15, 1733 (*Grub-Street Journal*, March 15, 1732)

M Doe-Roch, Patrick [pseud?], The Sequel Of Mr. Pope's Law-Case: Or, Farther Advice theron: In an Epistle to him. With a short Preface and Postscript. By a Templer. * *See the Publisher's Advertisement. With Notes Explanatory, Critical and Jocose. By another Hand, also a Brother of the Quill. The Second Edition, Revised and Corrected, and the Notes Enlarged. Lex benè administrat', summ' bon'; sed mal' administrat', pessim' malor'—Anglice. † The Law well administred, is the highest Good; but ill, the worst of Evils. ‡ For the Use of Madam — and Mademoiselle — of — Southward of Hampstead, and other

Ladies in whose Company the Author has formerly been. London: Printed by Anth. Gibbons, for the Benefit of the Author. M.DCC.XXXIII. (Price 2s 6d. i.e. for Verse 6d. for Notes 1s. and for Mr. Pope's Law-Case 1s.)

Rogers was unable to locate a 'first edition'. Nor have I, although *The Britwell Handlist* (London, 1933), *sub* Pope, lists what is apparently the 'first edition'. Both the 'Publisher's Advertisement' (pp. 3–4) and the doggerel poem are signed 'Patrick Mc Doe-Roch'.

A very puzzling item, apparently an attack only on Pigott, not on Pope. *Corr.* III. 355, n.1, suggests that Pope's 'There has been another thing, wherein Pigott is abused as my Learned Council, written by some Irish attorney' may be a reference to this pamphlet.

April 18, 1733 (*Grub-Street Journal*, May 10, 1733)

[Morrice, Bezaleel.] An Essay On The Universe: A Poem. [Three lines Latin.] London: Printed for John Oswald, at the Rose and Crown, in the Poultry, near Stocks-Market. MDCCXXXIII. Price 6d.

Praise of the *Essay on Man* whose authorship Morrice had not guessed.

November, 1738 (*Gentleman's Magazine*)

[Morrice, Bezaleel.] The Present Corruption Of Britons; Being A Paraphrase On the Latter Part of Mr. P—E's first Dialogue, Entitled, One Thousand Seven Hundred and Thirty-eight. [One line Latin.] London: Printed; and Sold by Thomas Gray in Exeter-Change; and by the Booksellers of London and Westminster. (Price Six-pence)

Dedication signed, p. [3], 'B. Morrice'. The Preface praises Pope's poem and admits that the following verses are a paraphrase of Pope's ideas and expressions. British Museum.

January 4, 1734 (*Grub-Street Journal*, January 10, 1734)

A Most Proper Reply To The Nobleman's Epistle To A Doctor of Divinity. To which is added, Horace versus Fannius; Or, A Case in Poinct. As Reported by Ben. Johnson. And The Belleman of St. James's Verses. London Printed: Sold by J. Huggon-

son, near Serjeant's-Inn, in Chancery-Lane. 1734. Price 6d.

F. G. in *Notes and Queries*, Ser. 5, XII, 477, noted that *Horace versus Fannius* first appeared in the *Grub-Street Journal*, No. 206, December 6, 1733 (see James T. Hillhouse, *The Grub-Street Journal* [Durham, North Carolina, 1928], p. 75), and adds, without offering any evidence, 'Pope reprinted it in the pamphlet [*A Most Proper Reply*], with a prefatory letter supposed to be written from Dr. Sherwin ...'

The pamphlet is a defence of Pope against Hervey's *An Epistle From A Nobleman To A Doctor of Divinity*, 1733. The 'Proper Reply' is a tasteless jumble of scriptural passages. *Horace versus Fannius* is entirely made up of quotations from *The Poetaster*, Act v, Sc. iii. 'The Belle-man of St. James's Verses' are little more than plagiarism of ll. 1–30, ll. 127–9, ll. 164–5, and l. 167 of Hervey's *An Epistle*, clearly intended as parody.

1715

Ninnyhammer, Nickydemus, F. G. [pseud.] Homer In A Nut-Shell: Or, The Iliad of Homer In Immortal Doggrel. By Nickydemus Ninnyhammer, F. G. [Two lines Latin.] London, Printed for W. Sparkes over against the Golden Lyon in Fetter-lane in Fleet-street. 1715.

Bond 43. This is a travesty of the first three books of the *Iliad*; the preface mentions Pope, Tickell, and Addison. See Sherburn, p. 141. With a new preface, this was reissued in 1720 as:

Homer Travestie: Being a New Translation Of That Great Poet. With A Critical Preface And Learned Notes. Shewing How this Translation excells Chapman, Hobbes, Ogilby, Dryden, Pope, and all other Pretenders. [Two lines Latin.] London: Printed for W. Boreham at the Angel in Pater-noster Row. 1720. Price 1s. 6d.

Illinois.

1738

[Paget, Thomas Catesby, Baron.] An Epistle To Mr. P— In Anti-Heroicks. Written in MDCCXXXVI. [One line Latin.] London, Printed in the Year MDCCXXXVIII.

Opens with an invocation to Pope. The second edition was published

in Paget's *Miscellanies In Prose And Verse. London: Printed in the Year M.DCC. XLI.* See Nichols, *Literary Anecdotes*, II. 115, and VI. 171, n.

November 8, 1733 (*Grub-Street Journal*, November 8, 1733)

The Parsoniad; A Satyr. Inscribed to Mr. Pope. London: Printed for Charles Corbet, at Addison's-Head, without Temple-Bar, 1733. [Price One Shilling.]

A dull satire on deists, bad churchmen, etc. Praise of Pope as man and satirist.

April 3, 1733 (*Grub-Street Journal*, April 5, 1733)

A Proper Reply To A Lady, Occasioned by her Verses address'd to the Imitator Of The First Satire Of The Second Book of Horace. By a Gentleman London: Printed for T. Osborne, in Gray's Inn, near the Walks. (Price Six Pence.)

A strong indictment of Lady Mary and a defence of Pope.

June 7, 1733 (*Grub-Street Journal*, June 14, 1733)

The Satirist: In Imitation of The Fourth Satire Of The First Book of Horace. [Two lines Latin.] London: Printed for L.G. and Sold by Mrs. Dodd without Temple-Bar, Mrs. Nutt at the Royal-Exchange, and the Booksellers of London and Westminster. MDCCXXXIII. [Price One Shilling.]

Also an edition with the imprint: 'Dublin: Printed by S. Powell, For George Risk, at the Shakespear's-Head, George Ewing, at the Angel and Bible, and William Smith, at the Hercules, Booksellers In Dame's-Street. MDCCXXXIII.'

A defence of satire, and of Pope.

September 30–October 2, 1742 (*London Evening Post*, Rogers)

Scriblerus [pseud.] The Scribleriad. Being An Epistle To The Dunces. On Renewing their Attack upon Mr. Pope, Under Their Leader the Laureat. By Scriblerus. [Two lines of verse.] London: Printed for W. Webb, near St. Paul's. 1742. [Price Six-pence.]

A defence of Pope and an attack on Cibber and the dunces. There is

an obvious indebtedness to the *Dunciad*, especially to Book IV. Reprinted in *The Scribleriad and The Difference Between Verbal And Practical Virtue*, ed. A. J. Sambrook, The Augustan Reprint Society, No. 125 (Los Angeles), 1967.

November 1, 1733 (*Grub-Street Journal*, November 15, 1733)

Scriblerus Maximus [pseud.] The Art of Scribling, Address'd to All the Scriblers of the Age. By Scriblerus Maximus. London: Printed for A. Dodd, without Temple-Bar. MDCCXXXIII. [Price One Shilling.]

Amusing ironic advice to various kinds of bad writers. Many of the dunces make an appearance.

December 4, 1733 (*Daily Journal*, Rogers)

Tit For Tat. Or An Answer To The Epistle to a Nobleman. [Two lines of verse.] London: Printed for T. Cooper, at the Globe in Ivy-Lane. MDCCXXXIV. (Price Six-pence.)

Contains only 'Tit for Tat', an attack on Hervey in reply to his attack on Pope. Contains four lines on Hervey's effeminacy not afterwards reprinted. Texas. The poem was included in:

February 7–14, 1734 (*Grub-Street Journal*, an advertisement for the J. Dormer edition below)

Tit for Tat. [Two lines of verse.] To which is annex'd, An Epistle from a Nobleman To A Doctor of Divinity. In Answer to a Latin Letter in Verse. Also The Review; Or, The Case fairly Stated on Both Sides. Wherein is shewn the true Cause of the foregoing Poems. Honi soit qui mal y pense. Motto of the Garter. London: Printed for T. Reynolds in the Strand, and sold by the Booksellers in Town and Country. MDCCXXXIV. [Price One Shilling.]

Reprinted in *Sawney and Colley (1742) and other Pope Pamphlets*, ed. W. Powell Jones, The Augustan Reprint Society, No. 83 (Los Angeles, 1960).

This includes not only 'Tit for Tat' but reprints Hervey's *An Epistle From A Nobleman*, 1733, with many small differences in punctuation, and prints a 45-line attack on Hervey, 'The Review; or, the Case fairly stated on both Sides'.

There is at Yale (not listed in Rogers) a very similar pamphlet with the title-page:

Tit For Tat. Or, An Answer To The Epistle to a Nobleman. [Two lines of verse.] To which is Added, An Epistle from a Nobleman To A Doctor of Divinity. In Answer to a Latin Letter in Verse. Some Evil-minded Persons having pirated Part of this Book, and impudently advertis'd it at One Shilling Price, Gentlemen are desired to beware of their mangled Scraps, this Original Copy with the Addition of the Nobleman's Epistle, &c. being never valued at a higher Price than Six-Pence. London: Printed and sold by J. Dormer, at the Printing-Office, the Green Door, in Black and White Court in the Old Bailey. [Price Six-Pence.] M.DCC.XXXIV.

This does not contain 'The Review', and a comparison with the Reynolds above reveals many obvious misprints.

March, 1735 (London Magazine)

Tit For Tat. Part II. By the Author of the First Part. Every Dog has his Day. To which is Added, The Latin Letter from a Doctor of Divinity to a Noble Lord, Burlesqu'd. With proper References to the Doctor's original Latin, inserted at the Bottoms of the Pages. London: Printed for P. Monger in the Strand, and sold at the Pamphlet-Shops of London and Westminster. Price 1s. M.DCC.XXXV.

Listed as unlocated in Rogers. Another attack on Hervey; there are no Pope references. Huntington.

February, 1734 (Gentleman's Magazine)

A Tryal of Skill Between a Court Lord, and a Twickenham 'Squire. Inscrib'd to Mr. Pope. [Ten lines of verse.] London: Printed and sold by J. Dormer, at the Printing-Office, the Green Door, in Black and White Court in the Old Bailey. [Price One Shilling.] M.DCC. XXXIV.

An attack on Hervey. Pope is mentioned, pp. 12–13. Texas.

January 17, 1734 (Grub-Street Journal, January 17, 1734)

The Tryal of Skill Between 'Squire Walsingham And Mother Osborne. An Eclogue, In Imitation of Virgil's Palaemon. To

which are added, Horace to Fannius, and an Apology for Printing a certain Nobleman's Epistle to Dr. S[her]w[i]n. [One line Latin.] London Printed: Sold by J. Huggonson, near Serjeants-Inn, in Chancery-Lane, 1734. [Price One Shilling.]

'The Tryal of Skill' is a political satire; Pope is mentioned favourably, pp. 13, 15. 'Horace to Fannius' is headed in the text 'To Lord Fanny. In Imitation of Horace to Barine'; it is a five-stanza satire on Hervey and his versifying. 'An Apology for printing the Nobleman's Epistle to Dr. S—w—n. By another Hand' is a lively 56-line satire on Hervey.

April 7, 1736 (*London Daily Post*, Rogers)

Two Epistles of Horace Imitated. London: Printed for T. Cooper, at the Globe in Pater-noster Row, 1736. (Price One Shilling.)

Epistle 1 is 'Inscribed to A. P. Esq;' (p. 1) and contains several flattering tributes to Pope. New York Public Library.

1717

A Walk From St. James's To Convent-Garden, The Back-way, Through the Meuse. In Imitation of Mr. Gay's Journey to Exeter. In a Letter to a Friend. London; Printed and Sold by James Roberts in Warwick-Lane, and Arrabella Morice next to the Rose-Tavern without Temple-Bar. 1717. (Price Six-pence.)

Sherburn listed this as unlocated in 'The Fortunes and Misfortunes of *Three Hours After Marriage*', *MP*, xxiv (1926–7), 91–109, and supposed it might refer to that play. It does not, however, mention Pope or the play, though there are several small hits at Gay. Harvard.

May 31, 1733 (*Grub-Street Journal*, June 7, 1733)

The Wrongheads: A Poem. Inscrib'd to Mr. Pope. By a Person of Quality. [Two lines Latin.] London: Printed for T. Astley at the Rose over against the North Door of St. Paul's; and Sold by R. Wellington without Temple-Bar. MDCCXXXIII.[Price 6d.]

Praise of Pope as a satirist in an imitation of the *Epistle to Burlington*.

INDEX

It was found impracticable to separate *The Dunciad*, 1728, *The Dunciad Variorum*, *The New Dunciad*, and *The Dunciad in Four Books*. 'Homer' has been used when the reference may be either to *The Iliad* or to *The Odyssey*. Pamphlets have their major entries under the author or pseudonym, if one is given. I cannot thank warmly enough Rodney Jilg, Esq., for his help in preparing this index.